MODELLING IN DATA BASE MANAGEMENT SYSTEMS

IFIP Working Conference on
Modelling in Data Base Management Systems
Freudenstadt, Germany, 5-8 January 1976

organized by
IFIP Technical Committee 2, Programming
International Federation for Information Processing

Program Committee
E. Benci, F. Bodart (Chairman), G. Bracchi, A. Cabanes, B. Douque, R. Durchholz,
M. Gallitano, C. Machgeels (Secretary), E. J. Neuhold, G. M. Nijssen, M. E. Senko,
T. B. Steel, R. W. Taylor.

NORTH-HOLLAND PUBLISHING COMPANY
AMSTERDAM • NEW YORK • OXFORD

MODELLING IN DATA BASE MANAGEMENT SYSTEMS

Proceedings of the IFIP Working Conference on
Modelling in Data Base Management Systems

edited by

G. M. NIJSSEN
Control Data Europe
Brussels, Belgium

1976

NORTH-HOLLAND PUBLISHING COMPANY
AMSTERDAM • NEW YORK • OXFORD

© IFIP-1976

North-Holland ISBN: 0 7204 0459 2

Published by:
North-Holland Publishing Company — Amsterdam
North-Holland Publishing Company, Ltd. — Oxford

Sole distributors for the U.S.A. and Canada:
American Elsevier Publishing Company, Inc.
52 Vanderbilt Avenue
New York, N.Y. 10017

Library of Congress Cataloging in Publication Data

IFIP Working Conference on Modelling in Data Base
    Management Systems, Freudenstadt, Ger., 1976.
    Modelling in data base management systems.

    "Organized by IFIP Technical Committee 2, Pro-
gramming, International Federation for Information
Processing."
    Includes index.
    1. Data base management--Congresses. 2. Com-
puter architecture--Congresses. I. Nijssen, G. M.
II. International Federation for Information Pro-
cessing. Technical Committee 2. III. Title.
QA76.9.D3I2 1976   001.6'442   76-25458
ISBN 0-7204-0459-2

Printed in The Netherlands

TABLE OF CONTENTS

EDITOR'S PREFACE

The first IFIP Working Conference on Database Management was held
in 1974, Cargese, Corsica; the second in 1975, Wepion, Belgium;
the third from January 5-8, 1976, in Freudenstadt, Germany (BRD).
Just as the previous two conferences, the third was attended by
some 60 invited participants, from various countries in Europe
and America. It was a pleasure to observe during the third
conference the increase in understanding of the basic problems
in Database Management. Mainly discussed during the conference
were concepts for the conceptual schema, and the papers on this
topic constitute the major part of these proceedings. Another
topic which got quite some attention was the gross architecture
for a DBMS. Furthermore, some time was spent on integrity
constraints and concurrency.

The papers included in these proceedings are arranged according
to the sequence of presentation. At the end of some papers, a
summary of the relevant discussion is given; such a summary is
produced by the author(s) of the paper.

The editor would like to express his appreciation for the excellent
work of the Local Arrangements Committee, Frau Günthör, Prof.
E. Neubold, Dr. H. Biller and Dr. E. Falkenberg.

Brussels, April 1976
G.M. NIJSSEN

Modelling in Data Base Management Systems, G.M. Nijssen, (ed.)
North Holland Publishing Company, 1976

A GROSS ARCHITECTURE FOR THE NEXT

GENERATION DATABASE MANAGEMENT

SYSTEMS

G.M. NIJSSEN
Control Data Europe
Brussels

Summary

Databases are in some way related to the reality. We therefore
start with the reality and analyze which steps have to be taken
before we arrive at the database and the database description.
During this analysis, information systems will enter the universe
of interest. Based on this analysis are the requirements for the
next generation GDMS. A design of the gross architecture for the
next generation GDMS is derived step by step. The Universe of
Discourse Schema or Conceptual Schema appears to play an essential
role in the next generation GDMS. Furthermore, a GDMS of the next
generation will provide the user with the freedom to select his
preferred mental model and language, while the physical aspects
are insulated in a special area. A GDMS providing the freedom to
select the mental model, and language, is called Coexistence GDMS.

Table of Contents

1. INTRODUCTION

With the increase of databases and the use of database management systems, the following questions may arise:

"What is the relationship between future information
systems and databases?"

"What is the role of a database management system in the
design, implementation, operation and modification phases
of future information systems?"

"What are the relationships between reality, database and
future information systems?"

"Why are present database management systems so complicated?"

An attempt to answer these questions is contained in the following sections.

2. UNIVERSE OF DISCOURSE

Searching for the answers, posed in section 1, in the present
day database literature, is quite a difficult job, if at all
possible. In the sequel we will try to answer the questions
by following a method which differs from the commonly available
database literature.

We prefer to start with those aspects which are inherent to any
information system, computerized or non-computerized, and delay
the introduction of computer oriented concepts until the point
where they need to be introduced.

2.1 PERCEPTION

The origin of an information system has to do with the need of
one and usually more persons to collect, note, process and
distribute data, related to a certain part of the reality.
The crucial question now is: what does mean: "data, related to
a certain part of the reality?"

Firstly, we have to be well aware that we can only collect data
about things we can perceive through one of our perceptors.
This can happen directly via eyes, ears, nose, etc., or indirectly via speedometer, radar screen, etc. In other words, it
may be impossible to collect data about the real reality, however it is possible to collect data about the perceivable reality. From this we may conclude (see figure 2.1.a) that via the
process of perception we "convert" the real reality into a
perceivable reality, and we are confined to collect, note,
process and distribute data regarding this perceivable reality.
Whether a certain element in the reality can be perceived has
to do with the ability to perceive. For indirect perceptions,
this means that the ability is increasing with the advance of
the technology. E.g. in 1930 one was not able to see a plane
above the clouds; the introduction of radar made it possible
to perceive a certain image of such a plane.

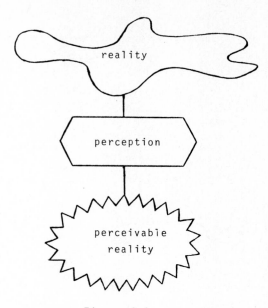

Figure 2.1.a

2.2 SYSTEMS ANALYSIS AND DESIGN

Between the perceivable reality and the description of the
database (often referred to as schema or conceptual schema)
one has to perform some of the most essential aspects of the
work, commonly referred to as systems analysis and design.
Although we have no intention to treat this topic in this
paper, we feel a need to discuss very briefly three distinguishable processes of systems analysis and design. These three
processes are:

- naming

- selection

- classification

Although one could treat these processes independent of each
other, it is very often the case in practice that the three
processes are quite strongly connected.

In order to illustrate the discussion with an example, we have
to make an assumption regarding the structure of the perceivable
reality. (By doing so, we are not trying to avoid the important
discussion on what precisely is the structure of the perceivable
reality; however this is not the appropriate place to elaborate
on it).

Let us a s s u m e that the perceivable reality consists of

        - a set of (atomic) elements,
        and
        - a set of relations

where the domains of the relations is the set of elements.

2.3 NAMING

For the time being, each element in the set of elements of the
perceivable reality is given an arbitrary name under the condition that a given name is assigned to only one element. This
means that there is a functional mapping from a set of names
to the set of elements. (see figure 2.3.a)

set of names   set of elements

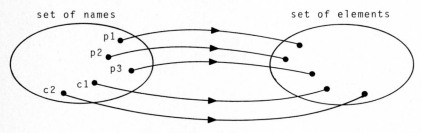

Figure 2.3.a

Furthermore, each relation of the perceivable reality is
assigned an arbitrary name such that the relation name is unique
for that relation within the set of relations.

We may now say that

      - each element in the set has a name (arbitrarily assigned)
      - each tuple in a relation has a name, which consists of
        the concatenation of the relation name and the names
        of the elements involved in this tuple,

or, all elements, both atomic elements and tuples, in our perceivable reality have a name.

In figure 2.3.b, the set of elements of the perceivable reality
consists of $\{$p1, p2, p3, p4, p5, p6, c1, c2, c3, r1, r2, r3, r4$\}$
and the set of relations is:

$\{\{$(p1,p3),(p1,p4),(p4,p6)$\}$ fa,

$\{$(p2,p3),(p2,p4),(p5,p6)$\}$ mo,

$\{$(p1,p2),(p4,p5)$\}$ ma,

$\{(p1,c2),(p2,c1),(p4,c3),(p5,c3)\}$ bo,

$\{(p1,c1),(p1,c3),(p2,c1),(p2,c2),(p2,c3)\}$ li,

$\{(p1,r1),(p1,r2),(p4,r3),(p5,r4)\}$ ow$\}$

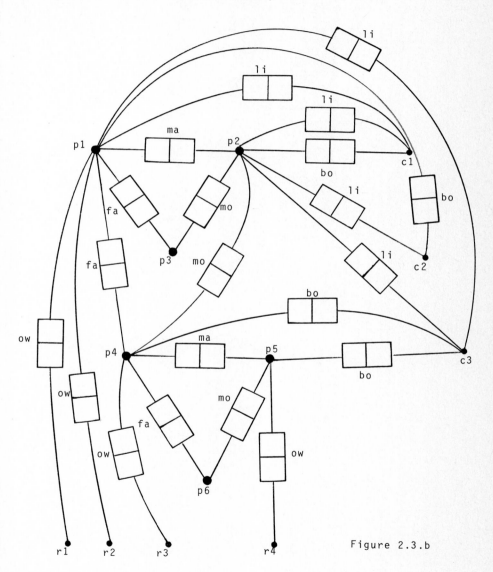

Figure 2.3.b

2.4 SELECTION

The perceivable reality is very, very, large. It is far beyond
the comprehension of a human being to talk intelligently about
all the elements of the perceivable reality. In all practical
situations one or more persons decide to concentrate on a very
small part of the perceivable reality. Said otherwise, one or
more persons agree to select a part of the perceivable reality
as their common frame of reference, or as their common Universe
of Discourse. (see figure 2.4.a)

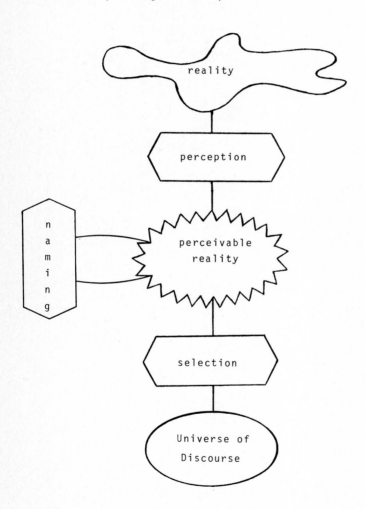

Figure 2.4.a

The process which brings us from the perceivable reality to the Universe of Discourse is called selection in this paper. The reason is that it is useful in the author's opinion, to stress the selection or decision aspect of that process. In many other scientific publications, this process is part of a wider process which is commonly referred to as "scientific abstraction" (Steel, reference 14, page 190).

Note.   The Universe of Discourse as described above has a close resemblance with the concept of "system of objects" as used by Kleene. He states "By a system of objects, we mean a (non-empty) set or class or domain (or possibly several such sets) of objects among which are established certain relationships". (reference 9, page 24)

Perception had to do with ability as we have seen before and technology; selection has to do with willingness or economy. In 1975 it would have been possible to measure every three months the blood pressure of all people above 45 in Germany; this could have resulted in considerably less deaths. However, willingness or economy have made the decision not to collect these data about the perceivable reality.

We will illustrate the selection process using the example as introduced in figure 2.3.b.

In the example as used before (figure 2.3.b), it is decided that the elements with name r1, r2, r3 and r4 are not of interest; furthermore, the set of tuples
    (p1,c1),(p1,c3),(p2,c1),(p2,c2),(p2,c3) li,
which tells us which persons have lived in which city, is de-cided to be outside the scope of interest. In general, the selection process removes from the set of elements and set of relations (which make up the perceivable reality), a certain number of elements and tuples; the result of this selection process is a set of elements and a set of relations on these elements for which it is considered to be of interest to collect data, to store data and to distribute data. This set of ele-ments and set of relations is jointly referred to as the Uni-verse of Discourse. The Universe of Discourse, which is the result of the selection process applied to figure 2.3.b, is represented in figure 2.4.b.

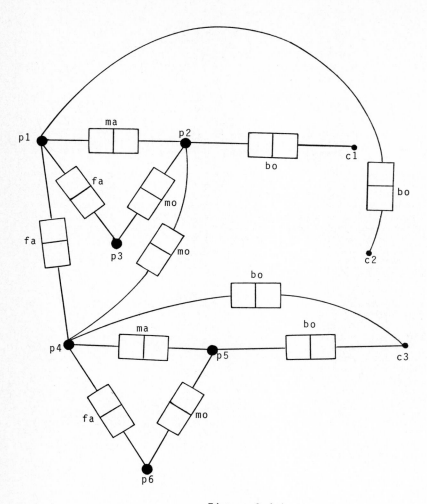

Figure 2.4.b

2.5 CLASSIFICATION

The set of elements and the set of relations of the Universe
of Discourse is, in many practical situations, too inhomo-
geneous. The set of elements and relations is therefore classified into a certain number of classes. (Please note that the
set of relations was already classified in figure 2.3.b)
The optimum number of classes is application dependent; in
general, a small number of classes and a large number of classes
cause inconveniencies; this effect is presented in figure 2.5.a.

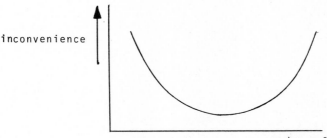

Figure 2.5.a

Classification is also used to increase the data correctness.
Suppose that p1 through p6 are names of persons, c1, c2, and
c3 names of cities, then we would accept that person p1 may
marry person p2, because both are persons. However we would
not like to see in the database that person p1 marries with
city c1. If we now classify the elements of the Universe of
Discourse into 2 classes, one being a class of persons
{p1,p2,p3,p4,p5,p6}, and one a class of cities{c1,c2,c3}and
then we may say that the relation "father" is only permitted
between a person and another person; or that a "marriage" is
between two persons; or that "born" is a relation between a
person and a city etc. In other words, classification of
the elements of the Universe of Discourse helps us to increase
data correctness.

Figure 2.5.b contains a classified representation of the
Universe of Discourse, in short UoD. Such a classified description of the Universe of Discourse (UoD) is an essential
part of communication among users, consultants, system analysts,
system designers and programmers.

G.M. Nijssen

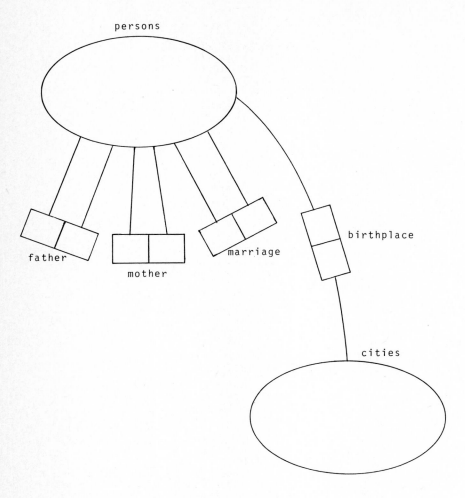

Figure 2.5.b

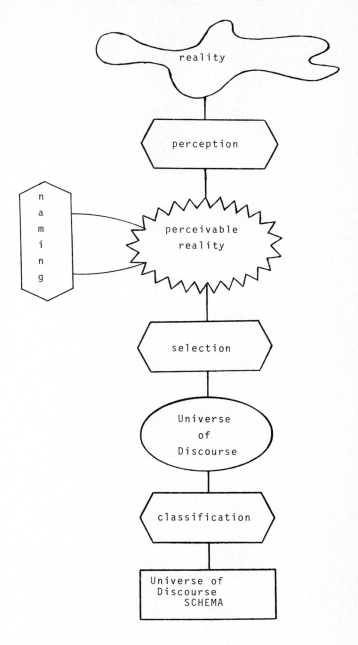

Figure 2.5.c

The description of the classes of elements of the UoD and the
relations among those classes, augmented with some additional
constraints, is called schema, or conceptual schema, or Universe
of Discourse Schema.

Remark.   The processes of naming, selection and classification
          are in practice often applied simultaneously. The
          sequence in this paper was only used to illustrate
          the concept "conceptual schema" with an example.

Classification is one of the most successful tools of human
intelligence, and is, wittingly or unwittingly, in use in
information systems. (See also Senko, reference 13).
The result of the classification process is presented in figure
2.5.c, where the Universe of Discourse Schema describes the
classes of interest in the Universe of Discourse.

2.6 UNIVERSE OF DISCOURSE SCHEMA

Starting from reality, we have arrived at the Universe of
Discourse SCHEMA, passing through the processes of:

- perception
- naming
- selection
- classification

In each and every information system, the designers and users
have agreed on a Universe of Discourse SCHEMA.

Note 1.   We want to emphasize that there has not been used any
          computer or data processing oriented concepts in any
          of the four above mentioned processes to arrive at the
          Universe of Discourse Schema.

Note 2.   Present database systems as well as the CODASYL data-
          base proposals can be characterized by having a Uni-
          verse of Discourse Schema, in which there are included
          several aspects which are alien to the Universe of
          Discourse, but inherent to computer concepts.
          (reference 3, 4, 5)

Note 3.   The ANSI DBMS report of February 1975 contains a con-
          cept which is intended to be the Universe of Discourse
          Schema; in that report the Universe of Discourse Schema
          is called Conceptual Schema. (reference 1)

SHARED DATABASE

As we have seen in the preceeding sections, one or more users
may agree to collect data about a part of the perceivable
reality. The description of the classes and other constraints
of their Universe of Discourse (UoD) is called UoD Schema.
The collection of data which describes the elements and tuples
of the selected part of the perceivable reality is the database.

3.1 DIFFERENT MENTAL MODELS OR USER VIEWS

Once a number of persons have agreed on the Universe of Discourse
which is common for them, it is possible to select a subset of
this Common Universe of Discourse which will be known to a
specific group of persons. However, such a specific group of
persons may prefer to see their subset of the Common Universe
of Discourse in their preferred mental model. In other words,
different groups of persons may see different subsets of the
Common Universe of Discourse and in different mental models or
views. (see figure 3.1.a)
This means that a group of persons will have a specific or User
view of the Common Universe of Discourse such that this specific
view is different in two aspects, namely:

- subsetting
- transformation

The user view corresponds to a subset of the Common Universe
of Discourse and this subset is possibly in an other mental
model than the mental model inherent in the Common Universe
of Discourse.

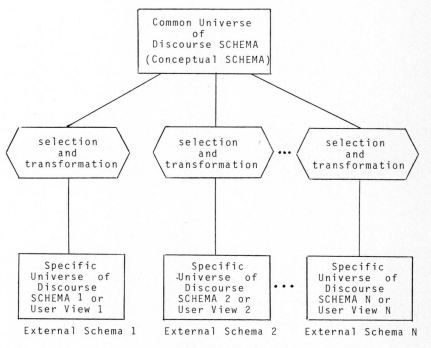

Figure 3.1.a

Note.   Present database specialists fairly often raise the follo-
        wing question:

        "Why is it not sufficient to provide only subsetting?"
        (In nearly all present systems and the CODASYL proposals,
        only subsetting is provided)

        One of the underlying assumptions of this question is that
        there is one mental model which is so superb that it is
        good for all users. This, however, turns out to be nothing
        more than an illusion, at least for the next ten years.

        I just want to refer to the debate on Network versus
        Relational (Ashenhurst, reference 2) and the upcoming
        debates of more semantic data models versus normalized
        Relational (Codd, reference 6).

        A mental model has a close analogy with religion, which is
        hopefully selected in freedom. We therefore believe that
        mental model freedom is an essential characteristic of
        future Generalised Database Management Systems. (GDMS)

        Another argument has a quite different source. Under the
        assumption that a user can make the best performance if
        he can operate with his preferred mental model, it is,
        with the increasing labour costs, an economical issue to
        provide various mental models, such that the user can select
        the one which maximizes his production.

3.2 DIFFERENT USER LANGUAGES

If users have their specific view of the Common Universe of Discourse, they want to store data of the User Universe of Discourse
in the database, and thereafter they maintain and select data.
If a computer is used to manage the data, then a user has various
options or languages to communicate with the computer in order to
get the data into the computer managed database or select data from
the computer managed database.

If a user prefers a mental model of the User Universe of Discourse,
consisting of a collection of tables (or normalized relations in
present database management jargon, see Codd, reference 6), then
he wants to use a language which can manipulate and select from
tables.   There are available today various languages which can
have as operands normalized relations or tables. (ALPHA, SQUARE,
SEQUEL, TAMALAN, CUPID). The common aspect of these languages
is that they operate on normalized relations; however they have
other characteristics which do make such a language convenient
for certain groups of users.   Some of these languages are easy to
learn by people without computer expertise or without being a
mathematician and as a consequence, this eliminates the interven-
tion of professional programmers to get data into and from the
database.
If a user prefers a mental model of the User Universe of Discourse,
consisting of a directed graph, then it is quite likely that the
user requests a computer expert (a professional programmer) to
write the update and selection procedures in a graph oriented language such as COBOL enhanced with a DML (Data Manipulation Language).
The professional programmer will use this language to navigate
through the directed graph, the user view or the User Universe of
Discourse (See CODASYL, reference 3, 4, 5).

There is a class of languages which permit to navigate from one node to another node in the graph. The common aspect of all these languages is often referred to as one-element-at-a-time logic. Fortran, COBOL and PL1 enhanced with a DML do all belong to this class of manipulation languages. However, it is well known that some groups of programmers prefer COBOL, some FORTRAN and others PL1 to navigate with the aid of a DML through a graph.

It may be expected that more and more users want to use a mental model or User Universe of Discourse, which is the same as the one commonly applied in everyday human communication (See Falkenberg, reference 8). Such a user view would bring the computer closer to the human being, with all known advantages. In that case, the people in France would like to use a language based on French in connection with such a user view, while people in Germany using the same user view as the French people would prefer to use a language based on German to manipulate and select data from their Universe of Discourse.

The arguments for having different languages, even for one and the same user view or mental model, are the same as those justifying many mental models as discussed in the previous section.

In figure 3.2.b various programs are added to the user views and Common Universe of Discourse Schema. The aim of all these programs is to update the data in the database or to select data from the database.

3.3 COEXISTENCE MODEL

In nearly all present database management systems as well as in the CODASYL and normalized relational database approach, a user has no freedom to select his preferred mental model; in these systems and approaches a user is forced to accept the one mental model supplied, although he may select a subset (of the classes) of the Common Universe of Discourse.

We are of the opinion that the next generation of Generalized Database Management Systems (GDMS) has to provide the user with the option to select his

- preferred mental model

and

- preferred manipulation language

Such a system provides the peaceful coexistence (Nijssen, reference 10, page 378) of the various data models and manipulation languages. We therefore have given this approach the name: coexistence model.

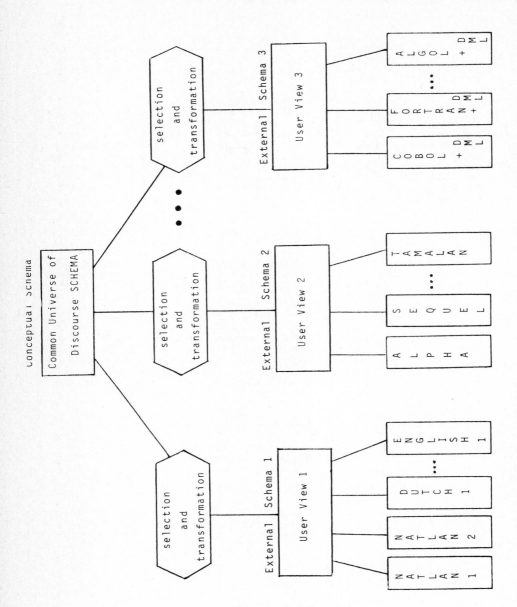

Figure 2.3.b

4. PHYSICAL DATABASE

In the previous sections we have discussed the descriptions of the (Common) Universe of Discourse Schema, and the various Specific Universe of Discourse Schemata or User Views and the various update and retrieval languages to operate on a Specific Universe of Discourse or User view. We must however not forget that we still need a computer to do the many jobs for us in the database world. One of the jobs a computer in a database environment does, is to store the data which represent the elements of the Universe of Discourse. So the computer has to know where and how to store the data on the physical storage devices. This means that the computer needs one or more algorithms for every set (or subset) of elements of the Common Universe of Discourse, which describe how and where these elements have to be stored, and which additional physical storage structures such as indexes, access paths, pointers, physical redundancy, etc. have to be built for each set (or subset) of elements of the Common Universe of Discourse.

In other words, there is a SCHEMA which describes the physical organization of the data representing the Common Universe of Discourse on the physical storage devices; this is called the STORAGE SCHEMA or INTERNAL SCHEMA.
Various kinds of things of the STORAGE SCHEMA such as indexes, access paths, pointers, physical redundancy have no counterpart in the Common Universe of Discourse. Furthermore, in order to optimize the computer resources, several groupings or aggregations of atomic elements and atomic tuples of the Common Universe of Discourse may be needed to be stored as a physical entity on the storage devices.

From this we may conclude that the STORAGE SCHEMA or INTERNAL SCHEMA contains constructs which are quite different from the constructs in the Conceptual Schema or Universe of Discourse Schema.

And this means that we need a description of the mapping from the UoD SCHEMA to the STORAGE SCHEMA and vice versa.

Note 1. In present database management systems, the User view or EXTERNAL SCHEMA contains constructs which in our approach would be classified as belonging to the STORAGE or INTERNAL SCHEMA. This means that in present database management systems a user program may reference constructs which are of physical nature. This would not be a bad thing, if it often were not necessary to modify the STORAGE SCHEMA in order to optimize the computer resources. The modification or change in the STORAGE SCHEMA is commonly caused by changing traffic patterns on the database or by hardware with different characteristics. If a user program may reference a physical construct, and this physical construct is changed in order to optimize computer resources, then this change requires a modification of the user program, or the famous reprogramming.

By migrating all physical constructs from the User view
to the Storage Schema, a program cannot be dependent
on physical constructs, hence one may change the
STORAGE SCHEMA without any reprogramming of the user
programs.

Note 2.   It may be argued that it could be possible to combine
the UoD SCHEMA and INTERNAL SCHEMA, and still have no
reference in the User Schema to any physical construct.

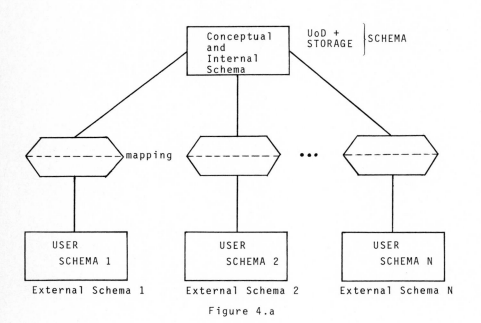

External Schema 1   External Schema 2   External Schema N

Figure 4.a

This is possible because the mapping between the combined UoD-INTERNAL SCHEMA and the USER SCHEMA may be
such that the User Schema part of the mapping does not
reference any physical construct. However, if a physical construct is changed in the UoD-INTERNAL SCHEMA,
then mappings have to be modified, because there are
in general many USER SCHEMAS and thus many mappings.
With a separation of UoD and INTERNAL SCHEMA, only one
mapping has to be modified if a physical construct is
changed.

Note 3.   From a methodological point of view, it would be an
accident if the UoD SCHEMA were the same as the
STORAGE SCHEMA, because they serve two quite different
aims. The UoD SCHEMA describes the Universe of Discourse in classes of concepts which have to provide:

   - completeness, preciseness
   - simplicity (to teach and to use)
   - independence preservation
   - evolvability

while the STORAGE SCHEMA has as aim to describe the
classes and population of the Universe of Discourse in
such a way that a certain function of computer resources (core, channel, disc), response time and insurance
is minimized.
Because the foregoing three notes have caused some misunder-
standing in some discussions with some database specialists,
we will rephrase it as follows:

From a pure economical point of view, it can be observed that
computer costs are decreasing and specialists costs are increasing. This has arrived at a point where it becomes attractive to trade off human resources and computer resources. It
is furthermore assumed that the UoD SCHEMA is a factor more
stable than the STORAGE SCHEMA, mainly because the STORAGE
SCHEMA aims at optimizing fairly rapid changing traffic patterns
on the database. If the logic of application programs were
bound to the STORAGE SCHEMA, then these programs would possibly
require reprogramming with every change in the STORAGE SCHEMA
or traffic pattern on the database.

The Universe of Discourse SCHEMA needs to be described by persons who really know the semantic or application aspects of that
Universe of Discourse.

The STORAGE SCHEMA needs to be described by persons who are real
specialists in the physical organization of data in a database.
This requires quite some special knowledge which will not be
known to the many people involved in the design of the Universe
of Discourse, nor can it be expected that such special knowledge can easily be taught to people whose prime interest is
the application, and not bit fiddling. Probably 70% of future
people have, in one way or the other, to do with the specification of the Universe of Discourse while much less than 1% of
future people will have to specify the STORAGE SCHEMA.
Figure 4.b represents the foregoing in a diagram. It is important to note that the Common Universe of Discourse SCHEMA is
independent of physical aspects of computer storage or any other
computer oriented concept; this is accomplished by the mapping
or transformation between the Common Universe of Discourse
SCHEMA and the STORAGE SCHEMA, which describes the physical or
storage aspects of the database. This means that two categories of persons, application specialists (writing the Common
Universe of Discourse Schema) and database engineers (writing
the Storage Schema) can do their job in their own territory.

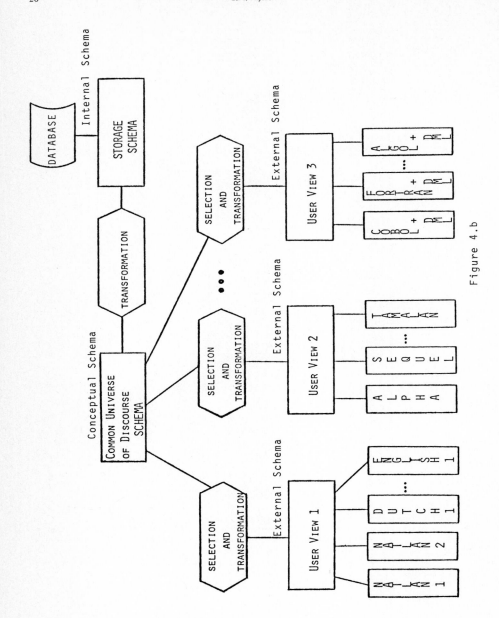

Figure 4.b

5. CONCLUSION AND SUMMARY

To summarize, we may say the following (see figure 5.a)

- a certain group of persons decides to collect data on a certain universe of discourse in order to be able to retrieve selected data

- the common universe of discourse is described (or documented) in terms of classes and constraints on these classes

- various user views can be described, using the user preferred model and possibly a subset of the Common Universe of Discourse

- each subgroup of persons may use his preferred language to have data enter his user view or to select data from his user view

- a database specialist describes the physical aspects of the database, which contains all the data associated with the Common Universe of Discourse

- once the schemata and mappings are available, the users can add data to, delete data from, and select data from the database

- present database management systems are so complicated because they were designed in the late sixties, a time when database technology was about to start.

G.M. Nijssen

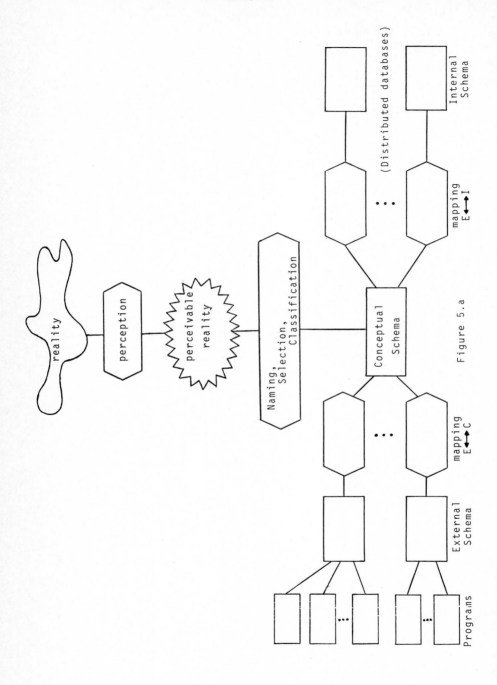

Figure 5.a

REFERENCES AND BIBLIOGRAPHY

1. ANSI

   Interim Report Study Group on Data Base Management Systems

   American National Standards Institute, ANSI/X3/SPARC DBMS
   Study Group, February 1975.

2. ASHENHURST R.

   A great Debate

   Communications of the ACM 17, June 1974, nr. 6, pp. 360

3. CODASYL

   Data Base Task Group April 1971 Report

   ACM New York, 1971

4. CODASYL

   DDL Journal of Development, June 1973 Report

5. CODASYL

   COBOL Journal of Development

   May 1975

6. CODD E.F.

   A Relational Model of Data for Large Shared Data Banks

   Communications of the ACM, vol. 13, June 1970, nr. 6

7. DURCHHOLZ R.   RICHTER G.

   Information Management Concepts (IMC) for Use with DBMS
   Interface

   In: Proceedings IFIP TC-2 Working Conference on Modelling
   In Data Base Management Systems, held in Freudenstadt, Germany,
   January 5-9, 1976.

8. FALKENBERG E.

   Strukturierung und Darstellung von Information an der Schnitt-
   stelle zwischen Datenbankbenutzer und Datenbank-Management-
   System

   Ph.-D Theses, University of Stuttgart, 1975.

9. KLEENE S.C.

   Introduction to Metamathematics

   Van Nostrand, Princeton, New Jersey 1952

10. NIJSSEN G.M.

    Data Structuring in the DDL and Relational Model

    In: Data Base Management, Proceedings of the IFIP Working
    Conference on Data Base Management, held in Cargese, Corsica,
    April 1-5, 1974, edited by J.W. Klimbie and K.L. Koffeman,
    North-Holland Publishing Company, Amsterdam 1974.

11. NIJSSEN G.M.

    Set and CODASYL Set or Coset

    In: Data Base Description, Proceedings of the IFIP Special
    Working Conference on data description languages: an in-depth
    technical evaluation of the CODASYL DDL, held in Wepion,
    Belgium, January 13-17, 1975, edited by B.C.M. Douqué and
    G.M. Nijssen, North-Holland Publishing Company, Amsterdam 1975.

12. NIJSSEN G.M.

    Two major flaws in the CODASYL DDL 1973 and proposed correc-
    tions

    In: Information Systems, December 1975, vol. 1, pp. 115-132,
    Pergamon Press.

13. SENKO M.E.

    Information Systems: Records, Relations, Sets, Entities and
    Things

    In: Information Systems, volume 1, nr. 1, January 1975,
    pp. 3-13, Pergamon Press.

14. STEEL T.B. Jr.

    Data Base Standardization: A Status Report

    In: Data Base Description, Proceedings of the IFIP Special
    Working Conference on data description languages: an in-depth
    technical evaluation of the CODASYL DDL, held in Wepion,
    Belgium, January 13-17, 1975, edited by B.C.M. Douqué and
    G.M. Nijssen, North-Holland Publishing Company, Amsterdam 1975.

Modelling in Data Base Management Systems, G.M. Nijssen, (ed)
North Holland Publishing Company, 1976

A Methodology for the Design of
Logical Data Base Structures

by

Ignacio Mijares* and Richard Peebles

Computer Communications Network Group
Department of Computer Science
University of Waterloo

ABSTRACT

An approach to the design of logical data base structures is presented, which recognizes two main parts. The first one consists in the construction of the logical data base structure from information provided by the user. This information includes not only functional dependencies, as in most of the current published work, but also includes the concept of static set dependency which is introduced here. Another important feature of the construction process is that two levels of association are recognized, allowing for two possible levels of abstraction in the data base structure.

The second part of the design approach analyzes some structural properties of the created data base. This is achieved by introducing a specific criterion to identify semantic views between pairs of attribute names.

ACKNOWLEDGEMENT

We thank Frank Tompa and Ernesto Villarreal for many helpful discussions that we had with them and we acknowledge the support of the National Research Council of Canada and of the Consejo Nacional de Ciencia y Tecnologia de Mexico.

* On leave from the Instituto Tecnologico y de Estudios Superiores de Monterrey (Mexico).

1.   INTRODUCTION

1.1 MOTIVATION

When the data base administrator begins the task of data base construction he is faced with thousands of separate pieces of information and he must somehow structure this data soup. It is now well recognized that the traditional intuitive methods lead to unmanageable problems of redundancy and consistency. What is needed then, is a simple step-by-step procedure for generating a hi-fidelity model of the organization's information structure. These problems have spawned the many data base models that we see today.

These data base models provide simplicity and a great deal of independence for current applications. Nevertheless, the data base administrator (DBA) and the programmers, still face non-trivial tasks such as the creation of the data base from scratch and the determination of logical access paths corresponding to different semantic views (of the existing) relationships. Current models are by and large syntactic and although some work has been done recently on data base semantics (9-15), the problems of data base creation and identification of semantic views have received little attention.

1.2 LOGICAL ACCESS PATHS IN THE RELATIONAL MODEL

To illustrate the problem faced by a programmer in dealing with the relational model (1,2,3,4,5,6,8) consider a data base pertaining to a retail organization in which sales information includes:

Attribute name	Meaning
S	sale number
C	customer name
P	product number
Q	quantity sold per sale
U	cumulative quantity per product per customer (aggregated over all sales)

This information is organized into the following relations in third normal form (key is underlined):

R1($\underline{S}$, C) , R2($\underline{C},\underline{P}$, U) , R3($\underline{S},\underline{P}$,Q)

Suppose that the user wishes to find all sales that led to cumulative values of 100. How should such a query be specified? First the user must think carefully about what this query means. For each occurrence of U=100 we will have a corresponding pair (C , P) obtained from R2. The "natural" meaning of the query is to find all sales where both C and P appear.

Initially the user may be tempted to specify such a query with the following SEQUEL (16) statements:

```
SELECT S
FROM R1
WHERE  C=
     SELECT   C
```

```
        FROM   R2
        WHERE     U=100
∩
SELECT S
FROM R3
WHERE  P=
        SELECT  P
        FROM   R2
        WHERE     U=100
```

This expression, however, would not give the expected answer because it would return all the sales involving a customer that has some cumulative equal to 100 and a product that has some cumulative equal to 100, which is different of returning all the sales involving a customer and a product whose specific combination has a cumulative equal to 100.

A query that would give the expected answer is shown below:

```
SELECT S
FROM r1 in R1
WHERE  C=
        SELECT          C
        FROM            R2
        WHERE           U=100
        AND             P=
          SELECT          P
          FROM            R3
          WHERE           S=r1.S
```

The above example illustrates that in order to describe a semantic view the user of the relational model must carry the semantics of the relations in his head. He must know that the expected answer will only be achieved by the second strategy.

There is a strong analogy here between navigating on pointers (as in the DBTG approach (7)) and navigating on operators of the relational algebra. The problem will be enormously compounded in very large data bases with hundreds or thousands of relations to deal with.

1.3 PREVIOUS WORK ON DATA BASE SEMANTICS

As we have noted, interest in the problems of data base semantics has been growing. However, this work has been mainly concerned with the representation problem rather than with the construction of the desired data base. No formal work has been done on how to assist the user (DBA) to iden-tify semantic views and their access paths. Similarly, a measure of quality of the set of elements selected to represent the real world has not been specified.

The work by Hainaut and Lecharlier (10) as well as the work by Deheneffe et al (11) identify the relationships between pairs of objects only, i.e. an association involving more than two objects must be represented as many binary relationships. This characteristic makes it very difficult (if possible at all) to represent naturally an object that is functionally dependent on an association of several other objects.

The paper by Schmid and Swenson (12) adopts a philosophy
similar to that described in the papers above and points out
that the relational model with the concept of functional
dependency alone is not completely adequate for expressing
some knowledge about the world. With this motivation a
model is derived in order to represent the semantics of the
world. However, since relationships are only represented
between pairs of objects, characteristics of an association
cannot be modelled. When representing the semantic
dependencies of their model by functional dependencies in
the relational model some semantics is lost and this brings
out interesting implications for the relational approach.
    Senko (18, 19) has developed a model (the information level
of DIAM II) that is based on labelled binary associations.
Thus, the addition of artificial nodes is required in order
to represent characteristics of an association. This situation makes it impossible to distinguish between characteristics of an entity and characteristics of an association. Furthermore, the model deals with single attributes
that are not grouped nor classified according to some
criteria.
    Tsubaki (20) has presented a multi-level data model
whose first level (Information Structure Model) is based on
the concepts of "Entity, Attribute, and Value" to represent
the semantics of the data base. In this model, relationships
are considered as entities and each attribute is defined to
have a unique role in the system. The idea of having no common attributes between two entity types is introduced. This
idea is similar to one presented here although the approach
to partitioning the set of attributes is quite different.
    Earnest (21) has proposed the superimposition of higher
level structures on the records and record interconnections
of a data base. This greatly simplifies the access to the
data base since the inter-record (inter-relation) connections need not be mentioned in the selection expressions. We
consider his ideas very valuable and go furhter along this
path by suggesting (in terms of his concepts) to have at
most one (default) structure for any set of attributes in
the data base. Although there is a common motivation between
our work and his work, there are significant differences
between the selection structures that he proposes and the
data model presented here.

1.4 OBJECTIVES OF THE STRUCTURAL ASSOCIATION MODEL

In the sections that follow we present a structural association model for data bases that can be added, as an extension, to most of the current data base models. We have
the following goals in mind.
a) First, we want to be able to reflect with the model the
   structure of the logical data base. Thus we did not intend to include all the details that may be considered as
   part of the conceptual schema but only those determined
   by the structural properties of the logical data base.
   For example, details like the fact that a person and
   his/her spouse must have different sex are not included
   in our model. By structural properties we mean those
   which determine the correct strategies to derive the existing semantic views. For example, sale number and
   cumulative per product per customer are not directly associated but there is a proper way to associate them in

terms of the logical data base structure.

b) Second we wish to make things as simple as possible for the users and for the Data Base Administrator. This criteria has led us to introduce concepts or classifications only when they were absolutely necessary.

c) Our third goal deals not with the representation problem of the model but the construction problem. We take a procedural approach and present some algorithms that, given some information by the user will produce the corresponding representation of the data base structure. These algorithms could be automated so as to allow the user to interactively describe a data base. Thus, in a way the input to these algoritms would be part of the Data Description Language corresponding to an implementation of our model. A more thorough analysis of the algorithms and their complexity can be found in (17).

d) Finally, in (17) we define a data base sublanguage and the algorithms to execute its commands in terms of the model.

The description of the model is given at the level of the Data Base Administrator, i.e., a casual user would not need to understand all the things presented here. It is also important to point out that we present here only what would be the basic core of the data base system upon which many other subsystems should be designed. For example, we do not discuss security, integrity, recovery and so on.

It is important to observe that our work is covered by the relational model in the sense that it can be described in relational terms and for that reason our model might be considered as an extension of it (i.e., our model can be superimposed onto a relational schema). However, we prefer not to assume any specific representation such as the use of relations since this tends to presuppose a whole set of decisions that we have not yet made. The same remarks are true for many current models.

We wish to emphasize that our work has been purely theoretical thus far and no implementation has been done.

In the following section we introduce the basic elements of the model and the algorithms to construct, in terms of the model, the logical data base structure. Finally we give a summary and conclusions for the paper.

2. STRUCTURAL CHARACTERISTICS OF THE MODEL

2.1. INTRODUCTION

The first step in structuring the data soup is to identify the most elementary type of association as that which exists among all the attributes that define a "singular class of entities" (SCE). This is a first level association which constitutes a building block for second level associations that exist among these singular classes of entities. At this second level we identify three relevant types of associations whose characteristics reflect the structural

properties of the data base. A set of "association graphs"
is used to represent all of the relevant associations that
are generated. These basic elements of our model allow us
to examine the information that can be derived by combining
different associations. This is easily accomplished with
the introduction of the "integrated graph" which is an
equivalent representation of the set of association graphs.
Since the means to describe the data base is fundamental to
any model we present two algorithms that map the user's
description of the world into singular classes of entities
and association graphs. SCEs and AGs can be considered as
"blocks of attributes" according to the definition given in
(23). In terms of the mental model proposed by Falkenberg
(24), SCEs and AGs can be considered as significations of
sets of associations while the concept of attribute, as
defined below, can be considered as a signification of a set
of objects. In terms of the conceptual model proposed in
(22) an SCE can be considered as an entity type, an AG as a
relationship type and attributes (to be defined) as properties.

2.2. SINGULAR CLASSES OF ENTITIES

The definition of entity given in (22) is used here: "An
entity is something of (that portion of) an enterprise that
is real or abstract, distinguishable and of interest for the
people of the enterprise". Each entity is characterized by
the values of a specific set of attributes, which are the
properties that completely characterize that entity. An
item is an occurrence of a value of an attribute. All the
entities characterized by a given set of attributes are said
to belong to one class of entities. In a class of entities, an attribute is singular if there may be only one
item of that attribute per entity of the class (i.e., it is
non-repeating). To clarify this definition, consider the
case of an entity representing a sale operation, the attributes SALESMAN-NO. and SALESMAN-NAME are singular attributes of the corresponding class of entities. However,
if there may be more than one salesman involved in the
operation, then those attributes are not singular.

In a class of entities, an attribute is unique if each of
its possible values may belong to only one entity of the
class, i.e. each item uniquely identifies the entity to
which it belongs. As an example, SALE-NO. and SALESMAN-NO.
are both singular in a class of entities representing sales
but only SALE-NO. is unique.

In a class of entities, a candidate key is any attribute
which is singular and unique in that class. Two different
entities may not have all items identical. Our model deals
with restricted classes of entities called singular classes
of entities (SCE) with the following restrictions:
a) All attributes in a singular class must be singular.
b) Each attribute belongs to one and only one singular
   class.
c) At least one attribute in each singular class should be a
   key.
d) Inside a singular class of entities, each attribute may
   not be functionally dependent on an attribute that is not
   a candidate key.

As a consequence of (b) the set of all possible attributes is partitioned in disjoint subsets which are the singular classes.

When translating a set of classes of entities into a set of singular classes, the information that cannot be represented inside the new entities, due to the above restrictions, will be represented in the form of "association graphs" which will be described shortly.

2.3 AN EXAMPLE OF SINGULAR CLASSES OF ENTITIES
If we are interested in information about sales of a given company we could enumerate a list of all the attributes in which we may be interested. Let us assume they are: SALE_FORM_NO, AGENT_NO, CUSTOMER_NAME, PRODUCT_NO, QUANTITY_SOLD, UNIT_PRICE, TOTAL_$_AMOUNT, $_AMOUNT, TYPE_OF_PAYMENT, BRANCH_OFFICE, DATE_OF_SALE, %_DISCOUNT, %_COMISSION.
Now, we might try to group them as follows:
Agent: (AGENT_NO)
Customer: (CUSTOMER_NAME)
Sale: (SALE_FORM_NO,   TOTAL_$_AMOUNT,   TYPE_OF_PAYMENT, BRANCH_OFFICE, DATE_OF_SALE, %_DISCOUNT, %_COMISSION)
Product   sold: (PRODUCT_NO, QUANTITY_SOLD, UNIT_PRICE, $_AMOUNT)
(where the first attribute in each group is the corresponding key)
The grouping shown above has a problem: in the class "Product sold", either attribute PRODUCT_NO is not a key or the other attributes are not singular because there may be many sales of the same product, and in consequence we have either many entities with the same key (same product), which is not valid, or an entity with many items of the same attributes, which violates the definition of singular attributes.
An easy way to overcome the problem is to split the class "Product sold" into three classes, as follows:
Product no: PRODUCT_NO, UNIT_PRICE
Quantity sold: QUANTITY_SOLD
Amount sold: $_AMOUNT
With these modifications our previous grouping meets the conditions of singular classes. Now, if we decide that we want to be able to know more information about customers we can add CUSTOMER_ADDRESS, CUSTOMER_TEL, and CATEGORY (if they are classified by volume of purchases or anything else as long as they belong to only one category). All these new attributes can be appended to the class "Customer" and it will still be singular.
Suppose now that we wish to keep a record of how many units of each product a customer has bought during the year (the cumulative of our first example). The cumulative can't be appended to the class "Customer" because a customer may not buy only one product throughout the year. On the other hand we can't append cumulative to the class "Product no" because each product must have a cumulative value as many times as customers have bought the given product. Therefore, we need a new singular class that will contain only the new attribute. Thus, our singular classes would look as follows:
Agent: (AGENT_NO)
Customer: (CUSTOMER_NAME, CUSTOMER_ADDRESS, CUSTOMER_TEL,

CATEGORY)
 Sale: (SALE_FORM_NO,   TOTAL_$_AMOUNT,   TYPE_OF_PAYMENT,
BRANCH_OFFICE, DATE_OF_SALE,%_DISCOUNT,%_COMISSION)
 Product no: (PRODUCT_NO, UNIT_PRICE)
 Quantity sold: (QUANTITY_SOLD)
 Amount sold: ($_AMOUNT)
 Cumulative: (CUMULATIVE)
       Informally, the objective in constructing the singular
classes is to identify independent entities in the user's
world and those attributes that simply describe properties
of those entities. The attributes within a class would have
no meaning to the user by themselves. The one attribute that
identifies the entity being defined is the key. The other
attributes cannot be entered into the data base without
reference to a key previously or concurrently entered.
Furthermore, if the key item is deleted the other items of
the given SCE occurrence must disappear as well.

2.4 ALGORITHM TO OBTAIN THE OPTIMAL SET OF SCEs
       Construction of the SCEs will not be a trivial task if
there are hundreds of attributes to deal with. Therefore a
simple algorithm is needed that will allow the data base administrator to generate SCEs on the basis of the user's
answers to some simple questions. The algorithm is based on
functional dependencies, it clusters attributes that are
dependent on one another. However , transitive dependencies*
are avoided by not seeking clusters of clusters. This should
be clear after reading the algorithm.
       The SCEs produced by this algorithm are optimal in the
sense that there are no transitive dependencies between any
pair of attributes within one SCE and no other set of SCEs
for the given attributes has smaller cardinality.
       In this and other algorithms we use the notion of
"covering" with the usual meaning. If A and B are two
n-tuples of binary digits then A covers B provided that A
has a 1 in every position that B does.

ALGORITHM
1) Assign a positive sequential integer (starting with1) to
     each attribute, in any way desired.
2) Build a matrix in which row (column) i corresponds to at-
        tribute i.   The (i,j)th element of the matrix should
        contain a 1 if attribute j is functionally dependent on
        attribute i (attribute i   attribute j). It should con-
        tain a blank otherwise.
3) Rename attributes in descending order of the number of
     1's in their corresponding rows.
4) Build a matrix, corresponding to this new numbering con-
     vention, as in step 2.
5) Merge equal rows, keeping track of all the attributes
     that correspond to a merged row. The attribute(s) cor-
     responding to each row at this stage is (are) the cor-
     responding key(s) of that row.
     Let n = the number of remaining rows after step 5.
     Also assume that there are four procedures:
     (i) "compound (i)" - returns TRUE if row i is cur-
     rently associated with more than one attribute and
     FALSE otherwise.
----
* C is transitively dependent on A if $A \rightarrow B$ and $B \rightarrow C$.

(ii) "merge (i,j)" - adds the attribute corresponding to row (i) with those already associated with row (j).
(iii) "mark (i)" - flags row (i) indicating that it has been absorbed into another.
(iv) "cover (i,j)" - returns TRUE if row i covers row i and FALSE otherwise.
The procedure then continues with:

```
6) FOR i=n STEP -1 UNTIL 1 DO
      BEGIN
            IF ¬(compound(i)) THEN
            BEGIN
                  FOR j=(i-1) STEP -1 UNTIL 1 DO
                  BEGIN
                        IF ¬(mark(i)) THEN
                        IF cover(j,i) THEN
                        BEGIN
                              merge(i,j);
                              mark(i);
                        END;
                  END;
            END;
      END;
```

7) The unmarked rows correspond to the optimal SCEs.

If we now apply this algorithm to the example of the sales data we obtain the matrices shown in figure 1. The entries in the matrix in part (a) are determined by obtaining simple functional dependency information from the user. Figure 1(b) shows the matrix sorted according to "row weight". Note that the renaming of attributes affect both, columns and rows, therefore the pattern of ones for a given attribute (row) may be different in the original matrix and in the sorted matrix. Step 6 of the algorithm simply asks us to start at the bottom row and search upwards for the first row that covers it. There are none and it is not marked. However, when we repeat this for the second row from the bottom we find that it is covered by row 2. Hence the notation in the "merged to" column to the right of the matrix.

Rows that are compound are not merged into higher rows thus avoiding transitive dependencies. Further, the procedure of sorting by row weight and seeking the "smallest" cover generates the close, base-level associations that we are seeking. Notice that some SCEs such as Cumulative and $-Amount are singletons because they are not properties of any single entity and because they have no further qualifying characteristics.

The result of step 6 is the set of "marked rows" indicated in the figure and the SCEs are the unmarked rows.

(Sale , Total-$, Branch, Date-Sale, Discount, Comission, Type-payment)
(Cust-name, Cust-category)
(Prod., Unit-Price)
(Cust-Address, Cust-Tel)
(Qty-sold)
($-amount)
(Cum/Prod/Cust)
(Agent-no)

	1	2	3	4	5	6	7	8	9	10	11	12	13	14	15	16	17	Order
1 Sale-form #	1		1			1		1	1	1	1	1	1	1	1			1
2 Agent #		1																5
3 Cust. name		1											1	1	1			2
4 Product #				1		1												3
5 Qty. sold					1													6
6 Unit Price						1												7
7 Total-$							1											8
8 $-Amount								1										9
9 Type Payment									1									10
10 Branch										1								11
11 Date-Sale											1							12
12 %-Discount												1						13
13 %-Comission													1					14
14 Cust. tel.														1				15
15 Cust. address														1	1			4
16 Cust. Cat.																1		16
17 Cumulative/Prod/Cust																	1	17

(a) Initial matrix of functional dependencies

	1	2	3	4	5	6	7	8	9	10	11	12	13	14	15	16	17	Merged to
1 Sale #	1	1	1			1		1	1	1	1	1	1		1	1		
2 Cust. name	1	1												1	1			
3 Prod. #				1		1												
4 Cust. address				1									1					
5 Agent #					1													
6 Qty. sold						1												
7 Unit Price							1											3
8 Total-$								1										1
9 $-Amount									1									
10 Type Payment										1								1
11 Branch											1							1
12 Date-Sale												1						1
13 %-Discount													1					1
14 %-Comission														1				1
15 Cust. tel.															1			4
16 Cust. cat.																1		2
17 Cumulative/Prod/Cust																	1	

(b) Sorted matrix of functional dependencies

Fig. 1: Example using the algorithm to obtain the optimal set of SCEs

2.5 ASSOCIATION GRAPHS (AG)

Having obtained the SCE's we must now define the more loosely coupled associations represented by the Association Graphs. An Association Graph is represented by the following diagram:

$\alpha_1, \ldots, \alpha_n$ and $\beta_1, \ldots, \beta_m$ represent keys of SCE's, and are called, respectively, "independent elements" and "property elements".

In modelling an association we are only interested in representing its most essential characteristics so as to keep things as simple as possible and to preserve its fundamental properties. Therefore, in an AG we represent the following information:

- All the elements in an AG are associated among themselves.

- Each property element is functionally dependent on the combination of all the independent elements.

In order to exist, an instance of an AG requires the existence of its independent part only. The AG's are to be viewed as templates. Instances of an AG are represented by occurrences of SCE's linked in the manner specified by the template. We do not care, at this point, how these links are represented. Henceforth we will use the term "association" instead of "instance of an Association Graph" whenever no confusion may arise.

2.6 TYPES OF ASSOCIATIONS

We distinguish three types of association.
1) Type I is characterized by the existence of a functional dependency between the independent element and each property element. In this type of association there must be only one independent element.

2) In type II associations there must be more than one independent element and each property element is functionally dependent on the combination of all the independent ones. The property part here represents characteristics of the association defined by the independent part.

3) In type III associations there must be more than one independent element and no property elements. It contains all the associations which are not of type I or type II. It is characterized by the existence of set dependencies (one-to-many relationships) between the participating SCEs and by the absence of functional dependency. (Note that one to many relationships in both ways correspond to many to many relationships).

It is interesting to note that SCE's can be considered and
represented as type I associations in which the key of the
SCE is the only independent element and all the others are
property elements.
    In the above algorithm and those following, it is as-
sumed that any attribute name cannot be the property of two
different sets of attributes unless one set is a subset of
the other or one set is derivable from the other by applying functional dependencies. More formally, this naming
restriction can be stated as follows: Each attribute name
is non-transitively (and non-pseudotransitively) fully
functionally dependent on at most one set of attributes. An
explanation of the terms used in the formal statement of
the assumption can be found in (13, 2). Observe that if
this assumption is violated the user faces a naming confusion because a given name may ambiguously represent a
property of two different sets of SCEs. Thus, this situation should not arise in appropriate naming schemas.
    It is also assumed that for any pair of attribute
names A and B it is not possible to derive, from the given
functional dependencies, that A,S ———→ B and
B,X ———→ A, where S and X are sets of attribute names and
at least one of them is not empty. A justification for
this assumption comes from the fact that models in DBMS are
composed of a structure division plus an integrity constraints division (25). Thus, the structure of a logical
data base may not necessarily reflect all the existing
functional dependencies since they are part of the integrity constraints. Therefore, for the construction of the
logical data base structure one may take into account the
biggest subset, of the existing functional dependencies,
that satisfies the second assumption described above. As
will be seen later on, there are some other desirable conditions for the naming schema. Further diiscussion of the
two previous assumptions can be found in (17).

2.7 ALGORITHM TO DERIVE ASSOCIATION GRAPHS
A methodology to map the information given by the user into
the corresponding set of association graphs is presented
here.

We will first give the algorithms and then apply them to
our example. It is suggested that the reader skim the algorithms and then refer back to them while following the
example. Given a set of different keys, each one corresponding to a SCE, the associations are derived as follows.

1.) Derivation of type I associations.

1.1) Identify functional dependencies among keys. (This can
be obtained from the algorithm to obtain SCE: each final
row, A, that covers another final row, B, implies that
A → B.

1.2) Create a set S containing all the non-transitive functional dependencies. For example, if A → B, B → C, and
A → C then S = (A → B, B → C)

1.3) For each functional dependency in the set S draw an as-

sociation graph as follows:
$$\text{If } A \longrightarrow B \text{ then} \qquad\qquad \begin{array}{c} A \\ \downarrow \\ B \end{array}$$

1.4) Merge association graphs with the same independent set:
$$\text{If} \quad \begin{array}{c} A \\ \downarrow \\ B \end{array} \quad \text{and} \quad \begin{array}{c} A \\ \downarrow \\ C \end{array} \quad \text{then replace them by} \quad \begin{array}{c} A \\ \downarrow \\ B,C \end{array}$$

2.) <u>Derivation of type II associations</u>

2.1) Build a matrix where each row/column corresponds to a key, as follows: We say that $Ki \xrightarrow{*} Kj$ if and only if for any set S, if $(S \longrightarrow Kj)$ is not transitive nor pseudotransitive then $Ki \in S$. (See (13) for an explanation of pseudotransitivity) Here again, derivable dependencies are ignored. In the matrix, the (i,j)th element must be 1 if $Ki \xrightarrow{*} Kj$, it must be blank otherwise. The elements of the matrix corresponding to a pair of SCEs such that one is functionally dependent on the other must be blank because their association has already been defined.

2.2) All diagonal elements must be blank. For each column find all the rows that cover it, i. e. have a one in that column, and generate an AG whose independent set contains the covering rows (at least one) and the property set the covered column.

2.3) Merge all AG with the same independent set as follows:
$$\begin{array}{c} ABC \\ \downarrow \\ D \end{array} \qquad \begin{array}{c} ABC \\ \downarrow \\ E \end{array} \qquad \Longrightarrow \qquad \begin{array}{c} ABC \\ \downarrow \\ DE \end{array}$$

3.) <u>Derivation of type III associations</u>

3.1) Build a matrix whose rows (columns) correspond to SCE's that do not appear in the property set of any type I or II AG. (Because if it appears in a property set then it will be associated to the other SCE's through its independent set).

All diagonal elements must be blank. The (i,j)th element must be 1, if Kj is "statically set dependent" on Ki $(Ki \xrightarrow{**} Kj)$ it is blank otherwise. We say that Kj is "statically set dependent" on Ki $(Ki \xrightarrow{**} Kj)$ if any value of Ki is <u>always</u> associated with the <u>same</u> set of values of Kj. That is, the set of values of Kj is permanently defined at the time when the event that produces a new value of Ki is completely defined. It is implicit that the set of Kj values (which may be empty) cannot change with time. As an example, SALE-NO. $\xrightarrow{**}$ PRODUCT-NO. because the set of products associated with a given sale is invariant after the sale is completely performed. The reverse (PRODUCT-NO. $\xrightarrow{**}$ SALE-NO.) is not true because the set of sales associated to a product changes with time and is not known at the time when a new product is available for sale.
This concept overcomes, partially, the semantic

limitation of functional dependencies as will be seen in an
example.

3.2) For each non-blank row (say i) build a non-directed
graph as follows:
- attribute i and all the attributes whose corresponding
  columns have a 1 in row i are the nodes.
- connect any pair of nodes between which references may
  be established when entering a new value for attribute
  i.
- a node with only one link connected to it is called a
  terminal node.

3.2.1) Generate a set for each path from attribute i to a
terminal node including in the set all the nodes traversed
in the path.

3.2.2) For each set generated in the previous step create an
AG whose independent set contains all the elements of the
set, if and only if there is no other AG with the same independent set.

In order to clarify the previous algorithm, we will apply
it to the set of SCE's shown below:

1)   E = Agent-no
2)   S = Sale
3)   C = Customer
4)   P = Product
5)   A = Address
6)   Q = Quantity sold per product
7) $ = Amount per quantity sold per product
8)   U = Cumulative per product per customer

General assumptions:

- Two customers may have the same address.

- One sale may include many products.

- One sale must include only one customer.

- Each customer must have only one address

- Credit for a given sale operation may be given to one
  or more agents.

The numbers correspond to those given in the algorithm.

1.) <u>Derivation</u> <u>of</u> <u>type</u> <u>I</u> <u>associations</u>.

1.1) The functional dependencies that can be identified from
the algorithm to obtain SCE are the following ones: (see
figure 1(b)).

The row of sale covers the row of customer: S $\longrightarrow$ C
The row of sale covers the row of address: S $\longrightarrow$ A

The row of customer covers the row of address: C ⟶ A

1.2) S = (S ⟶ C, C ⟶ A) is the set of non-transitive functional dependencies.

1.3) The AG corresponding to each element of set S are:

$$S \longrightarrow C: \quad \begin{matrix} S \\ \downarrow \\ C \end{matrix} \quad \text{and} \quad C \longrightarrow A: \quad \begin{matrix} C \\ \downarrow \\ A \end{matrix}$$

1.4) There are no association graphs with the same independent set and for that reason nothing can be merged.

2.) <u>Derivation of type II associations</u>

2.1) The matrix is built as follows:

- There is no key (K) such that K ⟶ E.
- There is no key (K) such that K ⟶ S.
- (S ⟶ C): element (2,3)=1.
- There is no key (K) such that K ⟶ P.
- (C ⟶ A): element (3,5)=1.
- (S ⟶ Ω, P ⟶ Ω): element (2,6)=1 and element (4,6)=1.
- (S ⟶ $, P ⟶ $): element (2,7)=1 and element (4,7)=1.
- (C ⟶ U, P ⟶ U): element (3,8)=1 and element (4,8)=1.
- All diagonal elements are blank.
- Since C is functionally dependent on S then elements (2,3) and (3,2) must be blank.
- Since A is functionally dependent on C and S then elements (3,5), (5,3), (2,5) and (5,2) must be blank.

The resulting matrix is:

	E	S	C	P	A	Ω	$	U
1) E								
2) S						1	1	
3) C								1
4) P						1	1	1
5) A								
6) Ω								
7) $								
8) U								

2.2) Column 1 is covered by no row
    Column 2   "
    Column 3   "
    Column 4   "
    Column 5   "
    Column 6 is covered by rows 2 and 4:
    Column 7   "
    Column 8 is covered by rows 3 and 4:

This gives the following AGs:

$$\begin{matrix} SP & \quad SP & \quad CP \\ \downarrow & \quad \downarrow & \quad \downarrow \\ \Omega & \quad \$ & \quad U \end{matrix}$$

2.3) SP and SP are merged into SP

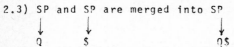

because their independent set is the same.

3.) Derivation of type III associations

3.1) Only S, P, and E can be rows (columns) of the matrix because they are the only SCEs that do not appear in the property set of any AG. Since S$\xrightarrow{**}$P and S$\xrightarrow{**}$E then elements (1,2) and (1,3) must be 1. Since there are no more static set dependencies, the following matrix is obtained.

	S	P	E
S		1	1
P			
E			

3.2) The first row is the only non-blank row:

- The nodes of the graph are S, P, E.
- When entering a new sale, references may be needed between sale and product and sale and agent.

This gives the following non-directed graph:

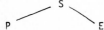

P and E are terminal nodes of the graph.

3.2.1) Since there are only two terminal nodes, then there are only two paths from S to a terminal node: (S,P) and (S,E).

3.2.2) The AG corresponding to (S,E) is: S, E
No new AG corresponding to (S,P) is created because there is already an AG whose independent set is precisely (S,P).

Now summarizing, we obtained the following association graphs:

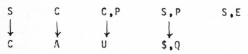

Note that the AG (S,E) was generated via the concept of static set dependency. Such data unit cannot be generated by algorithms based only on functional dependencies.

2.8 THE INTEGRATED GRAPH REPRESENTATION
The task of defining the structure of the logical data base is certainly much easier to do if we can deal with isolated partitions of it than if we have to consider the

data base as a whole at every step of this definition
process. Thus, the AGs and SCEs facilitate the definition of
the logical data base structure because they allow the
isolation of small parts of the data base at any given time.
This feature is remarkably valuable when considering very
large data bases.

However, it is not easy to comprehend the integration of
these parts (AGs and SCEs) and view the data base as a
whole. This is particularly important in trying to understand the operational characteristics of the data base ,
i. e. how data base accesses will be executed. To this end
we introduce the concept of an Integrated Graph (IG) that
explicitly shows the integrated structure.

The set of AGs and the integrated graph are equivalent
and can be derived from each other, according to the following rules:

- The integrated graph contains one labelled node for each
different SCE that exists in the data base.

- The upper part of an AG is represented by a special node,
called "junction box" (⬜), and solid branches to it from
each independent element.

- The lower part of an AG is represented by dotted branches
leaving the junction box corresponding to its independent
part and going to each property element.

Each junction box may correspond to a logical data unit
(relation, record) containing the keys of all the SCEs connected to the junction box. For this reason the term "data
unit" may be used to denote its corresponding junction box
whenever no confusion may arise.

Figure 2 contains the two alternative representations of
our example data base.

The integrated graph representation includes two
fundamental concepts that lead to a clearer picture of the
data base semantics.

a) Levels - Each node in the IG has a unique level, where
level is defined recursively as follows:

- All the SCEs that never appear in a property set are
level zero.

- Every box is in level k+1, where k is the maximum of the
levels of all the nodes connected to it through solid lines.

- Every property element is in level k+2, where k is the
maximum of the levels of all its independent elements. The
level corresponding to each element can be identified in
different ways in the graph. We use the convention shown in
fig. 2 (b). The way to determine levels in the IG is first
to find all the nodes without dotted lines connected to them
because they are all the level zero nodes. Then we can find
all the nodes of level 2 by finding all the nodes whose
dotted line is connected to a box that in turn is connected
(through solid lines) only to nodes whose levels have been
previously found. All the boxes that are connected only to
nodes whose levels have been previously found, i.e. 0 or 2,
are at level 1. Once all the level 1 and 2 nodes are found
we can repeat the same procedure to find all level 3 and 4
nodes, and so on. After finding the levels of all nodes the
graph can be rearranged as shown in fig. 2 (b). It is assumed hereafter that the IG does not contain a cycle whose
elements are in level 0 or 1 only. If this condition is not
originally met, some name refinement can be made in order to
satisfy it. This process is illustrated later. The proof

Ignacio Mijares and Richard Peebles

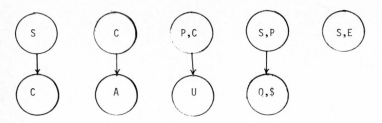

(a) A set of Association Graphs representing a data base.

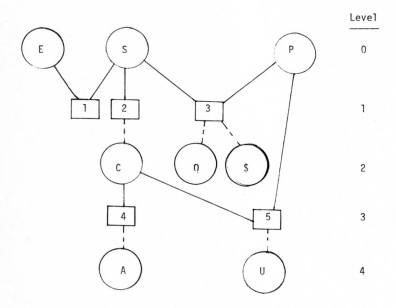

(b) An Integrated Graph representing the same data base.

Fig. 2: Different but equivalent representations of the same
data base.

that the level numbers are well defined can be found in
(17). Such proof is based on the second assumption stated
in Section 2.6.
   b) Legal paths - A legal path from node A to node B must
pass up towards the "root" (zeroeth level) of the IG then
down to level B. If the path runs through nodes $(A, X, , X_2$
$,..., X_n, B)$ then the level numbers of the nodes on the path
must monotonically decrease and then monotonically increase
to the level of node B. In figure 2 (b) there are two paths
from node C to node Q. The path $(C, 2, S, 3, Q)$ is legal but
the path $(C, 5, P, 3, Q)$ is not. The "degenerate" case where the
level numbers decrease only or increase only is permitted.
Between two nodes at level zero this rule will not work.
Here a legal path is one that connects the two nodes via an
alternating sequence of level zero nodes and level 1 junction boxes. In general the rule does not apply when the
change in monotonicity occurs at the lowest possible level
that allows reaching the destination. Thus, when there is
only one path between two nodes such a path is legal, i. e.
if there is a non-legal path between two nodes then there
must be at least one legal path between them. Since the
change in monotonicity that is not allowed is from increasing to decreasing in level number and since an atribute
name cannot be part of two property sets   then
any violation of the rule must be made by a subpath of three
nodes (attribute name, box, attribute name). Hereafter, the
term "non-legal subpath" will be used to denote a subpath of
3 nodes that violates the rule of legal paths. Obviously,
any non-legal path must contain at least one non-legal subpath. Observe that one non-legal subpath normally causes
multiple non-legal paths.

   This description of legal paths is useful for implementing the access algorithms and they also facilitate
the analysis of the data base structure by allowing the
precise identification of all the semantic views contained
in the data base. Intuitively they reflect the following
simple notions. Nodes at levels below 1 are properties of
some independent SCE or association of SCEs (possibly indirectly by being properties of properties, etc.). A legal
path is defined by seeking associations between these independent SCEs and by ascending or descending only within
the property group of one SCE or level zero association.
Now we are in a position to clearly define, in terms of the
proposed model, some useful concepts. Each path, between
two attributes, that includes only one box corresponds to a
direct association between them. If it includes more than
one box then it corresponds to an indirect association. The
"natural" association between two attributes is derived from
the (non-empty) set of legal paths connecting them. This
derivation is described below. A "non-natural" association
corresponds to each non-legal path joining the two attributes provided that it contains a non-legal subpath which
is not equivalent to any legal path. Finally, the set of
semantic views is equal to the set of natural and non-
natural associations. This is a subset of the set of direct
and indirect associations, which in turn is equal to the set
of all paths. Therefore, there is no one to one mapping
between semantic views and logical access paths. This allows
the determination of some semantic views involving at-

tributes that are in the property set of a type   II   AG,   as
shown   in   the   relational   example of Section 1.2. However,
those logical access paths that do   not   correspond   to   any
semantic   view   will   correspond   to   a sequence of semantic
views.
     The   retrieval   algorithm for semantic views traverses,
in parallel, all the legal paths between the attributes   involved.   Therefore,   the example query given in Section 1.2,
i. e. find all sales that led to cumulative values   of   100,
can   be   satisfied   by simply requesting the unique semantic
view between S and U, which could be specified as follows:
               RETRIEVE S(U=100);
The execution of this command implies the parallel   traver-
sal of the paths (U,5,C,2,S) and (U,5,P,3,S) which gives the
correct answer.   The user may   compare   the   two   constructs
used   to   specify the same query, i. e. the SEQUEL construct
in Section 1.2 and the one given above, and observe the simplicity obtained when dealing with unique semantic views.

It is easy to see that the structure of a logical data base
will be more clearly defined, i.e. more simply and with less
confusion,   when there is only one semantic view between any
pair of attributes, i. e. there is no   non-natural   association.   This   can   be   achieved   by   choosing an appropriate
naming scheme, i.e. by not representing two   different   attributes   with   the   same name. To clarify these ideas consider our example data base shown in Figure 2.   There   is   a
non-legal   path between C and P (C,5,P) but there is no non-
natural association between them because both the   non-legal
and   the   legal   path   (C,2,S,3,P)   correspond   to   the same
relationship. This is so, because U is a derivable   entity,
i.e. there should be a cumulative for each product bought by
a customer.   However, if U represented   the   opinion   of   a
customer   about a product (which may have not been bought by
the customer), then there would be a non-natural association
etween C and P, and in consequence there would be two semantic views between them. By refining the concept   of   product
(splitting   it into product-bought and product-surveyed)   or
the concept of customer (splitting   it   into   customer   and
person-surveyed)   we   could   assure   the existence of no non-
natural associations.   A formal method to achieve this   type
of   transformation   is given in (17).   When all the semantic
views are represented by natural associations, i.e. there is
only one semantic view between any pair of attributes, it is
possible to define a very simple data   base   sublanguage   in
which logical access-path specification is not required, and
it is also possible to view the   data   base,   for   retrieval
purposes,   as   one   single   table (relation, record). These
advantages are further clarified in (17).

3 SUMMARY AND CONCLUSIONS

3.1 SUMMARY
     The problem of designing logical data base structures has
been examined. In particular, a methodology was presented to
create the data base structure from information given by the

user. This information not only includes the concept of functional dependencies but also that of static set dependency.

An important characteristic of the structural association model presented here is the recognition of two levels of associations which allows the possibility of two levels of abstraction in the logical data base structure.

Finally, a specific criterion to identify semantic views was introduced as a framework for the analysis of the structural properties of the data base. It was also observed that the problem of logical access path specification can be considerably simplified in those data bases with only one semantic view between any pair of attribute names.

3.2 FURTHER WORK

The problem of different roles for a given attribute or for an SCE has to be studied in order to determine the best way of handling such situations.

A formal method must be developed to ensure that any data base can be transformed into an equivalent one containing only one semantic view between any pair of attributes. This transformation process can be called the "structural normalization" of data bases.

Many implementation ideas need to be considered in order to learn how much the proposed model would cost in space and time.

Finally, formal proofs for the graph generation algorithms are required to establish the fidelity of the structural representation.

REFERENCES

1) Codd E. F.
A relational model of data for large shared
data banks.
CACM, Vol. 13, No. 6, June 1970, pp. 377-387

2) Codd E. F.
Further normalization of the data base
relational model.
Courant Computer Science Symp. 6, Data Base Sys.,
New York City, 1971, Prentice Hall.

3) Codd E. F.
Relational completeness of data base sublang.
Courant Computer Science Symp. 6, Data Base Sys.,
New York City, 1971, Prentice Hall

4) Bracchi G., Fidelia A., and Paolini P.
A relational data base management system
Proceedings of On-Line 72 Conf., 1972

5) Codd E. F. and Date C. J.
Interactive support for non-programmers:
the relational and network approaches.
Proc. 1974 ACM SIGFIDET Workshop

6) Date C. J. and Codd E. F.
The relational and network approaches:
comparison of the application prog. interfaces.
Proc. 1974 ACM SIGFIDET Workshop

7) CODASYL DBTG April 71 Report

8) Codd E. F.
Recent investigations in relational data base sys.
IBM Research Report RJ 1385, April 23, 1974

9) Abrial J. R.
Data Semantics
Proc. of IFIP Working Conf. on DBMS, 1974

10) Hainaut J. and Lecharlier B.
An extensible semantic model of data base and
its data language.
Proceedings IFIPS Conf., 1974

11) Deheneffe C., Hennebert H., and Paulus W.
Relational model for a data base
Proceedings IFIPS Conf., 1974

12) Schmid H. A. and Swenson J. R.
On the semantics of the relational data model
ACM SIGMOD Int. Conf. on Management of Data,
May, 1975

13) Bernstein P. A., Swenson J. R., Tsichritzis D. C.
A unified approach to functional dependencies and
relations.

ACM SIGMOD Int. Conf. on Management of Data,
May, 1975

14) Earley J.
On the semantics of data structures
Courant Computer Science Symp. 6, Data Base Sys.,
New York City, 1971, Prentice Hall

15) Bukhari S. A.
A relational model for data bases.
Ph. D. Thesis, University of Waterloo

16) Chamberlin D. and Boyce R. F.
SEQUEL: a structured english query language
Proc. of ACM SIGFIDET Workshop, Ann Arbor, 1974

17) Mijares I. and Peebles R. W.
A methodology for the design of
logical data base structures.
University of Waterloo, CCNG-TR (to appear)

18) Senko M. E.
Data description language in the context of a
multilevel structured description: DIAM II with FORAL,
IBM Research Report RC 5073, October 9, 1974.

19) Senko M. E.
Specification of stored data structures
and desired output results in DIAM 11 with FORAL.
Conf. on very large Data Bases, Boston, Mass., 1975.

20) Tsubaki M.
Multilevel data model in DPLS
Presented at the Conf. in Very Large Data Bases,
Boston, Mass., Sep. 1975.

21) Earnest Ch.
Selection and Higher Level Structures in Networks
IFIP TC-2 Conference, Belgium, Jan. 1975.

22) Moulin P., Randon J., et al.
Conceptual model as a data base design tool.
IFIP TC-2 Working Conf. on Modelling in DBMS,
January 1976, Freudenstadt, W. Germany.

23) Adiba M., Delobel C., Leonard M.
A unified approach for modelling data in
logical data base design.
IFIP TC-2 Working Conf. on Modelling in DBMS,
January 1976, Freudenstadt, W. Germany.

24) Falkenberg E.
A uniform approach to data base management.
IFIP TC-2 Working Conf. on Modelling in DBMS,
January 1976, Freudenstadt, W. Germany.

25) Nijssen G. M.
A gross architecture for next generation DBMS,
IFIP TC-2 Working Conf. on Modelling in DBMS,
January 1976, Freudenstadt, W. Germany.

Modelling in Data Base Management Systems, G.M. Nijssen, (ed.)
North Holland Publishing Company, 1976

Information Management Concepts (IMC)
for use with DBMS Interfaces

R. Durchholz, G. Richter

Gesellschaft fuer Mathematik und Datenverarbeitung (GMD)

St. Augustin, Germany

Abstract: The paper is mainly concerned with detailing the background against which the conceptual system IMC is to be understood. Also, IMC is outlined informally as an axiomatic theory and the application of the theory to the general background developed in the first part is shown. Finally one derived concept from IMC is selected to give a taste of the power of the conceptual system. The selected concept is that of a spot, which has proven helpful in the clarification of several issues discussed now with DBMS. As an example, its application to the notion of "hierarchic data structure" is considered.

Contents

1. Introduction

Development of data base technology is gradually changing from a phase of experimentation and exploration to a phase of consolidation and systematization. A desire becomes apparent for a conceptual

foundation on which existing ideas can be understood and future
development can be based. In addition, such a conceptual foundation
has been recognized to be of considerable importance for
standardization efforts, which also recently have received increasing
interest.

A conceptual system which serves this purpose must - beyond inner
consistency - show adequacy to the problem. As adequacy can hardly be
proven by an a priori argumentation, several alternative candidates
should be designed and tried. IMC is claimed to be such a candidate.

IMC as it stands now is still under development. The present paper is
intended to explain the motivations for IMC and to illustrate by
means of selected features the IMC-approach and its potential.

2. General background for IMC

2.1. Notions of interface and channel

An overall view of data base management architecture has been
published recently in [ANS] and has been evaluated in discussions
both in scientific and in standardization committees. One of the
messages of this Interim Report is the statement, that "what any
standardization should treat is interfaces". From the context it is
clear that this statement is intended to refer to DBMS
standardization. For this purpose it makes explicit a point of major
importance. .e use of the word "interface" raises at least these two
questions: What is it, between ("inter") which an interface is
located? What constitutes an interface?

As concerns the first question, the "actors" adjacent to interfaces
are explicitly shown in the cited report as boxes representing
"people in specific roles" and "processing functions". Between these
boxes the interfaces are depicted by numbered solid bars. With such a
model for the description of information flow two fundamentally
different kinds of functional_units are distinguished: Units which
have the function to perform specified operations or to play a
defined role, and units which have the function to enable
communication between the other functional units by assuming

specified states (i.e. by "containing" data). This model view has also been adopted for the approach presented in the following. We will, however, replace the bar as interface symbol by a circle, to make this most important aspect more conspicuous. In previous investigations the above model view has already been applied in a project for operating systems standardization in [ABN]. It originates from an information system theory, which has been outlined e.g. in [FET]. In the mentioned applications the term <u>office</u> (Instanz) has been used for the process performing or role playing functional units, the term <u>channel</u> (Kanal) for functional units linking offices and enabling them to interact with each other by exchanging data.

These considerations will help us to discuss the second question by comparing the concept of interface in the Interim Report with the concept of channel as was just outlined. Such a comparison should lead to a more precise understanding of the term DEMS interface. Starting from here, an analysis of the interaction across DEMS interfaces finally yields the motivation to develop conceptual tools for talking about the things which are communicated.

In the Interim Report the symbol for an interface (identified by a number) may occur at more than one place in an architecture diagram (see e.g. [ANS], page I-9, interface 3). This indicates, that there is a distinction between an interface and a channel. A channel is defined by its surrounding offices which have access to it, unlike an interface, for which the surrounding offices seem not to be characteristic. The following interpretation brings them into connection: Offices communicating via a channel have to act according to common rules for the data traffic in the considered channel. All communication has to take place within these rules. The rules may or may not be explicitly stated - i.e. agreed upon or built-in. Not their origin but their existence is relevant in the present context. The rules however can be effective for more than one channel. So it makes sense to consider them by themselves, without regard to any particular channel. This leads to the conclusion, that by <u>interface</u> in fact the totality of rules is meant, which govern the traffic via a considered channel or the considered channels. One has to be aware, however, that very often a name of an interface is used to designate a channel where this interface is implemented, and vice versa.

2.2. Methods for interface description

Our purpose now is to develop a conceptual system for the description
of interfaces, more specifically, of interfaces considered in the
context of data base management systems. Such a description may
relate to an interface in an existing system as well as in a system
to be designed. We do not have specific interfaces in mind as long as
they are typical for DBMS, but for the sake of explicitness and
simplicity the kind of system preferably considered in this paper
will have two offices and one channel, where one of the offices is a
DBMS and the other is called "user" (see figure).

Figure 1

The "user" is meant to be any office using the DBMS, be it a
so-called end user, a program run, the DBA or whoever else.

For further simplification we will assume, that the offices
communicate by exchange of character strings only.

When we aim at concepts for the description of interfaces we should
be very clear about w h a t exactly is the subject of the
description. A first guess for instance could be that there is little
interest just in character strings floating to and fro through the
channel, but rather in the m e a n i n g conveyed by the character
strings. We will come back to this shortly.

Before that, another point concerning the subject of description
shall be worked out: I n t e r f a c e description should not make
reference to the internals of the offices involved. (Instead of
"internals of the offices" it would be more precise to say "internals
of the hardware (machines, animals, persons) filling the offices".)
Otherwise the description would possibly depend on inner changes of
the offices, even if they leave the behaviour unchanged. Furthermore,
for different channels with identical interfaces the descriptions
would possibly be different, depending on whether the offices
adjacent to the channel are of equal or different construction.

We will call the strict separation of behavioural from internal aspects the "principle of structured description" in accordance with the well-known structured programming, which is (nested) structured description of algorithms.

Although the advantages of the principle of structured description are well known and generally accepted, in practice aspects of construction ("implementation") very readily infiltrate interface considerations. It is therefore not superfluous to put strong emphasis on this point and to state once for all that in this paper we will n e v e r talk about office construction, if not indicated explicitly.

We now return to the topic of "meaning" mentioned above. If we want to talk about meaning, it should be indicated, the meaning t o w h o m is considered. Can we consider the meaning of character strings as attributed by the offices "user" or "DBMS"? Apart from the fact, that we would become entangled in futile philosophical disputes about whether a DBMS can attribute meanings to messages, this would be a violation of the principle of structured description, for the internals of the offices would be entered.

We are left with the possibility to consider "meaning" for the describer and the description reader. These are not offices of the system considered, although the same p e r s o n s may fill the office "user" at times. What kind of meaning can they associate with the character strings transmitted? Among various possibilities to approach this question the pragmatic way seems to be the one that is best suited, because it does not need to extend the context within which the interface is considered. The pragmatic understanding postulates that the meaning of a character string transmitted is the e f f e c t it has on the communication partners. Under the restriction not to consider internals of offices and not to consider any other reaction than character string exchanges, we can say that with the pragmatic view the meaning of a character string transmitted is the effect it has on subsequent character string exchanges.

Now it seems that we have been trapped in a circle: We started off with the desire not to talk just about character string exchange, but about the meaning of character strings. We end up with bending the issue back by saying that there is no meaning than that expressed by character string exchange.

This seemingly unsatisfactory result attains a quite different appearance when we take a closer look at the somewhat derogatory expression " j u s t character strings". Actually the effect on subsequent character string exchange can and as for DBMS also will be extremely complex. And, if we manage to describe it in such detail, that, given the history of character string exchanges, the reactions of the DBMS can be anticipated, and if this is done in a mentally economic way, is this not all what is really needed? In addition, it seems that any attempt to introduce "more" meaning than can be supported pragmatically will have adverse effects on the ease of communication about data base matters, for such extended meaning will involve more terminological and conceptual apparatus, which tends to obscure the real issue and to introduce ambiguity. Compare for instance the presently frequent reference to "reality".

Once we are convinced that interface description is best done by describing the effect of character strings transmitted on subsequent character string exchange, we have to look for a way to do this adequately. Three different methods are considered and evaluated.

The first method is the p h e n o m e n o l o g i c a l one. With this, the conceptual system for description of interfaces is based directly on "what is seen". This means, that one is talking in terms of character string exchange, which may include for instance character set, length, sequencing and interleaving of character strings, time delays and so on. Certainly this approach would have to go a very long way with many complicated abstractions before such esoteric things like "files" and "currency status indicators" could be described. So this method is likely to be inadequate.

Next we try two methods called "methods of imputed inner properties". These describe the interface as being between offices which act a s i f they possess certain inner properties. Mind, that this does not at all violate the principle of structured description. No claim is made about the actual internal nature of the offices. The imputation of inner properties is only a tool for description.

The distinction between actual and imputed inner properties is at the focal point of this entire discussion. It makes explicit the boundary between sound description methods and confusing reference to conditions on the environment not relevant to the subject under consideration. The problem is, that there are several aspects inherently or legitimately bordering the area of interface description: Usually from the outset everybody concerned agrees with the principle of structured description. Then, when it turns out that the phenomenological method is inadequate, one switches to imputed inner properties. But, as it is impractical to repeat all over again the word "imputed" (or an equivalent), the language in which the description is made does no more explicitly express this important distinction. This largely contributes to forgetting about it at all. In particular new-comers and people marginally concerned with the development will confuse the issue. To aggravate the situation, feasibility considerations are necessary in an interface design process and cause interest in implementation aspects. The chaos is perfect, if these are mixed up with imputed inner properties.

It should be mentioned, that the above is not just an academic exercise in semantic analysis, but can be substantiated through observation of most of the professional discussion going on in the data base field.

The word "imputation" has a negative flavour in English, which is of course not meant in the present use. In an earlier version the word "hypothesis" was used. As was pointed out in [WAG], this would be misleading and "model" would be much better. While this is true, the presently ubiquitous use of the word "model" does not recommend it for this purpose. In addition, although the literal translation of "hypothesis" to English ("supposition") has about the same meaning, the literal translation to German ("Unterstellung") is quite up to the point. This word, when translated to English, yields "imputation", but the German word is not always used in the negative sense.

One way to impute inner properties is to assume inner construction. In this case one would talk about various components of the offices, and how they interact with each other and with the environment of the office. Such an approach, although sometimes very appropriate for algorithms of limited complexity in the interaction with their environment, has nearly the same inadequacies for DBMS as has the phenomenological approach. In the next section we try as a last attempt, and actually that which is recommended, the approach of imputed_inner_power_of_imagination.

2.3. The universe of discourse

Let us recall that we are simply looking for an adequate mental
framework for the description of interfaces. When we say that we want
to impute for the offices a power of imagination, it should once
again be emphasized, that this is not a metaphysical claim, but just
an assumption for descriptional convenience. Also, in actual
technical discussion about data base matters, references to mental
powers of the user and even of the DBMS are creeping in at several
scattered locations and in an uncontrolled way. This seems to be much
more questionable than a deliberate, well-prepared and localized
introduction. According to the method of imputed power of imagination
the offices are thought of as having some of their imagination in
common. All communication is within the scope of the common
imaginations. The totality of imaginations that are subjects of the
communication is called the universe_of_discourse, UoD for short. For
an illustration see the following picture:

Figure 2

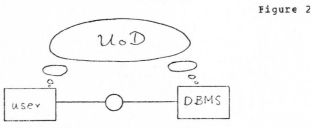

Although communication between the offices is w i t h i n the UoD,
a significant part of the dialog is devoted to c h a n g i n g   the
UoD.

2.4. The concept of construct

The initial task to find a conceptual system for the description of
interfaces can now be understood as the task of finding a conceptual
system to describe the UoD and its changes. At present we select for
consideration one single subject only, but one which is most
characteristic for DBMS. This is the entire information kept by the
DBMS for this one user. We call it the framework_construct. The
framework construct is known in detail by the DBMS, but not by the
user. Otherwise the user would not need to ask the DBMS about it.

Nevertheless the user refers to the framework construct when he communicates with the DBMS. The case for several users is considered below in this section.

The most salient feature of the framework construct is that it is not an undivisible whole, but that it consists out of parts. The parts are called <u>constructs</u>. Constructs may or may not be further decomposable into parts. Parts of constructs are also regarded as parts of the framework construct, hence they are constructs too.

Several alternatives may be considered for the composition of constructs from constructs. We have tried with some success to get along with two composition principles only:
- set aggregation
- set aggregation with additional unique naming of set elements.

Starting from these principles, we have derived a whole system of interdependent concepts (IMC), which gave us quite some interesting insight into the nature of several of the commonly used notions. For the development of the conceptual system a reasonable degree of precision and consistency was desired. This was carried out by developing a formal theory, for which the conceptual system under discussion is intended to be an application. Some concepts of this theory are outlined in section 3.

2.5. The universe of discourse for several users

The case for several users interacting with the same data base has not been taken into account so far. We will now append a few considerations on this case. If several users access the same data base, each of them must be aware of the others, because they interfere with each other. The questions now are: In what sense has a user to take into account his competitors and which are the tools he needs to react correspondingly?

We are now leaving our preferred diagram with one user only. The system diagram for several, say four, users is

Figure 3

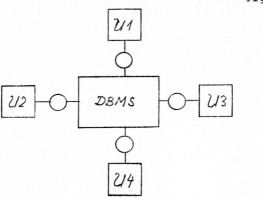

For each user there is one universe of discourse (UoD) for his
communication with the DBMS. Let us focus on one of the users - say
U1. U1 is faced directly with the DBMS. To him the other users make
themselves conspicuous through the reactions of the DBMS only. This
has to be understood in the very general sense, that messages from
the DBMS about constructs - say, as a result of a request - are also
reactions of the DBMS. U1 now has the choice to look at the DEMS
together with the other users as o n e office with built-in
stochastic sources.

Figure 4

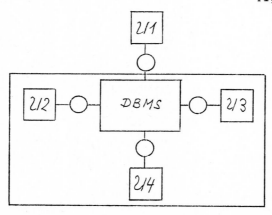

It is expected that the interference caused by the stochastic sources
will be a subject of discourse (among others) between U1 and the
DBMS. So for the description of this interface concepts are needed to

talk about the interferences (or possible interference) and precautions taken for them. There may be several ways to create concepts for this purpose. The most natural one seems to be to a s s u m e offices outside of the DBMS, which can be called (competitive as well as communicating) <u>users</u>.

It seems that nothing has been gained by first conceptually eliminating users and introducing them again as if they were a new invention. The difference however is, that the assumed users need not be the same offices as the actual ones. Not only can for instance several actual users be combined into one assumed one, but an actual user can be decomposed into several assumed ones (roles), if this helps simplify the description. Still more, the actual users can be decomposed and reassembled to form assumed users which are much easier to survey.

As the communication of two offices through one channel is a strictly sequential process, the system diagram above seems to eliminate concurrency by a conceptual trick. Unfortunately this is not the case. If the function of the DBMS is to be described - as e.g. is necessary for its design - all its channels have to be considered together. It is not sufficient to describe them one after the other. Under this view, the system diagram is converted to

Figure 5

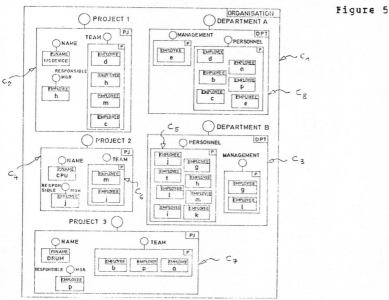

We have the result, that the description of the DEMS interface for a
single user needs to talk about sequential processes only, whereas
the description of the total interface of the DEMS towards its
environment and amalgamated from the interfaces of the various users
normally will require concurrent process description methods.

2.6. Physical representation of constructs

We will close this introductory section by a further limitation of
our scope of interest. In doing so we also relate ourselves back to
the starting point of the description of character string exchanges.
Within the imputed common world of constructs the communication
partners talk about constructs. This is done by exchanging construct
representations on physical media. (These we have become used to call
"data".) There may be and usually are several representations for the
same construct. The questions related to construct representation are
important ones and constitute an interesting field for research. In
the present paper however this topic is not under consideration.

3. Outline of formal IMC and its application

The formal IMC is an axiomatic theory the notions of which acquire
meaning only when they are interpreted. It is designed with the
intention to be interpreted within the conceptual framework developed
in the first section. In the sequel this conceptual framework will be
referred to as the "UoD-context".
In formal IMC we have two primitive notions, that is, notions which
have no definitions. They are atom and name. Atoms are to be
interpreted as non-decomposable constructs, names as the names
mentioned in the second composition principle of the UoD-context
(i.e. unique naming of set elements). The definition of a construct
then is recursively given by use of the formal counterparts of both
composition principles:

- An atom is a construct
- Any finite set of constructs is a construct
  (called collection)
- Any finite function from names to constructs is a construct
  (called a nomination)
- Anything which is not a construct by virtue of the above three
  rules is not a construct

Clearly this definition does not match exactly with the concept of
construct in the UoD-context, because it includes any conceivable
construct of any conceivable data base instead of the parts of the

present framework construct only. This extension cf the concept however is very convenient, for in the UcD cne will have tc communicate also about constructs that p o s s i b l y are parts of the framework construct (retrieval request) or ccnstructs that m a y or m u s t n o t (!) be part of future framewcrk ccnstructs (type declaration).

There is, however, a conceptual problem involved. It shculd be possible to distinguish one cf the many constructs to be the momentary framework construct. At present, we have nct means in formal IMC to express what distinguishes the framework construct frcm all other constructs and, moreover, tc talk atout the "present" cr "next" framework ccnstruct, or about framework ccnstruct transformation. In fact, this is an issue for extending the axicmatic theory. Such an extension will certainly invclve the intrcducticn cf new primitives and axicms. The reascn for not having elaborated such an extension is the lack cf time rather than unsurmcuntatle difficulty encountered in this attempt.

But even in its present state the theory already yields quite scme interesting derived concepts. One of them is the ccncept cf spct, as treated in more detail in next section. Another application is the currently much discussed concept of relation, the essence of which is rendered as a collective in IMC-terminolcgy (for details see [DRI]). This is identical with the relaticn concept of [HHT]. Furthermore, because in the IMC-approach there is no premature fixaticn and distinction of aggregation levels (e.g. like records, functions, cosets), this is a convenient basis for discussing the ccncepts cf type, population and cccurrence, although a really rigid treatment must be postponed until the concept cf framewcrk ccnstruct has received its formal characterization. However, one particular point can already be made: A construct is something that can be ccnsidered without reference to any type. The current terminology precludes this pcssibility by talking atout "instances" or "cccurrences" and thus making an automatic, at least implicit, reference to some type.

4. The spot concept as an illustrative example

A construct has its identity based only on its own properties rather
than on the properties of its environment, i.e. of its context. So
the number 7 is always the number 7 regardless of whether it is
considered the number of a house or the number of children or one of
the winning numbers of number lottery. The context of course is
different. What is that context? Consider the following example:

Figure 6

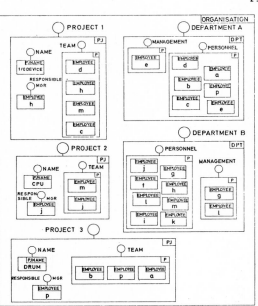

We focus our interest onto the construct j.   This construct is
embedded into three contexts. (By the way, that does not necessarily
imply multiple storing of the representation of the considered
construct.) To be able to distinguish the different appearances of
the same construct in a considered construct we say that construct j
is or appears at three spots.

In a representation of a construct - say, on paper, like in figure 6
- we may be able to point at a particular component of the construct
in a particular context and say "this". The relevant fact is, that

actually one does not point to a construct, but to a spot. If the
communication about spots is not via a common physical representation
and if consequently we cannot point with a physical pointer to the
spot, we need a conceptual counterpart for the physical pointer.

In formal IMC the spot is defined as the sequence of pairs, the first
of which consists of the empty name and the reference construct, the
last of which consists of the (in a collection: empty) name and the
construct "at this spot". The pairs in between are composed
analogously. (This definition of spot is only a slight modification
of the one already given in [DRI].) The last pair of a spot defining
sequence is also called the constituent at this spot. Referring to
fig. 6 the construct j appears at the following three spots in c_1:

$(-,c_1)$, (PROJECT 2,c_4), (RESPONSIBLE MGR,j)
$(-,c_1)$, (PROJECT 2,c_4), (TEAM,c_6), $(-,j)$
$(-,c_1)$, (DEPARTMENT B,c_3), (PERSONNEL,c_5), $(-,j)$

and e.g. in c_3 at the spot

$(-,c_3)$, (PERSONNEL,c_5), $(-,j)$

The lower case c's and j's stand for the respective construct, the
dash for the empty name.

It turns out, that this formal definition of a spot quite ably
captures the intuitive idea. However, it should be emphasized, that
the defining sequence of a spot is not intended nor suitable for
explicit use in a language, say for navigational purposes. It is
therefore necessary to identify spots other than by their defining
sequence. For the purpose of orientation and navigation in a large
construct a means for moving from spot to spot is to be provided at a
DPMS interface.

It may be useful to emphasize, that one and the same construct can
appear at several spots. This must not be confused with the idea,
that a type may have several occurrences (which are, however,
different constructs). Presumably that danger of confusion and a
feeling of still missing concepts were the reason for the authors of
[ANS] to put the word occurrence on page IV-8 between quotation

marks. However, they have recognized and indicated, that there is a
need for the concept of spot: "The objects defined in the conceptual
schema are not disjoint, in that ... the same "occurrence" of a
conceptual record may be in more than one conceptual record-set." In
IMC terminology this simply would read, that the same construct may
be at more than one spot. In the present context it is immaterial
that the construct is an occurrence of some type. Moreover it is
immaterial here, whether the multiple appearance of the same
construct is intended (by consistency constraints) or only by chance.
Spots at which the same construct appears are called parallel spots.

We think the spot concept is a very useful one in many data model
discussions. It should prove helpful by clarifying several
controversial or not well enough understood points, as is e.g. the
question of the power of data models.

As one example, when a data model is said to be hierarchic, such a
statement refers to a relationship between spots rather than
constructs. In a more general data model strong connections between
spots can be declared and are maintained by the system. Such
connections are e.g. that the constructs at the spots concerned are
identical (parallel spots) or that there is a "zero effort" access
path established between them. Both kinds of connections are realized
e.g. in the CODASYL model for a record construct which is a member of
two different coset occurrences and consequently appears at two
different spots. In a hierarchic model such connections cannot be
made. All system services are oriented toward following the spot
hierarchy. This hierarchy is given in a natural way by the very
definition of the spot concept, when we define a spot to be "above" a
second spot, if, in terms of sequences of pairs, the latter one (=
the spot "below") is an extension of the former one (= the spot
"above"). In the present context it is important to be aware of the
fact, that for a n y data model the spots of a construct form by
definition always a hierarchy in this sense of relative position. For
a data model to be called hierarchical or non-hierarchical the
relevant feature is, whether the system services follow this
hierarchy of spots or not. (Cf. also [PAR], where more care is
recommended for the use of the word "hierarchy" when several
hierarchies of different kinds are involved.)

As another simple example for the application of the spot concept let us consider a precise definition of the well-known concept of a record. It is clear, that the same construct which is a record in one context can be part of a record in a different context. So the property of being a record cannot in general be attached to the construct. For any particular data model, however, a set of spots can be defined, which identifies the records in this data model (under the condition of course, that in this data model one wants at all to talk about records). Formally, it would be sufficient to define these spots themselves to be the records.

A further application of the spot concept is the explanation of the fundamental ideas behind the currency concept of the well-known DBTG/DDLC proposal [CCL]. This has been elaborated in [DUB]. There the currency status indicators turn out to be of distinct nature: Whereas the "current of set" identifies one spot only in the whole network of cosets and records, all the other currency status indicators turn out to identify sets of spots.

Acknowledgement

A significant part of the ideas presented in this paper have been developed together with our colleagues W. Klutentreter and H. Simm of GMD. We are further indebted to the members of IFIP/WG 2.6, who encouraged us after a pre-presentation of parts of this paper to address a larger audience of experts.

References

[ABN] GMD/Arbeitsgruppe fuer Betriebssystemnormung: "Terminology for the description of models of job processing computer systems" (German). Gesellschaft fuer Mathematik und Datenverarbeitung, St. Augustin, 1971.

[ANS] ANSI/X3/SPARC: Interim report of the Study Group on Data Base Management Systems. Febr. 8, 1975.

[COL] CODASYL DDLC: Report June 73.

[DUR] Durchholz, R.: An analysis of the currency concept. Angewandte Informatik 17(6), June 1975.

[DRI] Durchholz, R.; Richter, G.: Concepts for Data Base Management Systems. In J. W. Klimbie and K. L. Koffeman (eds.): Data Base Management Systems, North Holland Publ. C., 1974.

[HHT] Hall, P. A. V.; Hitchcock, P.; Todd, S. J. P.: An algebra of relations for machine computation. IBM UKSC 0066, Peterlee, Jan. 1975.

[PAR] Parnas, D.: On a 'buzzword': Hierarchical structure. IFIP Congress, Stockholm, Aug. 5 - 10, 1974, North Holland Publ. C., 1974.

[PET] Petri, C. A.: Concepts of net theory. In: Proc. Symp. on Mathematical Foundations of Computer Science, pp. 137-146, High Tatras, 1973.

[WAG] Waghorn, W. J.: Discussion on Meeting IFIP-TC2-WG2.6, Jouy-en-Josas, Sept. 29 - Oct. 1, 1975.

Discussion

In the discussion several questions have been raised. The answers given here are not a direct transscript of the discussion, but reformulated to provide for a concise yet comprehensive reply.

Q.: Is only a l i m i t e d number of primitives assumed in formal IMC?

A.: Yes. Presently we have only two primitive concepts, atom and name. However, there are infinitely many objects which are atoms or names. As concerns extensibility of the theory, we assume a strategy very common in empirical sciences like physics: A theory is designed and tested for adequacy. To amend its inadequacies a new - although maybe not very different - theory is designed and tested again. This is an iterative process. In principle, each step results in an entirely new theory, which gives the flexibility to introduce any number of new primitives and axioms.

From the economic point of view it is recommendable to put not too much effort in formal work before a reasonable confidence in adequacy is established. This is, because formal treatment requires relatively much intellectual investment. Psychologically this might also be an obstacle to do the next step of the iteration process.

Q.: The structures you described are hierarchical. How can you express side conditions?

A.: Constructs do not in general have a hierarchical structure, because a construct may be component of several other constructs, none of which is component of the other. The impression of a hierarchical structure may have resulted from our representation technique, which shows the same construct several times if it appears in several contexts, that is, at several spots. Actually, this representation technique displays all spots separately, and in fact are the spots of any construct for any data model hierarchically organized. (Cf. also the paragraph on hierarchic data models in section 4.)

Conditions on constructs, as e.g. are employed to describe a set
of constructs for type declaration purposes, can be expressed in
any appropriate language chosen. Such conditions may require,
that the constructs at two different spots of a construct must
be equal. But they may also be much more general, depending on
the power of the declaration language.

Q.:   If records are defined to be just spots, how can you guarantee,
      that records of the same type have the same structural
      properties?

A.:   First, it should be remarked, that, although records in fact can
      formally be defined to b e spots, it will normally be more
      convenient to consider them as "constructs at spots". This is
      only to give the record concept a more customary appearance. The
      question involves two problems, which should be considered
      separately.

      The first problem is that of "same structural properties". We
      are used to the idea, that records of the same type have much
      the same "structure". If one tries to explain what is meant by
      "same structure", one will probably arrive at something like
      "same names at corresponding aggregation levels and same atom
      types in corresponding environments". But in a general approach
      all possible variations of what may be regarded "similar" to
      form a type must be taken into account. So it must be assumed
      that "of same type" or "of same structure" is arbitrarily
      defined for each DBMS.

      The second problem is that of recognizing the degree of
      arbitrariness that goes into the record concept of any
      particular DBMS. Although it is of course conceivable that we
      agree on a few common necessary (but not sufficient)
      characteristics for a record, it must be permitted for any DBMS
      to develop its own idea of what are records. Traditionally, with
      "record" is also associated the idea of a distinguished
      manipulation unit. This aspect may in specific cases be quite at
      variance with conventional ideas of "similar structure".

Q.: Is, what you are proposing, a semantic model? And how does it relate to the semantics as introduced in the previous lecture (Mijares and Peebles)?

A.: What is proposed is a system of concepts for the description of interfaces, in particular of interfaces as occur with DBMS. This is done by developing a general view on the description of a communication process (the UoD-context) and a formal theory (formal IMC). They are both connected by interpreting formal IMC in the UoD-context. Thus the mapping effected by this interpretation can be considered the semantics of formal IMC.

As concerns the relation to the previous lecture it is to be observed, that, although Mijares and Peebles give a rigorous definition of the semantics of a data base (in fact as an automaton), there remain some open questions which make a comparison difficult. One of the critical points is, that their concern about semantics seems to be directed mainly towards introducing enough structure into the relational model, so that modelling requirements of the user can be satisfied, which go beyond the expressive power of plain relations. This view basically amounts to call "semantics" any properties of the data base type, which are not expressible by only the relations of the momentary data base. At present, in DBMS discussions this is a very common usage of this word. We do not adhere to this usage, because we think, that one should stick to the meaning of the word as used in other disciplines, e.g. languages.

Data base keys, pointers and spots (Relation to paper of R. Engles)
(by R. Durchholz and W. Klutentreter)

In his paper on "Currency and Concurrency in the COBOL Data Base
Facility", R. Engles recommends elimination of the data base key and
substitution of the currency indicators by the more general device of
cursors. The concepts discussed are intimately connected to the spot
concept and it should be expected that reconsideration in the light
of the latter will provide some additional insight.

We will first identify a possible source of trouble caused by
elimination of the data base key without compensation. Then we will
indicate a way of understanding pointers as values for cursors.
Before we do so, we will however have to expand a little bit on the
discussion of the record concept, as given in the present paper,
section 4.

For simplification reasons, in section 4 above, a record is
considered to be given by o n e spot. Actually it would correspond
more closely to the intuitive idea of a record, if one would consider
it as being given by a s e t of spots. This set then is the set of
spots describing the record in its various contexts of
- one record type population,
- one area,
- several coset occurrences.
Mind that sets of spots describing records are disjoint.

We now consider the issue of eliminating the data base key. For a
full understanding of the role of the data base key the following set
of observations is relevant:
- A SCHEMA-NAME identifies the user's data base within the
  overall system.
- An AREA-NAME identifies the area in the data base.
- A DATA-BASE-DATA-NAME identifies the item in a record
  occurrence.
- However, a RECORD-NAME does not identify a record occurrence,
  but a record type population or even a record type. (This is
  one of the numerous terminological traps for beginners.)

- However, a SET-NAME does not identify a coset occurrence, but a coset type population or even a coset type. (Same remark.)

In the CODASYL proposal, the identity of a record occurrence is defined by its data base key. The identity of a coset occurrence is defined by its owner record occurrence, that is, indirectly by data base key too. Eliminating the data base key raises the question of what then defines the identity of record and coset occurrences. For instance, there may be two "identical" record occurrences (identical with respect to their contents) being members of two different set occurrences of different type. Are they the same record or different records? This question is vital for all operations like navigation or modification on coset membership as well as on contents. If the question of record and coset occurrence identity cannot be answered in a general and conceptually acceptable manner, one will probably stumble over many details when the proposal is elaborated. The proposed explanation of a record by means of the spot concept makes things easy: Two record occurrences are the same if and only if they are given by the same set of spots. This solution does in fact provide the desired conceptual clean-up, but it does not necessarily answer the practical question of how to handle identity of record occurrences at the programmers's interface level. R. Engles has tackled the question with the pointer concept. This approach is probed in the next paragraphs. We close the considerations on data base key elimination with the remark, that Engles' proposal is somewhat exceptional, as it does not recommend a compensation for the lost data base key. To our knowledge such a compensation in the form of a "record identifier" is offered in all other proposals, in particular, it is advocated by G. M. Nijssen. With such an identifier, the lost identity of record occurrences is made up for.

We now turn to the issue of pointers as values of cursors. The properties of cursors are well defined and their handling has certainly fewer difficulties than that of currency indicators. But here again we meet with the problem of record identity. For instance, when a user navigates two cursors on different routes through the data base, he may want to ask at times, whether the two cursors point to the same record. Engles says that "language is required to enable the COBOL program to determine ... whether two cursors contain the same pointer". This is obviously meant to say that identity of pointers entails identity of records and vice versa. (From an abstract point of view, one could say, pointers a r e records.) So our original question of record identity boils down to the question of what are pointers.

A first guess would be, that pointers can nicely be explained as being sets of spots, because we have this strong interdependence between the concepts via the record concept: On the one hand, a record is equivalent to a set of spots, on the other hand, it is equivalent to a pointer. However, there are problems with the gap pointer.

Whereas the null pointer can be understood as being the empty set (no spots) and the zero pointer can be understood as being a set of spots which are "above" record-spots, the gap pointer is not so easily explained. This may indicate, that the suggested explanation with spots does not really work. Alternatively, it raises the suspicion, that something is wrong with the gap pointer. And indeed, upon closer examination, this concept reveals a number of open questions. So it is not clear, whether one can have several gap pointers in sequence, or whether there is only "one gap" between any two records in a coset occurrence. Other questions are, whether a gap pointer loses its existence if the cursor is removed from it and what a NEXT command in the presence of gap pointers means. There are many more questions of this kind.

To all these questions answers can readily be given in one way or the other, but the point is, that each solution requires some arbitrary decisions which outrule possibilities not less natural than the ones adopted. A detailed illustration of the situation would render this paper too long, but the reader will easily realize the wealth of choices when he tries to give an answer to any of the above questions.

As a consequence of these observations, we propose to eliminate the gap pointer. Instead, on deletion or removal of a record, the cursor should go to the prior or next record, follow the removed record or assume the null pointer or the corresponding zero pointer. The choice between these possibilities may be attached to the cursors (at declaration time) or decided upon by the command (at execution time).

Modelling in Data Base Management Systems, G.M. Nijssen, (ed.)
North Holland Publishing Company, 1976

DIAM as a Detailed Example

of the ANSI SPARC Architecture

Michael E. Senko

Mathematical Sciences Department
IBM Thomas J. Watson Research Center
Yorktown Heights, New York

The notion of using levels of abstraction to understand, simplify and improve data base system architectures has a relatively long history. Notable early papers were published in 1969 by Madnick (1) and Meltzer (2). In these and other early papers, the level structure was determined by pragmatic rather than formal consideration of existing systems. This lead to technologically oriented separations utilizing concepts such as logical, physical and access method levels. In general, the levels and their components were defined in relatively gross terms.

The contribution of the DIAM I architecture (3) was not that it discovered the level structure approach, but rather that it gave *a detailed, relatively formal basis* for (a) the contents of a series of levels and (b) the mappings between these levels. In addition, it extended the work of Mealy (4) and Meltzer (2) with a detailed study of the semantic aspects of its data structure independent view of the real world, the Entity Set Level.

Recently, the ANSI SPARC Committee (5) has published new work on the definition of level structures. This work gave added stature to an External Schema Level above the levels formally defined in the DIAM I structure. It also gave clear recognition to the requirements for a canonical, data independent Conceptual Level describing the real world enterprise. This work and the earlier work of Levien and Maron (6), Langefors (7), Sundgren (8) and finally Abrial (9) on binary representations has provided the basis for further improvements in the original DIAM architecture. The new DIAM II architecture (10,11) contains (a) an *End-User Level* which fulfills the requirements desired by the External Schema of ANSI SPARC and (b) an *Infological (Conceptual) Level* based on modified binary associations. This level contains improvements in semantic integrity over DIAM I's Entity Set Level and the somewhat similar n-ary relational model.

The ANSI SPARC interim report is gives an excellent discussion of the functions to be provided by each of its three levels. However, it gives only a general description of the components of its levels using the relatively ill-defined, overlapping terminology of existing systems (records, fields, indexes, etc.). This has lead to descriptions that are comprehensive, but necessarily quite complex. In contrast, DIAM gives detailed, generalized descriptions not only for the contents of the various levels, but also the mappings between them. It does this in terms of a relatively small set of fundamental primitives. It may, therefore, provide a guide for the simplification and further refinement of the ANSI SPARC architecture. In this paper, we will draw the correspondences between the two architectures and indicate in greater generality the properties of the overall ANSI SPARC architecture.

THE GENERAL LEVEL STRUCTURES OF THE TWO MODELS

In Figure 1, we present the DIAM II "Double Funnel" diagram. The funnels opening toward the top and the bottom indicate that the system supports a greater variety of data structures at these levels than it does at the central Infological Level.

This "conceptual" level, as suggested by ANSI SPARC, is designed to be a canonical representation of the user's enterprise. In contrast, the upper End-User or External Schema Level is designed to support many user views and many program data structure views. The possibility of many user views provides for user efficiency and the possibility of many program data structure views provides for compatibilty with the data structures of existing programs. This external level of DIAM therefore exhibits some of the freedom for users called for by Nijssen in his paper at this conference on the COEXISTENCE model. It also provides the details required for creating such a mechanism. The lower level, the Internal Model, is designed to provide a general set of file organizations for computer efficiency.

The general requirements for functions at these levels are almost exactly the same for the two architectures. Since ANSI SPARC has not yet presented the details of the mappings between its levels, we will deal mainly with the correspondences in level content of the two architectures.

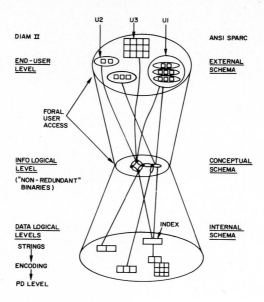

Figure 1 ANSI SPARC - DIAM II System Overviews

REAL WORLD REALM

Before discussing the Infological Level, we should first take note, as ANSI SPARC does, of the existence of a real world that we are seeking to describe. An informal discussion of the functions and characteristics of this real world will aid us in specifying the matching properties for the user levels of our architectures.

Using the Real World to Evaluate a Conceptual Level Model

In our information systems, we do not deal directly with the objects and concepts of the real world; we operate, instead, on user level "name structures" that are designed to stand for them. Like the theories of the physical sciences, these name structures are abstract formal models whose purpose is to reflect a certain class of imaginable real world situations as simply and accurately as possible. To compare the utility of such models, we must (as is done in the physical sciences) discuss how simply and how well they "match" the relevant properties of the real world.

This evaluation cannot be done within the framework of any particular formal model because each model is based on simplifying assumptions about the real world. The only tool that allows us to discuss all model assumptions is natural language, and it is this tool that we must use to evaluate formal models in terms of our knowledge of the real world. We can of course define certain natural language concepts more precisely to help us in our discussion, but in evaluations we must never enter completely into a simplified formal model and leave behind the power of natural language to discuss the models assumptions.

Terminology for Discussing the Real World

To provide a somewhat more precise basis for discussing the real world, ANSI defines five terms, Entity, Entity Set, Property, Fact, and Enterprise.

There is an essential correspondence between the ANSI and DIAM I definitions of *Entity* and *Entity Set*.

An *Entity* is an object, thing, or concept of interest to the enterprise.

An *Entity Set* is a set of Entities having one or more characteristics in common. (In DIAM II, these two primitives have been called Member and Member Group.)

A *Property* is a characteristic of an entity.

In the ANSI document, the discussion of *Fact* contains some inconsistencies. These inconsistencies later lead the document to state, again inconsistently, that a fact can be represented by a single Conceptual Field. The ANSI document (5, page II-15) states:

"A fact about an entity is an assertion that a property of that entity has a given value; for example, "name is Herb", "job title is programmer"..."

The definition is quite acceptable and it is in agreement with other definitions for *Fact*. It leads to a requirement that the representation of a fact requires two conceptual fields, rather the one field specified by ANSI later in its document.

Unfortunately, the examples are (a) incomplete, they are not examples of the definition, and, (b) they unnecessarily bring in the confusion factor of naming. As was stated earlier, in information systems we have to use names to stand for things. To parallel the definition above, we need names to stand for *at least three things* - the property, the entity, and the propery value. To parallel the definition "that a *property* of that *entity* has a given *value*", the example should state:

"the name (property) *of the person* (entity) is Herb (property value)".

The problem with both examples is that they do not indicate which entity the property is about. This is especially clear in the second example where we can ask:

"Which person has the job title programmer ?"

but it also applies in the first example, if we ask:

"Which person has the name, Herb ? "

In the physical world, we could of course point to these entities, but in an information system we must denote them by unique names, for example, the person with Employee Number equal to 01234. Now it is clear that we need two separate conceptual fields to represent a fact, one to contain the name of the entity ("01234") and one to contain the property value ("Herb").

A *Fact* as defined by ANSI involves three things (a) one property, (b) one entity the property is about, and (c) one property value. If the entity changes, then we are dealing with a different fact. The ANSI statement that:

"The same fact may be true of more than one entity...."

is in all instances inconsistent with the earlier definition because if the entity changes, we are dealing with a different fact. We will for the moment only note that the ANSI discussion of facts needs some refinement and return to the problem in our discussion of the Conceptual Schema.

THE DETAILS OF THE INFOLOGICAL (OR CONCEPTUAL SCHEMA) LEVEL

Much of the recent work in data base research has involved a "stripping off" of the characteristics of *individual points of view* on data structures to get the characteristics that are *common to all points of view*; that is, to get to *the underlying model*. One of the reasons for this work is that if information structures are specified in terms of common underlying characteristics instead of in terms of one point of view, then the major elements of the information structures will remain stable when we change to another point of view.

In DIAM, the use of this technique has allowed the definition of a relatively small set of primitives to cover a wide variety of detailed points of view (DBTG (12), IMS (13), relations, etc.). In discussing the Infological Level we will continue this work, trying to separate those things that are points of view from those that underlie many points of view.

A "Canonical" Conceptual Level

At the Infological Level or Conceptual Schema Level, one of our main desires is to find a cannonical form (that is, one standard form) for structuring the description of a specific enterprise. Now there are two ways of achieving this goal. One way is to allow only one place in the structure for each fact. The second (which ANSI suggests when it allows the contents of records to be non-disjoint) is to allow multiple places for each fact. For example, to allow the same conceptual field pairs to be stored in different conceptual records. This opens the possibility of having as many conceptual record types per entity type as there are combinations of entity type-property pairs. For most enterprises, this would clearly result in an impractical number of record types to be defined. The only recourse would be to define some rule which would algorithmically select one subset of conceptual records. It is difficult to conceive of some rule that would allow the contents of of conceptual records to be non-disjoint and still result in a set of record types all of which would be useful to the end-users of the system.

DIAM II selects the first course. The canonical nature of the binary structure is not violated by the ANSI example dealing with things like "gross revenue", "net revenue", and "taxes" which are interelated. In this case, any one can be derived from the other two. Since the choice of which pair to use is arbitrary, the most desirable guideline in this case seems to be use all three at the Infological level. This does not violate the requirement that fact storage be disjoint because we are dealing with three different facts. We should, of course, indicate at the Conceptual Level how the three facts are related so, at the lower encoding level, a choice of a particular pair as a basis for materializing the third concept might be made for storage and updating efficiency.

Difficulties with Record-Oriented Conceptual Levels

Having proposed a solution for this problem, one is still faced in record-oriented systems with further arbitrary choices. For example, Schmid and Swenson (14) note the arbitrariness in assigning attributes to n-ary relations. A similar situation occurs in the assignment of Conceptual Fields to Conceptual Records in the ANSI Conceptual Schema.

Another factor to consider is that we are interested in constructing a name structure that will support many points of view without being overly biased against or toward any one. In record-oriented systems one source of bias occurs when the user makes a tripartite classification of his concepts into "entities" (or "objects"), "attributes" ("properties" or "characteristics"), and "relationships" (or "associations"). Based on past experience, this classification seems like a reasonable one. An "entity" is something that is described by a record, an "attribute" is a field that describes an entity and occurs in only one record type, and a "relationship" is used to represent interactions between entities discussed in two or more different records. Note, however, how the definition usually relies on stored representation oriented concepts like records. But the major question is "Does this classification solve or cause more problems?"

On the *positive side*, Schmid and Swenson suggest that the classification assists in dealing with maintenance of data. However, at least some of the problem that their technique addresses might also be addressed in another way by recognizing that there are two reasons for changes of names, changes of names for objects (John's name is changed to Joe) and changes in names due to changes in relationships between objects (John moves from department, 420 to department, 430). This latter framework (involving two kinds of name changes) has the advantage that the time-dependent nature of these changes becomes evident. The second aspect, whether the system should maintain a list of values to check the names of entities but not of attributes seems to be decidable by the system.

There seems to be no other technical use for the detailed "entity, attribute, relationship" classification, although there is the psychological comfort that it is something we have always used and that it is based on differences found in existing record systems.

On the *negative side*, there is first the work that must be done to achieve the classification for each user. One only needs to read proposed guidelines in recent papers to become convinced that these decisions can be extremely difficult to make. Second, the classification is "point of view dependent" because each user's classification will depend on how much of the information structure his point of view takes in. If he is not interested in the description of a particular type of entity, then it will be reclassified as an attribute in his view. Of course, if his point of view changes then some of his entities, attributes and relationships will probably have to be reclassified.

In making our own judgement, we recognized most classifications have some utility, *but that each must be judged on its own merits and demerits*. With regard to the tripartite classification, we felt that less was better, and went to a two concept classification.

In DIAM I, we felt that we had removed some of the bias by avoiding the classification of fields into entity fields and attribute fields - we considered the underlying structure to be made up of fields containing only *Entity Names* which were connected together by *Role Names*. This gave the DIAM I Entity Set Model an added stability because it was never necessary to change an attribute field (like Department of Employee) to an entity field when the attribute field acquired attribute fields of its own (like Location of Department). Each field always contained an Entity Name, the only difference was that sometimes an Entity was described in great detail and sometimes it was not.

As far as we could see, the only difference in the system was that the user no longer had to classify things into two types - there seemed to be no less power in describing the real world. And since we had other independent means of dealing with physical representations, there was no advantage to be gained by retaining terminology whose characteristics were based on physical records.

Although the DIAM I structure did seem to have technical advantages with regard to stability, its vestigial record-orientation still lead to many facts being stored in one record. Also, like all other systems with record orientation, its transaction language required dramatically different syntax for dealing with inter- and intra-record associations. The syntax for inter-record associations with its seemingly artifical requirement for equals signs to match fields from the participating records was particularly disturbing. We, therefore, looked for a better structure. The DIAM II Infological Level Structure (10) that we arrived at is a modification of the binary association work of the authors mentioned earlier. The paper of Bracchi, Paolini, and Pelagatti at this conference has many notions in common with the DIAM II binary association model first presented in this earlier work.

This binary model seems not only to provide us with a better underlying structure, but also to give us a better handle on semantic integrity and on an unambiguous "almost English language" transaction language.

The terminology used in the original DIAM II paper is exact, but it differs from the ANSI SPARC terminology. We have, therefore, looked for definitions of ANSI terms such as "attributes", "identifiers", etc. which would allow us to retain the exactness of DIAM II Infological Model and yet bridge to ANSI.

The key to this bridging is to recognize that the distinctions between entities and attributes come into being *only when one adopts a particular point of view.*

In particular, when one's point of view is based on Employees, then Department becomes an attribute of Employees. When his basic viewpoint is Departments, then Employees become an attribute of Departments. In short, *the tripartite classification of things into entities and attributes is a function of point of view* (which varies with person and point of time). While it may be useful at the External Level, it should not appear in the underlying Infological (Conceptual) Level Structure.

Terminology for the Infological Level

When we recognize this, we can borrow and slightly redefine some of the ANSI terminology for "all realms" (5, page II-8) and construct a more natural bridge between the underlying information structure and the various user points of view.

To be clear about our definitions, we should first note a difference between a "set" and an "occurrence" (an element in a set). For the following discussion, a set contains occurences. Some of the concepts we define will be sets and some will be occurences. We will be careful to indicate which is which.

To define an information structure for an enterprise, we probably start by recognizing that the applications to be processed are most simply defined if the entities of interest are classified in a particular fashion. (For example, there is a certain set of entities to which payroll processing is applied. This set is frequently called EMPLOYEES.) We will call such application suggested sets, ENTITY-SET's, and we may give them formal ENTITY-SET-NAME's. (For example, EMPLOYEES, DEPARTMENTS, PARTS, COLORS, WEIGHTS, etc.) Whether we go to the trouble of giving them formal names known to the information sytem is a tradeoff question that we will deal with in a moment.

Names for Entities

The next step is, however, essential to the construction of an information system. We need some way of having at least one name to stand unambiguously for each entity of interest in each of the ENTITY-SET's. The way this is done is to have a "set of names" such that each name stands for at most one entity in our ENTITY-SET. Both ANSI and the DIAM terminology in this paper call the "set of names", an IDENTIFIER and the individual names in the set, IDENTIFIER VALUES. (ANSI also uses the term, DOMAIN for IDENTIFIER, but this term is redundant and we will not use it in DIAM II.)

Of course, to refer to an IDENTIFIER in our system, we will also have to give it a name, this name will obviously be an IDENTIFIER NAME. IDENTIFIER's have IDENTIFIER NAME's like EMPLOYEE-NUMBERS, DEPARTMENT-NUMBERS, PART-NUMBERS, COLOR-VALUES, WEIGHT-VALUES, etc.

Typical IDENTIFIER VALUES in each of these IDENTIFIER's are 012345, J45, 0786598, RED, 125, etc. We, ourselves, may do the work of assuring that each IDENTIFIER VALUE in an IDENTIFIER stands for only one entity or we may depend on some other agency to control the assignment. (For example, the Social Security Administration controls the assignment of IDENTIFIER VALUES in the IDENTIFIER with the IDENTIFIER NAME, SOCIAL SECURITY NUMBER.) In any case, we can, with certainty, refer unambiguously to any entity in the information system by giving the appropriate IDENTIFIER NAME and the appropriate IDENTIFIER VALUE within that identifier.

Representations for Facts

Having defined the means for giving unique names to entities, we will want to describe some of the entities in more detail. In particular, we want to state some FACT's about them. For this we require the definition of a FACT REPRESENTATION (a name structure for representing a FACT). This brings us back to our earlier discussion on points of view and underlying structures. We now want to define an underlying FACT REPRESENTATION in such a fashion that it is stable to changes in points of view and yet supports each point of view with a minimum of bias. In Figure 2, we present a FACT REPRESENTATION that seems to meet these requirements.

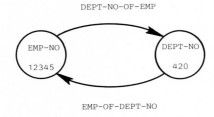

Figure 2 A FACT REPRESENTATION

In each of the circles, we have an Identifier Name above an Identifier Value. This combination provides a unique name for an entity in the enterprise. The reason we call the DIAM II Infological Level, a binary model, is because all of its facts are represented by associating names for *two* entities.

We would like to complete our definition of FACT REPRESENTATION by providing an easy bridge to the external point of view terminology of entities and their attributes. To do this, we need to say something about attributes. ANSI SPARC provides its definition of attribute in the context of definitions for roles and domains (5, page II-8). In this definition, it is not clear whether an attribute is a set construct or an occurence construct. One definition says "An attribute (conceptual field) is the representation of a property of *an entity*". In this case, it seems that an attribute is an occurrence construct. A later definition in the same section says "An attribute stands for a role and a domain; it is excellent practice for an attribute-name to contain both the role-name and the domain-name." In this case, it inconsistently appears that an "attribute" is a set construct analogous to role name and domain. The following definition seems to resolve these problems.

We will say that an ATTRIBUTE indicates how IDENTIFIER VALUES from one IDENTIFIER are used to describe entities named by IDENTIFIER VALUES from the same or a different IDENTIFIER. In this case, ATTRIBUTE is clearly a set construct. To refer to an ATTRIBUTE, we will give it an ATTRIBUTE NAME that is unique among the union of IDENTIFIER NAMES and ATTRIBUTE NAMES in the system. (The reason for this will appear in a later paper discussing the graceful evolution of attributes into entities.)

In the center of Figure 2, we have ATTRIBUTE NAMES (above and below) attached to arrows that point from the circle containin the name for the *Entity being described* to the circle containing the IDENTIFIER NAME and the IDENTIFIER VALUE standing for the entity doing the describing. The ATTRIBUTE NAME indicates the meaning of the description.

We can then give a definition of ATTRIBUTE VALUE by first noting that our specification of a FACT will always indicate which IDENTIFIER is in the circle that the arrow with a particular ATTRIBUTE NAME is pointing to. Since an IDENTIFIER NAME is always implied by an ATTRIBUTE NAME, we can say that an ATTRIBUTE VALUE of a particular entity is obtained by following an arrow with that ATTRIBUTE NAME and reading the IDENTIFIER VALUE in the circle at the other end.

We can now correlate with the ANSI terminology. A DIAM ATTRIBUTE correlates directly with an ANSI ROLE NAME. Since the term, attribute, is used more natural than role name in common English usage we prefer to use ATTRIBUTE for this construct. A DIAM II IDENTIFIER is equivalent to both the ANSI IDENTIFIER and the ANSI DOMAIN. We see no need to retain the redundant term, DOMAIN, in the DIAM terminology; and for simplicity, we will drop it.

In addition to being a slight improvement in definition, this FACT REPRESENTATION form allows us to support two different points of view about the fact without bias. In particular, if we start with *our point of view focused on EMP-NO*, and follow the arrow, DEPT-NO-OF-EMP, we find at its end the ATTRIBUTE VALUE, that is, "420". *On the other hand*, if we start with *our point of view focused on DEPT-NO*, and follow the arrow, EMP-OF-DEPT-NO, we find at its end one value for that attribute, "12345".

Of course, the attribute, EMP-OF-DEPT-NO, may have many values for a single department; but, just as in the real world, these are different facts so our fact representation form does not have to be extended to accomodate this situation.

More on Names for Entities

In beginning books on logic, particular attention is given to differentiating between "things" and "names for things". In information systems discussions, we do not make this distinction clearly and this frequently leads to imperfect definitions.

In our present terminology, "things" are called "entities". Since everything in the real world is an "entity" a "name" must also be an "entity" *and it is*. Names, however, constitute only a subset of the universe of all entities. In particular, the subset of names is defined by the fact that each of its members are used by someone *to stand in place of another entity*. (Elements in the "name subset" are usually representable by groups of alphanumeric characters.) From this definition, it is clear that names being entities can also have names *ad infinitum*.

In common English, when we assign a "name" to an entity that "name" becomes a special kind of "attribute value" of the entity. In particular, that attribute value may be used to uniquely identify that entity. Now there is no reason that a name for an entity be constructed from only one of its attribute values. There are cases where unique names can be constructed for entities from a combination of attribute values. A good example is DATE which is frequently identified by a combination of its attributes, those named DAY-OF-DATE, MONTH-OF-DATE, and YEAR-OF-DATE. Everyone would agree that the entities in the set, DATE, are as "real" (if not more "real") than the entities in the sets, DAY, MONTH and YEAR.

There are some cases which are at least equivalent in form, where some people will call the entity being named by a combination of its attribute values, a "dummy" or "artifical" entity. This usually occurs when the tripartite classification is being used as a system base. For example, when the underlying structure is being discussed in the terms, object and relationship (In COBOL terminology, the GROUP), it is often said that we have a "relationship" based on EMP-NO's and PROJECTS. To some authors, this seems to not be an entity because two related entities are part of its composition. Besides, a combination of names for two other entities has been used to form its name, on for an EMPLOYEE and one for a PROJECT.

The question is whether the difference between a relationship and an object is an underlying thing or whether it is simply in the construction of an identifier for an entity. If one reads the literature carefully, he almost always finds that the major distinguishing characteristic of a relationship is that it requires more than one name to identify it. For example, what happens if we decide to call the above relationship a TRANSACTION (which it was all along) and give it a TRANSACTION NUMBER. Does this change in identifier change the underlying structure which we wish to talk about? That is, have we changed a relationship into an entity by adopting a different naming convention, or were we talking about an entity all along? This problem is even more intriguing if we assume that two different people wish to hold the two different points of view at the same time. Which do we have then, a relationship or an entity?

In fact there seems to be nothing tó be gained by making the entity-relationship distinction in the underlying structure. The only distinction seems to be that some identifiers use the name of only one property of the entity (say, the EMP-NO of an employee) to identify it, and other identifiers use the names of more than one property (say, MONTH, DAY, and YEAR of DATE). All we need to handle this situation is to allow specification of identifiers which involve combinations of attributes.

For purposes of *semantic integrity*, the important thing to remember is that the combination of attribute values stands for a single entity. And that the attributes of that entity are *not* direct attributes of the entities named by the individual identifier values (Figure 3).

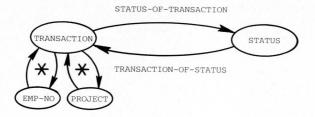

Figure 3

For example, if we assigned a STATUS to the transaction above, the STATUS would not be a STATUS-OF-EMP-NO, nor would it be a STATUS-OF-PROJECT. It remains a STATUS-OF-TRANSACTION. It is, of course, an *indirect attribute* of EMP-NO because the transaction is an attribute of EMP-NO, and STATUS-OF-TRANSACTION is an attribute of the transaction, but associating STATUS with EMP-NO in an n-ary without noting that EMP-NO is really only a portion of the name for a transaction leads, as Schmid and Swenson have pointed out, to *the inclusion of non-facts* in the system *with the same stature as facts.*

The DIAM II modified binary structure for facts with two places for entity names (identifier values) overcomes this problem as long as we recognize C that the name for an entity may be given by a combination of its attribute values.

There is at least one additional issue at the Infological Level that merits discussion. That issue deals with questions of the stature of Entity Sets and Internal System Identifiers for Entity Sets. The issue was brought up by Abrial (9) and has recently been clarified by Stephan Todd (15). In Abrial's paper, it was suggested that relationships externally identified by a combination of attribute values should have a one-field "internal identifier" known only to the system. At the last TC-2 data base conference, the DIAM paper (10) pointed out that this identifier is equivalent to an encoding. It also pointed out that there was no semantic requirement for an internal identifier. Whether such an internal encoding was used should depend solely on considerations of storage and decoding efficiency.

Todd, however, noted the possible requirement for an internal identifier that would remain invariant through changes of external identifiers. For example, if the system were concerned with DEPARTMENTS which were originally identified by DEPARTMENT NAME, the enterprise might at a later time wish to identify departments by DEPARTMENT NUMBERS. In such a case, it might be nice to have all the transaction programs phrased in terms of DEPARTMENTS rather than DEPARTMENT NAMES and to have the departments internally identified by a system identifier that mapped to either DEPARTMENT NAME or DEPARTMENT NUMBER.

There are several considerations in deciding the most appropriate solution and perhaps until further insight is available it will remain a matter of taste. The considerations include:

1. Arbitrarily requiring an internal identifier seems to restrict the efficiency options open to the data base administrator. That is, requiring an encoding or decoding for every interaction with the user seems to be unnecessary and often wasteful.

2. While it appears that the identifiers may be less stable than the entity sets, it is not clear that they are unstable enough to require special treatment for every identifier. There is also nothing to suggest that Entity Sets are significantly more stable.

3. The use of terms like DEPARTMENT in programs can be accomodated by the use of synonyms for the identifiers or they can be accomodated by the Member Group - Name Group mechanism presented in the previous TC-2 Workshop paper on DIAM II.

4. If the identifier does change, there is no reason why the original identifier could not be considered an internal coding. In this case, the penalty for encode-decode would only be incurred in the usual case where the identifier did change.

Parametrized Forms for Specifying an Infological level

Taking into consideration all of these aspects, the identifier and fact specification forms given in the earlier paper seem to be capable of covering all cases. They are:

```
ENTITY-SET-NAME entity-set-name

    [SYNONYM synonym]  .....


PREFERRED-IDENTIFIER OF entity-set-name

          ⎧ entity-set-name          ⎫
    IS    ⎨                  ·       ⎬
          ⎩ attribute-name-1 .....   ⎭

    CHECK-GENERATE-OPTION option-name


[IDENTIFIER OF entity-set-name

    IS   attribute-name-1 .....

    CHECK-GENERATE-OPTION option-name] ....
```

For example:

```
ENTITY-SET-NAME TRANSACTION

    SYNONYM ORDER-LINE

    PRIME-IDENTIFIER OF TRANSACTION IS TRANSACTION-NO

    IDENTIFIER OF TRANSACTION IS PART PROJECT SUPPLIER
```

The specification for a fact representation would be:

```
FACT ATTRIBUTE-NAME-1 attribute-name-1 FROM identifier-1

                   ⎧ 1 ⎫
    FUNCTION       ⎨   ⎬   [NICNAME nicname-1]  ....
                   ⎩ M ⎭

    ATTRIBUTE-NAME-2 attribute-name-2 FROM identifier-2

                   ⎧ 1 ⎫
    FUNCTION       ⎨   ⎬   [NICNAME nicname-2]  ...
                   ⎩ M ⎭
```

For example:

```
FACT ATTRIBUTE-NAME-1 DEPT-OF-EMP FROM EMP-NO

    FUNCTION 1 NICNAME DEPT-NO

    ATTRIBUTE-NAME-2 EMP-OF-DEPT FROM DEPT-NO

    FUNCTION M NICNAME EMP-NO
```

These are essentially the complete specification forms required for the Infological Level. Note that there is no need for a separate Relationship (or COBOL Group) specification to complicate the definition process. The only other comments are:

1.   The FUNCTION gives the number of attribute values that may be related with one instance of the identifier.

2.   The NICNAME allows us to give a short name to the attribute for use in the FORAL language. This short name need only be unique among the attribute names leading from the identifier. This is a well-defined way of achieving the "shorter, snappier, more locally mnemonic, synonym for the system attribute name" mentioned in the ANSI document (5, page II-9).

In Figure 4, we present a type diagram for the Infological Level. This could be used to guide the user in constructing transaction programs. While it is clear that such a type description would be too complex to display in many real situations with large numbers of attributes; the second choice, a normal catalog listing, should be no more complicated than listings for tabular or hierarchical files. It consists simply of a listing of the identifier names and their related attribute names.

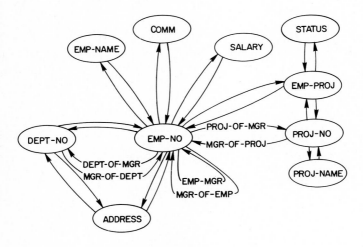

Figure 4 DIAM II - FORAL Type Diagram

INTERNAL SCHEMA LEVEL

DIAM II ACCESS PATH, ENCODING, AND DEVICE LEVELS

To provide a basis for discussing the correspondences between the two architectures at this stored representation level, we will give a short synopsis of the relevant three DIAM II levels.

Access Path Level

This level in DIAM is concerned with the definition of an efficient access path system for the information at the Infological Level. In DIAM I, three kinds of strings were defined and their encoding was defined in terms of Basic Encoding Units (BEU's) (16). The Stored Data Definition and Translation Task Group (SDDTTG) of the CODASYL Systems Committee has taken these concepts as a basis and expanded and modified them for the purpose of creating a general purpose data translator (17). In addition, the Denver Martin Marietta group has used DIAM I as a basis for a generalized data base system simulator (18). Again they have found the string and BEU concepts to be quite powerful in describing a wide range of data base system file organizations.

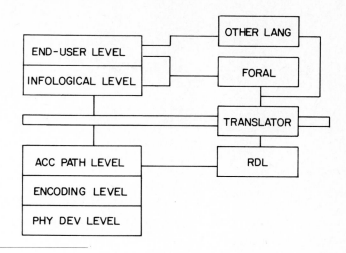

DIAM Level Structure

In DIAM II (11), we have *two* (instead of three) kinds of strings. We call them, *Type-Strings* (T-Strings) and *Instance-Strings* (I-Strings). I-Strings correspond closely to IMS-GIS segments and to DBTG single level records (as opposed to COBOL multilevel records). T-Strings correspond to IMS logical connections between records or segments of the same type or to DBTG Sets.

In DIAM (in contrast to either IMS or DBTG), there is no implication that either kind of string is encoded by the use of contiguity or chains. This choice should be, and in DIAM is, made more appropriately at a later and lower level of definition, the Encoding Level.

The I-String Specification requires five types of components.

    (1)   The I-String Name

    (2)   A List of T-Strings that this I-String is "ON"
           That is, which T-String collections this I-String is a member of.

    (3)   A List of T-Strings that start at this I-String

    (4)   A List of the Identifiers and Attributes contained on this I-String

And optionally,

    (5)   A List of the Fields required to represent the Identifiers and Attributes plus a mapping between the elements of the two lists

In the simplest case, (4) and (5) could be the same list, but in dealing with identifiers composed of multiple attributes and in the case where one identifier is related to its attributes in a M-1 or 1-1 manner (say, EMP-NO to DEPT-OF-EMP to ADDRESS-OF-EMP) attributes of more than one level may be contained in the same I-String and the more complex mapping is required.

In the normal case, however, the user would focus on a particular identifier (say, EMP-NO) and list any single-valued direct attributes that he wished on the string (say, COMM and SALARY). Each occurence of the I-String would then contain a particular identifier value (say, 012345) and the values of the specified attributes for that identifier value. (Figure 5)

The T-String specification requires six types of components.

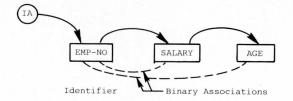

Figure 5   An I-String

(1)   The T-String Name

(2)   The Name of the I-String that this T-String is "ON"
       (or the fact that it is an Entry Point from the Catalog to the system's stored data base).

(3)   The element (an Identifier or an Attribute) that this T-String matches in the I-String it is "ON"

(4)   The Name of the I-String that appears on the T-String

(5)   A Boolean Statement qualifying the I-String instances that may appear on this T-String

(6)   Criteria for ordering the I-String instances on this T-String

In Figure 6, we present a combination of a T-String connected to an I-String. As can be seen from the figure, all the records on the T-String have the same format. ANSI SPARC "Form Extents" would be a natural outcome of the definition of T-Strings in DIAM. In fact, DIAM would have the capability for defining both disjoint and non-disjoint "Form Extents".

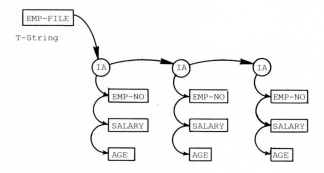

Figure 6   A T-String

Other Considerations

We must, of course, have a way of finding optimum paths in an access path network specified in terms of I-Strings and T-Strings. The required information can be from an appropriate catalog structure for storing the String parameters.

In the case of high level languages, entry to this catalog will be by way of attribute (or identifier) names. In essence, the high level language statement will call for accessing some attribute and the compiler will go to the attribute entry in the Infological Level Catalog to find the existing access paths to that attribute. With each Attribute Entry in the DIAM II Infological Level Catalog, we will have a list of the I-Strings that it is "ON". The next requirement is to store the remainder of the string specifications so that the compiler can trace from the I-Strings that the attribute is on back through T-Strings and I-Strings to a string that can be entered directly from the catalog. The string parameters with their "ON" specification allow this to be done in a straightforward manner.

In the process of tracing back the strings, the compiler will find the other parameters of the relevant strings so it can compile a decoding program for the BEU's used to encode the strings. In DIAM II, this parameterization information will be stored in an Acess Path Catalog which is separated from the Infological Level Catalog for search efficiency.

The representation integrity (3) and optimum search path selection (19) properties of DIAM I will remain. In particular, whenever the user enters a fact into the system, DIAM II will go to the Infological Level Catalog, find the appropriate ID-ATTRIBUTE pair, and under the attribute find all the I-Strings on which copies of this type of fact reside. It can then find the specifications of paths to these I-Strings by following the "ON" Entries in the Access Path Catalog back to an Entry Point. It can then follow these paths in the actual stored data base to find the locations where copies of the fact should be stored. In this fashion, it will be able to assure that all copies of a fact are maintained. In the case of retrieval, it will, of course, be able to select the optimum path to the fact using algorithms similar to those proposed for DIAM I (19).

These string definitions are based on the earlier DIAM I work; it is, however, interesting to note that both Nijssen (20) and Taylor (21) have proposed simplifications of the DBTG Set and Record definitions which would make them look very much like DIAM Strings. In a earlier paper, we have discussed how strings could be defined using a data base language called FORAL, the reader should refer to that paper (11) for further discussion.

Encoding Level

In DIAM I, the Basic Encoding Unit consists of four types of fields in the following order:

(1)   One *Label Field* which contains an encoding which is used to identify the the string type that this BEU represents.

(2)   One or more *APTR* (Association Pointer) *Fields* which point to the next member of a string that this BEU happens to be "ON"

(3)   One *VPTR* (Value Pointer) *Field* which points to the first of the elements (other strings, attribute names, or attribute values) that form this string.

(4)   a *TERM* (Terminator) *Field* that indicates the end of the string.

In DIAM II, the BEU and its parameters are unchanged. We cannot go into detail here with regard to the parameterization and factoring of DIAM BEU's. (This is done in Reference 16.) The main notion, however, is that the complete BEU's are placed in the stored data stream. Or, if all instances of a particular field in a BEU type have some regularity, this regularity may be expressed in the catalog and the field need not be stored in the data stream. It is then said to be "factored" into the catalog.

For example, if each I-String Instance is placed contiguous to the prior one in a particular T-String, then the APTR field in the I-String which points to the next I-String will always point to the first bit or byte "AFTER" the initial I-String. This information allows us to "factor" the APTR field into the catalog. Various factorings give us generalized lists, DBTG chains, IMS or GIS hierarchies, or single level records (n-tuples within relations). (Figure 7 presents a simple example of factoring).

Arrays in DIAM II

If DIAM II is to provide a basis for interfacing to a wide variety of procedural languages like FORTRAN, ALGOL, and PL/I, it should have the capability for representing arrays. Figure 8, we present a binary version of a complex array. The set of points (entities) in the main array, A, have the coordinates, X, Y, and Z. These are the attributes whose values serve to identify the entities of type A. These entities have two other attributes, one, T, stands for Temperature, and the second, B, is really another array that is nested inside A. It is a two dimensional array with coordinate attributes, U and V, and other attributes, Q and P.

We can tell that B is embedded in A because A is one of the components of its identifier (as indicated by asterisks in the figure). Although we cannot go into detail with regard to the FORAL language, it is possible to obtain a new array with Q and P added together to form a single scalar by the statement:

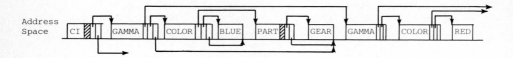

Figure 7a All BEU Information in Data Stream → Generalized List

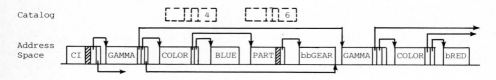

Figure 7b Fixed Length Attribute Values (Fields) ⇸ Value Terminator in Catalog

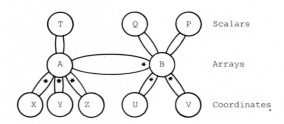

Figure 8

ARRAY <= A (X, Y, Z, T) FOR B (U, V; Q+P).

This statement is valid regardless of whether the array is represented in storage by the usual FORTRAN arrangement, or is so sparse that only the valid elements are stored with their coordinates (sparse representation). Not all array operations are this simple in FORAL, in fact most would probably be easier in an arithmetic language, but it is interesting to see such operations specified in terms of attributes rather than coordinate nesting (content addressing rather than location addressing). For example, to deal with a particular column Vi, we simply write a qualification limiting V to Vi.

It is interesting to note at this point that there has been considerable discussion in the literature on building a general data structure package based on arrays as primitive elements. Our discussion here indicates that arrays are just a special case encoding of binaries. Binaries, therefore, provide more general primitives than arrays for building data structures. We should base our data structure packages on binaries at the conceptual level the special case encoding to provide arrays.

Physical Device Level

Finally we need a generalized "access method" or "data base management system". Here we can retain the notions and parameterizations of FRAMES explained in detail in DIAM Note 1 (23). In this note, there are three major concepts:

(1) *Linear Address Spaces* which are allocated to devices

(2) *Contiguous Data Groups* which are groups of information containing BEU's that are all connected by contiguity. These CDG's are the things that are placed on the address spaces. In ANSI terminology, CDG's are called INTERNAL RECORDS. We will use this term in future papers.

(3) *Frames* which are composed of control fields, and bytes or other Frames. Frames provide the basis for defining placement and overflow algorithms.

By varying the parameters of these three concepts, it is possible to specify functions which provide the data structure properties of a wide variety of access methods including the IBM access methods ISAM, BDAM, SAM, and VSAM.

Defined Concepts for the ANSI Internal Model - Correspondences in DIAM

At the present time, only a small incomplete list of constructs have been defined for the ANSI Internal Model. The concepts deal only with rather macroscopic aspects of the Internal Model. They do not, for example, deal with the crucial problem of specifying the mappings between levels. There is, however, an extensive list of requirements appended to the Internal Model. In the following, we present the defined concepts along with a short extract of each definition. After each extract, we present a discussion of the ANSI concept in DIAM terms to indicate where simplification might be achieved.

In this discussion, we refer to the original DIAM article (3) for its discussion of the allocation of Linear Address Spaces to extents on devices. For the discussion of overflow handling and primary index specification, we refer to the FRAME parameters in DIAM Note 1 (23).

ANSI Record Encoding Constructs

INTERNAL FIELD (DATA ELEMENT) is the smallest named internal data object in the internal model. The value of an internal field is encoded and stored in a consecutive string of internal model space units (bits, bytes, etc.) It has magnitude, dimensionality, and a unit of dimension, or some non-quantitative interpretation.

This corresponds roughly to the collection of the lowest level BEU in the DIAM architecture. That is, it is a representation of the attribute value. Since this is only one special case of a BEU, DIAM covers more area with its BEU primitive, reducing the number of primitives.

INTERNAL FIELD AGGREGATE Internal fields may be aggregated, subordinate to an internal record, to reflect access strategies. There is no attempt to name, define, or characterize an internal field aggregate.

It is clear that this concept has no operational effect on the system architecture. Like one or two other ANSI constructs, it describes a *special case effect* of some file definition, but it plays no part in the file definition mechanism. It is a concept definition that must be read by any system user when he goes over the system documentation. However, he will never use it when he defines a file structure. Because of this, it is superfluous and the system description will be simplified if INTERNAL FIELD AGGREGATE never appears in the documentation. In DIAM, fields are aggregated in the normal process of defining an I-String.

INTERNAL RECORD (STORED RECORD) is a uniquely identifiable concatenation of related internal fields in the internal model. All of the values of internal fields in the occurrence of an internal record are stored in a consecutive string of internal model space units. The internal fields in one internal record may represent different types of facts about different entities, groups of facts about selections of entities, or other combinations.

This corresponds directly to the DIAM CDG (Contiguous Data Group), in future publications, DIAM will use the name, INTERNAL RECORD, because of its clearer meaning. It should be clear that facts require at least two fields for their representation.

ANSI space Allocation and Space Management Constructs

There is considerable overlap in the ANSI definition of the constructs, INTERNAL MODEL SPACE, INTERNAL RECORD AGGREGATE, and INTERNAL RECORD SET. We, therefore, group them together for discussion and comparison to the DIAM physical device level primitives, ADDRESS SPACE and FRAME. These simpler primitives seem to provide the desired space allocation and management properties in a general, well-defined manner.

INTERNAL MODEL SPACE is the abstraction of address space in which the internal data is stored. For the purpose of the internal schema, the internal model is represented as a flat, unbounded, multi-origin, linear address space. The unit of displacement can be modeled upon such things as bits, bytes, words, internal records, physical records, tracks, etc. Multiple copies of indexes or control blocks are visible in the internal model.

The INTERNAL MODEL SPACE corresponds closely to the DIAM collection of Linear Address Spaces. The main difference is that DIAM Address Space specification limits its displacement units to the physical subdivisions defined in the hardware system manual (bits, bytes, blocks, tracks, etc.). It places displacement units such as INTERNAL RECORDS that would normally be defined in a software manual into the FRAME specification. This provides a much clearer and greater separation of function in the DIAM architecture. In effect, information about such things as internal records need not be passed through the FRAME - ADDRESS SPACE interface. A more meaningful name for the concept, INTERNAL MODEL SPACE, would be INTERNAL ADDRESS SPACE.

The next two constructs, INTERNAL RECORD AGGREGATE and INTERNAL RECORD SET show a great deal of overlap. They can be covered by one construct. In addition they also have some ADDRESS SPACE properties that could be removed to simplify the construct without losing any system power.

INTERNAL RECORD AGGREGATE Internal records may be aggregated into blocks, pages, etc. usually to reflect access strategies. Space management, indexing, latency, sequence, or concurrency of reference, are among the many factors that affect access strategy. No name, definition, or characterization of an internal record aggregate.

INTERNAL RECORD SET (DATA SET) is a collection of zero or more occurrences of one or more internal record types, associated with a particular system addressing scheme, exhibiting a common internal data storage organization. A internal record-set is a collection of one or more space extents and form extents..

When these definitions are paired, it is clear that they are intended to cover something like the properties of a data set. One of the properties of a data set is that it is allocated over a number of extents - in effect, defining an address space. Both ANSI and DIAM separate out this address space allocation function with no loss of generality; it, therefore, need not be included here.

The second property that the constructs talk about is space management and record management within the address space. However, they provide no smaller constructs to allow the definition of these space and record management properties. In DIAM, the FRAME specifications provide the space and record management capabilities of access methods in a general fashion. In effect, a FRAME is defined as a subdivision of address space with well-specified record indexing and management properties.

With regard to terminology, it may be preferable to retain the flavor of the ANSI terminology rather than use the term FRAME for this construct. In this case, neither INTERNAL RECORD AGGREGATE nor INTERNAL RECORD SET seem to be appropriate since they talk about a group of records rather than about the management of records. Although longer, the term, INTERNAL RECORD MANAGEMENT SPACE, seems more meaningful.

SPACE EXTENT is a contiguous suballocation of address space of monotonically increasing address numbers that may contain zero or more occurrences of one or more internal record types. It can contain internal records from part of, from one, or from more than one form extent. The contents of a space extent are disjoint from those of other space extents.

In DIAM, this function occurs in the definition of ADDRESS SPACE's. When an ADDRESS SPACE is allocated to a device, those blocks, tracks, etc. on the device that happen to be contiguous implicitly form a SPACE EXTENT. It is not clear whether this aggregate requires an explicit label. Of course, if SPACE EXTENT is discarded, then the system loses no power, but it can be described with less terminology.

FORM EXTENT is a subdivision of an internal record-set that may contain zero or more occurrences of one or more internal record types. Each record type has the same internal record descriptors throughout the form extent. In a form extent, the properties of internal data objects are the same for all occurrences of the unit.

In this case, the ANSI construct describes a outcome of a file definition rather than a means for achieving it. In DIAM, the FORM EXTENT naturally occurs when a single T-String runs over a particular set of attribute values. To get two different encodings, the user would simple define two different T-Strings over the same attribute values. These strings could be allocated either to the same or different FRAMES. It seems that the properties of FORM EXTENT would be better provided by string definitions.

INTERNAL DATA BASE is a single, disjoint, integrated, named collection of internal record-sets described in one internal schema.

DATA BANK is the total collection of data known to be in the enterprise. Only operational, machine readable data.

These concepts again are used to describe the outcome of a file definition rather than to provide a mechanism for achieving it. They should be excluded from the discussion of file definition, but they might be useful in the more general documentation of the system.

With the suggested amendments, the ANSI construct definitions would now look like this:

INTERNAL FIELD is the smallest named internal data object in the internal model. The value of an internal field is encoded and stored in a consecutive string of internal model space units (bits, bytes, etc.) It has magnitude, dimensionality, and a unit of dimension, or some non-quantitative interpretation.

INTERNAL RECORD is a uniquely defined identifiable concatenation of related internal fields in the internal model. All of the values of internal fields in the occurrence of an internal record are stored in a consecutive string of internal model space units. The internal fields in one internal record may represent different types of facts about selections of entities, or other combinations.

INTERNAL ADDRESS SPACE is the abstraction of address space in which the internal data is stored. For the purpose of internal schema, the internal model is represented as a flat, unbounded linear address space. The unit of displacement can be modeled upon such things as bits, bytes, words, physical records, tracks, etc.

INTERNAL RECORD MANAGEMENT SPACE is a subdivision of an address space with well-defined properties for handling record overflow, record ordering, and record indexing.

T-STRING provides the basis for describing a set of records of the same format.

This completes the discussion of the simplified set of constructs required to provide the ANSI Internal Model. This set of constructs does not provide the detailed level of specification found in the DIAM model, but it does provide a simpler, less overlapping set of constructs for the general level of description that ANSI has given so far.

EXTERNAL SCHEMA LEVEL

DIAM END-USER LEVEL

By reviewing the DIAM documents in detail, it can be seen that the data structures used by existing languages such as FORTRAN, COBOL, ALGOL, PL/I, DL/I, DML, etc. can probably be described and therefore processed in terms of the DIAM internal schemas.

To present these data structures to an End-User, we would simply provide a similar, but simpler, mapper between the End-User Level and the Infological Level (Conceptual Schema). This mapper would use many of the software routines coded for the internal mapper, but would use fewer of them because it would need to deal only with the string (and perhaps some of the encoding) level mappings. It would not have to know about internal space management. This situation would save a great deal of otherwise redundant coding.

With regard to the ANSI External Model, the following definitions are given.

EXTERNAL FIELD is the smallest named external data object to which an application program can refer. It has a magnitude, dimensionality, and a unit of dimension, or some non-quantitative interpretation.

EXTERNAL GROUP is a collection of zero or more external fields and/or external groups.

EXTERNAL RECORD is a collection of zero or more external fields and/or external groups as viewed by an application program, to which concurrent accessibility is made available by a single primitive external data manipulation operation. By definition, all of the fields in an external record represent facts about the same entity. Each entity has an identity; therefore each external record has an identifier, such as employee number etc.
If an external record contains varying numbers of nested repeating external groups, then it could be called hierarchical.

EXTERNAL PLEX is a collection of zero or more external records and/or external plexes. The content of an external plex need not be disjoint from the content of other external plexes.

EXTERNAL-RECORD-SET is a collection of zero or more external records and/or external plexes, as viewed by an application program.

As implied by the earlier discussion, we probably do not require EXTERNAL PLEX and EXTERNAL GROUP in DIAM. The remainder of the terminology at this level could be used in the DIAM system.

SUMMARY

In this paper, we have indicated how DIAM II relates to the ANSI SPARC External, Conceptual, and Internal Schemas. In addition, we have presented some detail on how such a system would specify a wide variety of efficient file organizations for supporting existing data base systems.

ACKNOWLEDGEMENT

Discussions with Professor Janis Bubenko of the University of Stockholm have helped to correct and clarify a number of areas of this document.

REFERENCES

(1)   S. E. Madnick, J. W. Alsop: A modular approach to file system design. SJCC, 1969, 1-13.

(2)   H. S. Meltzer: Data base concepts and architecture for data base systems, IBM Report to SHARE Information Systems Research Project (August 20, 1969).

(3)   M. E. Senko, E. B. Altman, M. M. Astrahan, and P. L. Fehder: Data structures and accessing in data base systems. IBM Systems J. 1973, 12, 30-93.

(4)   G. H. Mealy: Another look at data, FJCC 1967, pp. 525-534.

(5)   FDT Bulletin of ACM-SIGMOD 7, No. 2 (1975) SPARC interim report, American National Standards Institute Document No. 7514TS01 (ANSI, Washington, D. C., Feb. 8,1975).

      C. W. Bachman: Trends in database management-1975. Proceedings of the 1975 National Computer Conference, pp 569-576 (AFIPS Press, Montvale, New Jersey, 1975).

(6)   R. E. Levien and M. E. Maron: A computer system for inference execution and data retrieval. Comm ACM, 1967, 10, 715-721.

(7)   B. Langefors: Information systems. Information Processing 74, 937-945 (North-Holland, Amsterdam, 1974).

(8)   B. Sundgren: An Infological Approach to Data Bases. (Urval nr 7) (National Central Bureau of Statistics, Stockholm, Sweden, 1973).

(9)   J. R. Abrial: Data Semantics. IFIP-TC-2 Working Conference on "Data Base Management Systems", Cargese, Corsica (North Holland, Amsterdam).

(10) M. E. Senko: The DDL in the context of a multilevel structured description: DIAM II with FORAL, Data Base Description, B.C.M. Douque and G.M. Nijssen (eds.). pp. 239-240 (North Holland Publishing Co., Amsterdam, 1975).

(11) M. E. Senko: Specification of stored data structures and desired output results in DIAM II with FORAL, Proceedings of the Conference on Very Large Data Bases (ACM, New York, 1975).

(12) CODASYL Data Base Task Group: Report to the CODASYL Programming Language Committee. (ACM, New York, 1971).

(13) INFORMATION MANAGEMENT SYSTEM IMS/360: Application Description Manual, Form GH20-0765-1, International Business Machines Corporation, Data Processing Division, White Plains, New York (1971).

(14) H. A. Schmid and J. R. Swenson: On the semantics of the relational model, Proceeding of the SIGMOD Conference, San Jose, California, 1975 pp. 211-223 (ACM, New York, 1975).

(15) S. Todd: Private communication. EEC Advanced Course on Data Base Languages, Freudenstadt, Germany, 1975.

(16) M. E. Senko, E. B. Altman, M. M. Astrahan, P. L. Fehder, and C. P. Wang: A data independent architecture model: four levels of description from logical structures to physical search structures. RJ 982 IBM Research, Yorktown Heights, New York, 1972).

(17) CODASYL Stored Data Description and Translation Task Group: Stored Data Description and Data Translation: A Model and Language (J. Fry, Chairman, University of Michigan, Ann Arbor). (to be published).

(18) L. Schneider: Quantitative Data Description. Proceedings of the SIGMOD Conference, San Jose, California (ACM, New York, 1975).

(19) S. P. Ghosh and M. E. Senko: String path search procedures for data base systems. IBM J. of Research and Development 18, 408-422 (1974).

(20) G. M. Nijssen: Presentation at IFIP-TC-2 Special Working Conference: "A technical in-depth evaluation of the DDL." Namur, Belgium January 13-17, 1975 (Proceedings published by North Holland, Amsterdam).

(21) R. W. Taylor: Observations on the attributes of database sets. Proceedings of the IFIP-TC-2 Special Working Conference, Namur, Belgium. January 13-17,1975 (North Holland, Amsterdam, 1975).

(22) M. E. Senko: An introduction to FORAL for users, version 2, parts I and II: basic information structure and basic query concepts. (IBM Research, Yorktown Heights, 1975).

M. E. Senko: An introduction to FORAL for users, version 2, part III: basic FORAL data base maintenance concepts (IBM Research, Yorktown Heights, New York, 1975).

(23) M. E. Senko and E. B. Altman: DIAM Note 1: A framework mode for implementing a record-storing facility, RJ 1365, (IBM Research, Yorktown Heights, New York, 1972).

DISCUSSION

At the conference, discussion occurred on three major topics of interest to this paper.

(1)   The ANSI SPARC definition of "fact".

(2)   Whether "Entity Set Names" or "Entity Name Set Names" should appear in the data base description (the Conceptual Schema) and in user's programs.

(3)   Whether a pure "binary" form or an "irreducible n-ary" form should be used as the basic element of descriptions at the Conceptual Level.

The ANSI SPARC Definition of Fact

The question brought up by Nijssen and others was whether the ANSI SPARC statement - that a fact was representable by *one* Conceptual Field - was satisfactory.

This topic was discussed in the preprint of this paper and the discussion has been amplified in this final revision. In particular, this paper suggests that a fact requires two fields, one containing the name of the entity the fact is about and a second containing the value of the property. (Generally, the third thing required, the "name of the property" is given in some fashion by the name of the field that contains the property value.)

The ANSI SPARC discussion assumes something which should be made explicit if SPARC's later remarks are to be agreed on by all workers. The thing that the ANSI discussion *implicitly* assumes is (a) that the field appears in a Conceptual Record and (b) that the Conceptual Record contains an Identifier Value that names the entity the fact is about.

Of course, the Identifier Value Field by itself also states a fact about the entity, but this fact form is a special case of the general rule. Best way to get a definition that correlates with the most prevalent form of fact is to use the *two Conceptual Field* definition. This definition covers the Identifier Value if we recognize that the Identifier Value field is serving the purpose of *two* fields, one for identifying the entity and one for giving the property value.

Definitions that leave important conditions out are of course open to misinterpretation. The ANSI SPARC discussion should, therefore, be changed to make the assumptions stated above explicit.

"The representation of a "fact" requires *two* Conceptual Fields, one to contain the "name of the entity being described" and one to contain the "value of the property" doing the describing."

Entity Set Names or Entity Name Set Names

At the conference, Prof. H. A. Schmid, Drs. Patrick Hall, and S. Todd along with others noticed that Figure 4, the DIAM II -FORAL Type Diagram contained the names EMP-NO and DEPT-NO. This was immediately interpreted to mean that this paper had retrogressed to ignoring Entity Sets in favor of Entity Name Sets. These two notions were addressed in the original Systems Journal DIAM paper and they continue to play a part in DIAM II. In essence, an Entity Set is a set of Entities in the "real world" and an Entity Name Set is a set of names for a set of Entities in the "real world".

A close reading of this paper or the conference preprint will find that the topic is discussed in detail and *at no time* does the paper forclose on the possibility of having names for Entity Sets, that is, "Entity Set Names" appear in the circles. In fact, the parameterization that appears specifically has the parameter, ENTITY-SET-NAME. Additionally, in the diagram, the circle, EMP-PROJ contains an Entity Set Name.

There are, however, some finer points in deciding whether to use either an Entity Set or an Entity Name Set to stand for a set of entities in a data processing system. These concern a tradeoff between (a) the number of names for sets that the system must store and the user must know and (b) the stability of programs. A system that uses both Entity Set Names (for example, EMPLOYEES) and Entity Name Set Names (for example, EMP-NO) will have to store about twice as many set names as the system that uses only Entity Name Sets Names. This places an additional load on the system and on the user because he must learn twice as many names. In a complex system, such additional loads could be crucial and should be taken into consideration. On the other hand, using both an Entity Set Name and an Entity Name Set Name for a particular set of entities lends additional stability to the system *if the relationship between entities in the set and their names changes.* IF IT DOES NOT, then nothing is lost by simply using Entity Name Sets.

In short, DIAM II handles both possibilities, and the user should make the tradeoff himself on a set by set basis depending on the anticipated stability of the name to entity relationship. This tradeoff is discussed in more detail in both the paper and the preprint.

Pure Binaries or Irreducible N-aries

Another topic of discussion involved the question of the better representation for a "basic fact" at the Conceptual Level. Over the years there have been two paths of progress on this topic. One path traveled by Levien and Maron and others has gone directly to the use of a pure binary form. The second path has traveled from some hierarchic or network form to flat files or n-aries *toward* pure binaries. DIAM has taken an intermediate path moving to flat files or entity descriptions and then jumping directly to a form of pure binary. The second path has recognized some of the difficulties with n-aries and tried to resolve them by going to smaller fact forms (irreducible n-aries) still in the spirit of n-ary relations. They give two reasons for halting at this intermediate stage. One is that there is an algorithm that allows the user to go from familiar flat files or n-aries to irreducible n-aries. It seems, however, if Delobel's statement at the conference is interpreted correctly, that such an algorithm will not work correctly unless it has additional information. The information that it requires seems to be what the pure binaries are. In effect, it seems that one has to know the answer before one can reduce n-aries. In this is the case, then there seems to be no reason for not stating the answer in pure binaries in the first place and avoiding the unnecessary work.

The second reason deals with the suggestion that pure binaries require the user to construct "excess entities"". This argument is illustrated in Figure 9.

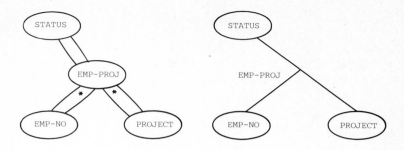

Figure 9

It is said that to give the property, STATUS, to the relationship between EMP-NO and PROJECT, in the binary approach that the user must create the "excess entity" EMP-PROJ. It is also said that the "excess entity" is unnatural and has no meaning in the "real world". Of course, to handle the same problem using irreducible entities, the user must create an irreducible n-ary which is not an entity. This "nonentity" somehow is considered to be more natural and to have more meaning in the "real world".

In a more technical sense, it can be seen that both forms in Figure 9 require the same number of names, four each. So that there is in no sense an "excess" in the binary form in terms of names, the final thing that the user must wrestle with. The irreducible n-ary form does, however, call for a heterogeneous set of constructs at the Conceptual Level. Some things are set of entities and others are sets of something different, irreducible n-aries. Whether these latter constructs are more "natural" than entities is a matter of opinion. In refering to Figure 10, we get some additional properties.

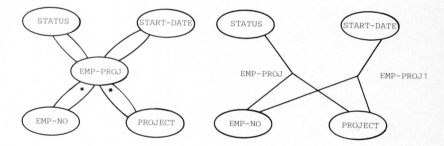

Figure 10

In Figure 10, we have added a second property, START-DATE. The addition of this property causes a greater divergence in how the two representations seem to work. In the binary case, the property is added easily to the "excess entity" EMP-PROJ, which looks even more real. In the irreduciable form however a new "excess irreducible n-ary" must be created. The number of names required to handle the change in Figure 10 differs. Pure binaries require only five whereas irreducible n-aries require six. On this technical basis, binaries seem to be simpler. A second consideration is the way in which EMP-PROJ relates STATUS and START-DATE in the binary form. In this case, they are clearly seen to be related by being properties of one "real world" entity. In the n-ary form, it is not clear whether they are related or not, one needs some additional information to find out. In this sense, the binaries have more semantic content.

Finally, a word about the word "natural". The thing that is easiest for us to do *on the basis of our past experience* seems to us to be most "natural". This may or may not be a good guide to what will be easiest or best to use in the future. In particular, one reason why binaries seem to be "less natural" is that in the past, we have thought about data processing in terms of flat files where less of the semantic constraints are specified.

(This is, of course, why hierarchies and networks are sometimes said to be "more natural".) When one goes to binaries, he must learn to specify the semantic information more explicitly. After some practice this process becomes easy and is no longer a problem. In doing this the user gets the advantage of being more explicit about the meaning of his information structure and, if FORAL is any indication, he gets the advantage of using a language that looks more like "natural" English.

Other points of view on this topic are discussed in the papers of Hall, Falkenberg, and Bracchi at this conference.

Modelling in Data Base Management Systems, G.M. Nijssen, (ed.)
North Holland Publishing Company, 1976

CONCEPTS FOR MODELLING INFORMATION*

Eckhard Falkenberg
Institut für Informatik
University of Stuttgart
Stuttgart, F. R. of Germany

This paper is concerned with the problems of structuring
and modelling information. The aim is to introduce concepts
which are adequate for the design of conceptual schemas and
which fulfill corresponding criteria. A method for modelling
information is proposed which is based on only two basic
concepts, object and role. The application of this system
of concepts is illustrated. A comparison with some other
approaches and a short evaluation are included in this paper.

1   THE AIM

In the present data base management research, there is a trend towards coexistence of different data models and languages within one
system. To reach this coexistence, as a gross architecture the conceptual-schema approach is proposed (ANSI-SPARC [2], NIJSSEN [14]).
Nevertheless, it is an open problem up to now what might be the most
adequate concepts just for the conceptual schema. Adequacy can mean
a lot of issues and criteria. Some of them are mentioned in the following.

We should be able to define the information contents of the application problem as precise as possible. For those precise definitions
we should be able to choose the simplest, most elegant and straight-
foreward solutions.

For the formal foundation of the concepts for modelling information
we should choose as few as possible basic concepts.

We should take into account that the types in a data base evolve in
course of time. This should not result in a permanent necessity of
reprogramming the manipulation functions and application programs.
This criterion we call evolvability.

Another important criterion we should consider is transformability.
This means that the concepts on the conceptual-schema level should
be chosen in a way, that the mappings between the conceptual schema
and the various other schemas - user schemas and internal schema -
become as simple as possible.

---

*   The presentation, given by the author at the conference in Freu-
     denstadt, is published elsewhere [11]. The present paper re-
     flects to some extend several discussion points of this confer-
     ence and has therefore the character of a postscript.

There are other criteria, like naturalness, comprehensibility, teachability and practicability. They are also important criteria, but
difficult to grasp and to proof.

It is the aim of this paper to give an introduction into concepts
which try to approximate these criteria of adequacy.

2   INTRODUCTION TO CONCEPTS FOR MODELLING INFORMATION

From a problem-oriented point of view, we can say that a data base
is the description of an abstract model of a piece of reality. This
description is performed by a language. It is an important and basic
premise of the approach presented in this paper, to distinguish very
carefully between (a) the abstract model of the application-specific
piece of reality and (b) the linguistic reference to that model. In
the literature, various terms are used for such an abstract model,
e.g. "object system" (SUNDGREN [18]), "things of the real world"
(SENKO et al. [16]), "information sphere" (FALKENBERG [10]). In this
paper, we will use the term universe of discourse. A universe of discourse consists of discrete elements. During a time period, a universe of discourse may change, new elements may be added, existing elements may be deleted.

To describe a universe of discourse means to signify (specify, identify) all its elements uniquely, by aid of specific linguistic expressions. Such an expression, signifying exactly one element of a
universe of discourse, we call a unique signification (more specific,
see FALKENBERG [11]).

Considering elements of a universe of discourse, we may distinguish
between (a) some kinds of fundamental elements and (b) some kinds of
semantic rules concerning these fundamental elements. This distinction is of practical importance. While fundamental elements are present in each application, the necessity to use the one or the other
kind of semantic rules depends on the application problem.

In this paper, we are only concerned with the question, what kinds
of fundamental elements there should be in a universe of discourse.
First, we give an introduction to the basic concepts and to some further concepts. Then we discuss some signification problems, in so
far as this is necessary in our context. Furthermore, we consider
changes of a universe of discourse.

2.1 BASIC CONCEPTS

A universe of discourse contains conceptual, mental units which are
distinguishable from one another, atomic and discrete in nature.
Those elements we call objects. When we ask for the information content of an object, the only knowledge we have a priori is that it
exists in our universe of discourse. Except that, an object has no
information content in itself. We get information content, if we say
something about the object, if we consider facts concerning this object, if we associate this object with other objects. For single,
atomic facts, for the smallest information-bearing* elements of a
universe of discourse, we use the term association.

---

*   term in colloquial sense

Informally speaking, an association contains and connects objects. We may now ask the question, what is the nature of this containment and connection. Is an association a set of objects or a tuple of objects or what? Before answering that question, let us look at the two linguistic expressions "W. A. Mozart was born in Salzburg" and "W. A. Mozart lived in Salzburg". If we assume the normal historical knowledge as universe of discourse, we see that each expression is a unique signification of an association between two objects. In both cases the objects are the same, "W. A. Mozart" and "Salzburg". Nevertheless, the associations are different, which is indicated by different verbs, "born" and "lived". Therefore, we cannot say that the only components of associations are objects. There has to be a further kind of components which we call <u>roles</u>.

We have now introduced the two basic concepts of our approach, namely the concepts object and role. Therefore, we call our approach the <u>object-role model</u>. Other concepts, in particular the concepts association and type, are definable by aid of these two basic concepts. The most fundamental aspects of the object-role model are described formally in the appendix. In the following, this model and some peculiarities of it are illustrated by examples.

2.2 ASSOCIATIONS

We have seen that the components of associations are objects and roles. Each object of an association plays a specific role within the association. It may be also the case that an association occurs as component of another association. In those cases we speak of <u>nested</u> associations.

Formally speaking, an association is defined as a set of object-role or association-role pairs. Within a universe of discourse, an object or an association may play several different roles, and also a role may be assigned to several objects or associations.

In the following, we give some examples of prominent cases. The unique significations we use to signify the associations are illustrated graphically.

In many application cases, associations are <u>binary</u>, that means they are sets of two object-role pairs.

Example:

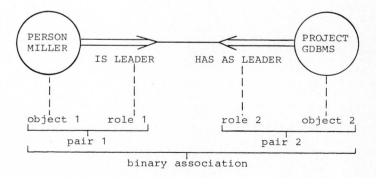

binary association

In this example two objects are associated, signified by "PERSON MILLER" and "PROJECT GDBMS". The person plays the role that he "IS LEADER" of a project, while the project plays the role that it "HAS AS LEADER" a person.

Not all application cases are as simple as the above example. In particular, sometimes more than two object-role pairs may be considered as one association, as one single fact.

Example:

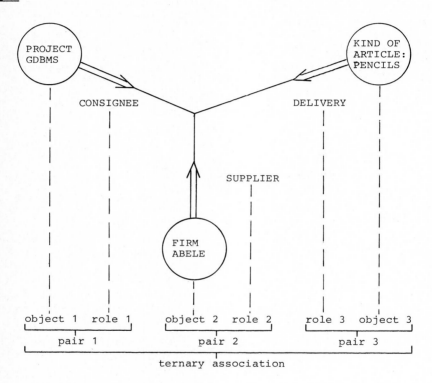

In this example we have three objects, signified by "PROJECT GDBMS", "FIRM ABELE" and "KIND OF ARTICLE: PENCILS". The role of the project is "CONSIGNEE", the role of the firm is "SUPPLIER", and the role of the kind of article is "DELIVERY". The three objects are, from a structural point of view, on the same level, because each object is associated to both other ones without preference.

There may be other cases, where such a preference exists. For example, we have the binary associations, that certain persons earn certain amounts of money per month. If we consider in addition the historical development of salaries, we have to add the dates, when those facts (persons earning amounts of money) begin or end.

Example:

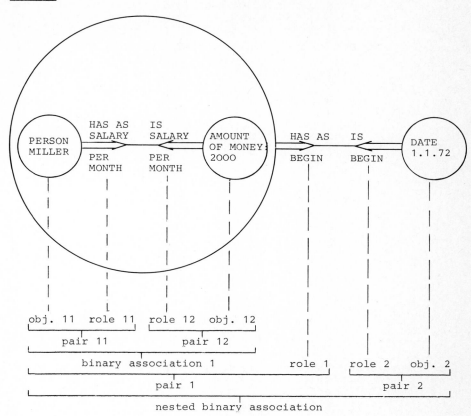

nested binary association

In terms of the object-role model, we can interpret this example as follows: There are two objects, signified by "PERSON MILLER" and "AMOUNT OF MONEY: 2000". The role of the person is that he "HAS AS SALARY PER MONTH" an amount of money, and the role of the amount of money is that it "IS SALARY PER MONTH" of a person. The whole salary association is associated to another object, signified by "DATE 1.1. 72". The role of the salary association is that it "HAS AS BEGIN" a date, and the role of the date is that it "IS BEGIN" of a salary association.

2.3 TYPES

It is usual in communication and, in particular, also in data base technology to deal with types of elements. An actually at a certain instance of time in the universe of discourse existing set of elements, belonging to a specific type, is called a population of that type. A single element belonging to a specific type is called an instance of that type (DURCHHOLZ [9]).

In our approach we distinguish association types and object types.
Association types may be defined by aid of the role concept in the
following way: Several associations belong to the same type, if the
sets of roles, occurring in each one of these associations, are identical.

Example:

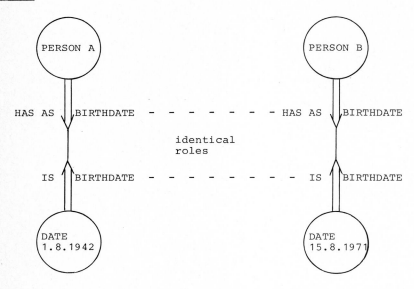

These two associations belong to the same type, because in both associations the same roles occur, signified by "HAS AS BIRTHDATE" and
"IS BIRTHDATE".

Also object types may be defined by aid of the role concept: Several
objects belong to the same type, if these objects play at least one
role in common. Following that definition in the above example, the
two objects signified by "PERSON A" and "PERSON B" may belong to the
same type, because they have a role in common, namely "HAS AS BIRTH-
DATE".

It is important to note that these definitions give in many cases a
good approximation of that what may be intuitivly called types. Nevertheless, these definitions are not at all binding. Normally, in looking at things from several points of view, one element of a universe
of discourse may be instance of several types. This means types may
be overlapping.

2.4 SIGNIFICATION ASPECTS

In the above examples, we have chosen relatively simple significations to signify the objects and roles of the represented associations uniquely. For example, we have assumed that the string "PERSON
MILLER" is a unique signification of an object. That assumption is
only valid if the individual name "MILLER" is unique within the

actual population of the object type named "PERSON". If this condition is not true, we need another signification, probably a more complicated one. For example, we may use several types of names like
"FIRST NAME" and "LAST NAME". The signification then probably becomes
unique.

Example:

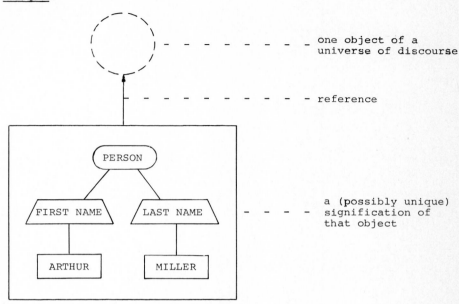

On the other hand, it is often possible to simplify the significations of roles. For example, if there are objects playing only one
role within the universe of discourse, and the significations of
these objects are chosen in an appropriate way, then this role may
be obvious and needs not to be signified explicitly.

Example:

In this example the roles of a salary association are not signified
explicitly, but implicitly by choosing the signification "SALARY
2000 PER MONTH" which is to some extend a mixture of object and role
signification.

There may be other cases where it is sufficient to signify the various roles in an association by just one expression. Such an expression is to some extend similar to the linguistic "predicate".

Example:

2.5   CHANGES OF THE UNIVERSE OF DISCOURSE

To change a universe of discourse means to add or to delete information-bearing elements to respectively from the universe of discourse.
This means for our approach that only <u>associations</u> may be added or
deleted. It is allowed that the associations to be added belong to
new types. It may also happen that the whole population of an association type will be deleted if this type is of no more interest. Changes of the universe of discourse mean therefore, that not only instances may change, but also the scope of interest, the types.

If only associations may be added or deleted, we have to answer the
question, how can we add or delete objects and what means that. To
introduce a new object into the universe of discourse means to add
new associations from which this object is a component. To delete an
existing object from the universe of discourse means to delete all
the associations from which this object is a component. We see that
objects are added or deleted <u>indirectly</u>, via associations. This is a
conclusion of the point that we consider an object in itself not as
information-bearing.

We might argue that we may be interested just only in the <u>existence</u>
of an object in the application-specific environment. But <u>in this</u>
case, we have introduced unconsciously and implicitly an information-
bearing element, namely the fact that our object exists in the environment. For conceptual clearness we should make this fact explicitly, that means we should introduce an existence association between our object and the object "environment".

3   COMPARISON WITH OTHER APPROACHES

In this section some points of comparison with other approaches and
some arguments about our approach are collected.

3.1   UNIVERSE OF DISCOURSE AND SIGNIFICATIONS

It is a matter of fact that in general one element of some universe
of discourse may be signified in various different ways (FALKENBERG
[11]). This is the main reason why we suggest to distinguish very
carefully between (a) the problems arising in structuring a universe
of discourse and (b) the problems arising in putting the linguistic

references to this universe of discourse. This distinction is an important premise for structuring and describing any relevant information content fairly precisely.

For example, let us consider a salary association between an amount
of money and a person having a first name and a last name. Let us for
a moment abstract from the signification problem, then we see that we
have an association between two objects, namely between a certain
amount of money and a certain person. The fact that we need a first
name and a last name (or probably something else like a personnel
number) to signify this person uniquely, belongs already to the signification problem. In this example we have the situation that the
unique signification of the one object (the amount of money) is simple, while the unique signification of the other object (the person)
is more complicated.

This attitude prevents us from having to answer the question whether
the first name or the last name earns the money directly, as illustrated in the following.

Example:

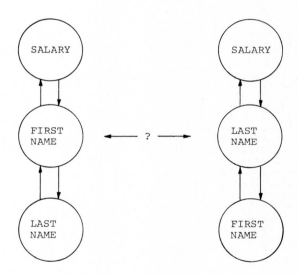

For our feeling, the information content of this problem can be defined more precisely if one follows the approach presented in this
paper (compare section 2.4; see on the other hand e.g. BRACCHI/FEDE-
LI/PAOLINI [4] p. 214 and SENKO [17], see also the "squidles" of
HALL/OWLETT/TODD [12]).

3.2 OBJECTS AND ROLES

We have seen that for the considerations about the universe of discourse two basic concepts are sufficient, namely object and role. In
other approaches, often a larger number of basic concepts are used,
like for example object, association, property and type (see e.g.

BENCI et al. [3]). It seems to us that for reasons of simplicity and
comprehensibility as few as possible basic concepts should be introduced.

The concept of object is well known from many other approaches. The
concept of role occurs in some less general form in the approaches
of CODD [7] and SENKO et al. [16] (role names). It has also some
similarity with ABRIAL's concept of access function [1].

3.3 PROPERTIES AND RELATIONSHIPS

A peculiarity of natural language is that one and the same fact can
be signified in various different ways. Let us consider, for example,
the two expressions "The house No. 11 is yellow" and "The house No.
11 possesses the colour yellow". Intuitivly, we could say that in the
first expression "yellow" is a property of the "house No. 11", while
in the second expression there is a relationship between the "house
No. 11" and the "colour yellow". But if we abstract for a moment from
the special linguistic paraphrase and ask what elements of our universe of discourse these expressions signify, we see that both expressions signify one and the same fact. The only point is that the one
linguistic paraphrase may be used more often than the other. Thus, we
may get the feeling that the one paraphrase is more "natural" than
the other.

It seems to us, that those linguistic peculiarities motivate the distinction between properties and relationships in many approaches (see
e.g. BENCI et al. [3], CHEN [5], HALL/OWLETT/TODD [12], MOULIN et al.
[13], SCHMID/SWENSON [15], SUNDGREN [18]).

We have good reasons not to provide that distinction on the conceptual-schema level. Namely, this distinction is often of fuzzy nature,
that means different users may come to different conclusions in clas-
sifying facts as properties or relationships. On the other hand, this
classification is often considered as obvious which means that it can
be dropped without loosing information.

There are even more serious problems with that distinction. Namely,
there may be some evolution event so that a type of facts which has
belonged, in the original universe of discourse, to the one kind belongs now, in the new universe of discourse, to the other kind. A
property may become a relationship or vice versa. Data manipulation
functions which deal with these types of facts and which refer to
this distinction will no more work after the evolution event. This is
the reason why the distinction between properties and relationships
results in a <u>lack of evolvability</u> (FALKENBERG [10]).

These considerations refer to the conceptual-schema level. On the
other hand, there may be user schemas where different linguistic
paraphrases are possible and, in particular, where the users may distinguish between properties and relationships.

3.4 BINARY ASSOCIATIONS

It is often argued that one can manage all problems of structuring
a universe of discourse by aid of binary <u>functional</u> association types
(see e.g. the CODASYL-set concept [6]). This is true but disadvantage-

ous in some cases. Namely, there may be an evolution event within the universe of discourse changing a functional association type into a relational one from the problem's point of view. If we want to save the functional approach in such a case, we have to introduce a new, additional object type (some people call it a dummy) which has now two new functional association types to the original two object types. The consequence of that is a lack of evolvability because those data manipulation functions dealing with the original association types, will no more work after the evolution event. Therefore, it is better to allow binary relational association types (ABRIAL [1], BRACCHI/FE-DELI/PAOLINI [4], SENKO [17]).

But we should not restrict ourselves to that binary concept because this restriction has some disadvantages. Let us consider an evolution event, so that a new object type has to be introduced into an existing association type (and thus modifying it). It may be the case that the trial to split the modified, expanded association type into several binary association types results in a loss of information (see CODD [7] p. 385). To avoid this loss of information we have to introduce another, additional object type. Again, like in the case mentioned above, the consequence is a lack of evolvability. Therefore, we should allow n-ary relational association types.

3.5 N-ARY ASSOCIATIONS

As an association is considered as a single, atomic fact, we cannot take any number of objects into an association. Therefore, when we say "n-ary", we do not mean CODD's approach [7], where in general several single facts are combined within one n-tuple, even in third normal form.

A possible criterion to decide how many objects are involved in an association, so that we can say this is a single fact, is the criterion of semantical irreducibility. Informally speaking, a semantically irreducible n-ary association type cannot be split into several association types with a smaller number of object types, without having to introduce an additional object type or without loosing information (see e.g. HALL/OWLETT/TODD [12], FALKENBERG [10]).

There may be problems with that criterion when it is applied uncritically (DELOBEL [8]). But normally, it may result in a good approximation of what we intuitively call a single fact.

Another problem is to decide whether an association, containing more than two objects, may have an internal nested structure or not. Because we should be able to define information contents precisely and straight foreward, and also for reasons of generality, we should allow nested associations.

4   SUMMARIZING EVALUATION

We have mentioned in section 1 some criteria of adequacy with regard to concepts for modelling information on the conceptual-schema level. Now we want to discuss the question, to what degree the concepts we introduced fulfill these criteria.

We have emphasized the importance of considering what are the smallest information-bearing elements of a universe of discourse, what are
single facts. We allow n-ary associations as well as nested associations. This is an approach which enables us to solve the problem of
structuring a universe of discourse in a precise and straight-fore-
ward manner. Another point we have emphasized is the clear distinction of the problems with regard to the universe of discourse from
the signification problems. Also, this point can improve precision.

We have introduced a fairly simple system of concepts. There are only
two basic concepts, namely object and role, by aid of which the others
are definable.

To fulfill the criterion of evolvability, we suggest (a) to avoid unnecessary distinctions like that between properties and relationships,
and (b) to allow (semantically irreducible) n-ary association types.

Transformability has to do not only with the considerations about the
universe of discourse, but also and, in particular, with the signification aspects. This point is demonstrated by the author elsewhere
[11].

With regard to naturalness, comprehensibility, teachability and practicability we dispense with arguments. They may be left to the judgement and taste of the reader.

REFERENCES

[1] ABRIAL, J.R.: Data Semantics, in Klimbie/Koffeman (eds.): Data Base Management, North-Holland 1974

[2] ANSI-SPARC: Status Report 1975

[3] BENCI, E. et al.: Concepts for the Design of a Conceptual Schema, IFIP TC-2 Working Conference on "Modelling in Data Base Management Systems", Freudenstadt, January 1976

[4] BRACCHI, G.; FEDELI, A.; PAOLINI, P.: A Multilevel Relational Model for Data Base Management Systems, in Klimbie/Koffeman (eds.): Data Base Management, North-Holland 1974

[5] CHEN, P.P.: The Entity-Relationship Model - Toward a Unified View of Data, Proceedings of the Conference on "Very Large Data Bases", Framingham, Mass., September 1975

[6] CODASYL-DDLC: DDLC Journal of Development, 1973

[7] CODD, E.F.: A Relational Model of Data for Large Shared Data Banks, CACM, Vol. 13, No. 6, June 1970, p. 377-387

[8] DELOBEL, C.: Discussion point on the IFIP TC-2 Working Conference on "Modelling in Data Base Management Systems", Freudenstadt, January 1976

[9] DURCHHOLZ, R.: The Concept of Type, Bericht ADF 11, Gesellschaft für Mathematik und Datenverarbeitung, St. Augustin, June 1975

[10] FALKENBERG, E.: Structuring and Representation of Information at the Interface between Data Base User and Data Base Management System, doctoral thesis, University of Stuttgart, June 1975 (in German; in English forthcoming)

[11] FALKENBERG, E.: Significations: The Key to Unify Data Base Management, Information Systems, Vol. 2 (1), April 1976

[12] HALL, P.; OWLETT, J.; TODD, S.: Relations and Entities, IFIP TC-2 Working Conference on "Modelling in Data Base Management Systems", Freudenstadt, January 1976

[13] MOULIN, P. et al.: Conceptual Model as a Data Base Design Tool, IFIP TC-2 Working Conference on "Modelling in Data Base Management Systems", Freudenstadt, January 1976

[14] NIJSSEN, G.M.: A Gross Architecture for the Next Generation Data Base Management Systems, IFIP TC-2 Working Conference on "Modelling in Data Base Management Systems", Freudenstadt, January 1976

[15] SCHMID, H.A.; SWENSON, J.R.: On the Semantics of the Relational Data Model, Proceedings of the ACM-SIGMOD Conference, San José, California, May 1975

[16] SENKO, M.E. et al.: Data Structuring and Accessing in Data-Base Systems, IBM Systems Journal, Vol. 12, No. 1, 1973, p. 30-93

[17] SENKO, M.E.: DIAM as a Detailed Example of the ANSI/SPARC Archi-
       tecture, IFIP TC-2 Working Conference on "Modelling in Data
       Base Management Systems", Freudenstadt, January 1976

[18] SUNDGREN, B.: Conceptual Foundation of the Infological Approach
       to Data Bases, in Klimbie/Koffeman (eds.): Data Base Mana-
       gement, North-Holland 1974

APPENDIX: THE OBJECT-ROLE MODEL

There are two basic concepts:

object o
role r

An association a is defined as a set of object-role or association-role pairs:

$$a = \{(x_i, r_i)\},$$

where $x_i = o_i \lor a_i$, $i \in I$, $/I/ \geq 1$, $o_i \in O$, $r_i \in R$, $a_i \in A$,

I index set: places of the association,
O total set of objects,
R total set of roles,
A total set of associations;

An association type A may be defined as a set of associations where each association contains the same set of roles:

$$A = \{a_j\},$$

where $j \in J$, $\forall i, j \neq k : r_{ij} \equiv r_{ik}$ for fixed $i \in I$ and $j, k \in J$,

$(r_{ij}$ or r_{ik} means the role r_i within the association a_j or

a_k , respectively) , $a_j \in A$,

I index set: places of the association type,
J index set: population of the association type;

An object type O may be defined as a set of objects, each of which plays at least one role in common:

$$O = \{o_k\},$$

where $k \in K$, $\forall k \; \exists \; r : \exists \; (o_k, r)$ for $k \in K$, $o_k \in O$,

K index set: population of the object type;

Modelling in Data Base Management Systems, G.M. Nijssen, (ed)
North Holland Publishing Company, 1976

DATA DESCRIPTIONS EMBEDDED IN CONTEXT

J. Ruchti
Eidg. Anstalt fuer Wasserversorgung,
Abwasserreinigung und Gewaesserschutz (EAWAG)
Eidg. Technische Hochschulen (ETH)
Duebendorf, Switzerland

Instructing a Data Base Management System about
its real environment requires a language capable
of communicating empirical facts about the real
world. A formalism is outlined which permits the
procedural description of empirical hypotheses
about the world.

Based on a model idea mapping each expression
with arguments onto an event in time involving
objects, the formalism is particularly suited to
relate data to time and to empirical context.

The formalism is intended to be a tool for
systems analysts and to improve the self
descriptiveness of data bases. An example is
given and the necessity of future semantic
interpretation of the empirical model is
discussed.

1. INTRODUCTION

The ANSI/SPARC interim report (1975) proposes that an enterprise
administrator write a conceptual schema as a formal model describing
the enterprise to a Data Base Management System. The conceptual
schema should be written in machine readable form. I introduce the
notion of 'conceptual language' as the means to write the conceptual
schema. It is the purpose of this paper to find some of the more
important features of such a conceptual language.

When speaking about something we should consent on our Universe of
Discourse (UoD). Speaking about a DBMS our UoD, at the conceptual
level, contains the following main components:

1. The DBMS with programmers, software, stored information
   about the UoD, and hardware.
2. EA, the Enterprise Administrator instructing the DBMS about
   the UoD.
3. eUoD, the external Universe of Discourse, which is often
   referred to as the 'real world'.

Thus UoD = {DBMS, EA, eUoD}.

A   schema   written   in   a   conceptual   language   should   meet   two
requirements.

-   Empirical truth: The human reader of the description of a
    conceptual schema   should   arrive at the same empirical
    interpretation as   was   intended by the author (EA) of the
    schema.
-   Semantic truth: A conceptual schema should conform to
    semantic rules defining data structures to the DBMS.

For a   simple   illustration   of   the   proposed   distinction between
empirical   and   semantic   truth   requirements we look at two record
descriptions:

    life (person, ssn, sex, date-of-birth, date-of-death)
    employee (name, company, date-of-employment, salary)

Both record descriptions are semantically correct, if we agree to
know what a record is and if we agree on the syntactic rule

    <record description> ::= <record   name>   (<record   field>
                             {,<record field>});

We   probably   have no doubt with respect to the empirical meaning of
the   life-record   description; we may agree that it is semantically
and empirically true.

But   there exist serious doubts which of a readers interpretation of
the description of the employee-record is true:

    1. interpretation.   employee-record   is   to   record   present
       employments and salaries of persons.
    2. interpretation. employee-record is to record the employment
       history of persons.

The example of the interpretation of the employee-record description
clearly   shogs   that a syntactically and semantically correct
description   is   not   necessarily   sufficient to document empirical
truth.

For an empirically true documentation we ought to supply the context
of ambiguous record descriptions. Such contextual information is
usually   found   in systems user guides or they just float as general
knowledge   in   the   human   environment   of   a DBMS. My proposal to
formalize contexts of record descriptions to the point of machine
readability pursues several goals:

-   Such   a   formalism should aid and guide a systems analyst in
    his task of describing a given environment.
-   The   formalism could be used to define integrity constraints
    on the data to be stored.
-   Potentially, formalized contexts could be easily stored as
    data in a DBMS and thus contribute to the self descriptive
    power of such a system.

The   enterprise   administrator   must   have a global knowledge of his
UoD, the enterprise. In particular he ought to be able to relate
data to the context of the external UoD, so that the DBMS will
render empirically relevant services to the enterprise.

For the enterprise administrator the conceptual language should be a tool of expressing his ideas about data in contexts describing the enterprise. As context plays such an important role, I shall use the term CONTEXT in order to name the basic modules of a conceptual language.

Enterprises are dynamic rather than static. Therefore CONTEXTS should be structured, they should reflect the 'time structure' of the UoD, and they should be updatable.

2. THEORETICAL FOUNDATION OF CONTEXTS

Following a definition given by Richards (1974) a description relates three items:

- an expression   Ixpx: 'there is an x such that px';
- an object   w: 'an object w';
- a point of reference : 'the utterer u of expression Ixpx
                    <u,t>   at time t'.

An expression Ixpx arises out of a pragmatic situation: u refers to an empirical object w by uttering Ixpx at t only if w satisfies px at <u,t>.
After utterance of an expression, Ixpx denotes on object w only if w satisfies px at <u,t>.

Thus a true interpretation of an expression requires knowledge not only of the expression but also of the point of reference. In addition the context of the utterance of an expression has to be known. We define the following elements as contextual:

- time of event: each expression Ixpx is related to an event e(p) involving an object w at event time t(I);
- neighbour events: to any event involving an object w there is at least one predecessor and/or one successor event involving the same object w. Two neighbour events can be described by two expressions.
- world lines: if we imagine a series of neighbour events on the same object connected by a line in time space, we arrive at the notion of Minkovski world lines (Carnap (1968)). A sequence of expressions describing a sequence of events on a world line shall be called a CONTEXT.

The proposal of CONTEXTS as a formal conceptual language attempts to take those simple ingredients of meaning into account. The syntax of CONTEXTS is outlined in Appendix A. Following up the example given in Appendix B we shall next discuss the empirical aspects of contexts.

3. EMPIRICAL INTERPRETATION OF CONTEXTS

At the empirical level CONTEXTS are not concerned with data structures. Instead, CONTEXTS

1. describe the structure of the external UoD which produces data;
2. enumerate those data which may be stored in a DBMS.

CONTEXTS are not programs. They are formalized hypotheses about possible patterns of events in the external UoD. In order to describe such patterns, CONTEXTS use formal declarations and statements, in appearance only similar to those of a programming language. In fact, CONTEXTS use freely syntactic elements derived from PASCAL (Jensen and Wirth (1974)), but most of these have to be interpreted empirically, in terms of the external UoD.

The following comments presume a first reading of Appendices A and B.

EMPIRICAL TYPES

Meaningful communication about the UoD requires explicit mention of individual elements of the UoD. At the conceptual level we most often do not reference individual elements but we prefer to refer to an element of a type, mentioning the type only.

Basic types. Much confusion can be avoided if we decide at the empirical level for each type (element) whether the type identifier denotes a material or an informational element of the UoD. The proposal of compulsory type declarations (MATTER/INFORMATION) forces us to distinguish between things and their names (and thus enables a machine e.g. to warn us in time if we attempt to store a real, live elephant in a DBMS).

Subsetting of types. Type declarations may also be used for subsetting types, thus offering the means of structuring the UoD by types of types.

Synonyms. The declaration of type synonyms is used to indicate that in a given context there occurr 2 or more different elements of the same type (Appendix B, ctx birth: the social security numbers of the child (ssn), the mother (wno) and the father (mno) are of the same type, but not identical).

Synonyms may also be used to change the identifier of the same element, as a context progresses (Appendix B, ctx womanhood: as a child grows to be a woman, we rename the identifier ssn of its social security number into wno; by this we avoid to say later that the woman gives birth to itself).

Free Types. Some types are declared free in the sense that we do not specify the values of their elements. Note that all types of MATTER have to be free types, because we cannot take material items into a description. Types of INFORMATION can be free (e.g. name in ctx life).

Bound types. Types of INFORMATION can be bound to a set of permissible values. Sex (ctx life) can be male or female only.

Identifiers. Types can also be bound to the field of a record description. Examples: social security number bound to ssn in record person (ctx life); contract bound to contract in record couple (ctx marriage). Types bound to the field of a record description are identifiers naming the world line described by the context containing the declaration.

PREDICATES

Event and state predicates are declared with respect to the types of their arguments. Predicates themselves are implicitly of type TIME. This means, that each predicate occurring in a statement symbolizes the time of an event or the time of observation of a state. For the sake of clarity it is often useful to declare a synonym of a predicate (e.g. syn birthdate = gives birth to).

STATEMENTS AND CONTEXTS

Each predicate expression (the simplest form of a statement) characterizes an observation of a state or an event involving individual elements of declared types.

A CONTEXT typically describes chronologically the events (and ensuing states) in which an element of a type participates. CONTEXT life (Appendix B) thus briefly describes some events in the life of a human which produce records to be kept by a civil servant in a city (hall) office.

Structure. CONTEXTS should be written in a structured way. This enables the author and the reader of CONTEXTS to concentrate on details at the appropriate level. Structuring may also prove useful for later partial updating of CONTEXTS.

Alternative hypotheses. The if...then...else-hypothesis states a condition for alternatives (ctx life: after birth and childhood, depending on your sex, you are going to manhood or to womanhood). The or-hypothesis leaves the decision, which way to go, to the future facts of real life (ctx childhood: you either die or you go through it; ctx manhood: you may die or you may begin or continue your cycle through marriage, divorce/widow).

Repeating patterns. The repeat hypothesis indicates potentially repetitious sequences of events.

Recording. Standard event record symbolizes the event of storing information into the DBMS. The statement <record ... (...) by ...> actually describes a point of reference: by..., the utterer and record..., the time of uttering.

Termination. Standard event terminate symbolizes the fact that a previously stored element has ceased to exist in the external UoD. The terminate statement is also an expression with a point of reference. Obviously, terminate may only operate on an identifier.

CONTEXTS are elements of the UoD. A CONTEXT written at the desk of the enterprise administrator is an element of the external UoD, presently without relevance to the DBMS.

As soon as the EA instructs the DBMS to read a CONTEXT, this CONTEXT will be an element of the DBMS.

Only after the EA instructs the DBMS to initiate a CONTEXT, the system will view the external UoD as defined by the CONTEXT. The CONTEXT now defines data structures to be built up between initiation and termination or replacement of a CONTEXT.

Referencing data stored previously under a by now terminated CONTEXT
should be pocsible by explicit mention of the context and its period
of validity.

4. NEED OF SEMANTIC INTERPRETATION OF CONTEXTS

CONTEXTS as a language to describe the conceptual schema have
volontarily been defined to express statements about the UoD in
terms of empirical notions rather than of data structures. We think
it should be the machines task to interpret CONTEXTS and to define
appropriate data structures. We intend to do the necessary research
along the folloging lines:

   - Improve the syntax of CONTEXTS.
   - Use the improved syntactic structure of CONTEXTS to define an
     appropriate system of relations.

The semantic data model of Abrial (1974) and the notions of
'semantic nets' and 'operational semantics' which are also used by
Weber (1976) may prove to be helpful.

The following few examples intend to hint very informally how the
syntactic elements of CONTEXTS can be interpreted semantically.

Each declaration of a bound etype imposes an integrity constraint on
the corresponding semantic data type with respect to the values this
type may assume. Thus, an empirically bound etype is semantically a
scalar type, adopting the term of scalar type from PASCAL.

An identifier, i.e. an etype bound to the field of a record
description, identifies the world line described by the CONTEXT
containing the declaration of the identifier. Semantically, such an
identifier is a record identifier, or the key of a relation.

Atomic relationships. Each expression describing an event involving
objects represents at the level of the expression a semantic 1:1{:1}
relationship between the arguments of the expression (ctx birth: one
sex is observed for one human).

Functions. But ctx life is valid for all humans of which data shall
be recorded. As a human is identified by a ssn, record person (among
other functions) defines a function from the identifier into sex.
Similarly, using Abrials (1974) definitions of access functions, we
have in ctx birth a function of an identifier (child) mapping onto
an identifier (woman). But when ctx birth is referenced from ctx
womanhood, we have an inverse access function from one woman to
children. In ctx marriage we define also mappings of a human onto a
marriage contract and a mapping from a man onto a woman. Marriages,
however, can be repeated in manhood or in womanhood. Therefore, in
the context of a single life, ctx marriage defines an access
function from a human to its marriage partners. But, considering all
recorded lives, ctx marriage defines a relation couple.

Structure. The grammar of CONTEXTS may semantically be interpreted
as a structured system of relations. Such an interpretation should
define the schema of a contextual data base within a DBMS, whereas
record descriptions, while contained in the contextual data base,
are the schema of the data base proper.

CONTEXTS themselves are blocks which may contain other blocks. It is noticed that recording statements - which are essentially record descriptions - may list record field identifiers which are introduced by blocks other than the block containing a record description. Further research should show if empirical structuring of CONTEXTS can be interpreted semantically for the normalization and/or for the definition of irreducible n-ary relations.

The few examples given - although not representative for the complexity of the proposed task - may suffice to understand that CONTEXTS - after more rigorous definition - can serve to reconcile the empirical and the semantic view of data.

5. DISCUSSION

The enterprise administrator, when writing a conceptual schema for a DBMS, must be capable of assuming two roles: he has to look as an empirist at the enterprise, the external UoD. The problems of the DBMS have to be approached with the view of the semanticist. The two complementary roles can not exclude each other. Therefore the different views (semantic/empiric) of researchers in the field do not necessarily exclude each other.

Nijssen (1976), Senko (1976), and Hall, Owlett and Todd (1976), as typical semanticists, voluntarily leave empirical notions of space, time and processes to interpreters of their abstract systems.

Benci et al. (1976) adopt a more empirical point of view. They devote a whole chapter to Real World Modelling in which they identify empirically relevant concepts. In particular they recognize the importance of 'the temporal and spatial content of the basic elements' of the real world.

Grotenhuis and van den Broek (1976) also investigate the properties of an Empiric Information Model in which they deal with time by using 'versions of information'.

CONTEXTS apparently take a purely empirical view. They stress the importance of time to the point of requiring procedural descriptions of the UoD. It is the empirical role of CONTEXTS to document agreement between humans (the enterprise administrator and his partners in the enterprise) on a model of the common Universe of Discourse. This role potentially contributes to the self descriptive power of a DBMS.

CONTEXTS are based on very few empirical notions such as types of elements of the UoD, events, time and two kinds of actors (the enterprise administrator and each utterer of a record are essentially actors). Therefore, the writer of a CONTEXT has much linguistic choice which presents the danger of bad terminology (the example given in Appendix B admittedly uses mediocre terminology). It is this danger which seems to call for linguistic research defining a library of basic definitional CONTEXTS. Although such research is beyond the scope of Data Base Theory, it could have stimulating effects on Data Base Research.

The need of semantic interpretation of CONTEXTS has been mentioned before.

6. REFERENCES

Abrial, J.R. (1974). Data Semantics. In: Data Base Management,
    edited by J.W. Klimbie and K.L. Koffeman. (North Holland,
    Amsterdam).
ANSI (1975). Interim Report Study Group on Data Base Management
    Systems, February 1975. (American National Standards Institute,
    ANSI/X3/SPARC DBMS Study Group).
Benci, E., Bodart, F., Bogaert, H. and Cabanes A. (1976). Concepts
    for the Design of a Conceptual Schema. (In this Conference).
Carnap, R. (1968). Symbolische Logik. (Springer, Wien).
Grotenhuis, F. and van den Broek, J. (1976). A Conceptual Model for
    Information Processing. (In this Conference).
Jensen, K. and Wirth, N. (1974). PASCAL User Manual and Report.
    (Springer, Berlin).
Nijssen, G.M. (1976). A Gross Architecture for the Next Generation
    DBMS. (In this Conference).
Richards, B. (1974). A Point of Reference. Synthese, 28, No.2, 361.
Senko, M.E. (1976). DIAM as a Detailed Example of the ANSI/SPARC
    Architecture. (In this Conference).
Weber, H. (1976). A Semantic Model of Integrity Constraints on a
    Relational Data Base. (In this Conference).

APPENDIX A: THE SYNTAX OF CONTEXTS

CONTEXTS

As the notion of context plays an inportant role in preserving the
empirical truth of data descriptions we shall use the symbol
'context' (ctx) as a reserved symbol identifying basic modules of a
conceptial language.

```
<context definition> ::= ctx <heading>  <block>.
<heading> ::= <identifier> {(<etype>:<etype>
              {;<etype>:<etype>})};
<block> ::= <declaration part>
            begin <statement> {;<statement>} end
```

Each block of a context contains a declaration part followed by
statements. The statements are disguised predicate expressions which
should be consistent with empirical experience. The symbols
occurring in statements may be taken from natural language. As
natural language may introduce sloppiness into descriptions it seems
advisable that the type of each symbol be declared before its use in
a statement.

ETYPE AND TYPE DECLARATIONS

Each type is to classify elements of our UoD, therefore we have to
provide the means of introducing more types than are commonly used
by information scientists. Since the conventional data types shall
be very useful at the semantic level of the conceptual schema, we
use, at the empirical level, the empirical etypes. They may be

declared as follows:

```
<etype declaration> ::= etype <etype definition>
                          {; <etype definition>};
<etype definition>  ::= <etype> = <etype expr> | <etype>
<etype expr> ::= record (<field description>) of <etype>
<field description> ::= <identifier> : <type>
<etype> ::= <identifier> | (<identifier> {,<identifier>})
```

Standard etypes are

MATTER, INFORMATION

of which other STANDARD and non-standard etypes and types are
derived:

```
etype TIME = INFORMATION;
      star = MATTER;
      molecule = MATTER;
      atom = molecule;
      animal = MATTER;
      human = ANIMAL;
      sex = (female, male) of INFORMATION;
      color = record (colour:PACKED ARRAY[1:10]
                              OF CHAR) of INFORMATION;
      number = INFORMATION;
      character = INFORMATION;
type  CHAR = character;
      REAL = number;
      INTEGER = number;
```

The declaration of etype color shows that the conceptual schema need
not necessarily know a etype definition when it is set up; instead,
a record description provides for latter input of the colour values
defining the etype. Note that the record description contains a
semantic element defining a string of 10 characters.

EVENT AND STATE PREDICATE DECLARATIONS

Predicates are 'empirical operands' on their arguments because they
symbolize an event involving objects. They are not semantic
operators because the action symbolized does not take place in the
DBMS, but in the external UoD.

At the present state of development of CONTEXTS all predicates are
assumed to be of etype TIME.

```
<predicate decl> ::= <pred kind> <pred definition>
                                {;<pred definition>;
<pred kind> ::= event | state
<pred definition> ::= <predicate> = (<pred typ expr>)
<predicate> ::= <pred component> {<pred component>}
<pred component> ::= {...} <identifier>
<pred typ expr> ::= <etype> {<etype>|<pred component>} |
              <pred component>{<etype>|<pred component>}
```

Events symbolize a change of state in which the events arguments participate:

```
event marries = (human marries human);
```

The following declaration is meaningful if we want to indicate that
addition is performed in the external UoD:

```
event plus = (number plus number);
      yields = (number yields plus);
```

States symbolize a state between two events:

```
state distance from ... to =
      (distance from molecule to molecule);
```

Events are insofar of etype TIME, as each event can be associated
with a single value on the time axis. States are insofar of etype
TIME, as we have to postulate a time of observation for each
recorded state.

SYNONYM DECLARATIONS

An etype or a predicate need be declared only once in a context.
Subsequent contexts may refer to them without declaration. However
it is possible to declare synonyms of etypes or of predicates after
declaration and in any later context.

```
<synonym decl> ::= syn <etype>{,<etype>}:<etype>
                       {;<etype>{,<etype>}:<etype>};
<etype> ::= <identifier>
```


Examples:
```
syn   metal: atom;
      angstrom: distance from ... to;
      woman, man: human;
      date of marriage: marries;
```


STATEMENTS

One or more statements follow the declaration part of a context.
Such an ordered sequence of statements represents a hypothesis of an
ordered pattern of events and/or of states in time.

The simplest statement is an expression; it has the same syntax as
the previously introduced <pred typ expr> (see predicate
declarations).

But also more complex statements are needed to describe patterns in
time:

```
<statement> ::=   <expression> |
                  begin <statement> {; statement} end |
                  <context>{(etype{,etype})} |
                  repeat <statement> |
                  if <statement> then <statement>
                              {else <statement>} |
```

```
                        <statement> {<alt><statement>}  |
                        <value substitution> |
                        <recording> |
                        <termination>

    <recording> ::= record <record name>
                    (<field description>{<field description>})
                                        by <etype>
    <termination> ::= terminate <record name>
                            (<identifier>) by <etype>
    <alt> ::= or | xor
    <value substitution> ::= <etype> := <etype>
```

DYNAMIC DESCRIPTION OF THE CONCEPTUAL SCHEMA BY CONTEXTS

After startup the conceptual schema of a DBMS is inexistent. The
system is now and at any later time ready to read a context:

```
        read <context>
```

The system will syntactically validate and store the context read.
The stored context will now represent one hypothesis about the UoD,
but it will not be in the conceptual schema. Only after the command

```
        initiate ctx <identifier>
```

the system will incorporate the hypothesis into the conceptual
schema in order to define the structure of data in the DBMS and to
control data flow to and from the DBMS.
The command

```
        terminate ctx <identifier>
```

will disable data input into storage with respect to the terminated
context. Data retrieval however may still refer to data stored under
the terminated context.
The command

```
        replace ctx <identifier> by <context>
```

is a combination of the termination and the read commands.

APPENDIX B: AN EXAMPLE

```
read ctx life;
etype   human = matter;
        city = matter;
        office = city;
        name = information;
        social security number
            = record person(ssn: integer) of information;
        sex = (male,female) of information;
        maritalstatus = (single, married,
                        divorced, widowed) of information;
```

```
syn     woman, man, child: human;
        wnam, mnam: name;
        wno, mno, ssn: social security number;
        ws, ms, cs: maritalstatus;

 {now follow declarations of contexts to be called by ctx life: }

ctx birth;
event   gives birth to = (human gives birth to human);
        is given = (human is given information);
state   with = (human with information);
syn     birthdate = gives birth to;
begin woman gives birth to child;
        child with sex;
        child is given name;
        child is given ssn;
        child with cs;
        cs:=single;
        record person(ssn; name: packed array[1:15] of char;
                      sex; birthdate;
                      cs; wno; mno) by office;
end birth;

ctx death(man: human; p: social security number);
event   dies = (man dies);
syn     date of death = dies;
begin
        man dies;
        terminate person(p, date of death) by office;
end death;

ctx childhood;
begin
      begin
      end     or    death(child,ssn);
end childhood;

ctx marriage;
etype document = matter;
        certificate = information;
        contract = record couple(contract: integer) of information;
event marries = (man marries woman);
state bears = (matter bears information);
        identifies = (information identifies information);
syn     date of marriage = marries;
begin
        man marries woman;
        document bears certificate;
        contract identifies certificate;
        ms:= married;
        ws:= married;
        man is given certificate;
        woman is given certificate;
        record couple(contract; mno; wno; date of marriage)
                      by office;
        record person(mno,ms,date of marriage) by office;
        record person(wno; ws; date of marriage) by office;
end marriage;
```

```
ctx divorce;
begin
      ms:=divorced;
      ws:=divorced;
      terminate couple(contract) by office;
      record person(mno; ms) by office;
      record person(wno; ws) by office;
end divorce;

ctx widow(wids: maritalstatus;
          widno: social security number);
begin
      wids:=widowed;
      record person(widno; wids) by office;
end widow;

ctx manhood;
begin
      man:=child;
      mnam:=name;
      mno:=ssn;
      ms:=cs;
      death(man,mno)
      or repeat begin marriage;
                      divorce or widog(ms,mno);
                 end;

end manhood;

ctx womanhood;
begin
      woman:=child;
      wnam:=name;
      wno:=ssn;
      ws:=cs;
      death(woman, wno)
      or repeat
         begin
            birth or begin marriage;
                         divorce or widow(ws,wno);
                    end;
         end;
end womanhood;

  { end of declarations
    begin of statements of ctx life:    }

begin
      birth;
      childhood;
      if sex = male then manhood;
      if sex = female then womanhood;
end life.

initiate ctx life;

{ end of example }
```

Modelling in Data Base Management Systems, G.M. Nijssen, (ed.)
  North Holland Publishing Company, 1976

BINARY LOGICAL ASSOCIATIONS

IN DATA MODELLING

G. Bracchi, P. Paolini, G. Pelagatti
Istituto di Elettrotecnica ed Elettronica
Politecnico di Milano

The functions and the required characteristics of the Conceptual
Schema in a multilevel data base system will first be investigated; on the basis of these characteristics, the network and the
relational models will be discussed.

Binary logical associations will then be shown to provide an appropriate semantic tool for data representation at the Conceptual
Schema level; the generality of this approach in modelling "difficult" situations will be discussed by means of examples.

A language for the binary conceptual schema will finally be introduced.

I - INTRODUCTION

The purpose of this paper is to discuss the most suitable data model at the Conceptual Schema level. This discussion has two aspects: selecting one model among
the different models that are presently under consideration (e.g. network, relational, binary), and solving particular problems inside the selected model.

The two aspects of the discussion are hardly separable since the choice of a particular data model depends on the solutions given to specific problems. For this
reason the paper has been structured in the following way:

1) Determination of the requirements of the Conceptual Schema through evidentia
   tion of the functions of the Conceptual Schema in the general operations of
   the database system (section II);

2) Development of a "logical" frame of reference that allows comparison of the
   different data models (section III);

3) Discussion of the Network and Relational approaches: the limitations of these
   models at the Conceptual Schema level are shown and the general characteristics of a more suitable data model are determined (sections IV and V);

4) A data model based on Binary Logical Associations is shown to provide the
   most suitable solution at the Conceptual Schema level; answers to open questions
   on such data model (e.g.: what types of Binary Associations should be allowed?
   Should the binary data structure be restricted by prefixed rules or should the
   Enterprise Administrator be as free as possible in the data structure definition?) are derived from the previous discussion (section VI). The functions
   and the characteristics of a language for this data model are finally determined (section VII).

II - CONCEPTUAL SCHEMA REQUIREMENTS

The role of a Conceptual Schema in DBMS architecture has been widely recognised
[1 - 3] , and the Coneptual Schema concept has been included in the recent ANSI-
SPARC interim report [4].

The resulting three-levels architecture, the terminology used to define the three levels of data definition, and the individuals who are responsible for each level of definition are shown in figure 1. The definition of the Conceptual Schema is viewed as a business operations responsibility rather than as an information systems' responsibility, and the person who carries this responsibility, i.e. the Enterprise Administrator, is more concerned with enterprise organisation than strictly with database organisation. It is important, in order to define the functions, the requirements and (as a consequence) the suitable data models for the Conceptual Schema, to recall that the Conceptual Schema is involved in the following two main processes:

1) Creation of the Conceptual Schema and of the Database.

In this process the Enterprise Administrator defines the information structure from his general viewpoint. This definition, the Conceptual Schema, is then utilized by the Database Administrator to define the Internal Schema, in which performance, space and optimisation considerations are present.
In order to define the optimal mapping between the Conceptual Schema and the Internal Schema, the Database Administrator utilizes additional information with respect to the information contained in the Conceptual Schema. The Enterprise Administrator "acts as an interface between the operations within the organisation, gathering information to ultimately be delivered to the Database Administrator to help solve performance problems..." [4].

2) Database Evolution.

This process has two aspects. The former is the necessity to change the Conceptual Schema as a consequence of changes in the enterprise itself. "The Enterprise Administrator must continually revise the Conceptual Schema to track the changing uses of information within the enterprise. Generally changes to the Conceptual Schema permeate the database environment causing schemas, mappings... to be modified" [4] . The other aspect of the database evolution process is concerned with the necessity that data reorganisation in the Internal Schema or in the External schemas do not cause changes in the Conceptual Schema, so that the effects of the reorganisation do not propagate into the whole system (data independence): "More frequently, however, the information usage of the enterprise as synthesized in the Conceptual Model may remain relatively stable..." [4].

An important problem, indeed, is to determine what changes should interfere with the Conceptual Schema.
So far we have recalled the fundamental characteristics of the Conceptual Schema as they are defined in [4] ; we will now more precisely discuss these characteristics referring to figure 2 :

          - The Conceptual Schema should be stable in order to obtain data independence (i.e., a change in the Internal Schema or the External Schemas would influence the mappings only); only the Enterprise Administrator is authorized to modify the Conceptual Schema.

          - As a consequence of the stability requirement any change of the Internal Schema, decided by the Database Administrator, is not affecting the Conceptual Schema.

          - The previous considerations are not only significant from an architectural point of view (by which we mean in this case a clear definition of roles between AA, EA and DBA, and consequently of data definition levels), since the fact that reorganisation leads from an old to a new Internal Schema without modifying the Conceptual Schema, means that something has changed that is contained (more or less explicitely) in the Internal Schema but is not contained in the Conceptual Schema.
In Figure 2 we have called the information that is contained in the Internal Schema but not in the Conceptual Schema "parameters". More precisely we say that the

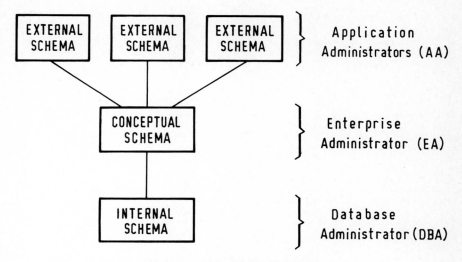

Figure 1 – Multilevel system architecture

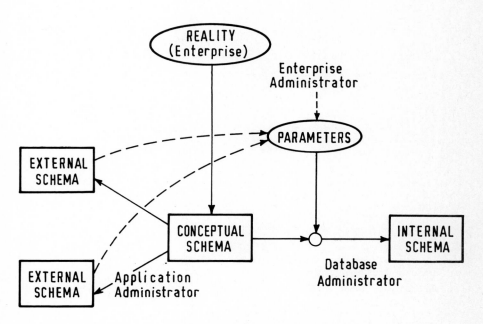

Figure 2 – Interaction among the three Schemata

Database Administrator obtains the Internal Schema from the Conceptual Schema plus
Parameters.

        - A crucial question about the Conceptual Schema is to determine what
information belongs to the parameters and what information belongs to the Conceptual Schema itself. The problem of the most suitable information model at the Conceptual Schema level can only be solved after the previous question has been answered.

        - The analysis of what sort of information the various existing data
models (Network, Relational) introduce at the Conceptual Schema level and the compatibility of the models with the functions of the Conceptual Schema is the object
of the following sections of this paper; this analysis leads to a definition of the
information that should be contained in the Conceptual Schema and consequently of
the role of the Enterprise Administrator.
From a general point of view, there is potentially a gain in data independence and
possibly a loss in performance if one transfers information from the Conceptual
Schema to the parameters. This transfer leads to the utilisation of a Conceptual
Schema model that is more different from the Internal Schema model; on the other
side, if one uses the same model at Conceptual and Internal Schema levels, only
a limited possibility of obtaining physical data independence is left.

        - The effect of the External Schemas on the parameters (indicated in fi
gure 2) implies the following consideration on the dynamics of the database: given
a certain Conceptual Schema and a set of parameters and an (optimal, as determined
by the Database Administrator) Internal Schema, a change in the External Schemas
or the addition of a new External Schema does not lead to a modification of the
Conceptual Schema (this is an aspect of logical data independence) but may lead to
a modification in the parameters, and as a consequence in this new situation the
Internal schema is not any more the optimal one and the Database Administrator may
decide for a reorganization.

III - A GENERAL FRAME OF REFERENCE FOR THE CONCEPTUAL SCHEMA MODELS

Any particular information model (for instance relational, network, binary, hierar
chical, etc...) forces the Enterprise Administrator to see the reality (that is
the information structure in the Enterprise) from a particular viewpoint; in the
multitude of aspects that characterize the Enterprise Administrator's view of the
information, he is forced to determine only those which are of relevance in the
particular data model considered. The frame of reference that we will develop here
does not pretend to represent the Enterprise Administrator's view without superim-
posing any restriction on it (even the natural language represents a restriction
to the natural view); however it is general enough to permit to consider the data
models that we will discuss as particular restrictions. This frame of reference
will be based on the concept of Logical Association (LA). A Logical Association
represents a logical connection seen by the Enterprise Administrator. From a mathematical point of view an LA is exactly a relation. The use we do of this concept,
however, is different from that of relation in the relational model [5] (see section V); this is a reason why we prefer to use a different terminology.

Let's consider m Sets of Concepts (SC) (we will later specify the meaning of Set
of Concepts; anyway it can be intended to have the same meaning as single or compound domain in the relational model).

An LA defined upon these m Sets of Concepts has the following characteristic

      a) $LA \subseteq SC_1 \times SC_2 \times \ldots \times SC_m$

Of course we could define a number of (semantically different) LA's upon the some
set of SCs. A Set of Concepts can be a Fundamental Domain (FD) (i.e. a set of atomic homogeneous values) or an LA :

      b) $SC = FD \lor LA$

The union of a) and b) defines recursively our frame of reference.

Example 1

Upon the following FDs:

C #	: Course Number	O#	: Offering Number
D	: Course Description		
S#	: Student Number	T#	: Teacher Number
G	: Grade		

we define the following LAs :

$$LA_1 \subseteq C\# \times D$$
$$LA_2 \subseteq C\# \times O\#$$
$$LA_3 \subseteq C\# \times O\# \times S\#$$

$C\#$, $O\#$, D, $S\#$, $T\#$, G, LA_1, LA_2, LA_3 are all SCs; the recursivity of the definition permits to define for instance :

$$LA_4 \subseteq LA_3 \times G$$

Example 2

Given the FDs: D : Day ; M : Month ; Y : Year , the Logical Association

$$LA_1 \subseteq D \times M \times Y$$

represents the (natural) SC 'Date', but in some particular application the following SCs could be of some utility :

$$LA_2 \subseteq M \times Y$$
$$LA_3 \subseteq LA_2 \times D$$

We will call descriptor of an LA the set of the "names" of the SCs upon which the LA is defined.
We have seen that a number of LAs can be drawn from each descriptor; not all the SCs defined in this way, however, are meaningful and, what is more important, not all the SCs are of interest to the users of a given database.
Moreover, the SCs are not independent from each other but they are correlated, since Concepts belonging to an SC may be derivable from concepts belonging to other SCs.

In example 1 if we know, through $LA_3 \subseteq C\# \times O\# \times S\#$, for each course in what offering it was given and from which students it was taken, we can derive, for instance, all the students who took a particular course (independently of the offering). If we know for each student which courses he took and in which offerings, and we know who was the teacher for each course in each offering, we can derive for each student which teacher he had. In the rest of the paper we will then call "data-deduction (or briefly "deduction")   the operation of extracting "smaller" concepts from "larger" ones; conversely the "data-induction" (or briefly "induction") will be the operation of building "large" or "more complex" concepts starting from "smaller"" and "simpler" ones.
The basic problem of a DBMS is that we want, of course, to store a finite number of concepts but we would like to give the users of the database the capability to deduce or induce all the concepts they are interested in.

In the early DBMS quite large and complex concepts were stored and directly presented to the users; in this way almost all the operations of the users were devoted to explicitly deduce or induce new concepts by means of programs. The problem was that minimal changes in the structure of the concepts stored in the database required a completely new definition of the deduction/induction process. This is the reason why the opportunity has been recognized of having a quite stable framework of SCs defined in the system (Conceptual Schema). The concepts actually stored can be different (as far as their descriptors are concerned)from

those of the conceptual schema (see [4] 'the conceptual schema may contain descriptors of objects that may be not represented by internal data...").

The process of data deduction/induction has two main parts:

1) deduction/induction of the SCs that represent the user's view of data from
the Conceptual Schema's SCs (that is External Schema definition), and

2) deduction/induction of specific concepts (in the application programs).

If part 1) of the process is defined once in the mapping and carried out automatically, the effort of the user is reduced.

Before investigating in depth the induction/deduction process, we want to point out
the fact that so far in our frame of reference we have never utilized the concepts
of key, identifier or similar and we have focused on a more logical property of
information, that is the possibility of building more complex concepts out of more elementary ones (FDs), independently of identification problems. We feel that
the historical development of data models, starting from physical implementation
problems, has often excessively tied the problem of data structure to the problem
of data identification. As we will show now, identification problems of course arise
when the user wants to utilize the database to retrieve, insert or delete a particular concept, but not when he defines the SCs which constitute his External Schema.

The induction/deduction process

We will now focus in a more precise way the problems connected with the induction/
deduction process. Let's suppose we have some SCs defined at the Conceptual Schema
level. An Application Administrator defines an External Schema, i.e. nothing more
than a new SC deducible or inducible from the SCs of the Conceptual Schema. If the
user wants now to retrieve data utilising that External Schema, he will simply de
duce/induce specific concepts of his SC from the concepts of the conceptual database (we use the term Conceptual Database to indicate the concepts, structured
according to the Conceptual Schema definition, that constitute the database. In
the relational model, for instance, the Conceptual Database has a tabular form).
If instead the user wants to update data, specific concepts for the Conceptual database must be deduced/induced from the concepts of the External Schema. As we
have partially pointed out before, there is a fundamental difference between the
operations at the SC level, that is the External Schema definition, and the operations at the specific concept level, that is retrieval or storage, because the
former operate only from the Conceptual towards the External Schema, whereas the
latter are bidirectional. This fact will be of some relevance in the discussion
of the characteristics of the SCs that should be contained in the data model at the
conceptual schema level.
Let's consider the following example, in which the FDs are the same as in example
1.

Example 3

The Conceptual Schema contains the following SCs:

$$C\# \ , \ O\# \ , \ S\# \ , \ G \ , \ T\# \ , \ SC_1, \ SC_2$$

where

$$SC_1 = LA_1 \subseteq C\# \times O\# \times S\# \times G$$
$$SC_2 = LA_2 \subseteq C\# \times O\# \times T\#$$

LA_1 associates to each course the offerings in which it was given and the students
and their grade; LA_2 associates to each course the corresponding offering numbers
and the teachers who taught it.

Let's define an External Schema with the following SC :

$$SC_3 = LA_3 \subseteq C\# \times T\#$$

If the user now wants to retrieve specific concepts of SC_3 such that $T\#$ is equal to a particular value, he actually deduces these concepts from the concepts of SC_2.

Let's suppose now that the user wants to insert data in the database through his External Schema; this means he wants to introduce in the database concepts belonging to his SC_3. However he can introduce in the conceptual database only concepts belonging to the SCs defined in the Conceptual Schema, i.e. he must deduce/ induce from the concepts of the External Schema concepts appropriate for the Conceptual Schema. In other words in inserting data we are logically following the reverse path with respect to the retrieval, and (this is the relevant fact) to the External Schema definition. The problem that arises is that not always from a deducible/inducible External Schema it is possible to deduce/induce complete concepts for the conceptual database. For instance, SC_3 is deducible from SC_2 but SC_2 is not inducible from SC_3; and in fact we could not use SC_3 to insert data.

Logical consistency

In order to completely deduce, from an External Schema, concepts for the conceptual database, strictly speaking, we should be able to completely determine all their components. It usually happens that we are not able to completely deduce the concepts of the conceptual database; a way to overcome this problem is to consider "undefined" the non specified components. However this technique presents some difficulties: mainly the concepts of the conceptual database should be, even if not completely determined, at least "identified" (i.e. distinguishable from the other concepts of the same SC); conversely, when we delete concepts from the conceptual database, even if their specification is not complete, we need to iden- tify them.

We call all these problems logical consistency and say that an operation on an External Schema that can't be carried out at the specific concept level is logically inconsistent with the database.

In other words the logical consistency problem is a problem at the concept and instance-identification level.

Physical consistency

In an analogous way we can define the physical consistency. Whenever we accomplish an operation on the conceptual database we must translate it into physical opera- tions, and the identification problem then arises. An operation on the conceptual database is said to be physically inconsistent if it can't be carried out because the necessary concepts can't be fully identified.

The choice of concepts for the Conceptual Schema

We will now focus our attention on the logical consistency problem and we will try to derive some suggestions for the characteristics of the Conceptual Schema concepts.

Two basic different strategies are possible :

1) to define large and structured concepts for the Conceptual Schema and to base the External Schema definition mainly on deduction processes.

2) to define small and not-structured concepts for the Conceptual Schema and to base the External Schema definition mainly on induction processes.

The first choice seems to be appealing for the following reasons :

- large concepts are better understandable, mainly if the database is large

- the deduction process for the definition of the External Schemas seems to be more natural and spontaneous.

The first reason seems undoubteadly to be true; about the second one, we have the following remarks:

a) Deduction of External Schemas from large concepts of the Conceptual Schema is a reductive way of interpreting the role of the External Schemas.
   If the External Schemas are themselves large concepts with a structure different from the one of the Conceptual Schema, two processes are actually needed:

   - to break the Conceptual Schema's concepts into smaller ones (deduction) and
   - to reassemble these small concepts to form the External Schemas (induction).

This double process doesn't seem quite easy: to realize this fact we suggest the reader to think of the logical problems he should face if, for instance, he had to define records for the External Schema assembling pieces of different records of a network Conceptual Schema.

In conclusion the use of structured concepts at the Conceptual Schema level permits a simple deduction only of those concepts of the External Schema that follow the same structure of the Conceptual Schema, and to strong limitations to the mapping (see Section V for an application of this criticism to the External Schema definition in the relational model).

b) The historical reasons to use large concepts (usually called records or, in a more "logical" way, entities and recently relations) derives from the fact that at the physical level the stored concepts need, for performance considerations, to be large and structured. The absence of a clear distinction between Conceptual and Internal Schemas led to the reproduction of the stored concepts at the Conceptual Schema Level. For instance, it appears that the network model is more similar to an Internal than to a Conceptual Schema (see Section IV).

c) As we clarified before, the possibility of utilising an External Schema to insert or delete data is based upon the capability to deduce/induce concepts of the Conceptual Schema from those of the External Schema or, at least, to identify them. If we have large concepts at the Conceptual Schema level and we deduce from them small concepts to define the External Schemas, it seems unlikely that starting from the External Schemas we can induce the large concepts of the Conceptual Schema or at least identify them.

To materialize this argument think of the following :

i) the Conceptual Schema is composed of a few large records; all the External Schemas that do not contain the identifiers of all the records whose pieces they use could never be used to insert/delete data.

ii) the Conceptual Schema is made of n-ary relations; all the External Schemas that do not contain the primary keys of all the relations whose domains are used could never be used to insert/delete data.

Remark c) is strictly connected with remark a); the more one requires the External Schema structure to be independent of the Conceptual Schema structure, the more the two remarks a) and c) are relevant .

All the previous remarks suggest that the second strategy for the conceptual schema, that is the use of small and non-structured concepts, is more suitable. An information model that is very close to this strategy is a model based on binary logical associations.

This approach has been already followed by various researchers, but it seems to us that some difficulties that have arisen in the utilization of binary relations derive from the lack of distinction between the (Conceptual) Schema level and the more physical levels. Another difficulty arises from the interpretation of a binary relational schema as a representation of the functional dependencies between keys and attributes as in the n-ary relational model. A third difficulty arises if one wants to ensure logical and physical consistency. In the following discussion of the network (section IV) and the n-ary relational model (section V) we will try to show that :

- the use of structured concepts at the Conceptual Schema level permits the solution of the consistency problems only if the External Schemas follow the same structure of the Conceptual Schema; otherwise the consistency problems are more difficult to solve than with relatively unstructured concepts at the Conceptual Schema level;

- the use of large records (network model) may lead to a lack of stability of the Conceptual Schema as defined in Section II;

- the use of a model based on logical associations (that is a model without identification problems) allows the Enterprise Administrator to be effectively more concerned with enterprise organisation than with database organisation because the model requires him to know logical information structure but not access oriented considerations;

- binary logical associations should not necessarily represent the functional dependency structure ;

- part of the information that is contained in more structured concepts can be derived by the database administrator by consideration of what we have called "Parameters" in Section II.

IV - SOME COMMENTS ON THE NETWORK MODEL AT THE CONCEPTUAL SCHEMA LEVEL

In the previous discussion on the appropriate concepts for the Data Model at the Conceptual Schema level a general criticism of the Codasyl [6] and ANSI Reports [4] with respect to the choice of the same (network) data model for External, Internal and Conceptual Schema was implied. We will discuss here the example on the network model given in [7] in order to show how the choice of the network data model is in contrast with the requirements for the Conceptual Schema as they are stated in section II of this paper.
A list of optimization areas in which the Database Administrator could practice his skill is given in [7, 8], for instance:

- field, record, set, pointer, index implementation techniques,
- placement of records, files or redundant data.

We call the choices in this areas "Performance Oriented". A second area of decision for the Database Administrator regards the fact that: "for each conceptual record in the conceptual schema there would be a corresponding internal schema declaration which answers the following questions: (1) is the record to be stored at all? (2) if it is to be stored, will it appear as a single linear record..?" [7].
We call the choices in this area "Access Oriented", because a decision on them is essentially dependent on the type of questions that the users will pose to the system, or, in a more general way, on what we have called "Parameters" in section II.

It follows from the discussion of the previous sections that at the Conceptual Schema level "access oriented" decisions should not be taken by the Enterprise Administrator.
The following discussion of the example (taken from reference [7]) has the aim of showing that the use of a network model at the Conceptual Schema level leads to the introduction of access oriented decisions at this level and that this fact is in contrast with the requirement of a "stable" Conceptual Schema.

The example is shown in figure 3a, b, c, d, which illustrate the modifications of the Conceptual Schema as a consequence of the variations of the Enterprise Administrator's view.
It is supposed that the Enterprise Administrator has the following reasons for modifying the Conceptual Schema :

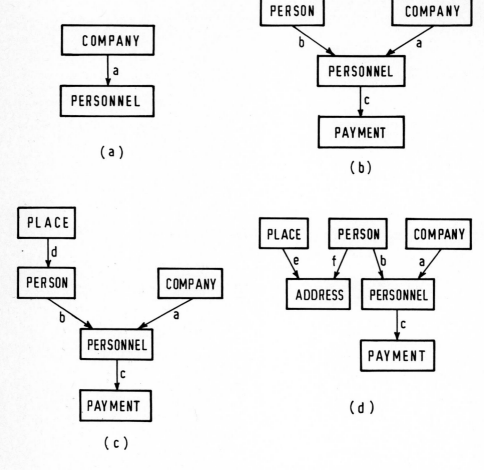

Figure 3 – Evolution of a sample Conceptual Schema

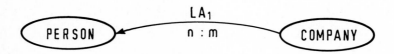

Figure 4 – The set of Concepts level

1) From a to b :

1.1) the detailed earnings of each employee were recognized to be of interest from time to time. In our frame of reference this means that a new Fundamental Domain (detailed earnings) is introduced in the Conceptual schema.

1.2) it was recognized that sometimes a person has a job in two different companies (the relation between Person and Company becomes many to many)

2) From b to c :

2.1) "This step came about when the Enterprise Administrator decided to factor the address of residence out of the person record" [7]. (An Attribute becomes an Entity)

3) From c to d :

3.1) Considering the past addresses and not only the current address of every person, the relation between "Person" and "Place" changes from n:1 to n:m. In a network model this leads to the creation of a new record, to the "entity splitting", and consequently to the "attribute migration".

The reasons for the Conceptual Schema modifications are then the following:

- Introduction of new data (reason 1.1), that is new Fundamental Domains. This modification is dependent on a change in the reality and it is acceptable in itself. In the example considered this change has only local consequences on the Conceptual Schema, but there could exist situations in which the introduction of new data causes a major modification in a Network Schema.

- Entity splitting (reason 2.1) because of a different use of the same data. This modification has generally an access oriented reason (in this case the request to access all persons living in the same place, for instance) and could be eliminated in a Conceptual Schema that does not have an access oriented view of data (by the way, the entity splitting process shows how the entity concept does not exist in reality [9]; in our frame of reference the entities used in the network model represent only an arbitrary subset of all possible Sets of Concepts).

- Necessity of transformation of a n:1 relation into a n:m relation (reasons 1.2 and 3.1). This point is the most interesting one. We must distinguish between two alternatives:

a) the transformation corresponds to a transformation of the reality (enterprise)

b) the transformation depends on a different view of the data by the Enterprise Administrator following access oriented considerations.

Let us consider for instance reason 1.2: if it was impossible before that a person had different jobs in different companies and now this fact becomes possible, it is acceptable that this modification of the reality has a consequence at the Conceptual Schema level, and the modification respects the "stability" requirement. In this case the Logical Association between Person and Company has changed its properties.

However, in the great majority of cases, the reason for the change is the following: the Enterprise Administrator knows from the beginning that the logical association is n:m, but in defining the Network Conceptual Schema he considers at first that the users will want to access Person via Company; he has to modify the Conceptual Schema when he realizes that the opposite access path is also required.

Some further considerations are derivable by examination of the modification 1 (from a to b) at the specific concept level. Suppose that the logical situation at the Set of Concepts level is the one represented in figure 4 (the arrow has no logical meaning but it only allows to associate a conventional posi-

tive direction to the association). Two possible representations of the corresponding conceptual database are represented in figure 5; in a network representation the modification implied by reason 1.2 leads from figure 6 to figure
7.

Note that :

- The representation of the conceptual database used in figure 5 is arbitrary;
  other representations are possible.

- The situations of figures 5, 6b, 7b correspond to the same logical association (conceptual schema) of figure 4, whereas the situations of figure 6b and
  7b correspond strictly to the schemas of figures 6a and 7a.

- The choice between the solutions of figures 6 and 7 is clearly access oriented; this choice should be a responsibility of the Database Administrator.

- Data Independence requires that the External Schemas defined on the Conceptual Schema are not influenced by a modification at the Internal Schema
  level; in fact, if the Conceptual Schema has the form shown in figure 4,the
  External Schemas are not affected by a change leading from the solution of
  figure 6 to the solution of figure 7 at the Internal Schema level.

- Suppose we are able to represent the "importance" of a particular access
  path by means of a function F (for the sake of simplicity we suppose F to
  be single valued) which represents, for instance, the frequency of specified
  queries, e.g.: $F(LA_1) = 0$ means that the query "find the companies where a
  given person works" is of no interest for the system (this idea was developed
  in $[9]$).
  The two solutions of figures 6 and 7 correspond to the following situations

  figure 6 : $F(LA_1)^+ \gg F(LA_1)^-$
  figure 7 : $F(LA_1)^+ \simeq F(LA_1)^-$

  The information represented by the function F is part of what we have called
  "Parameters" in section II.

From the above discussion we can derive that a data model,that permits the
representation of the pure logical associations among the data,satisfies the
stability requirement for the Conceptual Schema and allows a cleaner separation between the roles of the Enterprise Administrator and the Database Administrator than it is possible with the network model.

V – THE N-ARY RELATIONAL MODEL AT THE CONCEPTUAL SCHEMA LEVEL.

In the n-ary relational model the schema is a set of n-ary relations.
In an early definition $[5]$ an n-ary normalized relation was essentially a way
of representing in a flat structure a set of potentially hierarchical data.
Later definitions $[10-11]$ utilize the notions of functional dependency, 2nd
Normal Form (2NF) and 3rd Normal Form (3NF) to better characterize the relational model. An argument for the n-ary relational model is that the 3NF through
the notion of functional dependency is a non arbitrary "semantic" description of
the information stored in a database. Against this argument some observations
can be made; these observations will be grouped into three classes :

        1) Difficulties at the logical level: the 3NF (as well as other models)
doesn't solve the logical consistency problem without imposing strong limitations
to the possibility of defining External Schemas that follow a different structure from that of the Conceptual Schema; some of these limitations are not due to
the model itself, but they are in the very nature of the problem of logical consistency.

        2) Difficulties at the physical level: the solution to the physical
consistency problem requires the use of conformable representation $[12]$ at the
physical level; on the other hand conformable representations show disadvantages

Company	Person			Person	Company	
A	1 2 3	or		1	A	B
B	1 3 4			2	A	C
C	2 4 5			3	A	B
				4	B	C
				5	C	

Fig. 5 - Two representations of the conceptual database

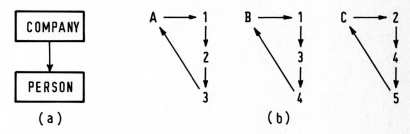

Figure 6 - Network representation

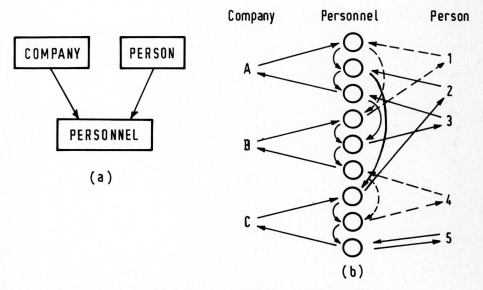

Figure 7 - Evolution of the network representation

under the viewpoint of performance.

        3) Necessity to consider the internal structure of the relations
that constitute the Conceptual Schema in the definitions of both the Internal
and External Schemas.

We will now discuss in details these three classes of observations and will
try to derive from them some characteristics of a suitable Data Model for the
Conceptual Schema.

1) Difficulties at the logical level

1.1) The first difficulty is widely recognized   [11] and consists of the fact
     that the way of the 3NF of describing functional dependencies is not uni-
     que: i.e.,despite the effort to make the 3NF definition to model a "clean"
     situation (in which zero, one or more (non-key) domains are fully dependent
     on one or more other (key) domains), sometimes this is not the case. The
     reason is that it may be impossible to break the functional dependency
     pattern in a "clean" way. An example, taken from [11] , is the following:

Example 4

Given the following Domains :
S = Student identification number
J = Subject
T = Teacher identification number
the relation (S,J,T,) where each Teacher teaches a Subject only, is in 3NF.

Its functional dependency structure is the following

The above structure doesn't follow the desired pattern.

1.2) Despite the apparent homogeneity of treatment of the associations among
     domains [13-14] , in the relational model there are two kinds of asso-
     tions among domains:

     a)   associations inside the same relation
     b)   associations among doamins of different relations.

This difference has the effect that, while it's easy to detect connections
inside the same relation, it can be quite hard to detect the implicit connections among different relations.

Example 5

Given the domains

S = (Supplier number), SN =(Supplier Name), ST (Status), C = (City)
            let's consider the splitting of the relation
SC= S, SN, ST, C

into the two relations

S = S, SN, C
C = C, ST

While in the relation SC the connection between the domains SN and ST is
explicit and direct, in the two relations S and C the connection is induced through a matching of values on the domain C in the two relations.

As a consequence, in any realistic schema with a certain number of
relations it can be very difficult to see all the possible (and eventually the best) ways to connect two domains which do not belong to the

same relation. This problem has already been realized by the researchers who tried to write complex queries in any alpha-like language: in fact most part of the qualification is not devoted to really qualify domains but to matching values of domains belonging to different relations, i.e. to "navigate" across different relations.

1.3) A serious problem is to control the logical consistency of all those domains which actually represent the same information but, by the process of successive normalization, are duplicated and scattered through many relations. In Example 5, which is very simple indeed, we should at least guarantee that the projections over the domain C(City) of the relations S and C yield the same set of values.

1.4) Let's consider again Example 5: the Conceptual Schema is constituted by the two relations in 3NF

S = $\underline{S}$, SN, C
C = $\underline{C}$, ST

and let's suppose we have defined an External Schema trough the following alpha-like expression :

(S.S, C.ST): $\exists$ S $\exists$ C (S.C = C.C).

Any attempt to insert data by utilizing this External Schema would fail. For if we try to insert, for instance :

<1058, 20>

we could insert < 1058, -, - > in S, but we could not insert < -, 20> in C, since undefined values for primary keys are not allowed.

On the other hand, if we had as Conceptual Schema the unique relation
SC = $\underline{S}$, SN, C, ST
and the following External Schema
(SC.S, SC.ST) : $\exists$ SC
the insertion of <1058, 20> at the user level would result at the Conceptual Schema level in the insertion of the n-tuple <1058, -, -, 20 >, and this is a perfectly legitimate operation.
Suppose now that the relation SC has the following functional dependency structure

This relation is in 2NF and not in 3NF, whereas the two relations' S and C are in 3NF (S and C are the solution to the problem of further normalizing SC).
We have obtained the, at first sight, surprising result that a 3NF Schema leads to logical inconsistency while a 2NF Schema is consistent with the same (insertion) operation.
This is due to the fact that, starting from the chosen External Schema, the concepts of the second Conceptual Schema are "identifiable", while the concepts of the first Conceptual Schema are not "identifiable".

The above observations show the following facts :

- The problem of ensuring the logical consistency of data-base operations cannot be solved in a general way by a particular Data Model imposing restrictions on the Conceptual Schema definition.

- Logical consistency is based upon a "similarity" between the actual structures of the given Conceptual and External Schemas; this "similarity" must permit the "identifiability" of Conceptual Schema concepts starting from External Schema concepts.

- The apparent absence of consistency problems of the 3NF is based on the

(arbitrary) assumption that the user's operations will follow the functional
dependency pattern. In the example of observation 1.4 this means that the user
is assumed to insert (delete) couples of <C, ST> but not couples of <S, ST>.

- It   is impossible to solve the logical consistency problem by imposing a
  "restricted" view of data structure, because there are users that will need
  to define External Schemas that have a different data structure from that of
  the Conceptual Schema; it is a more realistic solution to let the Enterprise
  Administrator free from restrictions in defining the Conceptual Schema, so that
  he can try to define a structure that most closely satisfies the user's view
  (it is possible, however, that in a number of situations this structure will
  follow the functional dependency pattern). An example of this approach will
  be given in Section VI.

2) Difficulties at the physical level

2.1) In order to ensure the physical consistency, the physical representation of
the relations is usually assumed to be "conformable" [12]. With our termino
logy we could say that the rules of conformability are introduced to ensure
the deducibility of the physical concepts from the Conceptual Schema concepts.
Let's discuss this point using Example 5 (relation SC in 2NF, relations S
and C in 3NF).
Now suppose that at the physical level we have a unique file to represent re
lations S and C (for instance, a sequential file, whose record are made of
the four fields S, SN, C, ST, ordered according to the values of S (this is
a non-conformable representation)). In this case it's impossible storing or
deleting information about the association between the domains C and ST without somehow interferring with the representation of the other information.
As another example let's consider the relation $S = (S, SN, C)$ and let's suppose that we want to use as physical representation a file made of hierarchical
records where C is the key and the couple S, SN is a repeating group: with
this file it would be impossible to insert a couple S, SN if the city is not
specified and on the other hand it's perfectly legitimate to insert a city
without specifying the value of S.
To summarize this point we can conclude that the absence of physical consistency problems in the relational model is due to the implied deducibility of
physical concepts from the concepts of the Conceptual Schema. This condition
is generally satisfied only by conformable representations.Not always the actual physical structure will be conformable (in the next point 2.2 some disadvantages of conformable representations are discussed) and in fact one of
the most widely used, i.e. the hierarchical, is not conformable in its very
nature.

2.2) We will now assume that the physical representation is conformable.
The association between domains of the same relation must be somehow physically materialized [12] by means of physical nearness, forward pointers,
backward pointers, etc.
The association between domains of different relations is indirect, i.e.
inducible via matching of values of common domains.
These facts lead to the following disadvantages :

a) Physical fragmentation of the database with duplications of the same
data. In the previous example we must have at least two files (correspond
ing to the relations S and C) in both of which the domain City is represented.

b) Multiplication of the physical operations needed. If, for instance, we
want to store information about a supplier including his Status, we must
insert an n-tuple in the file representing the relation S and another
into the file representing the relation C.
In a large database this multiplication of the physical operations needed
would dramatically increase.
This is actually a problem in all systems in which the user view of data

is different from the actual physical structure.
Peculiar to the conformable representation of an n-ary relational schema
is the fact that the Database Administrator has only limited possibilies
to prevent the situation.

The conclusions that can be derived from the above considerations are very similar
to those derived about the difficulties at the logical level: the analysis of the
relational model shows that the physical consistency problem can be solved by applying a strong limitation to the number of acceptable physical representations of
a relation in 3NF and consequently by limiting the possibilities of the Database Administrator; the acceptable physical representations are the conformable re
presentations; conformable representations, however, have some disadvantages.

Finally, we emphasize that :

1) the difficulties at the logical and physical levels that we have evidentiated
   on hand of the relational model are not due to the model itself but are in the
   very nature of the problem of logical and physical consistency;

2) in a given database the logical consistency problem gets worse when the user's
   view of the data structure (External Schema) is different from the Conceptual
   Schema;

3) the difficulty above can't be solved by a restrictive data model, because the
   user's view is tied to his information necessities, and it is better for the
   Enterprise Administrator to have a relative freedom in designing a Conceptual
   Schema that is structured according to the necessities of the majority of the
   users.

3) Internal structure of the relations

In order to define External Schemas the Application Administrator will consider
single domains of the relations and combine them into new structures (using our
terminology we say that he deduces/induces new Sets of Concepts from the relations). In other words he will look inside the relations at Set of Concepts
smaller than those expressed by the relations themselves.

In a similar way the Database Administrator must look at the connections among
domains inside the relations to have an idea of their importance and their use, in
order to operate the choices that are under his responsibility.

A question now arises spontaneously: since the people who use the Conceptual Sche
ma (the Database and Application Administrators) will actually look at the functional dependencies (or chains of functional dependencies) among the single domains
inside the same relation and across different relations, why not to use directly
the functional dependency model at the Conceptual Schema level?

In other words, since both the Database and the Application Administrators must
start with a deduction process, why not to break the relations into smaller units
(i.e. the n-ary concepts into binary concepts), once that it has been shown that
the 3NF doesn't solve in a general way the physical and logical consistency problems and it is not simple to read when the number of relations involved becomes
large?

The conclusion of this section is that small concepts like those expressed by the
functional dependencies are more suitable at the Conceptual Schema level; the
restriction on the Enterprise Administrator's view of data implied by a structure
based on functional dependencies, however, is not appropriate and different binary
concepts should be utilized. The next section will discuss this point.

VI - THE BINARY MODEL

As we explained in the previous sections, we came to the conclusion that the smallest concepts are the most appropriate for the Conceptual Schema [3, 9, 15] . The

smallest still meaningful concepts appear to be the Binary Logical Associations
(BLA).

Two kinds of problems arise now :

1) which should be the structure and the properties of Binary Logical Associations
   in the Conceptual Schema, and
2) is it always possible to describe the concepts of the Conceptual Schema in terms
   of Binary Logical Associations? This problem is the problem of handling non-
   binary associations.

Properties of Binary Logical Associations

We derive the properties of Binary Logical Associations from the discussion of
the previous two sections :

        a) The structure of the Conceptual Schema based on BLAs should not fol
low the functional dependency pattern. The reason for this property follows from
the whole discussion of Section V, particularly from observations 1.4, and 2.1,
2.2. In order to ensure that the Enterprise Administrator has the freedom of
choosing the most convenient BLAs we shouldn't put any restriction on them.

        b) Every functional characteristic (1:1, n:1,1:n, n:m) of the BLAs
should be permitted. The functional characteristicsof the BLAs shouldn't be relevant in the description of the structure of the Conceptual Schema; they could
be presented as a tool to give a better semantic explanation of the Conceptual
Schema, but they should not be determinant for the choice of the BLAs. However,
the functional characteristics have a major role in the mapping from the Conceptual to the Internal Schema.

For these reasons the Conceptual Schema should be built (at least in principle) by
two distinct and possibly orthogonal divisions: the Structure and the Constraint
divisions (in [2] also a Privacy and a Concurrency division were proposed). The
Structure division should be free from constraint considerations, as stated above.
The Constraint division contains the functional characteristics of single associations (this fact substitutes single identifier definitions of other data models),
and other properties of "Association-Constructs" (path equivalence, for instance,
Composite Keys, etc.).

This is coherent with the discussion of section IV, particularly the last example:
there are many different ways of representing an n:m association at the physical
level (the choice between them, as we have shown, is "access oriented"), but at
the Conceptual Schema level the representation should be unique to satisfy the sta
bility requirement.

        c) Fundamental Domains and not Role Names should be the Elementary
Sets of Concepts [16]. This property follows from observation 1.2 of Section V,
and eliminates the distinction between inter-and intra-relation associations.
The resulting Conceptual Schema becomes more readable. Note that the consistency
problem presented in observation 1.3 of section V is modified but not solved in
the binary model.

Handling non-binary associations

Let's face now the second question we asked at the beginning. The problem here is
not to investigate if there exist Sets of Concepts that are not binary (because
they exist of course). What we have to see is whether there exist Sets of Concepts
that can't be induced from BLAs.

We will discuss this question through examples :

        - Concepts that naturally seem to be non-binary

Let's take a classic counterexample against the binary model : i.e. the "Date".
Everybody knows that the concepts of date is a ternary logical association made

up of Day, Month, and Year. There are two ways of reducing this concept to a binary form :

a) to create nested binary relations, as for instance the following

We detected some disadvantages with this first method, mainly :

1) It's arbitrary to chose any particular way of nesting the BLAs.The following could also be chosen, for example :

2) Nested binary relations create same problems to deal with, since they need to be treated in a different way than the other ones.

3) Nested binary relations actually create a distortion of the reality. In fact, as we have seen in section III, Examples 1 and 2, to say that M and Y together are associated with D is a legitimate way of describing the reality, but it is not the same as to say that Y, M, D together are a Date.

In conclusion nested bynary relations are a representation of the reality, but they are not equivalent to n-ary Sets of Concepts.

b) To create Internal Sets of Concepts, whose elements have no meaning by themselves but have the function of linking together concepts belonging to different Sets of Concepts. For the date we have

The set of concepts "Date" can be considered, as far as the conceptual database is concerned, as a set of "unique names" each of which identifies a date. The use of the same word "Set of Concepts" in the Frame of Reference of Section III and in the Binary Model could cause some confusion in the reader.

The Frame of Reference was defined as :

$$\text{F.R.} \begin{cases} LA \subseteq SC_1 \times SC_2 \times \dots \times SC_m \\ SC = FD \ V \ LA \end{cases}$$

In the Binary Model the nested solution could appear <u>formally</u> as more correspondent to the Frame of Reference, because this solution can be defined recursively by

$$\underline{\text{Nested}} \atop \underline{\text{Binary}} \begin{cases} BLA \subseteq SC_1 \times SC_2 \\ SC = FD \ V \ BLA \end{cases}$$

whereas the use of internal Sets of Concepts (ISC) leads to the following model :

$$\underline{\text{Binary Model}} \quad \begin{cases} \text{BLA} \subseteq \text{SC}_1 \times \text{SC}_2 \\ \\ \text{SC} = \text{FD} \lor \text{ISC} \end{cases}$$

In this model both FDs and ISCs are non-derived elements and no recursivity is needed: the model is formally different from the Frame of Reference .However, considering the representation capabilities of the models, it appears that the Binary Model proposed here is more able to express non-binary concepts like those of the Frame of Reference. This fact was shown on the example DATE; formally we have for that example :

$$\text{FD} : \text{DAY, MONTH, YEAR}$$

$$\text{F.R.} \quad \begin{cases} \text{DATE} \subseteq \text{DAY} \times \text{MONTH} \times \text{YEAR} \\ \\ \end{cases} \quad ; \quad \underline{\begin{array}{c}\text{Nested}\\\text{Binary}\end{array}} \quad \begin{cases} \text{BLA}_1 \subseteq \text{DAY} \times \text{MONTH} \\ \text{DATE} \subseteq \text{BLA}_1 \times \text{YEAR} \\ \text{or the other two possi-} \\ \text{ble solutions} \end{cases}$$

$$\underline{\text{Binary Model}} \quad \begin{cases} \text{ISC} = \text{DATE} \\ \text{BLA}_1 \subseteq \text{DATE} \times \text{DAY} \\ \text{BLA}_2 \subseteq \text{DATE} \times \text{MONTH} \\ \text{BLA}_3 \subseteq \text{DATE} \times \text{YEAR} \end{cases}$$

Uniqueness and symmetry of solution lead to prefer the Binary Model.

- The problem of Composite Keys

We remind that keys (identifiers) definition is considered in the Binary Model as a constraint definition.
From the point of view of Structure definition the problem is the same as the previous one and leads normally to the introduction of an Internal Set of Concepts. Let's consider the following example (taken from [11]) :

> Fundamental Domains : PERSON, SUBJECT, POSITION
> Candidate Keys : (PERSON, SUBJECT) or (SUBJECT, POSITION)

We introduce the ISC EXAMINATION and the resulting Structure in the Binary Model is :

In the Constraint division the functional characteristics of the involved BLAs and the fact that couples (PERSON, SUBJECT) or (SUBJECT, POSITION) are unique can be defined; note that this type of constraints is automatically checkable in the Binary Model.

Some comments on Internal Sets of Concepts

We wish to point out that the new sets of "unique names" introduced and the new binary associations have exactly the same properties as the other FDs and BLAs and that they can be treated in the same way.
The only differences are :

> a) the values of the Internal Sets can't be retrieved by the users (since they are internal unique names and they have no meaning for the outside world);
> b) the values of the Internal Sets are not physically stored in the database.

We emphasize that the Internal Set does not introduce particular difficulties at the Conceptual Schema level, because it corresponds to the natural view of Set of Concepts, and it is not bound to a dummy physical record. In this sense the word Internal has only the meaning that the content of this Set of Concepts is already expressed in other, more elementary Sets of Concepts.

An example of a Binary Conceptual Schema

Let's consider the Binary Schema shown in Fig. 8,

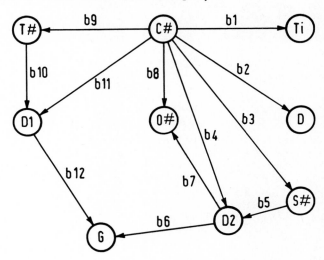

Figure 8- A sample Binary Schema

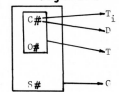

Fig.9

where the FDs are the same as in Example 1, Ti is Title, D1 and D2 are Internal Sets of Concepts.

Let's also suppose that the functional dependency structure is the one represented in Fig. 9.

We outline again that the Binary Conceptual Schema and the functional dependency structure are defined on the same data but they represent a very different reality.

In the Binary Conceptual Schema of Fig. 8 the Enterprise Administrator is expressing the fact that starting from a C# he would like to know its Title and Description, all the Teachers who taught it, all the Offerings when it was offered and all the Students who took it; that, given C# and T#, he would like to know the Grades that the Teacher gave in a specified course; given C# and S# he would like to know in which Offerings the Student took the course and his Grades.

It should be superflous to outline that we do not mean that the above Schema is more meaningful or less arbitrary then the functional dependency structure. The meaningfulness can be decided by the Enterprise Administrator only and it can't be decided by the DBMS designers. As far as the arbitrariness is concerned, both structures, once defined, are somehow arbitrary and impose limitations to the definition of the External Schemas; the difference is that these limitations in the Binary Schema are decided by the Enterprise Administrator, who will try to satisfy the user's necessities, while in the second case (functional dependencies) they are implicit in the data model.

In the definition of the Internal Schema corresponding to the Binary Conceptual Schema the Database Administrator will try to define a structure that represents the given Conceptual Schema and takes care of the parameters; in the case of the functional dependency structure and of the corresponding 3NF Schema he would try to optimize considering the possible conformable representations.

It should be evident that the result of the two processes would be generally different (only a particular "parameter" configuration could lead to the same solution in the two cases) and that, if the Enterprise Administrator has defined a "good" Binary Schema, that is a Schema corresponding to the effective information requirements of the Enterprise, the performance in the case of the Binary Schema could be better.

In the next section we will briefly describe a language to ask queries of a Binary Conceptual Schema. What's the usefulness of such a language? From a conceptual point of view it defines the operations allowed on the database. The semantic of each operation on the External Schemas should be expressed in terms of this language (and translated into operations on the Conceptual Database).

From a practical point of view two choices are possible :

- effectively translating the application program's operations on the External Schema into instructions of this language, or

- bypassing the Conceptual Schema level and directly interpreting the External Schema operations in terms of Internal Schema (physical) operations.

The first choice is more data-independent, the second is more efficient.
Anyway we will not care here about this point; the Conceptual Schema language has here a more theoretical interest thant an effective interest as a programming language.

VII - A LANGUAGE FOR THE BINARY CONCEPTUAL SCHEMA

The first remark we will make is that, since the Binary Logical Associations are mathematically binary relations, any language convenient for the n-ary relational model is convenient for the Binary Conceptual Schema too. In particular the Alpha Language $\begin{bmatrix} 11 , 17 \end{bmatrix}$ could be used. However, we can take some little advantage from the fact that we already know the structure of the relations we are dealing with (i.e. they are binary). In particular the "navigation" across relations could (and should) be, at least syntactically, simplified. The basic idea is the following : let's suppose we have three FDs, say A,B,C, and two binary logical associations $b_1:(A,B)$ and $b_2:(B,C)$. If we want the couples A, C corresponding to the same value of B, in an alpha-like language we should write:

$$b_1.A, \ b_2.C \ : \ b_1.B = b_2.B.$$

In a binary conceptual schema we could more readably write the above expression in the following way :

$$A,C \ : \ A \longrightarrow b_1.B \longrightarrow b_2.C$$

It's not our aim discussing here the precise syntactical properties of the conceptual schema language; in the rest of this section we will instead give an example of a query both in an alpha-like language and in a modified language with the aim of suggesting the way in which a Binary Conceptual Schema could be utilized.

Let us suppose we want to retrieve all records "student" for all the students who took the course number 125 more than 4 times and obtained a grade "A" at least once. The following TARGET and QUALIFICATION can be written (omitting the quantifiers) :

- alpha-like language

  TARGET : $b_2.S\#$

  QUALIFICATION : $b_3.S\# = b_2'.S\# \land b'_3.C\# = 125 \land b'_3.C\# = b_4'.C\# \land b'_2.S\# = b'_5S\# \land b'_4.D_2 = b'_5.D_2 \land$ ICOUNT $(b'_4.D2) > 4 \land b'_5.D_2 = b'_6.D_2$

  $\land b'_6.G = A$

- modified language

  TARGET : $S\#$

  QUALIFICATION : $C\# = 125 \to b'_3.\ S\# \land$ ICOUNT$(C\# \to b'_4.D2 = S\# \to b'_5.D2) > 4 \to \to b'_6.G = A$

This modified language can also be utilized, as well as the alpha language [11], in order to define hierarchical or network External Schemas.

VIII - CONCLUSIONS

An architecture of a DBMS based on three levels (External, Internal and Conceptual Schema), as it is now widely accepted, generates the problem of determining suitable data models at each level. In this paper we have tried to deduce the characteristics of the most suitable data model at the Conceptual Schema level. The requirements for the Conceptual Schema that seem to be relevant for the data model have been outlined; one crucial requirement is the "stability", that is the characteristic of the Conceptual Schema to be unaffected by variations at the Internal or External Schema levels. This property is strongly connected to the separation of roles between the Enterprise Administrator and the Database Administrator, and consequently to a clean separation of "logical", "address oriented", and "performance oriented" choices.

In order to discuss this separation a general frame of reference for the "logical" description of information has been developped, and on the basis of this frame of reference some aspects of the network and the relational models have been discussed. The network model has been shown to contain "address oriented" information and therefore not to be completely suitable for the Conceptual Schema. The relational model has been shown to introduce some restrictions on the logical view of data through the concept of functional dependency; these restrictions are negatively influencing the work of the Enterprise Administrator without ensuring the exclusion of consistency problems.

We have tried to illustrate that a model based on Binary Logical Associations is the most suitable at the Conceptual Schema level and we have shown that a language developped for the relational model may work on the Binary model as well; some syntactical modifications are however strongly recommended.

We feel that some improvements to this work will derive from a careful analysis of the "mapping" problems between the Conceptual and the other Schemas. Our principal aim here has been, more than to solve all specific problems that arise, to clarify the nature of the Conceptual Schema and the limitations to the achievement of data independence.

REFERENCES

1. Astrahan M.M., Altman E.B., Fehder P.L., Senko M.E., (1972) "Concepts of Data Independent Accessing Model" Proc. ACM-Sigfidet Workshop.

2. Nijssen G.M. (1976), "A Gross Architecture for the Next Generation DBMS", this book.

3. Bracchi G., Fedeli A., Paolini P. (1974) "A Multilevel Relational Model for Data Base Management Systems" in : "Data Base Management", Klimbie and Koffeman eds., North Holland, pp. 210-225.

4. ANSI (1975), "Interim Report ANSI/X3/SPARC Study Group on Data Base Management Systems" ANSI, February 1975.

5. Codd E.F. (1970) "A Relational Model of Data for Large Shared Data Banks" CACM 13, No. 6, pp. 377-387.

6. Codasyl (1971), "Data Base Task Group 1971 Report" ACM New York.

7. Bachman C.W. (1975) "Trends in Data Base Management" Proc. National Computing Conference, pp. 569-576.

8. Langefors B. (1969), "Some Approaches to the Theory of Information Systems", BIT 3, N. 4.

9. Bracchi G., Paolini P., Pelagatti G. (1975) "Data Independent Descriptions and the DDL Specifications" in : Data Base Description, Douqué and Nijssen eds., North Holland, pp. 259-267.

10. Codd E.F. (1971), "Further Normalization of the Data Base Relational Model" Courant Computer Science Symposia 6, "Data Base Systems", Prentice Hall, New York.

11. Date C.J. (1975) "An Introduction to Data Base Systems" Addison Wesley Publishing Company.

12. Date C.J., Hopewell P. (1971) "Storage Structure and Physical Data Independence" Proc. ACM- Sigfidet Workshop.

13. Codd E.F., Date C.J. (1974) "The Relational and Network Approaches: Comparison of the Application Programming Interfaces" IBM Research Report RJ 1401.

14. Codd E.F., Date C.J. (1974) "Interactive support for Non-Programmers: the Relational and Network Approaches" IBM Research Report RJ 1400.

15. Abrial J.R. (1974)"Data Semantics" in "Data Base Management, Klimbie and Koffeman eds., North Holland, pp. 1-60.

16. Senko M.E. (1975) "Data Description Language in the Context of a Multilevel Structured Description", in "Data Base Description", B.C.M. Douqué and G.M. Nijssen (eds.), North-Holland, pp. 239-257.

17. Codd E.F. (1971)"A Data Base Sublanguage Founded on the Relational Calculus"Proc. 1971 ACM-Sigfidet Workshop on Data Description, Access and Control.

Modelling in Data Base Management Systems, G.M. Nijssen, (ed.)
North Holland Publishing Company, 1976

A CONCEPTUAL MODEL
FOR INFORMATION PROCESSING

F. Grotenhuis, J. van den Broek
N.V. Philips Industries
Department of Information Systems and Automation
Eindhoven, Netherlands

A conceptual model for information processing, consisting
of a model for both information and processing.
The underlying concepts of the models are discussed. The
concepts and a possible formal language for information
are worked out. The processing model is discussed to the
level of detail necessary to describe the interference
problems of processing and information.

CONTENTS

1. INTRODUCTION

Based on the conviction that the understanding of information processing systems
has to precede the understanding of data base management systems, this paper presents a model for information processing, consisting of a model for processing and
a model for information (data).
We like to introduce some ideologies which we adopted after exploring the manifold
problem areas. Some of the principal problems can be illustrated by the observation
of the development stages of an information system.
It seems obvious to start with a <u>conception</u> of the system, by describing the global structure. Some people call this architecture, others call this the info-logical description. On this level, an information system appears as a network of
functional modules (components) and a data and control flow between those modules
(components).
The next step is the construction of the components, by defining the algorithms,
which also implies a certain structure. This step sometimes is called the data-
logical definition.

The last step is to decide how the system is going to be implemented and how to
deal with the different aspects of the hardware like: efficiency, integrity etc.

It would be nice if the transition between steps would run smoothly. Unfortunately
we discover that the notions used at a certain level are not present in the next
level, with the result that the concepts of a lower level creep into a higher level.
In the worst case even "black boxes" have to be accepted.
Another inconvenience is that the "blueprints" at the various levels look different
having different structuring concepts etc.

As we feel that this situation may not be very attractive for a user, we adjudge
him the following ideology:
a user wants a plain view through his information system, based on his own concepts
- for all levels which are relevant to him
- and for all aspects of that system
Thus, our intention is not to force unfamiliar concepts upon the user.

2. BASIC PRINCIPLES

As it is our aim to describe as precisely as possible a model for information processing, it seems useful to start with a short discussion about <u>models</u> in general,
to clarify what we mean by a conceptual model.
This discussion is primarely based on the introduction of the concept of models by
(Kleene 52) and (Bertels, Nauta 74).
Moreover we introduce the notion of <u>coherent structuring</u> which also has to be clarified.

2.1 Models

We distinguish three types of models i.e.
+ empiric model
+ conceptual model
+ formal model

The system we want to model is called the object system (Langefors 73).
The <u>empiric model</u> corresponds to the entities of the object system. The <u>conceptual</u>
<u>model</u> cooresponds to the notions (concepts) with which we can classify the entities
of the object system. The <u>formal model</u> corresponds to names or tokens to express
these notions (concepts). Each model can be expressed by means of a language. Thus
the formal model is expressed by a formal language.

Sometimes it will be useful to subdivide the conceptual model into a intuitive (conceptual) model and a precise (conceptual) model.

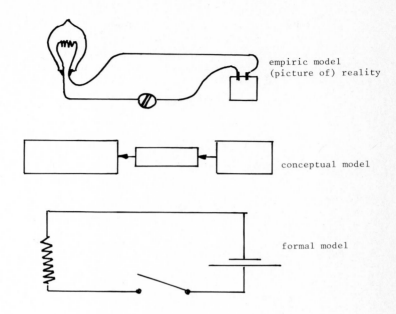

empiric model
(picture of) reality

conceptual model

formal model

2.2 Coherent structuring

This notion means that a user must be able to recognize his own concepts, in the description of his information system. These concepts must be valid on all levels and for all aspects of that system. With aspects we mean, functionality, reliability, efficiency, privacy, etc.
The notion of 'level' corresponds with the division of a system into subsystems. For reasons of simplicity (Popper 36) we want to restrict the number of distinct concepts. On the other hand we do not want to restrict the viewpoint of a user which implies that we do not want to put any restriction on the information system. These considerations lead to the concept of coherent structuring which means that congruent structures will appear on each level.

> *Examples*
>
> *In the real world we recognize coherent structures in the organization of an enterprise. Management is organized in the same way for each level and the various aspects as financial, technical etc. will show the same pateern on each level.*
>
> *It would be nice if we decide for a "branchless" programming language to conceive "branchless hardware" too. If the hardware is structured coherently with the "programs" then one is able to*

replace smoothly software by hardware or vice versa.

The structure of the data used in a program should be coherent with the structure of the program.

The introduction of coherent structures for various viewpoints and levels might contribute to a better understanding of the information system and also to concepts of higher level languages, semantic levels in programming and structured programming (design).

2.3 The approach of this paper

The approach choosen in this paper is such that the topics are discussed first from an empiric point of view, afterwards this discussion is repeated to formulate a conceptual model.
Then this conceptual model is formalized.

3. A SKETCH OF THE MODEL OF INFORMATION PROCESSING

The complete model under consideration is related with facets like, processing, information, etc. Because of the intermixed relationship between those facets in a precise manner it is useful to present first a sketch of the model.
A way to achieve this is to follow the chain of thoughts of an information-engineer whose object system is the "real world", (thus the information-engineer does not belong to this "real world"), and whose aim is to design an information processing model of which the realisation is called an information processing system. The purpose of an information system is to provide information about the world the information engineer is modelling (Langefors 73).

The information engineer takes the following steps which are illustrated by figure 1 and described hereafter.

step 1: The empiric model

> The information engineer observes the real world and recognizes objects such as products, stores relationships between the various objects etc. Moreover he recognizes activities. He selects those items which are relerelevant for him.

step 2: The intuitive conceptual model

> As the information engineer cannot handle the items itself, he is using a model of the items. The items are mostly represented by a form (e.g. the description of a car).
> He also uses forms to describe activities on items (e.g. the sale of a car). Thus he is creating an abstract system which is a mapping from his empiric model. For some objects and activities that abstraction has already been made in real world such that he recognizes forms as objects in the real world.
>
> He might have observed activities on forms.
> Hence his intuitive conceptual model consists of the concepts of forms and activities on forms. A place of activity may be a department, a desk of a man, a mechanical device or any combination.
> The activities are more or less independent of each other and proceed simultaneously, producing new forms which are forwarded to other places of activities giving the impression of streams of forms coming from and going to places of activity. If several streams of forms are fed into one place of activity one may recognize the problem of interference.
> A place of activity is concerned with a certain function, described in a so called statute.

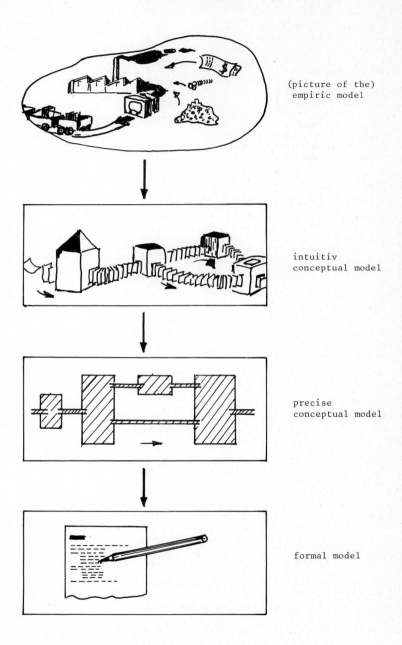

(picture of the)
empiric model

intuitiv
conceptual model

precise
conceptual model

formal model

Fig.1: informationstreams and processing units

The execution of such a function takes a certain amount of time. Because
of the fact of introducing "time" the model represents a proces which implies that we have to deal with states of the objects described in the model. Thus introducing the concept of version.
Various versions of forms may be kept for later processing or repeating
processing. Hence one needs a notion of archiving or registering.
The overall picture of the information system shows that the places of activity are composed of other places of activity, which could be considered
as being nested activities.
Simarly structures appear in the streams of forms: A department deals with
packets of forms, which are, at a lower level, divided into separate forms,
handled by subdepartments, where in the next level employees are dealing
with parts of the form.

Furthermore the function of a boss can be seen at each level of activity.
A boss is not actually taking part of that activity but keeps things going.

Step 3: The precise conceptual model

From the intuitive conceptual model we can derive a precise conceptual model to be used by the information engineer. First of all the information
engineer will restrict himself to that part of the information system that
is to be automated. The notions used in the intuitive model are now replaced by precise concepts for places of activities, streams of forms and various aspects.

Processing units.

Places of activity are replaced by processing units.
A processing unit has the following characteristics:

The procedure of a processing unit is described in a work-instruction.
This work-instruction cannot be modified by the procedure itself, thus the
processing unit is preconditioned.

The processing unit is always 'on' (receptive) i.e. if data is presented
to a processing unit, it will be processed.

A processing unit is always subordinated to another processing unit: a
discipline processor, which can influence only the state of the processing
unit (being busy or not).
The ultimate discipline processors are the start and stop buttons.
The disciplinary actions to be taken on receipt of disciplinary messages
are described in the discipline instruction of a processing unit.
Processing units can be connected to other processing units, thus it is
possible to construct a net of processing units.
The processing units in a net are working indepently. This means that time-
delays have no influence on the transformations described in the work-instruction. Those transformations are considered to be "time-less" and
therefore represent mathematical functions.

The information streams.

Forms which have a meaning for a place of activity will represent information for that place.
Therefore a stream of forms can be regarded as a stream of information in
the conceptual model.
The stream of information can be described by the connector between two
processing units. This connector takes care of the transfer of information
from one processing unit to the other. Consequently the time-delay is solved in the connector.
Only one type of information is associated with a connector. The connector
handles only one unit of information at a time.
Depending on the level of abstraction of the processing unit, this unit of

information may consist of a single value or an information structure.

Example

The connectors for a processing unit that produces invoices from orders are described as ORDERS and INVOICES. Within this processing unit, other processing units are nested which handle the information nested in ORDERS and INVOICES e.g. ORDERLINES and INVOICELINES.

Each connection in a net of processing units is predefined (known in advance). This implies that the streams of information are preconditioned.

Resuming: The conceptual model of an information system can be expressed by streams of information going to and coming from processing units.
The concepts of information streams and processing units are equivalent, depending on the situation, however, the accent can be put on one of the two.
The processing units and their associated information streams can appear in different types:
- A batch-type with a constant stream of information
- A control type of processing unit which deals with incidental information
- Processing units which split and merge information streams or monitor the traffic.

A special type of processing units is introduced: the register processor.

The functions of the register processor is to keep the information, supply copies on demand, add more up to date information to the already existing information, thus creating a new version of the information.

Step 4: The formal model

The information engineer needs a formal language to describe his information system. For the description of information we refer to the detailed information model. The formal language to describe the processing units is left out of this paper; we limit ourselves to the more detailed concepts of a processing unit.

4. THE INFORMATION MODEL

Because of a lot of confusion about objects, entities, individuals, properties etc. it seems to be valuable for a better understanding to start this subject with the empiric model too.

4.1 The empiric information model

4.1.1 Mapping of objects into the information system

The informatin engineer – the person who designs an information system – tries to model the business world for describing an information system. Hence the information system is a mapping of the business world of which the objects are mapped by means of text. Objects may be concrete objects as well as sets of concrete objects, or abstract objects etc. Thus in an information system we manipulate with texts being mappings from objects.
An object belongs to an objectsystem (Langefors 73).
In our view this objectsystem can be the real world of business as well as e.g. operating systems etc.

In this paper we refer to objectsystems dealing with the real world.

4.1.2 Connection between objects and texts

The text must be connected in some way to the object.
There are two possibilities to achieve this.
The first one is to attach a token, which is a unique one within the objectsystem, to the object and to the text. This token is often called a name.

Example

*A social security number is attached to a person and will
appear in the text describing a person in the social-secu-
rity- information system.*

The second possibility for connecting objects with text is that we do not need a token or name but the semantics of the text is sufficient to connect the text and the particular object. It seems to be that there are certain restrictions on this thesis, see e.g. (Zemanek 70).

Example

*An object that represents an association between two named
objects can be expressed by the concatenation of both names,
thus does not need a token itself.*

4.1.3 The role of an object

A particular object can be mapped into different texts, because the object is used in different objectsystems or more roles are envisaged in one objectsystem.

Example

*A person is mapped into another text in a social security
system as in a company-employee system. Even the names indicating that person may be different.
For instance there may exist a social security number and
an employee number of that person. The connection may or may
not be described.*

The mapping of an object into a text we call a role.
Thus we recognize a particular person in the role of patient, employee or passenger etc.

4.1.4 The properties of an object

The object, in a certain role, is described by the properties belonging to that particular role.

Example

*Consider an object, say a house placed at Ripendale 254 in
Grenoble, France.*

*A person who wants to live in that house is interested in
the role of "living conditions" concerning that house.
Therefore he is going to do measurements on the house.
He will measure e.g. number of rooms, price of rent, esthe-
ticision of architecture, size of garden etc.*

The properties can be observed i.e. can be <u>measured</u>.
Consequently there may exist a proper interrelationship between the various observed properties of an object.

Example

*An interrelationship can be expressed between the weight of
a person and his length.*

These proper interrelationships are a type of so called consistency constraints.

4.1.5 Associations between objects

In the real world we discover that two or more objects may be associated with each
other. This association can be seen as an (abstract) object itself to which properties are attached.
There also exist constraints regarding the association between objects.

Example

*There exists an association between a car and its owner.
A constraint could be that a car is owned only by one owner.
Another one could be: Every owner has only one car.*

*The association between a patient, a doctor and a clinic
can be an object of observation.*

4.1.6 Versions of information

A repeating observation of an object could lead to different values of measurements. Thus introducing the concept of version of information.
Indeed the term information includes eternity: Knowledge, and thus information
about objects, increases as time goes on. From the foregoing we can derive that
the manipulations on information consists of:
+ inspecting of information
+ addition of information
+ rectification of data or improvement of information.

Existing information cannot disappear or be changed, changing could be regarded as
falsification. Thus the quantity of information is always growing, we only have to
decide explicitly what is the scope of interest we are dealing with.

Examples

*The information that John and Ann once are married will never
disappear although they are possibly divorced now.*

*A salary increase of 10% does not remove the old salary.
The new version and the old one still exist, only a new version of information is added.*

My scope of interest of employees is e.g.: all the employees which belong on the first of January 1975 to my department.

4.1.7 The representation of objects

Let us consider an object named Jack Brown, in the role of employee of company X. The employee for the objectsystem in consideration can be expressed by

"the salary of Jack Brown"
"the sector he is working in"
"the date he became an employee"
"the qualification being a graduate or not".

Thus the object named Jack Brown could be represented in the role as employee.

Example

NAME	SALARY IN $	SECTOR NAME	SINCE YEAR	GRADUATION YES OR NO
JACK BROWN	15.000	ADMINISTR	1945	YES

Remark: This is an instanteneous description of Jack Brown in his role as employee of company X. At this instance of time he has the salary of 15.000$ and is working now in the administrative sector. He will always be a graduate and the time he became an employee is also a fact.

We can consider more objects in the same role as employee of company X.

Example

EMPLOYEES OF COMPANY X				
NAME	SALARY IN $	SECTOR NAME	SINCE YEAR	GRADUATION YES OR NO
JACK BROW	15.000	ADMINISTR	1945	YES
DICK GREEN	10.000	SERVICE	1954	NO
MARY BLUE	20.000	SERVICE	1954	NO

In this case one may think of the columnnr NAME contains unique texts being the names of the corresponding employees.

4.1.8 The composition of information

In an information system we often have to deal with information in various levels of abstraction (Hoare 72).
This implies that an element of information at a certain level can be considered as an entity while in the next step a more exact observation leads to the recognition that this element is composed of a number of elements, possibly of different types.

> *Example*
>
> *A more detailed view of an order is that it is composed of an orderheader and several orderlines.*

The composition of information starting from the information about known objects results also in compound information.

> *Example*
>
> *From the information on the children of a person, his cars, his education, the information element "complete person" can be derived.*

4.2 The conceptual information model

Based on the notions described in the empiric model of information we now come to more precise concepts.

4.2.1 The mapping of objects into info-points

Instead of using a table representation as a means of expressing ourselves we choose for a spacial approach. So we can deal with sets of points in a space. The space we call info-space and the points are called info-points. Each info-point is a mapping of an object **x**) into this info-space.

The values 97, Brown and 15.000 are called the components of the info-point which represents the person Brown in the role of (a particular) employee. The texts "employee-number", "family-name" and "salary" are called component names (see also Bosak 62).

---

x) An object belongs to a certain objectsystem. Thus an info-space represents a part of the objectsystem. This particular info-space represents no information for another objectsystem.

Example

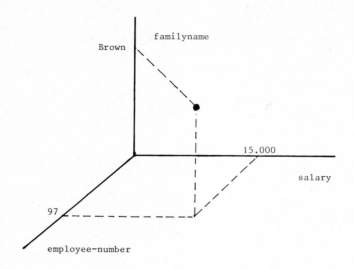

Info-space of employees with one employee with

employee-number: 97
family-name   : Brown
salary   : 15.000

4.2.2 The connection between objects and info-points

Every info-point has to correspond with one and only one object. In our example, if the company has 14.000 employees, then these should be represented by 14.000 info-points in the info-space. The <u>identifying-space</u> is a (sub)info-space in which no info-point corresponds with more than one object.

Example

> *The identifying space indicated with employee number full-fills this definition, because every employee in real world has a unique employee-number.*

The foregoing definition includes that there may be more than one identifying space within an info-space. Moreover the identifying space may be equal to the info-space.
The components of the identifying space are called the identifying components and thus the identifying components are the connection between the object and the info-point.

Examples

ARTICLE RELATIONS		
article containing	*article contained*	*number*
X 33	A 14	3
X 33	A 17	1
A 14	A 17	2

The identifying space is formed by the two components: "article containing" and "article contained".

MARRIAGES	
husbands	*wifes*
John	Mary
Peter	Ann

There are two identifying spaces formed by "husbands" and "wifes", if we accept monogame marriages only.

STRING-QUARTET			
1st violins	*2nd violins*	*tenor-violins*	*violincello*
Wolfgang	Amadeus	Johan	Sebastian
Robert	Ludwig	Leopold	Bertholdi
Robert	Ludwig	Leopold	Kurt
Guiseppe	Johan	Arthuro	Paganini

The identifying space in this example consists of the complete info-space viz. the four names of the quartet-members.

4.2.3 The info-point as a role of an object

Different roles of objects are expressed by different info-points. The identifying spaces of the info-spaces representing the same object may be the same or may differ.

Example

A person may play the role as: a patient identified by a patientnumber, a civilian identified by a registration number and a taxpayer also identified by the civilian registration number:

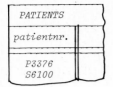

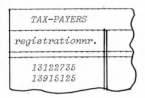

*Remark: the connections between info-points belonging to dif-
ferent info-spaces will be explained in the chapter
dealing with associations.*

4.2.4 The components of an info-point

The components of an info-point are expressed by values. The set of possible values for a component is called the <u>component domain</u>. Because various components
of different info-points might have the same domain it is useful to be able to refer to a domain by a name: the <u>domainname</u>.

Example

*The domain of registrationnr. of CIVILIANS can be described
as "a number between 1 and 99999999".
The domain of sex of PERSONS can be expressed by the values
'male' and 'female'.*

4.2.5 Associations between info-points

The associations between info-points are expressed by associations between identifying components. The association may be associations between info-points in the
same info-space or in different info-spaces. Moreover an association may exist between two or more info-points. An association is an object itself.

Example

CARS		PERSONS		CAROWNERS	
carnr.		registrationnr.	name	car	owners
A123		1001		A123	1001
Z 71		1002		Z 71	1002
Z 72		1003		Z 72	1001
		1005			

The association between cars and persons expressing the object
ownership of a car, is described in the info-space CAROWNERS.
This info-space contains the components car and owner which are
connected to carnr. of CARS and registrationnr. of PERSONS.

It is obvious that the connections between the components of the associated info-
points are subject of constraints.
This constraint can be expressed by the interrelatinship of the value sets of the
components.
In the foregoing example the car of CAROWNERS is the identifying space. This means
that a car has only one owner, and an owner may have more than one car. The constraint that the value set of carnr. of CARS is equal to the value set of carnr.
of CAROWNERS, expresses that every car has an owner. The constraint that the value
set of owners of CAROWNERS is a subset of registrationnr. of PERSONS expresses that
a car is owned by a registrated person.

Example 2

The association of patients and civilians as described in the
example of paragraph 4.2.3, could be expressed as follows:

PERSONS	
CIVILIANS	PATIENTS
registrationnr.	patientnr.
13122735	P3376
13914124	–
13915125	S6100

If we declare that CIVILIANS to be the identifying space, this
declaration implies that at a given moment of time a person
may be a patient represented by a patientnr. Because not every
person needs to be a patient, the value of the patientnr. can
be "not relevant". Furthermore it can be stated that each patient
is a civilian.

4.2.6 The version of information

New events or new measurements on the objectsystem result in new information, which is added to the already existing information. Thus a version of information is valid during the interval between two succeeding measurements or observations. This implies that information has to be kept in what we call registers. The characteristics of a register are: new information is added to already existing information, only copies of the information are delivered, and the consistency of the information belongs to the realm of the register.

Addition of one or more info-points to an info-space results in a new version of the set of info-points, called info-set, of the info-space. This new version of the info-set exists apart from the previous versions. Thus several versions of an info-set may exist at a given moment of time and are equally usable. The different versions are identified by an info-point is determined by the version of the info-space only one version of an info-point will appear.

Furthermore we introduce the notion of most recent version of an info-space. Thus the most recent version of an info-point appears at least in the most recent version of the info-space.

The notion of version can be extended to a group of info-spaces, in which group the info-spaces are associated in some way.

4.2.7 The representation of info-points

Based on the concepts, described in the previous paragraphs, we can summarize the items with which we can represent the info-points.

Info-points are described by info-spaces which are constructed out of components. Those components which are associated with a component domain that describes the set of possible values.

The connection between info-points and objects can be declared by naming the identifying components.

Associations between objects are represented by associations between their identifying components. The representation of the version of an info-point appears in the version of the info-space.

4.2.8 Composition of info-points

A composition can be considered as an info-point to which one or more info-spaces are connected.

Example

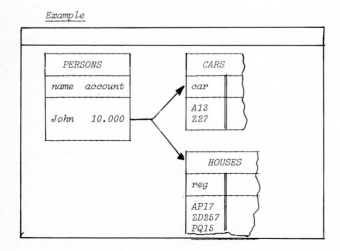

The possesion of a particular person is composed of the info-point representing that person and the info-spaces CARS of person and HOUSES of person belonging to that particular person.

The result of such a composition is called an <u>info-structure</u>.

Info-structures may represent informationstreams on various levels of abstraction. Informationstreams are always tree-structures. Nets of information are described by the associations between info-spaces.

4.3 The formal information model

In the following paragraphs a more formal description is given of the concepts of information as described in the previous chapter.

4.3.1 The description of the info-space

We refer to an info-space by an <u>info-name</u> and to the constituing components by a <u>component-name</u>.

The general formal of the info-space description is:

<infoname> : (<componentname$_1$>,<componentname$_2$>,....)

<u>remark</u>: the notation< >represents meta-brackets, between which a name can be described.

> *Example*
>
> *PERSONS : (REGISTRATIONNR,LENGTH,WEIGHT)*

The interpretation of a component-name is within the context of the info-name, thus we refer to a component by:

<infoname> o <componentname>

in which "o" represents the connector of the names.

4.3.2 The description of the identifying spaces

The identifying spaces of an info-space are defined by the identifying components. An info-space may have one or more identifying spaces and an identifying space may contain one, more or all components.

The declaration of the identifying space(s) of an info-space can be seen as a condition added to the definition of that info-space. Thus the format of the info-space definition is

<infoname> : (<componentname$_1$>,<componentname$_2$>.....|

<identspace$_1$>,<identspace$_2$>......)

identspace can be replaced by:

<componentname$_a$>⊗<componentname$_b$> .....

The symbol ⊗ indicates an "and" (=concatenation) between the components.

> *Example*
>
> *TIMETABLE : (HOUR,ROOM,TEACHER,SUBJECT* |
> *HOUR ⊗ ROOM,HOUR ⊗ TEACHTER)*

4.3.3 The role of an object

Different roles of objects are expressed by info-spaces with different descriptions. The different info-spaces can be seen as <u>decompositions</u> of an info-space.
On the other hand the "total view" of an object, represented by an info-space, can
be regarded as a <u>composition</u> of the "sub-views" which are also represented by info-
spaces.

Example

PERSONS : (REGNR.,NAME,DOMICILE,MILITARY-RANK|*REGNR.)*

CIVILIANS : (REGNR.,NAME,DOMICILE|*REGNR.)*

SOLDIERS : (REGNR.,NAME,MILITARY-RANK|*REGNR.)*

The registernumber of the soldiers and the civilians are con-
tained in the set of registernumbers of the persons.
The next paragraph gives a precise formalism to express the
various relationships between the info-spaces.
The info-spaces CIVILIANS and SOLDIERS are decompositions
of the info-space PERSONS, while PERSONS is a composition of
the info-space CIVILIANS and SOLDIERS.

In the case that we make a composition of info-spaces of which the sets of identifying components are different, we need the value 'not relevant' for the composite
info-points.

Example

Not every civilian is a soldier and therefore not every person
has a military rank.
Thus introducing persons whose MILITARY-RANK = 'not relevant'.

4.3.4 The component description

With each component, a componentdomain is associated; each componentdomain has a
<u>domainname</u> and describes the set of possible values.
The association between a component and its domain is declared as follows

<infoname> ∘ <componentname> ⇒ <domainname>

Example

PERSONS ∘ LENGTH ⇒ INTEGER-A

The values belonging to a domain are noted as:

<domainname> := { <values> }

Examples

INTEGER-A:= { 40,41,................250 }

SEX = { MALE, FEM. }

TEXT := { <alphabetic, max 10 characters> }

4.3.5 The description of associations

4.3.5.1. Associations between info-spaces

As mentioned before, associations between info-points in info-spaces can be expressed by relations between value sets.
The notation used for a value set is

$$\{<name>\}$$

If the valueset of one component must be indicated,

name   could be replaced by

$$<infoname> \circ <componentname>$$

If the valueset of more components must be indicated, name   could be replaced by

$$<infoname> \circ (<comp_1> \otimes <comp_2> ...)$$

The associations between the valuesets can be expressed by the known set-operations such as:

$$\{<name_1>\} = \{<name_2>\}$$

$$\{<name_1>\} \subseteq \{<name_2>\}$$

$$\{<name_1>\} \cap \{<name_2>\} = \emptyset \text{ etc.}$$

Example

$$PERSONS : (REGNR, SALARY | REGNR)$$

$$CARS : (CARNR, PRICE | CARNR)$$

$$CAROWNERS : (CARNR, OWNER, YEAR | CARNR)$$

$$\{CAROWNERS \circ CARNR\} = \{CARS \circ CARNR\}$$

$$\{CARONWERS \circ OWNER\} \subseteq \{PERSONS \circ REGNR\}$$

4.3.5.2 Subsets used in associations

A constraint on a valueset can be described by a function to be applied on that valueset, resulting in a subset.
The general notation for this constraint is

$$<infoname> \circ <componentname> | <function>$$

Examples

$$EMPLOYEES : (EMPNR, SALARY, SEX | EMPNR)$$

$$MALES : (EMPNR, SALARY | EMPNR)$$

$$\{MALES \circ (EMPNR \otimes SALARY)\} =$$

$$\{EMPLOYEES \circ (EMPNR \otimes SALARY) | EMPLOYEES \circ SEX = 'MALE'\}$$

In this example the info-descriptions of MALES and EMPLOYEES are different.
If the info-descriptions were equal we could reduce the notation to

$$\{MALES\} = \{EMPLOYEES | EMPLOYEES \circ SEX = 'MALE'\}$$

Another constraint is described in the following example:

HIGHSAL : (EMPNR,SALARY EMPNR)

$\{$HIGHSAL$\circ$(EMPNR $\otimes$ SALARY)$\}$ =

$\{$EMPLOYEES$\circ$(EMPNR $\otimes$ SALARY)

              EMPLOYEES $\circ$ SALARY >'50000'$\}$

In the next example the conditional function is left out, resulting in a kind of projection.

SALARIES : (EMPNR,SALARY$|$EMPNR)

$\{$SALARIES $\circ$ (EMPNR $\otimes$ SALARY)$\}$ = $\{$EMPLOYEES $\circ$ (EMPNR $\otimes$ SALARY)$\}$

4.3.6 The description of version

As the version of an info-point depends on the version of the info-space, we can express the interval during which the version of an info-point is valid, by means of the values of the version of the info-space at the begin and at the end of the interval.

For this reason we introduce two special components FROM and UNTIL which are added to each info-space.

FROM has the value of the version of the info-space when the version of the info-point came to existence.

UNTIL has the value of the last version of the info-space where this version of the info-point was still valid.

The general format of the description of an info-space is:

<infoname> : (<components>,FROM,UNTIL$|$

              <identspace> $\otimes$ FROM,

              <identspace> $\otimes$ UNTIL

The component UNTIL may contain the value 'unknown' if the version of the info-point is the most recent version.

Example

CARS : (CARNR,MILEAGE,FROM,UNTIL$|$

          CARNR $\otimes$ FROM, CARNR $\otimes$ UNTIL)

CARS			VERSION 24
CARNR	*MILEAGE*	*FROM*	*UNTIL*
A15	12000	20	23
A15	14000	24	unknown
A16	11000	19	unknown
A17	30000	12	21
A18	15000	12	unknown

In this example the most recent version of CARS contains:

```
A15    14000
A16    11000
A18    15000
```

The version of a set of associated info-spaces can be expressed in a similar way. The versions of the separate info-spaces are considered as properties in the info-space that represents the network.

```
<infoname>:(INFOSPACE,VERSION,FROM,UNTIL|

          INFOSPACE ⊗ FROM,INFOSPACE ⊗ UNTIL)
```

Example

NETWORK			VERSION 3
INFOSPACE	VERSION	FROM	UNTIL
CARS	7	1	3
CARS	11	3	unknown
PERSONS	9	1	2
PERSONS	17	2	unknown
CAROWNERS	4	1	unknown

The current version of NETWORK implies the versions:

```
CARS        11
PERSONS     17
CAROWNERS    4
```

4.3.7 The representation of info-points and data

Resuming, the general formats of the description of info-points are[*]:

INFOSPACE

$<infoname>$: $(<componentnames>,... |<identcomponents>,...)$

$<componentname> ⇒ <domainname> := \{<set\ of\ values>\}$

$<identcomponents> :: <componentname_1> ⊗ <componentname_2>...$

ASSOCIATION BETWEEN INFOSPACES

$\{<infoname> ∘ <components>\} <setop> \{<infoname> ∘ <components> | <function>\}$

$<components> :: (<componentname_1> ⊗ <componentname_2> ...)$

$<setop> :: =,⊂,⊆,..$

[*] remark: the metanotion :: denotes "can be replaced by".

The definitions describe mathematical sets.
The values may refer to objects in the real world, in this case we call the set
an <u>info-set</u>. The identification part is then known as a name or token for that object in the real world.
If this connection does not exist we call the set a <u>data-set</u>.
A data-set may be the result of a projection of an info-set in which the identifying space of the info-set is not involved.

> *Examples*
>
> *EMPLOYEES:(EMPNR,SALARY,TAX,BLOODGROUP*$|$*EMPNR)*
>
> *EMPLOYEES defines an info-set, the projection*
>
> *EMPDATA : (SALARY,TAX,BLOODGROUP*$|$*SALARY,TAX,BLOODGROUP)*
>
> *represents a data-set*

If in the definition of an info-space, the constraint of uniqueness is left out,
the definition refers to a "group" of values which are not necessarily unique. The
general definition of such a "group" is

<groupname> : (<components>,...)

> *Example*
>
> *SALARYDATA : (SALARY,TAX)*

4.3.8 The description of information structures

In this paragraph the formal notation of information structures is discussed.
Then some operations are indicated to derive an information structure from defined
info-spaces.

The general format of the description of an information structure is derived from
the description of an info-space by describing an info-space as one of the components.

> *Example*
>
> $\langle infoname_3 \rangle$: *(<components$_1$>,...(<components$_2$>,...*$|$
>
>   *<identcomp$_2$>)*$|$*<identcomp$_1$>)*

The info-space described by <components$_2$>,... is related to the info-point identified by <identcomp$_1$>.
Thus the identifying space of the nested info-space consists of the concatination
of both identifying spaces.

> *Example*
>
> $\langle infoname_1 \rangle$: *(<components1>,...*$|$ *<identcomp1>)*
>
> $\langle infoname_2 \rangle$: *(<components2>,...*$|$ *<identcomp1>⊗<identcomp2>)*

Example

ORDER : (ORDERNR,CUSTNR,(ARTNR,QUANT|ARTNR)|ORDERNR)

Intersections

From an info-space various info-structures can be derived by the <u>intersection</u> operation.
The intersection divides an info-space in more info-spaces such that all info-points in a section have the same value for the <u>intersection</u> function that was applied on the info-space.

\<infoname\> : \<infoname\> ∘ (\<function\>,\<components\>,...|\<function\>)

Examples

Given the info-space:

EMPLOYEES : (EMPNR,DEPTNR,SAL,TAX|EMPNR)

the following info-structures could be derived:

EMPLOYEES   DEPTNR:EMPLOYEES   (DEPTNR,(EMPNR,SAL,TAX|EMPNR)|DEPTNR)

EMPLOYEES   SAL:EMPLOYEES   (SAL,(EMPNR,DEPTNR,TAX|EMPNR)|SAL)

EMPLOYEES   NET:

EMPLOYEES   ((NET:=SAL-TAX),(EMPNR,DEPTNR,TAX|EMPNR)|NET)

EMP ∘ DEPT = EMPLOYEES ∘ (DEPT,(SAL) | DEPT)

5. THE PROCESSING MODEL

In this chapter a more precise conceptual model for processing is described.
We introduce a mathematical machine called <u>P-machine</u>.
Then a <u>P-processor</u>, being a program working as a P-machine, is indicated.
A formal description of these two concepts is not within the scope of this paper but the concepts serve to discuss the streams of information.

5.1 The mathematical machine (P-machine)

In this paper the description is limited to a physical model of the P-machine and an illustration of the nesting of P-machines.

5.1.1 The P-machine

The P-machine can be represented by the following picture:

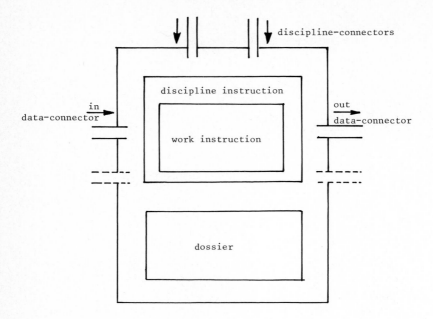

Picture of the P-machine

The components of a P-machine are:
- one and only one discipline-in-connector
- one and only one discipline-out-connector
- at least one data-in-connector
- at least one data-out-connector
- one and only one discipline instruction
- one and only one work instruction
- one and only one dossier
- one and only one clerk to carry out the work

The workinstruction contains a sequence of indivisible instructions which describe the algorithme of the transformation.
The workinstruction is embedded in the discipline-instruction which has the same characteristics as the workinstruction.
The discipline-instruction describes the disciplinary actions, e.g. the actions to be taken at a start or stop signal.
The workinstruction is not influenced by the discipline-instruction.

The dossier serves as a prospective memory, it represents the state of the P-machine together with the work- and discipline-instructions.

Information is exchanged with other P-machines, via the in and out-connectors.
With each connector one type of information is associated.
The information can be transferred only in one direction.
A connector can be looked at as a medium (being a P-machine) that transfers the accessrights of information form one P-machine to the connected P-machine (handshaking).

5.1.2 Nesting of P-machines

P-machines can be connected in such a way that the network of P-machines behaves
like a P-machine.
An example of such a network is given to illustrate this.

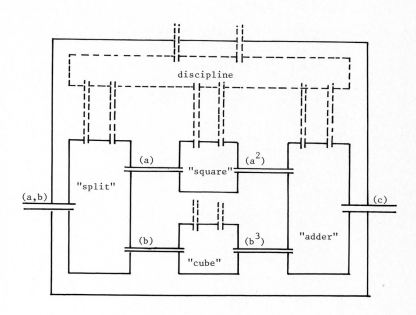

*Via the in-connector of the outermount contour, the two-tuple
(a,b) is brought in.*
*The P-machine "split" transfers (a) and (b) to the P-machines
"SQUARE" and "CUBE" resp.*
*In these P-machines the input is transformed into (a^2) and (b^3)
which values are fed into the "adder" giving the output
$c = (a^2 + b^3)$.*

*The discipline connectors of each P-machine is connected to a
P-machine acting as discipline-P-machine for the network.
Hence the network represents a P-machine with one discipline-
in and one discipline-out-connector, and the data-in-connector
associated with (a,b) and one data-out-connector associated with
c such that $c = a^2 + b^3$.*

5.2 The P-processor

A P-machine can be considered as a conceptual model for the P-processor.
Reversely, the P-processor can be considered as a "program" working according
to a P-machine.

Because P-machines can be connected to a network, the concept of P-processors introduces a high degree of parallellisme.
Moreover this concept allows the description of the sequencing of informationstreams in order to solve the problem of interference.

With each connector of a P-processor an info-stream is associated.
The info-stream consists of <u>info-elements</u> and the P-processor handles one info-
element at a time. This info-element may be an info-point or an info-structure.

We might consider the action of a P-processor as a transformation of one info-
space to another info-space.

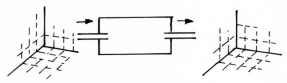

It is not sufficient to associate an info-space to a connector.
It has also to be declared what the size is of the info-stream (the number of info-
elements), on which P-processor has to operate.
Therefore we introduce the concept of a <u>P-job</u> associated with a P-processor.

5.2.1 The concept of P-jobs

A P-job is the work done by a P-processor, according to its work-instruction, on a
defined quantity of information.

> *Example*
>
> *An illustration taken from real live could be: "The digging
> of your garden".*
> *"Digging" is associated with a work-instruction and "your
> garden" expresses the quantity on which this activity is
> defined.*

The information in the info-stream belonging to a P-job is indicated by means of
two <u>separation brackets</u> appearing in info-stream.
The opening bracket named <u>brac</u> the closing one called <u>ket</u>.

The brac's and ket's are recognized by the P-processor, and their existence is expressed in the workinstruction of the P-processor.
The brackets may enclose zero, one or more info-elements.

A P-job may be defined on one and only one info-element of the info-stream, in
which case the brackets are used implicitely.

The operations associated with the brackets may appear implicitely or explicitely in the workinstruction of the P-processor.
In general the brac brings the P-processor in its initial state and the ket in its final state.

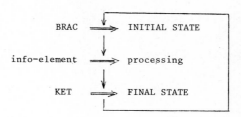

Example

> *In the P-JOB defined as summarizing a number of values, the BRAC will initialize SUM and the KET will make SUM available.*

5.3 Description of infostreams

An info-stream is described in association with a connector of an P-processor.
As a general notation can be used:

<processorname>∘<connectorname>⇒<infostream>

The P-JOB may be defined for one and only one info-element, which is described as

<infostream> :: (<info-element>)

As notation for a group of info-elements, being a subject of the P-JOB, is used:

<infostream> :: $\left[(\text{<info-element>})\right]$

The info-element may consist of an info-point or an info-structure.

<info-element> :: (<infoname>)

<info-element> :: (<infoname$_1$>,(<infoname$_2$>)) etc.

If an info-structure is described at a lower level of abstraction, it falls apart into two or more info-streams

$(\text{<infoname}_1\text{>},(\text{<infoname}_2\text{>})) \Rightarrow$

$(\text{<infoname}_1\text{>}) \wedge \left[(\text{<infoname}_2\text{>})\right]$

> *Example*
>
> *Consider the info-spaces:*
>
> *EMPLOYEES :(EMPNR,DEPT,SAL EMPNR) and DEPARTMENT :(DEPT DEPT)*
>
> *from which the following info-structure can be derived*
>
> *EMPLOYEES   (DEPT,(SAL) DEPT)*

*The P-job to be described is the summarizing per department
of the salaries paid within that department, and this for all
departments.*

We could refer to this P-job as:

  (DEPT,(SAL) DEPT)   *PROC1*   *(DPET,SUM DEPT)*

Detailling of proc1 results in:

  (DEPT,(SAL) DEPT)   *PROC11*   *(DEPT,(SAL) DEPT) (BRACKETS)*

  (DEPT,(SAL) DEPT)   *PROC12*   *(DEPT,SUM DEPT)*

  (DEPT,SUM DEPT) (BRACKETS)   *PROC13*   *(DEPT,SUM DEPT)*

Detailling of proc12 results in:

  (DEPT,(SAL DEPT)   *PROC121 (DEPT DEPT (SAL)*

  (SAL)   *PROC122 (SUM)*

  (DEPT DEPT) (SUM)   *PROC123 (DEPT,SUM DEPT)*

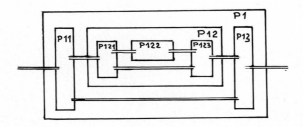

5.4 Interference

The problems of interference arise in an informationsystem if the same information
is used in different informationstreams.

Example

*The informationstream that produces a survey of employees
will interfere with the addition of information concerning
employees.*

The interference problem has to be recognized in the design of the informationsystem and the solution has to be described.
The result is a preconditioned traffic control system, in which interference is
not possible, thus the informationsystem is deterministic.

There are three concepts involved the problem of interference:
- the P-job
- the version of information in the register processor
- the traffic rules be described in P-processors

The P-job associated with a register processor can be of three different types:
- A P-job which only inspects information in the register
- A P-job in the register. The new information is the result of a new observation
  of an object or the result of a transformation. The existing information of an

object is never "overwritten" by <u>new</u> information of that object
- If the existing information is not correct, a correction actions has to be started, thus introducing a type of P-job which can rectify the incorrect information, probably by overwriting.
The correction actions can be considered as a replay of real-life history.

A P-job uses one and only one version of information.
A add-type P-job uses also one version of information and creates a new version
which becomes available to other P-jobs at the end of the P-JOB.

The interference of information is solved by the postulate that P-jobs never will
interfere.
It is obvious that the concept of version allows simultaneous use of information
by P-jobs of the inspect type, in combination with P-jobs of the adding type.
Simultanity of P-jobs of the adding type, on the same information could be solved
in several ways. The discussion on those solutions is not in the scope of this
paper. The solution is defined by means of P-processors which act as traffic control processors.
We will conclude with a scetch of a register processing subsystem to illustrate
the above mentioned concepts.

Example

*A general picture of the traffic, around a register processor,
is indicated by the connecting lines between the register processor and the "new", transformation, and inspect processors.*

*As more processors of a certain type are connected with the
register processor, the connectors of the register processor are
extended with processors which act as traffic controllers, with
connectors for each individual processor.*
The functions of the control processors could be described as:

*A: sequencing of the P-jobs of the inspect type according to the
priorities defined for each connector.*

*B: sequencing of the P-jobs of the add type, in which interference
of the P-jobs is prohibited.*

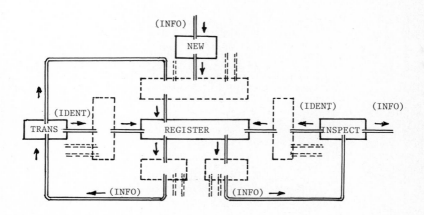

6. BIBLIOGRAPHY

(Bertels, Nauta 74)   C.P. Bertels; D. Nauta
                           The meaning of model in sciences (Dutch)
                           Wetenschappelijke Uitgeverij, Amsterdam 1974

(Bosak 62)   Codasyl development Committee
                           (Language Structure Group)
                           An Information Algebra
                           CACM 5/4/190-204, April 1962

(Brinch Hansen 73)   P. Brinch Hansen
                           Concurrent Programming Concepts
                           ACM Comput. Surveys 5/4/223-245; 1973

(Codasyl 73)   Conference on data systems Languages
                           DDL Journal of development, June 1973

(Codd 70)   Codd, E.F.
                           A relational model for large shared data banks
                           C.A.C.M. 13/6/377-387, June 1970

(Dijkstra 74)   E.W. Dijkstra
                           Guarded commands, non determinancy
                           and a calculus for the derivation of program EWD-418

(Dijkstra,   E.W. Dijkstra, C.S. Scholten
 Scholten 72)   Parallelism in Multi-record Transactions EWD-338

(Fabry 74)   R.S. Fabry
                           Capability based addressing
                           C.A.C.M. 17/7/403-412, July 1974

(Grotenhuis,
 Van den Broek 75)   F.J. Grotenhuis, J. van den Broek
                           Processors: An information system
                           structuring concept (will appear)

(Hoare 72)   C.A.R. Hoare
                           Notes on Data Structuring
                           in Structured Programming
                           O.J. Dahl; E.W. Dijkstra; C.A.R. Hoare
                           Academic Press 1972

(Kleene 52)   S.C. Kleene
                           Introduction to metamathematics par. 8, 14 and 15
                           North-Holland Publ. Co. Amsterdam, The Netherlands 1952

(Langefors 73)   B. Langefors
                           The informatio structure of
                           a collection of e-messages
                           TRITA-IBADB 1011   1973

(Popper 36)   K.R. Popper
                           The logic of scientific discovery
                           Hutchinson of London (rev. ed. 1968)

(Zemanek 70)   H. Zemanek
                           Some Philosophical Aspects of Information Processing
                           In: The Skyline of Information Processing ed. H. Zemanek
                           North-Holland Publ. Co. Amsterdam, The Netherlands, 1971

Cross reference

The emphasis in our paper is the description of information and related problems rather than the problems concerning data-bases.
The articles in these proceedings can roughly be devided according to the foregoing point of view. Some papers deal with the object-system which is the "real world" ("enterprise" etc.) and others are more concerned with "data-base" as an object-system, which could be seen as already an abstraction of the real world.

A cross-reference is made taking into account those papers which are in some way directly connected to our concepts.

G. Nijssen : the requirements put on future DB-systems

R. Peebles e.a. : the first paragraphs dealing with a model for data-bases

R. Durchholz : his approach, see also the phenomenological facet

M. Senko : the paragraphs dealing with the real world realm and the info-logical level

E. Falkenberg : his paragraph concerning the foundations of the method

J. Ruchti : related are the paragraphs on components of meaning. Moreover there exists a remarkable correspondence between his "contexts" and our abstractions and structured information

G. Bracchi e.a. : seems to be a compromise between an "information approach" and todays computer restriction

E. Benci e.a. : the paragraphs dealing with the foundations, the design methodology, especially the abstractions in data structures called the global way of considering the data and processes

P. Hall e.a. : seems to have a lot of similarities with our paper

H. Weber : we remark some relationship with the paragraph on data-semantics

L. Kalinichenko : we recognize some correspondences between his 4-level approach and our paper

T. Steel : apart from his formalism there seems to be a relationship with respect to the information model as is described in our paper.

Modelling in Data Base Management Systems, G.M. Nijssen, (ed.)
North Holland Publishing Company, 1976

CONCEPTS FOR THE DESIGN OF A
CONCEPTUAL SCHEMA

E. Benci★, F. Bodart★★,
H. Bogaert★★, A. Cabanes★★★

The studies and researches on data bases concerned chronologically
the following topics :
- Definition and setting-up of large files manipulation software.
- Definition and setting-up of DBMS involving the automatic manage-
ment of certain information properties (CODASYL, SOCRATE).
- Information theoretical studies involving the logical-physical
independence notion, and the associated languages (CODD, DELOBEL,
NEUHOLD, DATE & HOPEWELL).
Now, there is a trend toward including the preliminary part of
the system analysis in the data base design itself. This paper is
within this framework :
- Methods for description of an information set independent of
any access structure and software.
- Methods for description of evolution rules of an information set.
The description language of the users sub-structures is not considered, neither is the manipulation language (except for a few
rules in the examples).
Such a description tool should be a necessary preliminary to the
realization of any design tool of a data base system. It must
also be considered an important part of a "system analysis and
design language". Indeed, it is on the one hand the means for expressing the synthesis of the systems analysis and design phase,
and on the other hand the initial frame of reference for the implementation studies.

I. THE CONCEPTUAL ORGANIZATION AS THE RESULT OF THE ANALYSIS PROCESS

We call *conceptual organization* the result of the system analysis and design
phase. This result is a complete (as complete as possible) image of the organization phenomena of interest which will be represented by the information system.
The specific object of this paper is to define the formalism allowing the description of the conceptual organization. This could lead to a broader approach of the
conceptual structure included within the conceptual organization than those generally developed in the literature [2], [20]. Indeed, let us consider the ANSI/
SPARC definition of the conceptual schema.
"It represents the enterprise's view of the structure it is attempting to model in
the data base. This view is that which is informally invoked when there is a dis-
pute between the user and the programmer over exactly what is meant by program
specifications".
In this statement two problems can be emphasized :
- the conceptual schema as an integrated view and a bridge between the external
schema and the internal schema.
- this integrated view as the result of an analysis and design process.
In this paper the second problem is chosen to be focussed.

★   I.R.I.A. - Paris
★★ Institut d'Informatique - Namur (Belgium)
★★★ Conservatoire National des Arts et Métiers - Paris and Institut d'Informatique,
    Namur (Belgium).

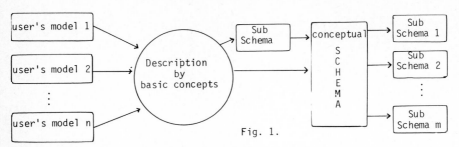

Fig. 1.

The users perceive the real world by means of models (cfr. fig. 1) : mathematical models, logical models, analogic models, descriptive models, etc. The information of each model can be *described* by basic concepts such as : entities, associations and properties.

At a *data* level, the information content structured by the previous basic concepts has to be formally represented. The conceptual schema aims at describing users' models associated with a given reality (for instance an enterprise or a subset of it).

Generally, sub-schemata (or external schemata) are deduced from the conceptual schemata. But, there are often sub-schemata that will exist before the design (or re-design) of the conceptual schemata.

The conceptual structure describes the following elements

$$
\text{Conceptual organization}
\begin{cases}
\text{- Conceptual structure}
\begin{cases}
\text{- Conceptual data base} \\
\text{- Integrity constraints}
\end{cases} \\
\\
\text{- Evolution rules}
\end{cases}
$$

The conceptual structure contains the description of the data set (conceptual data base) and of their properties (integrity constraints).

The evolution rules describe the set of operations that modify the state of the data base ; in this respect, they describe the interaction of the information system with the environment.

The description of a conceptual structure with the help of a given language is called a conceptual schema.

A rough architecture of the system is depicted in   figure 2 where it can be observed that :

(i)   there is a mapping between the conceptual structure and the access structure. (we call internal schema the description of the access structure with the help of a language.)

(ii)   the integrity constraints which are described from the conceptual data base are mapped, on the one hand, onto internal procedures of the DBMS and, on the other hand, onto part of application programs.

(iii)   the evolution rules are mapped onto application programs.

(iv)   the users' substructures can be deduced either from the conceptual structure or from the access structure.

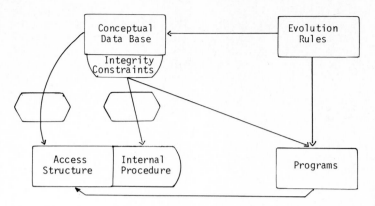

Fig. 2.

The roles associated with the conceptual organization are the following :
- Informational model of the real world.
- Reference model for the system analysis and design, and for the data base imple-
  mentation.
- Reference element toward implementation.
- Documentation tool of the data base and reference element for the users at the
  time of operation of the information system.

II. REAL WORLD MODELLING

The a priori of focusing on the conceptual structure as the result of an analysis
and design process leads to starting to structure the information as it is perceived
in the real world.
Afterwards, the structure of information obtained will be integrated and represented by the conceptual schema.

1. Real world concepts

We will call *real world objects* a set of things whose behaviour can be observed
through stimuli. The objects are defined relative to these stimuli. We will call
perceived real world the set of models or representations that helps to conceive,
structure and control the real world objects. On the one hand "immediate experience, real life" have their own *representation* systems ; on the other hand experience is structured or theorized and leads to more formal *representations* where
the syntax as well as the vocabulary are highly standardised, simpler and more rigorous. We assigned to the *conceptual model* the purpose of representing the perceived real world in terms of information. i.e. :
- as far as the computer scientist or the implementor is concerned this means the
  information as what is giving shape (*) to a certain knowledge but yet remains
  distinct of it,
- as far as the individual within the organization is concerned, the conceptual
  model will be the expression of his tool-language.

The conceptual model is thus an *interface* between an analyzed structure and an implemented structure. The content of it has a different meaning for the computer
scientist and for the organization.
- (i)   The representations handled by the individuals in the organization (i.e. the
        perceived real world) belong both to real life and to various theoretical
        models. Therefore, it is not easy to have an integrating view of information
        in the perceived real world.

(*) ARSAC, J. : La science informatique, Paris, Dunod, 1970.

This difficulty is remedied by the use of standard models and tool-languages that every organization tends to build (Accounting model, professional language, ...)

(ii) The representations the implementors work on are not of the same nature. Here, the form of   information is important as well as the rules for derivation of the formal relations between them.

Therefore, and certainly as a starting point, it is important to use a description tool of the conceptual organization, namely a formalism, which is as *neutral* as possible both from the semantic and implementation point of view.
In order to show it we shall consider two models :
- a set of concepts which underlie the basic structure of the perceived real world.
- the formalism used for the conceptual organization.
The mapping of the former onto the latter   is intended to show the interaction of the perceived real world structure (the semantical aspects) and its representation.

2. The basic structures of the real world

We assume that the immediate experience of the real world leads people to recognize that it may be completely described with entities, properties and associations between these entities (*).
It is beyond our scope to establish the criteria and the rules by which one can decide what is an entity and what is a property in the real world. People embedded in the organization decide for it and are more able for the commodity of his control to recognize something as an entity or, on the contrary, as a property.

2.1. The basic elements of the perceived real world

We will consider, for the reason developed above, a minimum number of concepts to structure the real world :

- *Entity* : An entity is what an individual or group (e.g. : an organization, a firm, a group of scientists,...) sees as a *whole* having an existence of its own. (As a system or element of a system, an entity is characterized by : a set of quantitative and qualitative properties, and a permanent behaviour ; the number of properties and the permanency of the behaviour being function of the level of resolution.
  Examples : A client, a product, a plant, ...

- *Association*: An association is a set of two or more entities where every one plays a given role. An association may possess different properties. The existence of an association is contingent on the existence of the entities it relates.
  Examples : "Owner" is an association between the entities "person" and "vehicle". "Order line" is an association between an "order" and a certain "product".

(*) The basic concepts used to describe the perceived real world will be taken as axioms but are none the less justified by the following points :

  1) They are based on common sense (structuring the real world is nothing else than identifying entities, associations between these entities, and properties of these entities).

  2) The theory of systems which claims to describe with great generality the models of the real world is based on the same concepts (while the names are different) e.g. [17].

  3) Predicate calculus relies on similar concepts [16]. Let us mention that this approach of describing the perceived real world was already proposed (though with some differences) by Langefors [18] and by Sundgren [23], and was also retained in [12].

- *Property* : A property value belonging to an entity or an association is a quality that the individuals attribute to this entity or this association. The existence of the attributed property values is contingent on the existence of the entity or the association concerned.
Example : A property value of my pen is to write in blue color or to be very cheap. For an association : the quantity of an order line.

2.2. Concepts of types

Entities, properties, associations are the basic concepts which underlie the agregate concepts of types. We will simply define :
- *Type of entities* : it is a *set* of entities (as defined supra).
- *Type of properties* : it is a *set* of properties. The definition space of this set is always a set of entities, and/or associations referred to by the set or properties.
- *Type of associations* : it is a *set* of associations. The definition space of this set is always the set(s) of entities referred to by the set of associations.
One of the aims of an analysis and design methodology is precisely to develop the ways by which these sets shall be determined.

2.3. Identification of basic elements of the perceived real world

Every concept that has been pointed out is generally identified and designated by a name in the real world. Usually as far as representation is concerned we assume that the name of an entity in the real world is a property of this entity. Yet, sometimes there will be no specific identification in the organization or there can be several different names (synonyms). This will raise some problems in the representation process of the real world concepts.

2.4. Temporal and spatial content of the basic elements

The entities, properties, and associations of the real world have implicit or explicit spatio-temporal specifications in the organization. The temporal and spatial *location* will be considered first, the temporal and spatial *dimension* of the properties coming after. (It is important to mention that these spatio-temporal specifications should lead to checking the underlying integrity constraints).

a) Location in space and time

While the location in space does not make problems, certain ambiguities do shroud the temporal location. The latter has a different nature if we consider
(i) the existence duration or validity duration of a basic element,
(ii) the date at which something or some events are observed in the real world.

Observation date

In order to analyse or control a system in the real world, the observation dates of the phenomena are taken into account. In fact, the dating is necessary since in general the observation or the control of real processes is not realized continuously (or on line). It should be noted that the dating considered here is quite a different problem from both the scheduling of the implemented system activities and the date of creation of an entity in the real world.
Generally, a specific date is associated with a property but exceptionnally one date only can be attached to an entity when all its properties are always observed at the same date.

Existence duration or validity duration of a basic element

Another kind of temporal measure is the duration of existence of an entity and an association. This duration comes straight forward from the definition of the entity - which states the existence of the entity - The existence duration can be given partially either by a period or by a date of creation ; completely by the

date of creation and the period or by the date of creation and the date of destruc-
tion of the entity or the association.
It is clear that the existence of a property value related to an entity (or an
association) is the existence of the entity but that the property value can have
a specific validity duration in the real world less than the existence duration.
(e.g. : the price of a product is valid for three months or the oak is green during
spring and summer).

b) The temporal dimension

All quantitative property values are defined by dimensional characteristics and
by the units in which the value is measured.
Example : Speed = km/hour has as dimension L divided by T i.e. unit of length by
unit of time. Acceleration : L divided by T^2.
Time   is an important dimension, it defines traditional concepts such as :
State variable i.e. without temporal dimension but located in time (cfr. supra),
Flow variable i.e. variable with an explicit temporal dimension together with a
location in time. Example : annual overhead costs.

III. THE CONCEPTUAL MODEL : REPRESENTATION OF THE REAL WORLD

Three aspects will be successively considered in the conceptual organization :
data structure, integrity constraints, evolution rules.

1. Data structure

1.1. Formalism for a conceptual organization

Several formalisms can be used to describe the conceptual organization, especially
as far as the conceptual structure is concerned. (e.g. [7], [11], [13], [14]).
Numerous recent works have shown that the formalism of the relation, by its simplicity and its generality, is remarkably adequate to describe the static state of a
"conceptual" data base. This is not the case when describing its evolution. To
this purpose, the notion of relation family is introduced :
R_1^1 .... R_1^i is a series of relations defined on the same components, indexed by
$i \in I$ and written $(R_1^i | i \in I)$. If R^i is defined on the sets A, B, C, it is quite clear
that the families $(A^i | i \in I)$, $(B^i | i \in I)$ and $(C^i | i \in I)$ have to be defined.

An operation on a relation is a function f_j^i such that $R^{i+1} = f_j^i(R^i)$ and R^{i+1} are
obtained either :

- by addition of a n-tuple to R^i
- by suppression of a n-tuple from R^i
- by modification of a n-tuple of R^i
- by equating with R^i (identity operation).

A *conceptual data base* B^i is a set of relations indexed by the same value $i \in I$.
$$B^i = \{R_1^i, R_2^i, \ldots, R_q^i\}$$
A conceptual data base B^{i+1} is obtained by applying to each relation $R_n^i \in B^i$
one of the possible operations
$$B^{i+1} = \{R_1^{i+1}, R_2^{i+1}, \ldots R_q^{i+1}\} = \{f_1^i(R_1^i), f_2^i(R_2^i), \ldots, f_p^i(R_q^i)\}$$
Nota : A relation R_h^i can be empty.
We will call :
(i) *type* of relation, of set... a family of relations, sets, ...

(ii) *evolution rules* the definition of the allowed operations on a base B^i.

1.2. Representation of entities, associations and properties

If it is relatively easy to accept the concept of entity as a basic element of the model of the perceived real world, this is not the case when we want to represent this concept in an information model. As a matter of fact the identification and designation of an entity can only be done by the property values related to it. Further, the existence itself of an entity can only be represented by the existence of the set of property values. This same argument can be transposed to the associations. Therefore, the existence of an entity or association is represented in the conceptual structure as a n-tuple of a relation. Nevertheless, an identification problem arises since several n-tuples could contain the same data in one relation.
Example : The relation PERSON (NAME, CH.NAME, TOWN) is ambiguous since it could contain two Smiths, Peter, Washington.

An unambiguous identification mechanism is necessary to represent the real world entities in the conceptual structure.
Accordingly :

- If there is in the real world some property which identifies unambiguously an entity,   then   this entity could be identified in the conceptual structure by the data representing the property.

- On the other hand, there are some entities of the real world which cannot be identified by a property (real world concept) without ambiguity ; in order to take this case into account, the concept of *s-entity* will be created in the conceptual structure. (The *s* indicating that this concept is a substitute for the entity in the conceptual structure.) Basically, an *s-entity* represents the *existence* of a real world entity. A *type of s-entity* will be a component of the types of relations declared in the conceptual structure. (The s-entity is similar to the concept of surrogate in : "Relations and Entities", by P. Hall, J. Owlett and S. Todd.) The set of values of the component is not known in the organization, but it is given by a mechanism described in the conceptual data base (*).

Summarily, the conceptual structure is made up of three types of basic elements :
- the type of *data,*
- the type of *s-entity,* and
- the type of *relation.*

The real world basic concepts are perceived by the types of properties one of which is the existence property. The types of properties are represented by types of data and types of s-entities for the existence. The types of data and types of s-entities are organized by types of relations.

1.3. Designation in a conceptual structure

The problem of representing the perceived real world is more precisely expressed when the concept of designation is introduced.

(*) In an implementation model a data base key corresponds to the concept of s-entity. [1], [5], [14].

- Definition : *Designation* is defined as the specification of an element in a set
  or a subset belonging to the given set. This specification can be effected in
  one of the following three ways :

  - *Designation in the organization*, (or ORG-DES), is the specification of a set
    name known in the organization and of one or several values of this set. If it
    is accepted that in the organization the elements of a certain set are codi-
    fied (e.g. character string), then a ORG-DES is composed of a set name and one
    or several codes of the elements. Those are generally called constant, immediate
    value, descriptor, etc.

  - *Designation in the base*, (or BASE-DES) is the specification of one or several
    elements of a set by the definition of its position relative to the other in-
    formation of the conceptual data base.
    Such a designation requires a designation language which depends on the forma-
    lism used to describe the data base.
    Example : We shall consider the relation :
            PRODUCT (PN, DT, P)
    such that the n-tuple (pn, dt, p) $\in$ PRODUCT if the price p of the product pn
    was defined at date dt. The identifier of the relation is (PN, DT). An ORG-DES
    is (PN, 1235) and designates a number (1235) of product (PN). A BASE-DES is :
            {np | $\exists$ p [(p = 1,000) $\wedge$ PRODUCT (np, ., p)]}
    which designates a set of product numbers for which the unit price was or is
    equal to 1000. We note that $\exists$ p [.... = 1000] is a ORG-DES.

  - We define *designation by generating function*, as the designation by a set name
    and a function name.
    This function applied to a set name has as image one or several elements of
    this set. Another parameter of the function is the index i of the data base,
    because, for different values of i, the function provides different elements
    from the set. Such designation will be named GEN-DES.
    Example : Consider the relation INVOICE (IN, TOT) such that (in, tot) $\in$ IN-
    VOICE if the invoice with number *in* has the total *tot*.
    The identifier is IN.
    If it is wanted to create a couple (in, tot), and to add it to INVOICE,*tot* and
    in must be known.
    Let us assume that the invoice numbers are automatically generated by a pro-
    cedure applied to the base and called NEW-IN.
    The parameters of NEW-IN will be "IN" and i (i is implicit). If (TOT, 1025)
    is an ORG-DES of an element of TOT, then (NEW-IN (IN), (TOT, 10125)) is the
    designation of the set where NEW-IN (IN) is a designation by a generating func-
    tion.

1.4. Basic elements of the conceptual structure

The designation concepts will be used here to define the basic elements of the
conceptual structure.

- *Type of data*
  A type of data is a family of sets an element of which can be designated by
  ORG-DES, BASE-DES or GEN-DES. The values in those sets are known by the data
  base system as well as by the host organization. A data type has one or several
  names (synonyms). It can possess one or more formats in the organization.

- *Type of s-entity*
  A type of s-entity is a family of sets the elements of which can be designated
  by BASE-DES or GEN-DES. Individually, the elements of these sets can only be
  'known' by the data base.
  The type of s-entity of the conceptual structure corresponds to the type of entity of the real world by :

(i) the generating function of the s-entity type,
(ii) the name(s) of the s-entity type.

- *Type of relation*
A type of relation is a family of relations the components of which are data-
types or s-entity-types. This is the only means chosen to represent the semantic
association of the perceived real world.
A relation type is characterized by a unique name (It does not seem necessary
to define synonyms).

1.5. Time representation in the conceptual structure

The introduction of time at the conceptual level leads to distinguish the following problems :
- the representation of the real world time,
- the time representation of the evolution of the conceptual structure.
The latter, the information system dynamics, is treated by the design of the evolution rules that are mentioned in the following. (cfr. III.) The former is concerned with the temporal structure of the perceived real world which was already considered. Its representation in the context of the conceptual structure basic elements does not raise particular problems :
- The representation of the dimension and the units of measure of properties can
  easily be done by introducing the data type "measure unit" in a relation.
- The representation of the dating is related to the representation of an entity,
  association, and property. This can be done in the conceptual structure by a
  data type.
- The same is true for the existence and the validity duration.

It must be noticed that the links between the existence and the validity duration
of the entities, association and properties will be stated as integrity constraints.
Example : Assume the relations :
        PRODUCT (PN, DT1, P)
and CUST-SALES-VA (CUST N, PER, SAL-VA).
The key of the first relation is PN, DT1 pointing out that there are several versions of a same product. It could be important to know that DT1 is a date and P is
the associated data. This is also important in the second relation where PER indicates the validity period of the sales-value associated with the customer number
CUST N.
We will notice that the introduction of time in a DDL raises no specific problems.
For a DML, the syntactical problems have already been investigated [2], [7].
Further, if the DML can effect the classical operations (ordinal, cardinal) it will
allow the manipulation of time. Nevertheless, for chronological data bases life
could be eased by developing specific operators both at the DDL level and at the
DML level.

2. Integrity constraints

The development of data base systems puts an increasing emphasis on security
and integrity constraints. Several factors explain this increasing interest. A
first factor lies in the fact that the setting-up of a data base normally introduces a time delay between, on the one hand, the data collection and storage activities and, on the other hand, the processing of the application program. A
second factor lies in the integration of multiple files in order to limit their
dispersion, the data redundancies, the maintenance difficulties and the inconsistency of the information system.
This leads to set the problem of the "intrinsic" validity of the data available to
the user. The intrinsic character comes from the fact that the validity here considered depends neither on the operating reliability nor on ill-will ; it depends
on the integrity constraints (logical constraints) pertaining to the data and the
processing.

2.1. Definition

In the conceptual structure, the integrity constraints are predicates defined on elements of the conceptual structure in order to provide the user with correct data as output of his applications programs (insofar as those are syntactically and semantically correct).The integrity constraints limit both the set of possible values that types of data or types of relations can include, and the set of possible operations on the data base.
The correct data are those which must conform to some properties of the real world pointed out by the user in terms of his own model of the real world.

The problem of measuring the validity degree raises important questions beyond the scope of this paper. Indeed, the enforcement of the integrity constraints cannot guarantee a complete validity if only because the constraints themselves rely on data. They simply aim at reducing the chance of errors. We will give a few comments about this definition :

- It is not restrictive as to the nature of the properties. For example, it does not allow to discriminate between a condition relative to the format of a data, and a condition expressing under a complex algebraic formulation the set of the possible values of the data.

- What is generally called integrity constraints refers either to the control procedures which are part of an application program in the conventional approach (as compared with data bases) or to those which are verified in the organization. In the data base approach, the numerous controls, the interactions between these and their a priori setting-up must increase the consistency of the data base and, hence, that of the information system.

- The integrity constraints are not relevant for the updating of data only : any evolution rule which may be applied to the base must refer to them.

- The way of expressing an integrity constraint is in close relationship with the model chosen for describing the data structure. That model will certainly have to be completed by additional language elements in terms of its possibilities.

- The problem of integrity constraints in the framework or the conceptual structure will be confined essentially to the definition of a tool (language) for expressing them. Indeed the constraints are specified by the analysis of the real world, but their enforcement resorts either to the organization or to the system. The description of the integrity constraints must, however, include the aspects that will bear on the implementation conditions (response time, interaction of constraints, deadlock conditions, ...)

2.2. Description of the integrity constraints

In the following, the analysis is not intended to be comprehensive. It only aims at characterizing the most frequent integrity constraints.
A first approach will not take into account the space-time structure within which terms of a predicate describing an integrity constraint are expressed. As far as a static data base is concerned, it must be totally consistent at any time. The examination of the integrity constraints, thus, is limited to the analysis of different types of expressed conditions without reference to the conditions under which the enforcement of the constraints is processed.

a) Integrity constraints defined on a type of data

(i)   Constraints concerning the possible values of a type of data, when these values do not depend on other types of data in the base. There can be different conditions defining the set of the possible values of a type of data, e.g. :
        - enumeration of the set of values, possibly including the unknown value and the non-existent value.

- definition of the boundaries of the set.
- definition of the generating function ("computing function") of the set of
  values. That function could be an algebraic expression, the parameters of
  which should be specified (e.g. : smoothing parameter for time series).

(ii)   Specification of the format(s) of a type of data.
       The same data can be coded in several ways within the same organization.
       These different ways must be described regardless of which will be chosen
       for the access structure. When this is decided upon (a problem we are not
       interested in) ... the necessary transcoding will be defined by examining
           different external codings and their use within certain "evolution rules".
       The specification of the format - as usually understood (binary, decimal,
       alphanumerical format) - together with the definition of the set of the pos-
       sible values provide a general specification of the format of the type of
       data.

(iii) Cardinality
       This type of constraints specifies the number of possible values (given
       maximum, minimum, average ...) of a type of data in the conceptual base.
       This constraint may be a parameter for the physical implementation.

It is sometimes interesting to discriminate between the integrity constraints defined on a single type of data used in several types of relations (e.g. constraints
concerning the values of the turnover) and the integrity constraints related to
a type of data belonging to one type of relation. (e.g. constraints on the turnover as defined in the framework of the relation "Exported Products"). The second
case could be regarded as a constraint concerning a type of data depending on a
type of relation.

b) Integrity constraints defined on a type of s-entity

In the set of integrity constraints defined on types of data one can only retain
those concerned with cardinality. Indeed, it follows from the definition of the
s-entity that the formats as well as the values taken by the s-entities are not
known in the organization.

c) Integrity constraints defined on a type of relation

(i)   Defining a type of relation is *in se* an integrity constraint, as it implies
       that any type of data is a component of at least one type of relation, and
       therefore, any updating of the data base should verify the definition of
       the relations. This tautological property corresponds to the "relational
       consistency" property of the ANSI/SPARC report.

(ii)   One can specify as a constraint that a sub-list of the list of the compo-
       nents of a relation are mandatory components of the relation : the values of
       these components may not be unknown.

(iii) Other types of constraints : specifying that the values of a type of data of
       a relation is conditional to the values of one or more other types of data.
       The modes of that specification may be similar to those mentioned for the
       values of a type of data, namely : by enumeration, by definition of the
       boundaries, by   definition of the computing function.

Example : consider the type of relation : CUSTOMER

CUSTOMER(CUST-NR, ORD-NR, PROD-NR, Q, P, LV, GSACO, IGSA, MG)
Definition of the types of data :
        CUST-NR : customer number   Q : quantity
        ORD-NR : order number   P : price
        PROD-NR : product number   LV : Value of an order line

```
GS-CUST-ORD : Gross sales per customer per order (monetary terms)
TGS-CUST : total gross sales per customer
MG        : margin per customer.
```
Knowing the sets of the possible values of Q and P it will be possible to obtain
the sets of the possible values of LV, GS-CUST-ORD, TGS-CUST and MG by using the
following functions :
```
value of a line  =  quantity  x  price
GS-CUST-ORD      =  Sum of the LV of an order
TGS-CUST         =  Sum of the GS-CUST-ORD of a customer
MG               =  TGS-CUST  x  0.3
```
Each of these functions defines an integrity constraint applied to one *part* of the
relation.
For an *occurrence* of the relation, it would also be possible to define integrity
constraints specifying :
the set of the prices of a given product :
    if PROD-NR = pro *then* p ∈ {100, 125, 130}
the set of the quantities of a given product that may be ordered
    if PROD-NR = pro *then* min quantity = 10
                               max quantity = 15

(iv) The constraints of cardinality
      As to the relation itself one may define cardinality constraints that spe-
      cify the number of n-tuples of the relations (given number, minimum, maxi-
      mum, average number), conditional or not to the cardinality of one or seve-
      ral other relations.
      As to one part of a relation one may define cardinality constraints that
      specify the number of possible values of a component of the relation, de-
      pending on the values of one or more other components of that relation. For
      instance, one could specifiy a maximum number of ordered products per order.
      Two important particular cases should be noted : on the one hand, the cons-
      traints specifying a functional dependency between components, and on the
      other hand, constraints pointing to the sub-list of components of a relation
      defining the *key* or *index* of the relation (the second is a special case of
      the first).
      These conditional cardinality constraints are easily expressed by means of
      the projection operator of a relation on its components and on values.
      We will note :
      - that these constraints are expressed either on the entire relation, or
        some part of it, or on a single n-tuple of the relation.
      - that the projection operator of a relation on some components and/or value
        of it allows to specify the parts of a relation.

d) Integrity constraints defined between relations

(i)   Specification of values
      Example : Consider the relations :
           WAREHOUSE (WH-NR, STORAGE CAPACITY)
               key : WH-NR : Warehouse number
           INVENTORY (WH-NR, PROD-NR, STORAGE-CAPACITY, QT-ON-HAND)
               key : WH-NR, PROD-NR
      Two integrity constraints could be defined between the two relations : a
      first one specifying that the storage capacity of a product in a warehouse
      is a function of the storage capacity of the warehouse : a second one, spe-
      cifying that the total sum of the warehouse capacities on all products is at
      most equal to the whole capacity of the warehouse.

(ii) The constraints of *cardinality*
      Example : Consider the relations :
           SALESMAN (SALESMAN-NR, NAME, AREA, PROD-NR, GROSS-SALES)
           CUSTOMER (CUST-NR, NAME, TOWN)
```
```

A constraint of cardinality can be defined stating that the number of sales-men is less than the number of customers :

CARD (*Projection* Relation : SALESMAN *on* Domain : SALESMAN-NR)
≤ CARD (*Projection* Relation : CUSTOMER *on* Domain : CUST-NR)

(iii) Constraints of *inclusion*

This type of constraint specifies that the values of a component (type of data) of a relation are included in the set of values of a component of an-other relation.

In particular such a constraint allows to express the MANDATORY clause of the CODASYL report.

Example : Consider the relations :

CUSTOMER (CUST-NR, NAME, TOWN)
CUST-ORD (ORD-NR, CUST-NR, PROD-NR, Q, ...)

A constraint of cardinality can be defined expressing that the cardinal of the set {CUST-NR} of the relation CUST-ORD is at most equal to the cardinal of the set {CUST-NR} of the CUSTOMER relation :

CARD (*Projection* Relation : CUST-ORD *on* component : CUST-NR)
⊂ CARD (*Projection* Relation : CUSTOMER *on* component : CUST-NR)

This implies that a customer order may be recorded in the base if it is re-lated to a customer. In the case of a new customer, the updating of the CUSTOMER relation will be processed before the recording of the order.

(iv) Constraints of equality and other constraints of comparison.

These are similar to the constraint of inclusion. It will be noted that the sets to be compared are obtained by the application of relational operators such as projection, composition, ...

e) Constraints of confidentiality

We will restrict ourselves to outline the possibilities offered by the relational model for expressing the confidentiality constraints. Four sets of elements form the bases of these constraints :
- the set F1 of the persons (and, possibly, the application programs) having auth-orized access to the data of the conceptual data base.
- the set F2 of the possible operations on the base :
   F2 = {read, add, modify, suppress, read and add, read and modify, ..., no action} ;
- the set of data which can be accessed. The whole data base, a type of relation, a n-tuple, ...
- the set of conditions : a condition is a predicate that must be verified in or-der to gain access. It is nothing else than an integrity constraint in a dynamic environment.
   These conditions could be function of :
   - the values of the components of the relation to be accessed,
   - the values of the components of other relations,
   - the parameters, external to the procedure,
   - the use of the operations.
The confidentiality constraints can be represented by the relational model.
- To this aim, we will define a type of relation for each type of operation. The components of these relations would be, on the one hand, the set of the identi-fiers of those persons related to the operation type, and on the other hand the set of the data involved in this type of operation. The elements of this set would be identified as follows :
   - conceptual data base : conceptual data base name,
   - sub-set of the base   : sub-set name,
   - a type of relation   : relation name,
   - n-tuple of a relation : relation name/value of the n-tuple identifier,
   - part of a relation   : relation name/names of components and values on which the relation has to be projected.
- the expression of the conditions will be made with the help of a property des-cription language.

The conditions imposed on the context in which the data are accessed and on the use of these operations refer to the events characterizing a procedure. In fact, these conditions place the confidentiality constraints in a dynamical context.

3. Consistency context and evolution rules

For instance let us consider an integrity constraint expressing that the total sales for a customer must be equal to the sum of the amounts invoiced. This constraint does not have to be checked at all times. It could be checked only at the *end of a period*, when the client's *balance* is computed : in other words this constraint has to be checked at a given time (or over a given period), and is conditional to one or more specific application(s).

This implies that the consistency of the base does not have to be absolute. So, the span of verification of the conditions may be limited in time to the consistency context of an application.

Let there be the predicates p_1, p_2, ... p_q, applied to all/some parts of the data base or of the host organization elements. Different values of p_1, p_2, ... p_q and the value of P determined by $p_1 \wedge p_2 \wedge p_3 \wedge ... \wedge p_q$ have been drawn in the following figure for different values of I (index of time).

	1	2	3	4		i			I
	T	T	F	T		T			p^1
	T	F	T	T		T			p^2
	T	T	T	T		T			p^3
	T	T	F	F		T			p^q
	T	F	F	F		T			P

If P is true, the data base is *consistent*, if not, the data base is partially consistent with respect to the true predicates.

For a particular application, it is not required that all predicates be true. A given subset of predicates assigned to that application (or group of application) is called the *consistency context* of the application : only the predicates in this subset must be true.

Example :
- Consider the applications :
  - product prices updating,
  - computing of the invoices for the current orders.
- The types of data are the following :
  - OR-NR : Order number   STATUS : $\begin{smallmatrix}0\\1\end{smallmatrix}$ indicator
  - CUST-NR : Customer number
  - PROD-NR : product number   P : price
  - PROD-NR : product number   GS-CUST-PR : Gross sales per customer per
  - DT1 = DT2 = DT3 : Dates (in days)   product
  - TOT : Total of an invoice
  - PER : Period
  - Q : quantity
  - P : unit price
- The types of entity
  - LN : line-number
- The relations :
  - CUR-ORD (ORD-NR, LN, PROD-NR, Q) : current order line.
  - CUR-CUST-ORD (ORD-NR, CUST-NR, DT1, STATUS) which relates the current order numbers to the customer number, the date of ordering, and the indicator STATUS

(1 if the order is already processed and 0 if not).
- PROD (PROD-NR, DT2, P) which gives the price per unit for every product and every date of update.
- INV (INV-NR, ORD-NR, DT2, DT3, TOT) which associates the number INV-NR of an invoice with the order number ORD-NR, as well as with the ordering date,the invoicing date and the invoice total.

Further, one considers : CT (DT, NC) where (dt, nb) $\in$ CT if nb is the number of updates at the date dt. (This number may be zero but all the dates are existent.) On the other hand, it is assumed that the organization rules force us to compute the invoices if the update of the product prices has been processed. The consistency context of the updating application for the day d is :

$$P_1 \land \forall \, dt \, [\, CT(dt, .) \qquad dt < d \,].$$

P_1 is a condition not described here and the second part means the updating has not yet had to be processed.
The consistency context of the invoicing application is :

$$P_1 \land dt \, [\, CT(dt, .) \quad dt = d \,]$$

The second part of each of the two contexts is contradictory with that of the other.

The integrity constraints can be classified in three groups with regard to their processing as required by a given application : the external, internal and mixed integrity constraints.
The *external* integrity constraints are those which are applied only to the entry parameters of the application, namely : to the data which are necessary to the application and not included in the base.
Consider for example the ordering procedure.
For an order k, the parameters of the procedure will be the four-tuples : (k, line numbers, product number, quantity). An external integrity constraint will verify that there are not two lines within a same order with the same line number and the same product number. The integrity constraints relative to the format of the parameters are also external constraints.
The *internal* integrity constraints are those which are applied to the data already recorded in the base ; they must be verified at the time of processing of the application. Example : Before computing a customer balance, one should have checked that the gross sales figure for this customer over a given period is equal to the sum of the amounts invoiced. The constraint of cardinality, the constraints relative to counters, ... are other examples of internal constraints.
The *mixed* integrity constraints are applied both to the parameters of the procedure and to the data of the base. Example : When booking an order one will check that the order number is different from all the order numbers already recorded in the base. Likewise, one will check that the customer number stated in the order already exists in the base. The comparison of the current data with a recorded data constitutes another example of mixed integrity constraints.
It follows from this analysis that the dynamical aspect of the constraints does not have to be expressed in a properties description language (statical point of view) : it will be part of the procedure description. Therefore, a language will be used for the description of the evolution rules.

4. Evolution rules

The integrity constraints are actively embedded in the sequence ⟨ decision - processing of operation(s) on the data base ⟩ , either when a decision leads to the activation of a constraint, or when a constraint triggers a decision.
We will call *event* any decision which triggers the processing of an operation on the base (⋆). An event is either at rest or activated. The activation of an event

---

(⋆) Create, suppress, modify ...

can be due, either to the host organization (then it will be an *entry event*), or
to a particular state of the base. In this latter case, one will discriminate between the events which trigger the operations, being internal to the base (*internal
events*), and those which are known by the organization (called *result events*).
Let us consider again the booking procedure for a customer order. It can be illustrated by the following figure :

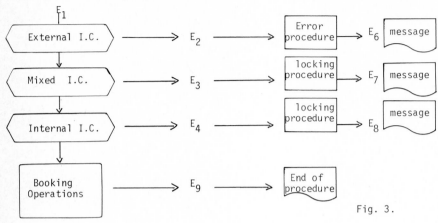

Fig. 3.

with :

External IC	: constraints on format, non-redundancies ...
Mixed IC	: existence in the base of the products ordered and the customers, etc.
Internal IC	: constraint on the solvency of the customer, authorization to trigger the procedure, ...
E_1	: entry event
E_2,E_3,E_4,E_5	: internal events
E_6,E_7,E_8,E_9	: result events

Aiming to greater generality, it is possible to define the events activated by the
organization and which only trigger procedures without interaction with the base.
These will be called *external events*. They are not directly of interest to us since
they allow to describe the organization evolution, independently from the conceptual structure. They have to be taken care of by a description formalism of the organization *sensu lato*.

Parameters : In most cases, parameters are associated with an event. For instance,
the event E (decision to create a product) is accompanied at least by a product
number (if the unit price is unknown). Hence, the event E shall come with the
triplet (a, b, c) where a is a designation of product number, b is a designation
of date, and c a designation of unit price.
In many cases, an application or procedure will be triggered by the simultaneous
activation of several events, and possibly by several groups of events.
Moreover, it has been stated that the procedure A_i will necessitate several parameters 1, ...k ..., r. The presence of the set of all the parameters is thus necessary for each group of events. Some events will have no parameter, others will
have part of the set. Let us note that the end of a procedure can also be considered as an event.
Summarily, an evolution rule can be defined from the following set of necessary
information :
- the name of the evolution rule,
- the group(s) of trigger events,
- the parameters associated with these events,

- the external integrity constraints (on the parameters),
- the internal integrity constraints (on the data of the base),
- the mixed integrity constraints,
- the expression of the consistency context,
- the event(s) induced by the application processing,
- the parameter(s) associated with these induced events,
- the elementary processing operations as such.

Accordingly, the concept of evolution rule is necessary to describe the dynamics of an information system, and in particular the dynamics of the integrity constraints. The latter's processing is necessarily executed in a context of ⟨ event - actions ⟩ sequences. The data relative to the ⟨ event - actions ⟩ sequences correspond to the temporal location properties (dating, existence and validity duration) and to the space location (★)

We limited the exposition of the evolution rules to the expression of the dynamics of the integrity constraints. However, it must be emphasized that the description of the elementary operations plays a particular role. In the same way that the conceptual model is an instrinsic description of the information independent of any implementation considerations, the evolution rules constitute an intrinsic description of the processing, independent of any operating mode (batch, real-time...)

The design methodology of an access structure as function of the conceptual structure and of the applications is substituted by an approach where the applications are first decomposed into evolution rules and operating modes. The following figure explains the parallelism of nature and design between, on the one hand, the evolution rules and the conceptual structure, and, on the other hand, the access structure and the programs. (Fig. 4.)

CONCLUSIONS

In this paper we have used a relational model to describe a conceptual schema. We have shown that this model allows to represent the three elements of the conceptual model (the data structure, the integrity constraints and the evolution rules) with a small number of concepts (the relation) and mechanisms (operations on the relations).
We have also shown that this model implicitly contains the elements of a system analysis and design methodology : the relevant concepts have been isolated - although the methodology as such was not considered - ; the elements of a description language of these concepts have been presented ; finally the definition of a global way of considering the data and the processes has been attempted.

The points still to be studied relate to the integration of this tool - or a similar one - in a unified methodology for the setting up of computerized information systems. The bridging tools - and if possible optimizing ones - between the conceptual structure and the best access structure - whatever this latter's model can be - are yet to be defined. Presently they do not exist.

Given their non-existence could it not be that the elaboration of a conceptual model will be a negative element as far as the global economy of designing and implementing a computerized information system is concerned ? Indeed this would on the one hand nearly duplicate the elaboration of the access model and on the other hand the conceptual model would not fulfill its role as a means of expression of needs. The next step will be to investigate the realm of the tools establishing a bridge from the conceptual structure to the access structures.

(★) cfr. supra II-2.4.

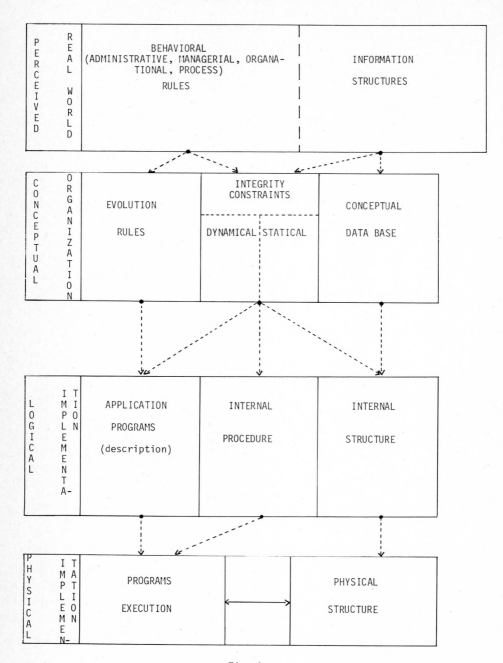

Fig. 4.

REFERENCES

[1] ABRIAL, J.R. : Data Semantics, in "Data Base Management", J.W. Klimbie and K.L. Koffeman (Ed.), North-Holland Publ. C°, 1974.

[2] ANSI/SPARC : Report on Data Base Management Systems, 1975.

[3] BRUCE, Bertram C. : A Model for Temporal References and its Application in a Question Answering Program, Artificial Intelligence 3 (1972), 1-25

[4] CABANES, A. : Cours "Banques de données", Institut d'Informatique, Namur ; Conservatoire National des Arts et Métiers, Paris, avril 1975.

[5] CODASYL : DDL Journal of Development, June 1973.

[6] CODASYL : Data Base Task Group , 1971 Report, Communications of the ACM, New York, 1971.

[7] CODD, E.F. : A Relational Model of Data for Large Shared Data Banks, Comm. ACM, 13 (1970).

[8] CODD, E.F. : Normalized Data Base Structure : A Brief Tutorial, ACM, SIGFIDET Workshop, 1971.

[9] DATE, C.J. and HOPEWELL, P. : File Definition and Logical Data Independence, IBM UK Laboratories Ltd, Hursley Park, England, May 1971.

[10] DELOBEL, C. : Contribution théorique à la conception et l'évaluation d'un système d'information appliqué à la gestion, Thèse d'Etat, Université de Grenoble, 1973.

[11] DEHENEFFE, C., HENNEBERT, H., PAULUS, W. : Relational Model for a Data Base, Proc. IFIP Congress 1974, North-Holland Publishing Company, 1022-1025.

[12] DEHENEFFE, C., HAINAUT, J.L., TARDIEU, H. : Individual Model for a Data Base, in "Data Structure Models for Information Systems", Proceedings of the International Workshop, May, 27-30, 1974, Namur, Coll. : Travaux de l'Institut d'Informatique n° 3, P.U.N., Namur, 1975.

[13] FALKENBERG, Eckard : Time-Handling in Data Base Management Systems, Internal CIS-Report 07/74.

[14] HAINAUT, J.L., LE CHARLIER, B. : An Extensible Semantic Model of Data Base and its Data Language, Proc. IFIP Congress 1974, North-Holland Publishing Company, 1026-1030.

[15] HUITS, M.H.H. : Requirements for Languages in Data Base Systems, in Douqué, B.C.M. and Nijssen, G.M.(Ed.) : Data Base Description, North-Holland/American Elsevier, Amsterdam, New York, 1975, 85-110.

[16] KLEENE, S.C. : Mathematical Logic, John Wiley & Sons, Inc., New York, 1967.

[17] KLIR, J. and VALACH, M. : Cybernetic Modelling, Illife Books Ltd, London, 1967.

[18] LANGEFORS, B. : Information Systems. Proc. IFIP Congress 1974, North-Holland Publishing Company, 1974.

[19] NIJSSEN, G.M. : Set and CODASYL Set or Coset, in Douqué, B.C.M. and Nijssen, G.M. (Ed.) : Data Base Description, North-Holland/American Elsevier, Amsterdam/New York, 1975, 1-75.

[20] NIJSSEN, G.M. : Data Base Management Language and System, March 1975 (Control Data Europe (unpublished).

[21] Introductory Report : "Data Structure Models for Information Systems", Proceedings of the International Workshop, May, 27-30, 1974, Namur. Coll. : Travaux de l'Institut d'Informatique n° 3, P.U.N., Namur, 1975.

[22] STEEL Jr., T.B. : Data Base Standardization : A Status Report, in Douqué, B.C.M. and Nijssen, G.M. (Ed.) : Data Base Description, North-Holland/American Elsevier, Amsterdam/New York, 1975, 183-198.

[23] SUNDGREN, B. : The Infological Approach in the Design of Data Bases, in "Systemeering", Ed. Lundeberg, M. and Bubenko, J. ; Studentliteratur, Lund, 1975.

[24] WANG, C.P. : Parametrization of Information System Applications, Research Report R.J. - 119, IBM. Research Laboratory, San Jose, 2973.

Modelling in Data Base Management Systems, G.M. Nijssen, (ed)
North Holland Publishing Company, 1976

RELATIONS AND ENTITIES

Patrick Hall*, John Owlett and Stephen Todd
IBM United Kingdom Scientific Centre
Neville Road, Peterlee,
County Durham, SR8 1BY, UK.

Considered as a candidate for the conceptual schema, a relational
system has many nice features.   There are however some
difficulties, particularly if keys are used and it is desired
to change them.   Such difficulties do not arise in a system
based on entities, but other problems do.   We argue that an
appropriate data model, basically relational in flavour, can
be obtained by marrying these two systems.

To do this we present an approach to relations which avoids some
of the machine oriented features of earlier relational systems;
this approach underpins the Peterlee relational system.   We then
discuss the relevant aspects of entities, and conclude by seeing
how these meet together to give a unified data model.

---

*   Current Address: British Ship Research Association,Wallsend,Tyne and Wear,UK.

1.   INTRODUCTION

This paper describes the results of a search for a data model. We have
concentrated on the conceptual schema (in the sense of the ANSI interim report
(1975)) and we do not cover the external or internal schemata.

Two candidates are considered - the relational model and the entity model - and
we show how the advantages of both can be combined into one system. In addition,
we discuss irreducible relations (following Rissanen and Delobel (1973)) and
recommend their use for the conceptual schema.

The relational model of file organization was essentially propounded by Grindley
and Stevens (1968) but it gained its main impetus from the work of Codd (1970).
It is a powerful high-level model, able to express complicated relationships in
a convenient way.   We use an improvement on the usual idea of relation, giving
a formal definition of order independent columns based on Hall, Hitchcock and
Todd (1975).

Entities were discussed in a data modelling context in the early sixties
(CODASYL (1962), Markowitz, Hausner and Karr (1963)) but, like relations,
made their impact some time later, in this case in a paper by Mealy (1967).

We have found that it is in the identification of individual objects that the
approaches display their weaknesses.   The usual relational model cannot denote
an individual object independently of its attributes.   The binary entity model
on the other hand is often forced to handle entities for which there is no
sensible parallel in the real world.

The model we propose allows the modelling of entities in an n-ary relational
framework.   Domains may be value sets (as in current relational models) or
entity sets.   The elements in entity sets are *surrogates*, which are data model
representatives of the entities of the application.   We consider an alternative
to this - the use of tuple identifiers - but conclude that it is a less suitable
solution.

Another notion introduced is that of an *irreducible* relation.   The idea is that
relations should be decomposed by projections so that each tuple in the
conceptual model represents a "basic fact" in the application.

Certain concepts appropriate in the conceptual schema are mentioned but not
fully covered.   The most important of these concerns constraints: the point is
made that if powerful constraints are to be expressed simply, the data definition
and data manipulation languages cannot be fully separated.

The paper is principally a discussion of relations at the conceptual level.   It
is realized that in both the external and internal schemata many concepts are
necessary that we reject at the conceptual level.   For example, an efficient
implementation may make use of both field and record ordering.

2.   RELATIONS

§2.1 Domains and Selectors

One of the ideas motivating the relational approach is that machine-oriented
features should not obtrude into our data model.   Consequently the order of
the records within a file or the order of the fields within a record should not
be a part of the model.   In relational terms this means that the ordering of the
tuples (or rows) and the ordering of the components (or columns) must both be
immaterial.   The first requirement is easy to satisfy - a relation is a set of
tuples and a mathematical set has no notion of ordering.   The second is a little

more difficult - traditional mathematics usually uses component numbering, and database systems usually order the columns even when attribute names are also provided.

Associated with each component there is a *domain* - the set of values which the component might take - and Codd (1970) suggested that the domain name might be used to identify the component.   This works well unless we have more than one component taking values in the same domain - in such cases the domain name must be qualified by a distinctive rôle name.   Such a system is using the domain name to do two quite different things: firstly to denote a domain of values and secondly to identify a component of a relation.

We separate these two functions completely and associate a *domain* and a *selector* with each component.   A domain is a set of possible component values, and a selector is a name which uniquely identifies its component.   A domain may be associated with many components, but a selector cannot be associated with more than one component in any given relation.

Having made this distinction we always reference a component using its selector and, in our model, do not regard the components of a relation as being ordered in any way.   This point of view, is perfectly consistent with traditional mathematical usage, as we shall see in §2.3.

Since Codd's initial paper, a variety of systems based on relational ideas have been developed, and they have confused the notions of domain and selector. Making a clear distinction (as is done in the PRTV (Todd (1976))) results, we believe, in a better understanding of relations and it has also helped in the solution of the problem known as domain-name inheritance, as discussed in (Codd (1971), 10).

§2.2 A Pictorial Representation

Relations such as we have described above can still be represented as tables with rows or columns, where we must be careful not to attach any significance to row order or to column order.   At the head of each column we put two names - a selector name and a domain name.

When we consider such a table, we can view it in two ways.   The first of these emphasizes the rows.

P D_P	R D_R	T D_T	V D_V
a	c	f	j
b	e	i	n
d	h	m	q
g	l	p	s
k	o	r	t

We regard the selectors as being the primitive set; a tuple (such as the one highlighted) associates a value with each selector. It still gives the same value for a given selector if one reorders the rows and columns. Consequently

R D_R	P D_P	V D_V	T D_T
o	k	t	r
h	d	q	m
c	a	j	f
e	b	n	i
l	g	s	p

represents exactly the same relation.

Alternatively, we can concentrate on the columns.

P D_P	R D_R	T D_T	V D_V
a	c	f	j
b	e	i	n
d	h	m	q
g	l	p	s
k	o	r	t

This is the same relation as before but this time we regard the tuples as being a primitive set and the selectors as giving a value for each tuple.

These two ways of viewing a tuple correspond to the tuple function formulation of relations of §2.3 and the component function formulation of §2.4. The informal approaches illustrate the duality of the more formal techniques.

§2.3 The Basic Relational Model

The usual mathematical analysis of the concept of an n-tuple is as follows. Given a set S of n indices, and a domain D_s for each index s, an n-tuple is a function which associates with each index s a value in D_s. (More formally, an n-tuple is a function $t:S \to \{D_s:s\epsilon S\}$ such that, for all $s\epsilon S$, $t(s)\epsilon D_s$.)

One of the simplest sets of indices that could be used is the set of the first n integers. There is however no reason why this set should be chosen and any set of indices, ordered or not, will do. We adopt the above definition as our definition of tuple, using selector as a synonym for index.

The set of *all* tuples, for a given choice of selectors and corresponding domains, is called the Cartesian product (or type) and denoted by $\underset{s\epsilon S}{\mathsf{X}}\, D_s$.

A relation is a subset of the Cartesian product: in other words, a set of tuples of the same type.

§2.4 Duality

In the basic model we view tuples as functions, mapping selectors to values. If we wish, we can regard the selectors as being the functions, mapping tuples to values.

Suppose R is a relation of type $\underset{s \in S}{\times} D_s$. Then, for all $s \in S$, we can define $\hat{s}$: $R \rightarrow D_s$ by

$$\hat{s}(t) = t(s),$$

and we call each $\hat{s}$ a *component function* of R.

We then define

$$\hat{R} = \{ \hat{s}: \quad s \in S \}$$

and call $\hat{R}$ the *dual relation* of R.

If we had defined a relation to be a set of component functions, we could have obtained the tuple function version by a similar process. This dual formulation does not capture naturally the notion of purging duplicate tuples - if we impose a condition to make sure that purging takes place, then the formulations are equivalent.

§2.5 Changing a Key

The relational model we have presented is a more suitable candidate for the conceptual schema than is a model in which the components are ordered. We would argue however that it is still not completely appropriate since an object is represented in the model simply by a collection of values.

As an example, we consider the concept of changing a key. By a key, we mean a component, or set of components, whose value uniquely determines a tuple in a relation. Changing a key has long been accepted as a special case in relational languages (see Codd (1970)).

A well known example of a key is the personnel number. What happens if we announce that, in a company's database, a particular personnel number is to be replaced, wherever it occurs, by a new one? Have we recorded a change to someone's personnel number or have we recorded his dismissal and replacement by a new employee (who happens to have the same name)? There is no way to tell.

There may of course be severe implementation problems in making the change, but in considering a data model we are more concerned about the ambiguity of meaning. We need some concept of "person" or "individual" in the system to remove the ambiguities. Then in the one case we would change an individual's personnel number; in the other case we would create a new individual and give him the same details as the one he replaces, which we then delete. (If the system can link to the person himself, who doesn't change, rather than to his personnel number, which might, then the use of individuals might also help with the implementation difficulties).

Such requirements for individuals lead us to the consideration of entities.

3.   ENTITIES

§3.1 What is an Entity?

Students of data semantics use the word 'entity' a lot in an attempt to capture the notion of something in the world, about which we might want to talk in discussing a database.   It is fairly easy to convey to someone the general idea of what an entity is, but much harder to give a rigorous definition.

The problem is one of circularity.   Chambers' dictionary, (editor Macdonald (1972)), describes an entity as "something with objective reality";   what then is a "thing"?   A thing is "an entity;   that which exists or can be thought of". We must abandon the attempt to define entities and be content with axiomatizing them - with giving properties that are satisfied by all entities (or by the class of entities), assuming these as primitive, and using them in our discussions.

One property that is shared by entities is that they can be named, cf Senko, Altman, Astrahan and Fehder (1973).   These names are just representatives of the entity, and need not be visible outside the system.   Knowledge of the use of names is vital to communicating with a computer.   We cannot store a person inside a computer - there are many ways in which we can store a name for him.

§3.2 Surrogates

It has been suggested by Langefors (1966) that "the object may be regarded as being simply the bundle of property values associated with it".   In §2.5 we discussed one objection to this - a further objection is that the set of values of genuine interest to an application may not determine the object uniquely. If, for example, we are only interested in people's names and addresses, how do we distinguish between two people of the same name living at the same address?   It is traditional in information system~ invent a special property which will uniquely identify distinct individuఁ   ~, for example, Langefors (1968)).

Following these lines it has been suggested by Engles (1972) that "associated with each entity set is an attribute whose value is in one-to-one correspondence with the entities.   We will call this attribute the identity attribute ....
Examples are part-numbers, man-numbers, order-numbers, etc."   Once again this doesn't seem completely satisfactory.   The identity attribute is more intimately associated with the entity than are the other attributes, and it needs to be distinguished from them.   It seems unreasonable to insist that a user invent personnel numbers, when all he wants to do is to record new people, distinct from all other people in his model.   (Even when personnel numbers are in use, we may want to register names and salaries of new employees before they are assigned a number.)   Furthermore, problems are caused when he wants to change these numbers (see §2.5).

Changes to the names of entities haven't been required by programming languages in the past - it is no doubt possible to re-name such entities as the integers and to count '2,1,5,7,3,8,6...' but such a change would be traumatic.   In data-bases similar changes can be equally traumatic but people still want to make them - they feel that since it was they who originally assigned the personnel numbers they have the right to change them.   They certainly need to be able to correct mistakes in the data.

Consequently, in our data model we have a collection of unique objects which act as the representatives of the objects in the outside world.   These represent-atives are called *surrogates*.

(In an implementation of an entity based system, the unique identity of an
entity is manifest in some system-given "internal identifier".   This identifier
may be reserved purely for internal use or it may be visible to the user. Abrial
(1974) has made a clear distinction at this point.   The database key of DBTG
(CODASYL (1971)) appears to have been an attempt to handle this problem.)

The term 'surrogate' very neatly captures what is intended - every entity of the
outside world is associated with a surrogate which stands for that object in the
model.   If we wish to refer to an object in the model, we refer to its
surrogate using one or more properties to identify uniquely the surrogate
required.

The diagram shows various manifestations of an entity.

external schema row of table		
conceptual schema surrogate	enterprise administrator	"real world" entity
internal schema record id.	realm of machine	realm of enterprise administrator

The entity itself is represented by a surrogate in the conceptual database, by a
record identifier in the internal database, by the row of a table in one of the
external databases, and as a vague cloud in the mind of the enterprise
administrator.

3.3 The Basic Entity Model

As a first approximation to a conceptual schema we might, following Mealy (1967),
take a set of entitites, a set of values, and a set of data-maps. Entities we
have already discussed, values are objects which *for the purpose of the applica-*
tion in question we do not regard as entities, and data-maps relate entities
either to values or to other entities.

Two points are worth noting.   Firstly, there is no absolute distinction between
entities and values. To a car manufacturer, a colour is merely an attribute of
one of its products: to the company that made the paint, a colour may well be an
entity.   In most applications numbers will be values: to a number theorist they
are definitely entities, each with its own properties.

Secondly, and more importantly, we have at the moment only one entity set; any
distinctions between entities are implicit in the data-maps. In defining and
manipulating entities it is convenient to be able to address subsets of the
totality of entities. The prime need for entity sets is in the defining of
data-maps, to separate out those entities for which a particular data-map is
applicable.   Thus a natural mathematical step, given Mealy's model, is to

partition the entities using the domains of definition of the data-maps, with atomic entity sets being defined by the partition generated by the totality of data-maps.

Several papers (eg Hainaut and Lecharlier (1974)) do develop entity sets along these lines. Most other approaches, however, begin with distinguished sets of entities rather than the totality of entities. It is important to note that *some entities may be members of more than one entity set*. For example we may wish to think of men and women as separate entity sets in one context, but think of them together as people somewhere else. Thus we have to admit that the class of entity sets is closed under the normal set operations of union, intersection and difference.

A possible source of confusion when considering entity sets as the domains of data-maps is the presence of partial knowledge. There is a distinction between a data-map being inapplicable to an entity, and its being applicable but of unknown value. In defining data-maps one is clearly concerned with applicability versus inapplicability, and not with undefined values. A discussion of undefined values is beyond the scope of this paper: for our purposes it is sufficient to consider a single undefined value, an element of every entity set (as was done in the Information Algebra of CODASYL (1962)).

§3.4 Excess Entity Sets

Using the entity model gives us the opportunity to identify individual objects clearly. Unfortunately, if only binary data maps are allowed, it also requires us to identify individuals we don't need for our application.

A company might, for example, store its products in warehouses, where each product is stored in several warehouses and each warehouse stores several products. The database might store how much of each product is stored in each warehouse.

The dependency in this example can be expressed pictorially as

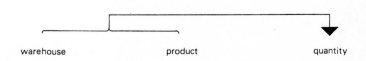

warehouse   product   quantity

In a binary entity model we must form a new set consisting of (surrogates representing) product-warehouse pairs, and base our data-maps on this. While this introduces no ambiguity it does mean that we have to have entity sets in our schema which have no intrinsic meaning to the application.

Thus the binary model requires an artificial analysis. It is because of this unnaturalness that binaries are not considered appropriate for the conceptual schema.

This problem of excess entity sets which afflicts the binary entity model does not affect the relational approach. What we would like to have is a combination of the features of relations and entities so that we can have entity surrogate sets in the schema when we need them, and only when we need them.

4.   A COMBINATION

§4.1 Preamble

In section 2 we urged that domains and selectors be clearly distinguished and
that we avoid using the one name to denote both.   In this section we are urging
a similar distinction: in many relational systems personnel numbers and the
like are doing two jobs.

i)   They act as invariant values which act as surrogates
            for individuals, and which can appear at several
            places in the database to provide links.

ii)   They act as unique identifiers under user control
            which can be used by him to identify an individual
            easily.

If we wish to distinguish between these rôles then we must introduce entity-
surrogate sets into relational theory.   The entity-surrogate can then play the
first rôle, and the keys playing the second rôle become ordinary values.

§4.2 Entity Sets as Domains

We require that entity sets be defined as separate domains of a basic type
distinct from the types of value sets (such as numbers and character strings).
These entity sets contain entity-surrogates, internal identifiers which are
allocated by the system on request (at the creation of a new entity), and then
remain invariant until the removal of the entity from the system. Entity domains
would then be used in relations in the standard manner.   The important usages of
entity domains would be in recording the properties of an entity, and in the
recording of relationships between entities.

For example, suppose that we are analysing a personnel system.   We are concerned
with PEOPLE (an entity domain), and their NAMES (a value domain).

We then form a relation

EMP_NAME (person :   PEOPLE,
          name   :   NAMES)

to record the names of individual PEOPLE.   (We would also have other relations to
store other information such as the addresses of these people.)   To record
managerial relationships, we would then define

MANAGES (manager :   PEOPLE,
         worker   :. PEOPLE)

To query who manages whom, we cannot use just the relation MANAGES since it
contains only internal identifiers, and these are not allowed any external manifes-
tation.   We must combine the information from MANAGES and EMP_NAME, matching the
component "person" to the components "manager" and "worker".   Then we list the
related names.

§4.3 Irreducible Relations

It is common practice in data processing to collect all attributes of an entity
together into one record.   The assumption is that they will often be required
together.   Also, doing this permits the record to be used as a surrogate for
the entity.

This practice has been carried into the general use of relations. Such ideas as third normal form (Codd (1971),9) break up records only in cases of transitive dependence. Again a tuple is often a surrogate for an entity, and further reduction is difficult.

In a conceptual schema, it is desirable to hold only basic facts. That such and such a person has age 49 years and that he has salary £6900 are two separate facts, and should be considered separately. This makes data independence simpler to maintain (addition of a new attribute is done by addition of a new relation rather than redefinition of an old one). It also helps to increase concurrency, since transactions accessing different attributes of an entity can be seen to be accessing different relations.

To guarantee that only basic facts are held in tuples, the concept of irreducibility of relations is introduced. A relation is *irreducible* if it cannot be broken down by projection into several relations of smaller degree in such a way that these relations can be joined to reconstitute the original relation. This concept is of long standing in algebra (Burnside (1911)) and has been used by Rissanen et al (1973) in the context of the internal schema.

As an example, consider a relation RESULTS, as described in Date (1975).

person PERSON	subject SUBJECT	position POSITION
A	X	1
A	Y	1
B	X	3
B	Y	2
C	X	2

We might project this to give two relations.

person PERSON	subject SUBJECT
A	X
A	Y
B	X
B	Y
C	X

person PERSON	position POSITION
A	1
B	2
B	3
C	2

On joining these projections, the result contains a tuple

person PERSON	subject SUBJECT	position POSITION
B	Y	3

that was not in the original.   Similarly, any other way of breaking down the
original relation gives the same problem.   Thus RESULTS is irreducible.

An example of a reducible relation is a typical employee relation:

```
EMPLOYEE (person    :    PEOPLE,
          pn        :    PERSONNEL_NUMBER,
          name      :    NAMES,
          mgr       :    PEOPLE)
```

This can be reduced to

```
EMP_NUM  (person    :    PEOPLE,
          pn        :    PERSONNEL_NUMBER)

EMP_NAME (person    :    PEOPLE,
          name      :    NAMES)

EMP_MGR  (person    :    PEOPLE,
          mgr       :    PEOPLE)
```

It is only at the conceptual level that irreducibility (and often even entities themselves) are important.   At the external schema and the internal schema we might produce

```
EMPLOYEE1     (pn            :    PERSONNEL_NUMBER,
               name          :    NAMES,
               mgr_name      :    NAMES)
```

The operation of inserting a new tuple to EMPLOYEE1 would create a new surrogate in PEOPLE and update EMP_NUM, EMP_NAME and EMP_MGR at the conceptual level.

A tuple in an irreducible relation represents a "basic" fact. It is desirable that all relations in a conceptual schema be irreducible. Irreducibility (like third normal form) is an intensional property of a relation and cannot be system checked.   It is a form of constraint, but unlike the constraints of §5, it is an integral part of the schema. Generally systems analysis produces irreducible relations;   the problem is not how to do the reduction but how to avoid the temptation to group facts.   In cases where irreducible relations are not produced naturally, there are no clear rules to define the "best" reduction of the set of relations.   It is interesting to note the production of a set of irreducible relations is similar to the production of a non-redundant covering of functional dependencies (Rissanen et al (1973) and Bernstein, Swenson and Tsichritzis (1975)).

(Note also that the use of irreducible relations eliminates the need for undefined values.   However, as in §3.3, we must be careful in modelling the distinction between undefined and inapplicable values.)

An irreducible relation will never have a key set that is less than all but one of the components.   In many cases, irreducibility will force the entity/ binary relation approach. This is not always true, as in the example RESULTS.

§4.4 Tuple Identifiers

An alternative approach to the provision of entity domains in relations has been considered: this is the use of tuple identifiers.   The idea is that every tuple has an identifier, and that this can be used as an element in another tuple. Thus in the personnel case we might define

```
EMP_NAME    (name          :       NAMES)

EMP_NUM     (person        :       EMP_NAME,
             pn            :       PERSONNEL_NUMBER)

EMP_MGR     (person        :       EMP_NAME,
             mgr           :       EMP_NAME)
```

We do not find this a satisfactory approach to the conceptual schema for two reasons:

1)   Every entity must be represented by a tuple whose
        identifier is used as a surrogate.   This confuses
        the existence of an entity with its properties.

2)   One of the properties of an entity must be chosen
        as the principal property of the entity.   The
        tuple identifiers from the relation giving this
        property are then used as the entity-surrogates.
        This choice is not always easy to make. (Should we
        take the name or number of an employee? Even
        worse, should we take the husband or the wife as

the principal property of a marriage?)

Whichever we choose we lose symmetry.   The only
way to retain symmetry is to abandon all hope of
using irreducible relations, and make sure that all
properties of an entity are kept in the same
relation.

5.   FURTHER COMMENTS

The ideas discussed so far are not intended to give a complete view of relational
systems as we understand them.   Several other points are well worth mentioning
but cannot be covered in detail.

1)   Constraints

It is commonly recognized that constraints must be
specified within the conceptual schema, rather than
expecting programs to maintain consistency.   We
agree with this view, and consider that the full
power of the DML should be available for the
specification of constraints.   Thus a complete
separation of DDL and DML is impossible.

2)   Complex Domains and Hierarchies

In manipulating data it is often necessary to allow
more complexity than is required at the conceptual
level.   In particular the DML should handle
complex domains (such as Cartesian products and
power sets of other domains) and hierarchical
"group by" type commands.   We haven't found
any case where these are needed to define a conceptual schema, except in conjunction with the
DML for constraint definition.

3)   Measures of Existence

Some attributes of entities give a "measure of
existence" of how many or how much of this entity
there is.   For example, a warehouse may well be
interested in how many paper clips are in stock,
but not in the individuality of each clip.   The
mapping that gives this quantity can be considered
to be of a special type.   It must be decided
whether such a map should be given special status
within the conceptual schema.

4)   Time and Ledgers

So that a system can be audited, or recovered
after a crash, some out-of-date data must be
retained.   In fact there is a case for never
erasing data completely (unless legislation or
considerations of security require it) - though
it may of course be stored on a medium of very
slow access.   This implies that a ledger must
be kept of past data and transformations of it,
see Bjork (1975).   In considering a ledger,
particular care must be taken to distinguish
between an entity and its surrogate - the times

at which the one exists may not be the same as the times
the other does.   For example, when an employee retires,
his surrogate may cease to exist in the company's
information system although he himself continues to exist.

6.   CONCLUSION

Of the many models suggested for the conceptual schema we have selected and
discussed two - relations and entities - and have seen limitations to both.   The
limitations we discussed could be overcome by including entity-surrogates within a
relational framework, and we recommended doing this by allowing entity-surrogate
sets as domains.   We further recommended that the conceptual schema should
contain only irreducible relations.

We have not given precise construction details - indeed we have listed some
important topics which there was no space to cover - but we believe that entitized
n-aries are the most promising basis for a conceptual schema that we have encountered.

7.   REFERENCES

1   J.R.Abrial
    "Data Semantics"
    Data Base Management (edited by J.W.Klimbie & K.L.Koffeman)
    North-Holland, Amsterdam, 1974

2   ANSI/X3/SPARC
    Study Group on Data Base Management Systems
    Interim Report, February 1975

3   P.A.Bernstein, J.R.Swenson and D.C.Tsichritzis
    "A Unified Approach to Functional Dependencies and Relations"
    ACM-SIGMOD International Conference on Management of Data
    San Jose, California, May 1975, pp.237-245

4   L.A.Bjork, Jr.
    "Generalized Audit Trail Requirements and Concepts for Data
    Base Applications"
    IBM Systems Journal, 1975, No. 3, pp. 229-245

5   W.Burnside
    Theory of Groups of Finite Order
    Cambridge University Press, Cambridge, 1911

6   CODASYL Development Committee
    Language Structure Group
    "An Information Algebra"
    Communications of the ACM, Vol.5, No.4, April 1962, pp.190-204

7   CODASYL
    Data Base Task Group Report
    April 1971

8   E.F.Codd
    "A Relational Model of Data for Large Shared Data Banks"
    Communications of the ACM, Vol.13, No.6, June 1970, pp.377-387

9   E.F.Codd
    "Further Normalization of the Data Base Relational Model"
    Data Base Systems, Courant Computer Science Symposia No. 6
     Prentice-Hall, Englewood Cliffs, New Jersey, 1971, pp.33-64

10   E.F.Codd
     "A Data Base Sublanguage founded on the Relational Calculus"
     Proceedings of the 1971 ACM-SIGFIDET Workshop on Data Description,
     Access and Control, San Diego, California, November 1971

11   C.J.Date
     An Introduction to Database Systems, pp. 109-110
     Addison-Wesley, Reading, Massachusetts,1975

12   R.W.Engles
     "A Tutorial on Data-Base Organization"
     Annual Review in Automatic Programming, Vol.7, Part 1
     Pergamon Press, Oxford, 1972, pp.1-64

13   C.B.B.Grindley and W.G.R. Stevens
     "Principles of the Identification of Information"
     Proceedings of File 68, an IFIP/IAG International Seminar on
     File Organization, Amsterdam, November 1968, pp. 60-68

14   Jean-Luc Hainaut and Baudouin Lecharlier
     "An Extensible Semantic Model of Data Base and its Data Language"
     *Information Processing 74 (*edited by J.L.Rosenfeld*)*
     North-Holland, Amsterdam, 1974

15   Patrick Hall, Peter Hitchcock and Stephen Todd
     "An Algebra of Relations for Machine Computation"
     Conference Record of the Second ACM Symposium on Principles of
     Programming Languages, Palo Alto, California, January 1975
     pp. 225-232

16   Borje Langefors
     Theoretical Analysis of Information Systems
     Studentlitteratur, Lund, Sweden, 1966

17   Borje Langefors
     "Elementary Files and Elementary File Records"
     Proceedings of File 68, an IFIP/IAG International Seminar on
     File Organization, Amsterdam, November 1968, pp. 89-96

18   A.M.Macdonald (editor)
     Chambers' Twentieth Century Dictionary
     W. & R. Chambers, Edinburgh, 1972

19   H.M.Markowitz, B.Hausner and H.W.Karr
     SIMSCRIPT - A Simulation Programming Language
     Prentice-Hall, Englewood Cliffs, New Jersey, 1963

20   George H Mealy
     "Another Look at Data"
     AFIPS Conference Proceedings, Fall Joint Computer Conference
     Vol.31, pp.525-534

21   J.Rissanen and C.Delobel
     "Decomposition of Files, a Basis for Data Storage and Retrieval"
     IBM Research Report No. RJ 1220, San Jose, California, May 1973

22   M.E. Senko, E.B. Altman, M.M.Astrahan and P.L. Fehder
     "Data Structures and Accessing in Data-Base Systems"
     IBM Systems Journal, 1973, No. 1, pp. 30-93

23   S.J.P.Todd
      "Peterlee Relational Test Vehicle: a system overview"
      IBM Systems Journal, Vol. 15, No. 3, August 1976

Since the acceptance of this paper, another approach to grafting entities onto a
relational system has been given by Chen.   His paper would be relevant reading
for anyone interested.   The full reference is:

      Peter Pin-Shan Chen
      "The Entity-Relationship Model - Toward a Unified View of Data"
      ACM Transactions on Database Systems, Vol. 1, No. 1, March 1976, pp. 9-36

POSTSCRIPT

Many of the papers given at the conference had a similar approach to ours, in
that they gave a set-theoretic model for schema definition, with a bias towards
the systems analytic use of the schema.   The computing use of the conceptual
schema as a "common schema" to supply a bridge between internal and external
schemata was not emphasized in these papers.

Our ideas are within the so-called "3-concept" framework, and are very similar
to the ideas of Benci et al [BBBC] and Moulin et al [MRSSTT].   Our 'entity
set' is roughly equivalent to the 'type of object' or 'type of entity' of BBBC,
'entity type' of MRSSTT, 'entity name set' of Senko et al (1973), and 'type' of
Biller and Neuhold.   Our 'value set' corresponds to the 'type of property'
or 'type of data' of BBBC, and 'property' of MRSSTT;   it occurs implicitly in
various other contributions.   Our 'domain' finds its equivalent in terms like
'type' and 'fundamental domain' though there are differences.   Our 'relation'
corresponds to the 'relation' of most contributions, though some people have a
special word for relationships between entities and values (eg Senko's
'attribute').   Our distinction between components, selectors and domains was
not usually matched in its full elaboration - the nearest equivalent occurs in
Durcholz and Richter's nominations.

Our 'surrogate' found a rough equivalent in 'internal identifier' as used by
Senko, and Bracchi et al, though no contribution closely matched the term.   The
word 'surrogate' was disliked by some, because of connotations of 'substitute because the real thing is unavailable' -. these connotations are unfortunate and
were not intended, since our surrogates are representatives where the real thing
cannot represent itself.

Two major areas of discussion relevant to our paper were raised.   The first
concerned the choice of binary or irreducible n-ary relations, and the second
concerned the validity of distinctions between "entity" and "value".

The binary/n-ary controversy seems the less important.   Proponents of the
binary approach point out its greater simplicity, those of the n-ary approach do
not like the artificiality of introducing extra domains during systems analysis.
Neither simplicity nor artificiality can be quantified, and it seems unlikely that
there is a "right" answer to the problem.   The artificial domains that must
be introduced in the binary case are the same as the n-ary (n>2) relations in the
irreducible n-ary case.   Thus the controversy could be resolved by allowing
tuples to be used as entities (ie relations used as domains).   However, this
relaxation of first normal form causes significant theoretical complications, and
nobody at the conference advocated such an approach.

In Senko et al (1973), the point is made that all entities can be named, and the authors associate at least one entity name set with every entity set.   The elements of an entity name set have a unique external representation.   There is not always a natural external name, as is pointed out in §3.2 of our paper. When it is possible to associate with each object in a domain a unique external name, and these names do not vary with time, it is convenient to use these names to identify the objects;   furthermore there is no falsification of the systems analysis in so doing.   These domains are the value domains.   When the use of such names is not possible, some internal names (our "surrogates") must be used to identify the objects.   Domains for which this is necessary are entity domains.

The distinction between value and entity domains can be viewed in terms of signification (cf Falkenberg).   For value domains there is always a very simple direct signification using the name, and this signification always signifies the same object.   For example, 'personnel number 12345' will always signify the same personnel number.

For entity domains signification is more complex.   'The person with personnel number 12345' is not quite so simple;   in addition, the person signified may change or the signification become invalid (ie empty).   Sometimes a signification as complex as 'the person with no personnel number yet, and name 'John Smith', whom the person with personnel number 12345 interviewed on date 6th January 1976' may be necessary to identify someone.   It is even possible that there will exist objects for which there is *no* unique signification - two objects for which every fact recorded in the database for one is recorded for the other too.   The database still records that there are two such objects.   They may later become identifiable again, if an extra fact is recorded about one (it cannot matter which one) and not the other.   (An example of this unlikely state of affairs might be two orders to a supplier for the same quantity of the same product;   the two orders originated on the same day from the same department and were charged to the same budget.   They become identifable if a mistake is diagnosed and one of the orders is cancelled.)

We wish to emphasize that the distinction we draw between entity and value domains is based on analysis of the objects themselves.   It is not the rôle a domain plays in a relationship (eg as the range of a function) that determines whether it consists of entities or of values: relationships may exist among any family of domains.

ACKNOWLEDGEMENTS

We would like to thank Terry Rogers and Mavis Price for their help.   Terry, as our manager, gave us advice and encouragement throughout the writing of this paper, and Mavis typed the various versions of it for us.

APPENDIX

Overlapping Domains

Much interest was expressed at the conference in the ideas of domains and constraints, and the problems of overlapping domains. The idea of restricting the elements of a component of a relation to lie in a particular domain is indeed a type of constraint. Whether a constraint of this kind is considered as a constraint or as the use of a domain is merely a point of view. An example was given at the conference concerning "people" with a property "sex" and companies with a property "number of employees". We define "legal units", which may be either people or companies, and which have a property "solvency" (solvent or bankrupt). Each legal unit has a property "legal unit type", which specifies whether the legal unit is a person or a company. Diagrams of such situations can be confusing, but here is an attempt.

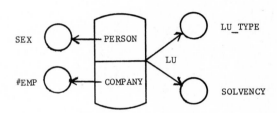

The constraints can be defined in a mathematical style by

(i) α: LU $\rightarrow$ LU_TYPE
(ii) β: PERSON $\rightarrow$ SEX
(iii) γ: COMPANY $\rightarrow$ #EMP
(iv) δ: LU $\rightarrow$ SOLVENCY
(v) PERSON $\cup$ COMPANY = LU
(vi) PERSON $\cap$ COMPANY = $\emptyset$
(vii) PERSON = α^{-1}(person)
$(viii)$ COMPANY = α^{-1}(company)
(ix) LU_TYPE = {person, company}

In a system which insists on non-overlapping domains, LU must be defined as a domain, and formulae (ii), (iii), (vi), (vii) & $(viii)$ considered as a (redundant) set of constraints. They make use of the sets PERSON and COMPANY; we can avoid naming these sets by regarding β (resp:γ) as a partial function from LU to SEX (resp: #EMP), dropping (v) & (vi), and rewriting (vii) & $(viii)$ as

(x) α^{-1}(person) $= \beta^{-1}$(SEX)
(xi) α^{-1}(company) $= \gamma^{-1}$(#EMP)

In a system which permits definition of domains in terms of other domains, PERSON and COMPANY can be defined as basic domains; (v) is then a definition of the domain LU, $(i) - (iv)$ are definitions of the relation types of α, β, γ&δ in terms of the domains.

Whatever type of system is used, some set of formulae equivalent to *(i) - (ix)* must be given.   Attempts to distinguish between formulae that define domains and formulae that are to be called constraints may be necessary in order to define the schema in some particular system, but they are less appropriate in the conceptual schema.

Modelling in Data Base Management Systems, G.M. Nijssen, (ed.)
North Holland Publishing Company, 1976

CONCEPTUAL MODEL AS A DATA BASE

DESIGN TOOL

This paper is the result of deliberations of an IRIA (★) study group.
Took part in the elaboration of it :

P. Moulin, J. Randon, M. Teboul : E.D.F.-G.D.F. (STI) 21, rue Joseph
Bara 92132 ISSY-LES-MOULINEAUX (FRANCE)

S. Savoysky : L.C.P.C. 58, boulevard Lefebvre 75732 PARIS (FRANCE)

S. Spaccapietra : Institut de Programmation 4, place Jussieu
75005 PARIS (FRANCE)

H. Tardieu : C.E.T.E. Zone industrielle 13290 LES MILLES (FRANCE).

ABSTRACT : Among the motivations for constructing a "conceptual model" we want
to emphasize those concerning the design of a data base.
In the first part, concepts and rules to achieve this goal are proposed. They
are associated to the steps of the modeling process.

1) At the perception stage :
   ★ ENTITY : An entity is something of (that portion of) an enterprise real or
             abstract, distinguishable and of interest for the people of that
             enterprise.
   ★ RELATIONSHIP : A relationship is a connection of interest for the people
                   of the enterprise, between two or more entities.

2) At the induction stage :
   ★ PROPERTY : A property is a characteristic of an entity or a relationship.
   ★ VALUE : A value realises a property.

3) At the abstraction stage :
   ★ ENTITY-TYPE : An entity-type is an abstraction representing a collection of
                  similar entities.
   ★ RELATIONSHIP-TYPE : An relationship-type is an abstraction representing a
                        collection of similar relationships.

In the second part are discussed: Codd's relational model, CODASYL and ANSI
proposals, according to the purpose we assign to the "conceptual model".

1 - INTRODUCTION

Among the motivations for constructing a conceptual model we want to emphasize
those concerning understanding, description and analysis of the real world.
So we think that the concepts used must have the capability to be the basis of
a data base design methodology and facilitate "enterprise administrator" (1)
and "end users" communication.

(★) IRIA : "Club Banques de Données" - Domaine de VOLUCEAU 78150 ROCQUENCOURT
                                                                (FRANCE)

The question then arises :

> Shall we have a dependence between the conceptual model and the internal
> model, such that the conceptual model is limited to the present state of
> the "internal" technology ?

If yes, we shall conclude as the ANSI/SPARC study group that "richness of real
world relationships is beyond the capability for modeling".

If no, the transformation between conceptual model and internal model has to
be made non automatically by the "data base administrator" : the conceptual model
may then represent the richness of the real world and so has no implementation in
the data base.

Our answer is the second one. We think that the coneptual model must not be
influenced by the present time DBMS implementation possibilities. The conceptual
model is directly derived from the universe of discourse according to a method
of investigation of the "real world".

The concepts we propose are associated to different steps of the modeling process

- <u>perception</u> of the "real world", which is composed of entities and
  relationships between these entities.

- <u>induction</u> which permits to discover properties of entities and relationships.

- <u>abstraction</u> which permits to classify entities and relationships.

In the present paper we shall introduce these basic concepts and some rules
associated with them. In a second part, we shall discuss CODD's relational model,
CODASYL proposals and ANSI proposals according to purposes we assign to a conceptual model.
Although integrity constraints are part of a conceptual model, they will not
be studied in this paper.

2 - CONCEPTS

The proposed concepts are classified in three stages : perception, induction,
and abstraction.

2.1. Perception stage

. ENTITY
An entity is something of (that portion of) an enterprise that is real or
abstract, distinguishable and of interest for the people of that enterprise. An entity is an atomic element for the people of that enterprise.
By convention it is not divided because a part of it will not be of
interest for that enterprise.

Examples : - these bolts

- this petrol

- the PARIS storehouse

- the NAMUR storehouse

- this employee

RELATIONSHIP
A relationship is a connection of interest for the people of the enterprise, between two or more entities.

Note : A relationship can exist if connected entities exist and only if
they do.

Examples : - these bolts are stored in the PARIS storehouse.

- this petrol is stored in the NAMUR storehouse.

- by this number 0123 order, the PARIS storehouse has to
deliver 1000 number 9876 bolts to Mr John Green.

- the NAMUR storehouse has to deliver 1000 number 9876 bolts
to the CHARLEROI production unit.

2.2. Induction stage

From perception and according to the utilization of the information, an
inductive mental process, permits to discover the <u>relevant properties</u>
of entities and relationships.

PROPERTY
A property is a significant characteristic of an entity or a relationship.

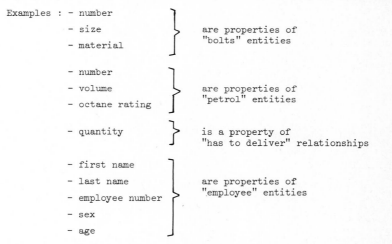

Examples : - number
- size   are properties of
- material   "bolts" entities

- number
- volume   are properties of
- octane rating "petrol" entities

- quantity   is a property of
              "has to deliver" relationships

- first name
- last name   are properties of
- employee number "employee" entities
- sex
- age

Note 1 : The relevant properties of entities and relationships may change
with time.

Note 2 : What is an entity, a relationship, a property ?
First of all, the system analyst has perceived the entities of
interest for the people of the enterprise. These entities are
the basic elements of the enterprise universe of discourse. Some
of these basic elements are involved in compound elements, which
are the relationships.

Entities and relationships have characteristics, some of these
are of interest in the enterprise, and so they will be the
relevant properties. A property has no meaning by itself. To be
significant a property must be associated with the qualified
entities or relationships. For example, the property "color"
of "cars" entities differs from the property "color" of "political
parties" entities.

When the system analyst will found something which looks like a
property, he will have to answer the question : is that really a
property, is it not a new entity or a new relationship ? The answer
cannot be given without knowledge of the enterprise universe of
discourse and must be given according to it. For example "employee"
may be :

- a property of "person" entities
- or an entity
- or a relationship between the entities "person" and "company".

. VALUE
A value gives a real existence to a property. A value realizes a property.

Note : "unknown" is a possible value.

Examples : - the value represented by 1234   ⎫
     -   "   "   "   " 5678   ⎬ are values of the property "number"
     -   "   "   "   " UNKNOWN   ⎭

     - the value represented by 92   ⎫
     -   "   "   "   " 97   ⎬ are values of the property "octane rating"

     - the value represented by SCHMIT   ⎫
     -   "   "   "   " DUPONT   ⎬ are values of the property "name"
     -   "   "   "   " UNKNOWN   ⎭

Note : Conceptual model is not concerned with representation of values.
That belongs to internal model domain.

2.3 Abstraction stage

At that stage we shall define disjointed classes of :

- similar entities having the same properties

- similar relationships, having, if necessary, the same properties.

These classes are determined according to the utilization of the information
and discriminative properties and/or values of properties.

Why disjointed classes ?

- An entity belongs to one class and only to one. So an entity has one and
only one generic name and relationships cannot be masked by an entity
class.

- A relationship belongs to one class and only to one. So a relationship
has one and only one generic name.

These two rules may help to construct "real world" structure and to get a
non ambiguous view of (that portion of) the enterprise for "enterprise
administrator" and "end users".

Note : These rules make classes of entities not very different from the
ANSI/SPARC concept of "underlying conceptual record".

ENTITY-TYPE

An entity-type is an abstraction representing a class of entities
(collection of similar entities, having the same properties).

Note : - Entities are occurrences of entity-types.

-   Entity-types are defined according to the relevant properties
    of the observed entities and, if necessary, discriminating
    values of some of them.

Examples : - STOREHOUSE is the entity-type representing the class of
entities: Paris storehouse, Namur storehouse, Aix storehouse,

-   EMPLOYEE is the entity-type representing the class of
    entities: Mr Schmit, Mrs Dupont, Miss Jone,...

- Let us suppose that bolts and petrol are the only products used
  in that enterprise.

  If the property "to be combustible" is a discriminative one for the
  people of (that portion of) the enterprise, we shall define two
  entity-types ("BOLT" and "PETROL").

  If that property is not discriminative and if there are not any
  other discriminative properties, then only one entity-type will be
  defined ("PRODUCT").

. RELATIONSHIP-TYPE

A relationship-type is an abstraction representing a collection of
relationships connecting n entities belonging to the same n entity-types
and having, if necessary, the same properties.

Note : - Relationships are occurrences of relationship-types.

-   A n-ary relationship-type (relationship) connects n entity-types
    (entities). n is often greater than two.

Examples : - Binary relationship-type

Relationship-type STOCK connecting PRODUCT and STOREHOUSE
entity-types.

. 10 000 number 9786 bolts are in stock in the Paris
  Storehouse.

. 15 000 number 9786 bolts are in stock in the Namur
  Storehouse.

. 1 000 m3 of number 0123 petrol are in stock in the
  Namur Storehouse.

are binary relationships occurrences of the relationship-
type STOCK.

- 3-ary relationship-type

Relationship-type TO-DELIVER connecting PRODUCT, STOREHOUSE
and PRODUCTION-UNIT entity-types.

. The Namur storehouse has to deliver 10 000 number 9786
  bolts to the Charleroi production unit

. The Namur storehouse has to deliver 5 000 number 9786
  bolts to the Aix production unit

. The Aix storehouse has to deliver 15 000 number 9788
  bolts to the Aix production unit

are 3-ary relationships occurrences of the relationship-
type TO-DELIVER.

- 4-ary relationship-type

Relationship-type ORDER-ITEM connecting ORDER, CUSTOMER,
PRODUCT, STOREHOUSE entity-types.

. by the order number 0123, the Paris storehouse has to
  deliver 1 000 number 9786 bolts to Mr John Green.

. by the order number 0123, the Namur storehouse has to
  deliver 10 000 number 9786 bolts to Mr Jean Dupont.

. by the order number 1234, the Aix storehouse has to
  deliver 100 m3 of number 0123 petrol to Mr James Schmit.

are 4-ary relationships occurrences of the relationship-
type ORDER-ITEM.

2.4. Relationship-type consistency rules

Relationship-type definition process is controlled by two kinds of consistency rules : checking rules and decomposition rules.

2.4.1. Checking rules

A relationship-type property must be meaningful with regard to all
the entity-types connected by that relationship-type. If a property
has meaning only for some of the entity-types connected, then that
property does not belong to that relationship-type.

Example : If the property "due quantity" means the quantity of a
          product that a storehouse has to deliver to all the produc-
          tion units, then this property cannot be a property of the
          relationship-type TO-DELIVER.

If a property of a relationship-type is not entirely defined with
regard to entity-types connected by that relationship-type, then
that property does not belong to that relationship-type.

Example : If the property "due quantity" is the quantity of a product
          that a storehouse has to deliver to a production unit,
          then this property is not entirely defined with regard to
          entity-types PRODUCT and STOREHOUSE.
          So that property cannot be a property of the relationship-
          type STOCK.

2.4.2. Decomposition rules

The purpose of decomposition rules is to transform, when it is possible, relationship-types in less n-arity other ones. So, only basic
relationship-types are holden in conceptual model.

The decomposition of relationship-types has two major goals namely :

- better understanding of the universe of discourse
- integrating at an early stage of conception a particular type of integrity constraints which has a great impact on structuring the conceptual model.

In order to understand these two points we have to come back earlier in method.

We have pointed out entity-types and relationship-types with the criterion that they are of interest for the people of the enterprise. An other way to express this criterion could be that these concepts applied to the enterprise have a great stability in the enterprise.

In the same manner a particular type of integrity constraints has a major impact on structuring the conceptual model : functional dependencies play a major role in optimizing the conceptual model for three reasons :

- Looking for functional dependencies in relationship-types allows the designer to better understand his universe of discourse.
- Functional dependencies if they have the same stability as entity-types and relationship-types should be integrated at a very early stage of conception.
- Although internal model is not in our scope, reducing n-arity of relationship-types is very helpful because most of the DBMS have no hability to process relationship-types with a n-arity greater than two. N-ary relationship-types $(N > 2)$ remaining after decomposition will be reduced at the internal level by a compromise which always has consequences on performances.

First case, a function exists between two entity-types.

Example : The relationship-type ORDER-ITEM connects ORDER, CUSTOMER, PRODUCT, STOREHOUSE entity-types.
If a product may be stored in one and only one storehouse, there is a function between PRODUCT and STOREHOUSE. Then ORDER-ITEM will be decomposed in :

. PROD-STORE connecting PRODUCT and STOREHOUSE

. ORDER-ITEM-1 connecting ORDER, CUSTOMER, PRODUCT.

If an order concerns one and only one customer, there is a function between ORDER and CUSTOMER.

Then ORDER-ITEM-1 will be decomposed in :

. ORD-CUST connecting ORDER and CUSTOMER

. ORDER-ITEM-2 connecting ORDER and PRODUCT.

So the 4-ary relationship-type ORDER-ITEM will be decomposed in three binary relationship-types PROD-STORE, ORD-CUST and ORDER-ITEM-2.

Second case, a function exists between an explicit or implicit relationship-type and an entity-type.

Example : If a product may be delivered to a customer only by the nearest storehouse which stores that product, then there is

a function between an implicit relationship-type connecting
PRODUCT, CUSTOMER entity-types and STOREHOUSE entity-type.

So ORDER-ITEM relationship-type will be decomposed in :

. DELIVERABILITY connecting PRODUCT, CUSTOMER, STOREHOUSE

. ORDER-ITEM-A connecting ORDER, PRODUCT, CUSTOMER.

2.5. About some notions used in other models

We want to discuss briefly some notions used in other models. We think they
are out of the scope of our paper because they are integrity constraints or
belong to external or internal model.

. Identifier, key, ... : An identifier of an entity-type (relationship-type)
is a property of that entity-type (relationship-type) any value of which
belongs to zero or only one occurrence of that entity-type (relationship-
type). An occurrence of that entity-type (relationship-type) can always be
distinguished from any other by the value of identifier property.

We think that the quality of a property to be an identifier is an integrity
constraint (integrity constraints are parts of the conceptual model, but
are not in the scope of our paper).

. Access path : in the conceptual model, properties and/or relationships can
be an access path to entities, and none of them are privileged.

We think that external and/or internal models are concerned with privileged
access path, not the conceptual model.

. Security : we think that security constraints in the meaning of ANSI/SPARC
belong to the external model.

3 - ANALYSIS OF CODD'S MODEL, CODASYL AND ANSI PROPOSALS

3.1. Analysis of CODD's model

We present a critical analysis of the relational model proposed by Codd
according to our proposals, because of the considerable influence it has
in the data base field, chiefly at conceptual level.

This study is made, keeping in mind the goal of giving facilities for
designing data bases and not only "real world" modelling.

3.1.1. The relation concept

The relational model has not the concept of entity-type. It expresses it by
a relation between attributes which are the properties of the entity-type.
The justification given by CODD in its first paper (3) seems to us subjec-
tive.

But we see an objective reason for keeping a distinction between entity and
relationship : a main quality of a relationship is that it exists if all the
connected entities exist and only if they do. This is a basic integrity
principle associated with our relationship concept.

Let us consider the occurrence of the STOCK relationship-type :

10 000 # 9786 bolts are in stock in the Paris storehouse.

If one of these connected entities or both are suppressed, this relationship disappears.

On the contrary, an entity keeps existing even if one or several of its
properties are suppressed. Thus, the entity PERSON Dupont always exists
with the same meaning even if for instance the property telephone number
is unknown.

So the properties of an entity play a different role than the entities
connected by a relationship. In a relationship we cannot have unknown
elements on the contrary to relational model (4).
We think that **dependence** upon elements is of prime importance and consequently we make a difference between the concept of entity and the concept of
relationship.

An other reason to have two concepts is that the third normalization may
lead to construct relations having no interest in the enterprise world.

Let us have the relation EMPLOYEE (<u>employee #</u>, last name, department #,
department manager #)
Codd's normalization leads to define <u>two</u> relations :

    . EMPLOYEE (<u>employee #</u>, last name, department #)

    . DEPARTMENT (<u>department #</u>, department manager #).

The new relation DEPARTMENT may have no interest for the people of the
enterprise.

Our proposal is :

    . first, defining entity-types of interest for the people of the enter-
      prise,

    . then defining the relationship-types between these entity-types.

As the decompositions rules are applied only to relationship-types, no new
entity-type is defined.

3.1.2. The key concept

The key concept is introduced by CODD to normalize the relational model.
We saw in 2.5. that this notion is not necessary at the structure level in
the conceptual model. We think that to express this notion with integrity
constraints is clearer. We show in 2.4. that with out the key concept a
free ambiguity conceptual model may be constructed by applying consistency
rules including CODD's normalization.

3.2. Critical analysis of CODASYL proposals as a conceptual model

The main problem when studying CODASYL proposals as a conceptual model, comes
from a probable misusing of the proposals which are in fact internal-model
oriented - Our objective is to demonstrate the unability of CODASYL to
satisfy the conceptual model specifications as they appear in the ANSI-SPARC
Report.

The CODASYL proposals considered in this paper, are the DDL specifications
as they appear in the April 73 report. These specifications have already
been analyzed at the IFIP-TC2 meeting in January 75. Our objective is to
reanalyze the main results of this meeting according to our proposals.

3.2.1. <u>Comparison of the concepts used in our proposals and CODASYL</u>
       <u>proposals</u>

A critical analysis of CODASYL concepts will attempt to show the following
points :

. CODASYL concepts are not "clean".

. CODASYL concepts do not fit the conceptual model.

a) <u>CODASYL concepts are not "clean"</u>:

The objectives of CODASYL group to make easy the programming of data base
and to keep only implementable concepts led the participants to propose
some "unclean" specifications. The following criticisms are those of the
TC 2 group :

- in a set an owner cannot be member

- repeating groupsare an other way to define sets

- the DB key is the only direct access to records

- the program cannot use any fields as an access key

- a set may contain many records-types.

This list is not complete. It shows that CODASYL proposals should be
cleaned even in the present philosophy.

b) <u>CODASYL concepts do not fit the conceptual level</u> :

Our proposal is based on "entity-type" and "relationship-type" as fundamental concepts.

CODASYL proposal is based on "record-type" and "set-type". We shall analyze the main differences between these concepts.

RECORD : "a record is a named collection of zero, one or more data items
          or data aggregates. There may be an arbitrary number of occurren-
          ces in the data base of each <u>record-type</u> specified".

SET   : " a set is a named collection of record-types".
          A set shall have one <u>owner</u> and zero or many ordered <u>members</u> ;
          one occurrence of record can only appear once in any occurrence
          of set.

ENTITY-TYPE : "an entity-type is an abstraction representing a collection
              of entities having the same properties".

RELATIONSHIP-TYPE : "a relationship-type is an abstraction representing
                    a collection of relationships connecting entities
                    belonging to n entity-types and having, if necessary,
                    the same properties".

The above definitions are directly derived from CODASYL and our proposals.
In the case of SET (as in the case of RELATIONSHIP-TYPE), it should be
noted that these two concepts describe a collection of occurrences of set
(or relationship), an occurrence of set (or relationship) is by itself a
set (in a mathematical sense) of records (or entities).

. <u>Critical analysis of the concept of record</u>

At the conceptual level, we manipulate entities which belong to entity-types. The concept of record could be quite near the concept of entity, if the record type were only used to define entity-type, excluding all CODASYL specific concepts as group, vector,...

. <u>Critical analysis of the concept of set</u>

The set concept covers actually two features :

- access path

- functional binary relationship.

We precise here that access path has nothing to do with conceptual model. The relevant feature of the set is the set as a functional binary relationship.

We shall then consider that representing real world with functional binary relations is a very constraining modelization because :

1) There are many non functional binary relationships

2) There are many n-ary relationships (connecting together more than 2 entity-types)

3) A set, as it is, cannot have properties.

       * Constraint 1) is solved by creating an extra RECORD and two sets instead of one ; example :

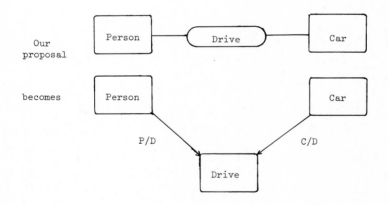

Our
proposal

becomes

we notice that :

. The 2 sets P/D and C/D are mandatory automatic

. The record "Drive" has not at all the same conceptual meaning as records "Person" and "Car". The record "Drive" may have no specific field.

* Constraints 2) is much more difficult to solve.
The representation of n-ary relationships generates a lot of troubles
in a CODASYL schema if designed without care.

Example :

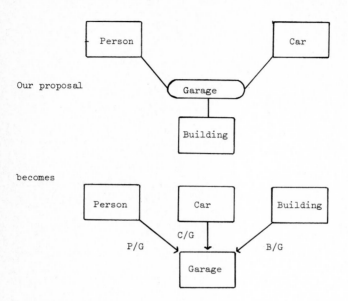

Our proposal

becomes

- The three sets P/G, C/G, B/G are mandatory automatic
- The record "Garage" has not at all the same conceptual meaning
  as records "Person", "Car", "Building".

An internal analysis of functional relations that do not exist in
CODASYL, should allow to normalize this relationship. If, for
instance, a car can park in only one building, the schema becomes.

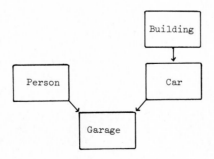

＊ Constraint 3) can be bypassed in giving specific fields to record
created to establish the relationship. Nevertheless, the meaning of
these fields is entirely depending on the simultaneous existence of
all records participating to the relationship which is not the case
for a field belonging to a record representing an entity.

We see that using the record and set concepts obliges the data base
designer to describe integrity constraints at a very early stage of
conception. These integrity constraints are only due to the impossibi-
lity of CODASYL to take in account the whole complexity of real world.

3.2.2. CODASYL can be chosen after "cleaning" as an internal model mapped in a non automatic way from a conceptual model constituted by our proposal

a) It is quite evident that we do not dispose, at the moment, of informatic
tools (DBMS) which can proceed much more complex structures than those
described in CODASYL.

b) It is also quite evident that real world to be modelized, supposes the
disposal for the designer of much more complex structuring tools.

We feel that conceptual model problem of today is the dependence between
the conceptual model and the internal model.

We think that the conceptual model has not to be limited to the present
state of the "internal"technology. So the conceptual model has no implementation in the data base and the transformation between conceptual model and
internal model has to be made, non automatically using a precise method
based on principles close to CODD's normalizations.

3.3. Critical analysis of ANSI conceptual model proposals

This study is voluntarily limited on concepts of ANSI proposals which are
concerned by the comparison with our ones. The considered concepts are those
we find in the two realms : Real World and Conceptual Model.

3.3.1. Concepts of the Real World

a) Property

It is important to notice that, at real world level, we only need
concepts associated to the perception of the real world (entities and
relationships). Others concepts are associated to the induction or
abstraction stage of modeling : those belong to conceptual model. Indeed
at real world level we observe entities and relationships between these
entities, but as soon as we think over them and try to represent them,
we pass at conceptual level.

Thus property which "plays a role in describing an entity", as ANSI-SPARC
report says, must belong to conceptual model, more especially as this
property is not really discerned in the real world but is induced by
observation of the real world.

So it is for the others concepts in keeping with property : fact, value,
domain,...

b) Entity

This concept is almost the same in the two different proposals. They
insist in the same way on the notion of : "interest for the people of the
enterprise".

As there is not a unique way to discern real world we agree with the
assert : "The scope of an entity is arbitrary".

However we remark that we cannot "define and name" an entity at this level
we can only do it in conceptual model.

c) Relationship

We disagree with the part of the definition of a relationship : connection between properties of entities. At the perception level we distinguish entities and connections between these entities. We need properties
to describe entities and relationships. On the other hand kind or direction of connection are included in the description of the relationship,
they would be found at conceptual level.

d) Entity-set

The entity-set is not a concept associated with the perception level.
It is a result of a mental operation to describe and organize the real
world. So it must not appear at the real world level.

3.3.2. Concepts of conceptual model

We find in this realm such terms as record, group, field. They seem to be
very close to hardware and software considerations. So it is not very
desirable to use them in conceptual model.

We analyse subsequently these concepts in more details.

a) Conceptual record

The fundamental criticism we can generally make is that ANSI-SPARC has
kept, at conceptual stage, all the ambiguity inherent in the different
levels of perception of the real world.

It is obvious that people may have different perceptions of the real
world. If we agree that the conceptual model is a representation of the
enterprise, this representation has to be constituted by integration and
not by addition of different users sight. We shall find these sights in
the external model.

The enterprise is single, the conceptual model is also single. All
ambiguities must be deleted. To avoid ambiguities we shall retain the
less level of different perception since all perception of upper level
is a relationship between entities of less level.

Thus our entity-type agree with the "underlying conceptual record" of
ANSI-SPARC report.

On the other hand we can note :

- Notion of identifier is not necessarily a part of conceptual model
  (Cf § 2.5.). However we can find it as a useful information for the
  mapping conceptual schema internal schema.

- In sofar as conceptual model describes the enterprise in a single and
  exhaustive manner, we are opposed to redundancies in this model.
  Different representations issued from the same conceptual model can be
  redundant. Redundancies in the model itself could uselessly be a factor
  of insecurity.

- It seems to be misplaced to say that "a conceptual record is the object
  that is logically stored, retrieved, or deleted" (ANSI-SPARC report
  page IV.10). We prefer to avoid these notions of data manipulating at
  this level.

b) Conceptual field

This concept is in ANSI-SPARC report, the correspondent, at the conceptual level, of the property in the real world. We have eliminated the notion of property in the real world so we discuss here both these concepts. We remark that our proposal allows to use a single word :
Property when ANSI-SPARC report uses : Property, Attribute and Conceptual Field. In addition, the notion of fact, which expresses an action of mapping between a property and its domain, should not appear among the concepts of conceptual model.

These remarks made, the concept of property may be the similar in both proposals. This is also right for value.

A difference however exists. Our proposition says that a property applies itself not only on entities but also on relationships. We found this notion in the ANSI report but it is not clearly stated.

On the contrary, the notion : role of a property does not appear in our proposal. We ought to examine which existing roles we take into consideration at conceptual level.

c) Conceptual group and conceptual plex

We find in the use of these two concepts the inconvenience we discussed with conceptual record. They introduce ambiguities in conceptual schema because these concepts are used to describe the different levels of perception other than conceptual record. So we disagree with utility of these concepts in the conceptual model. They may eventually appear in the external model as description of each application sight.

d) Conceptual record—set

We think that "for the sanity of the enterprise administrator" and to avoid ambiguities classes of entities and relationships must be disjointed. So we desagree with "the contents of a conceptual record-set need not be disjoint from those of other conceptual record-sets".

3.3.3. Definition of the conceptual model

We think that the conceptual model must be defined with regard to the real world and applications which permit to select in the real world entities of interest for the enterprise.

This process of definition must be independent of particular implementations. Once conceptual model is defined, we complete it with useful information for the mapping between conceptual model and internal model. However, these informations will only be as indications and not as specifications (ANSI-SPARC report page IV.32).

We think that, in contrary of ANSI-SPARC report, no references at internal model have to be done when defining the conceptual model.

On the other hand, we ascertain that the ambiguity conserved at conceptual level by ANSI-SPARC definition of conceptual record and conceptual record-set does not enable to give any rules on the definition of the conceptual model. Only recommendations can be made.

On the contrary, the elimination of ambiguities allows definite rules helping a correct definition of the conceptual model.

4 - CONCLUSION

The choice of the three concepts : entity-type, relationship-type, property for the "conceptual model" is proposed to facilitate the real world understanding. What from the real world is defined as an entity, a relationship, a property is arbitrary and the choice is made according to the utilization of the information in the enterprise. Some rules may be helpful to this choice and they are under investigation.

This model often called "trinity model" is sometimes said to be "too natural". We have tried to demonstrate that it is sufficient as a conceptual model. It is possible to map it in other models such as relational model, CODASYL or ANSI proposals, if it is not chosen as the final conceptual model. The contrary seems more difficult.

The three concepts and the consistency rules help the data base designer to investigate the real world in a right way, and better investigation provides a better stability for the "conceptual model".

At last, these concepts are absolutely free of DBMS implementation constraints.

5 - ACKNOWLEDGEMENTS

The study group would like to thank H. Heckenroth and D. Nanci co-authors of (10) for numerous very helpful and pleasant discussions. We would also like to thank G.M. Nijssen for providing valuable suggestions for improvement of this paper.

6 - BIBLIOGRAPHY

(1) ANSI/X3/SPARC : Interim Report (75-02-08)

(2) Bachman C.W.   : "The programmer as navigator" CACM (November 1973)

(3) Codd E.F.   : " A relational model of data for large shared data banks" CACM (June 1970)

(4) Codd E.F.   : "Understanding Relations" FDT Bulletin of ACM-SIGMOD Vol 7 number 1 (1975)

(5) CODASYL   : "Data Base Task Group Report" ACM (New-York - 1971)

(6) Deheneffe C., Hainaut J.L., Tardieu H : "Individual Model for a Data Base" Proc. Data Structure Models for Information Systems Workshop, (May 1974, Namur). Travaux de l'Institut d'Informatique n° 4 P.U.N., NAMUR, 1975.

(7) IRIA/INSTITUT D'INFORMATIQUE DE NAMUR, "Rapport Introductif du Séminaire Modèles de Structures de Données" (May 1974).

(8) Nijssen G.M.   : "Data Structuring in the DDL and Relational Model". Proc. IFIP TC 2 working conference-Cargese (April 1974).

(9) Senko M.E.   : "Data description language in the concept of a multilevel structured description : DIAM II with FORAL". Proc. IFIP TC 2 working conference-Wepion (January 1975).

(10) Tardieu H., Heckenroth H., Nanci D. : "Etude d'une méthodologie d'analyse et de conception d'une base de données". CETE/IAE Aix (May 1975).

CROSS - REFERENCE

What are the concepts needed at the conceptual level ?

Two schools of thought appear at the Freudenstadt working conference :

- 2 concepts school : RELATION and DOMAIN
- 3 concepts school : ENTITY-TYPE, RELATIONSHIP-TYPE and PROPERTY
  (using our terminology).

In this "cross-reference" we do not want to compare these two schools of thought, but we will try to propose a synopsis of the "3 concepts" presentations.

I	II	III	IV
our paper	RELATIONS AND ENTITIES P. HALL J. OWLETT S. TODD	CONCEPTS FOR THE DESIGN OF A CONCEPTUAL SCHEMA G. BENCI H. BOGAERT F. BODART A. CABANES	GENERAL TERMS Introduction to the final discussion session by J.M. GALLITANO
ENTITY-TYPE "is an abstraction representing a collection of similar entities"	ENTITY-SET "the elements in entity-sets are surrogates..." "every entity of the outside world is associated with a surrogate which stands for that object in the model"	TYPE OF ENTITY "a type of object is identified by a type of entity which identifies it only in the conceptual structure"	SIMPLE (underlying) CONCEPTUAL RECORD "a collection of zero or more conceptual fields representing an entity. This record can be a binary relation or any other form that is irreducible
RELATIONSHIP-TYPE "is an abstraction representing a collection of similar relationships"	RELATION "...associated a domain and a selector with each component. A domain is a set of possible component values, and a selector is a name which uniquely identifies its component"	RELATION "a type of association is represented by relation(s)" "a type of object is represented by relation(s)"	COMPLEX CONCEPTUAL RECORD "a collection of zero or more conceptual fields or records representing an entity (simple or complex) It can be an n-ary relation, any other type of relationship an event or other complex structure"
PROPERTY "is a characteristic of an entity or a relationship"	DOMAIN (value-set)	TYPE OF DATA "a type of property is represented by one, or more type of data"	CONCEPTUAL FIELD "the smallest named conceptual data object that represents an idea or a fact perceived about an entity (or thing in the enterprise).

There is in (III)   a distinction between the basic elements of the perceived
real world (object, association, property) and the basic elements of the conceptual structure. The concept of <u>object</u> disappears and is replaced by the concept
of <u>entity</u> which allows <u>identification</u> of object but is "basically a component
of a relation". Objects are <u>represented</u> by relations in the conceptual structure.

This concept of entity seems to be close to the notion of "surrogate" in (II).

In (IV) it is proposed a three concepts school subset of ANSI/SPARC. These
concepts are general enough to include those of (I) , (II) and (III) . But
they seem to us insufficiently selective to be helpful tools to the system
analyst when he investigates the enterprise universe of discourse.

Modelling in Data Base Management Systems, G.M. Nijssen, (ed.)
North Holland Publishing Company, 1976

ON THE SEMANTICS OF DATA BASES:

THE SEMANTICS OF DATA MANIPULATION LANGUAGES

H.Biller, W.Glatthaar, E.J.Neuhold

Institut für Informatik, Universität Stuttgart

D-7000 Stuttgart, Herdweg 51

1. Introduction

The discussion of the semantics of data base management systems requires, first of all, a clarification of the term semantics as it is
used in the area of data base management systems.

The data in a data base system can be regarded to represent information (facts) about the real world (see for example /Sundgren 71/).
The users are interested in these facts and they want to manipulate
them according to the rules as they are understood in their application environment. To represent this slice of reality which is to be
manipulated in a data base we introduce an abstract model of the real
world. The semantics of the data base, i.e. its meaning to the user,
can now be regarded as the interpretation of the data contained in
the data base and of the data manipulations in the framework of the
abstract world model. One state of the abstract model represents the
users abstraction of the real world as it exists at a specific instance of time. The transitions between the different abstract world
states reflect the dynamic changes as they arise in the users world.

On this basis we can now define the formal semantics of data definition and data manipulation languages found in data base management
systems. Using the theory of formal languages a data definition
language can be viewed as a set of expressible DDL-programs, or
schemata. A formal semantic description of a data definition language
now assigns to each DDL-program a class of abstract world states.
Since a DDL-program itself defines a set of possible data base states
(i.e. data configurations as they may exist at some specific instance
of time in the data base) we can now observe that the (formal)
semantic description of a data definition language specifies for all
the data base states the semantic interpretations as they are allowed
in the framework of the abstract world model. In a previous paper
(/Biller 75a/) we have shown such a formal semantic description,

based on CODASYL DDL /CODASYL 73/.

A data manipulation language can also be viewed as a set of expressible DML programs. Each such program describes manipulations on the data base which may be categorized as information retrieval processes,
updates of the data base, and processes for deducing information from
the data contained in the data base. In other words, DML-programs specify the interactions between a data base system and its users. A formal semantic description of a data manipulation language assigns to
the data manipulations appearing in a DML-program corresponding manipulations in the abstract world model. That is, the formal semantic
definition of a data manipulation language describes for all the data
manipulations arising during a DML-program execution the semantic interpretations as they are allowed in the framework of the abstract
world model. However, for this description the abstract world model
has to be expanded into a memory model, which formalizes the communications with the external environment (i.e. the users). A detailed
description of this model as well as of the manipulations which may
be performed on the memory model, i.e. the allowed state transformations, can be found in /Biller 75b/.

Besides specification of the formal semantics of the data definition
and data manipulation languages in the framework of the abstract
world respectively the memory model, we may also specify the formal semantics with respect to the meaning these languages have for
the implementor of the data base management system. These realization
semantics assign, on the one hand, to each schema a class of storage
states in a storage model, on the other hand, they assign to each DML-
program a class of transformations between states of the storage model and other (successor) states.

The formal description technique for realization semantics of DDL's
has been developed in /Biller 75a/ and applied to a subset of CODA-
SYL DDL. The realization concepts as they are needed for data manipulation languages will be discussed in this paper and utilized for
the description of a subset of CODASYL DML /CODASYL 71/.

Given a precise semantic definition for both the user and the implementor of the data definition and data manipulation languages it
is possible to prove the correctness of an implementation based on
the formal description. Since the data in the computer storage re-

present the abstract states, a correspondence between the memory
transformations assigned by the interpretation to a DML command and
the transformations of the storage states must exist. This correspondence is specified by a <u>verification</u>, i.e. a function which
assigns to storage transformations memory transformations and thereby defines the intended meaning of these storage transformations.

Since the semantics of the DDL form the basis for the development of
the semantics of the DML a short resumé of /Biller 75a/ is given in
chapter 2. In chapter 3 we first introduce the memory model, then
discuss the extension of the storage model needed for the definition
of a realization of the CODASYL DML, and finally define the realization of some of the DML commands.

We have chosen the CODASYL data definition and data manipulation
languages because we feel that these languages are widely known and
are also of such complexity that their formal description represents
a strenuous test of the power of any description technique. In addition, the numerous discussions about the semantics of these proposals
(see for example the discussions at the TC-2 Wepion conference /Dou-
qué 75/) show that the English language descriptions are not sufficient to enforce a common understanding of the different language
features. When such discussions can be based on a formal semantic
description any misunderstandings can easily be resolved. Furthermore, the formal semantic description exposes the many interdependencies existing between the concepts of DDL and DML and it illustrates the heavy amount of implementation knowledge which is required from all the users of these languages.

For the description of the formal semantics of the data definition
and data manipulation languages the mathematical semantics as introduced by Scott and Strachey (/Scott 70/, /Strachey 73/) has been
used. We have chosen this technique because it offers a number of
advantages as compared to the operational semantics used in some
earlier papers (e.g. /Biller 74/). Among these advantages are:
1) The mathematical semantics offer a unique technique to represent
   both the declarative and algorithmic concepts of the various
   languages. In operational semantics the static aspects of recur-
   sivly defined objects cannot be defined by equations. They rather must be discovered during the runtime of an abstract machine.

2) In the course of a semantic definition it is very simple to change
   the level of detail in such a fashion that only as much detail as
   needed for a specific purpose is introduced in the description of
   some concept.
3) Semantic descriptions can be repeated at different levels of detail, as for example, the abstract world semantics and the realization semantics selected for the data base area. The similarity between the different levels remains close enough to allow
   for well structured verification processes and equivalence proofs.
The notation used in this paper is summarized in the Appendix.

2. Static Aspects of the Data Base

The allowed objects and the interdependencies existing between them
in the perceptible world are described by certain classification
rules. These rules thereby specify the static structure of the world.
In the data base which models this world the static structure is defined by the schema, which can be considered as a sentence of a data
definition language (DDL). In this chapter we introduce a subset of
the CODASYL DDL and give a short summary of its interpretation both
from the viewpoint of the implementor and the user. A more complete
description may be found in /Biller 75a/.

2.1 Syntax of the DDL

The clauses in CODASYL DDL can be divided into three different
classes, namely clauses which describe the logical structuring of the
data, clauses which describe implementation features, and clauses
which give information needed for the proper execution of DML commands. For example, clauses involving areas consider parts of the
physical store and are therefore of the second type. Clauses of
the third type are the LOCATION MODE and SET SELECTION clauses. Since
we regard areas not to bear meaning for the user they are ignored by
his interpretation of the schema. But nevertheless the area concept
influences the interpretation of DML commands and must therefore be
included in the DDL as shown in chapter 3. We will also show that by
the inclusion of data base keys at the user level conflicts arise
which have the consequence that manipulations based on this implementation oriented concept should not be included in a DML. In the
CODASYL DDL we have record entries which describe the possible (record) objects and set entries which describe set objects. A set object

consists of several record objects which belong together in some
sense. The following syntax is taken with some small changes from
/CODASYL 73/. We have selected all clauses which describe the logical
structuring and added one format of the LOCATION MODE clause and some
of the clauses concerning areas.

SCHEMA NAME IS schema-name
    {AREA NAME IS area-name}...
    ["record-entry"]...
    [SET NAME IS set-name-1
      OWNER IS record-name-1
      ORDER IS LAST
      [MEMBER IS record-name-2 OPTIONAL MANUAL
        SET SELECTION IS THRU set-name-2 OWNER IDENTIFIED BY

$$\left\{ \begin{array}{l} \text{CURRENT OF SET} \\ \text{DATA-BASE-KEY EQUAL TO data-base-identifier-1} \\ \text{CALC-KEY EQUAL TO data-base-identifier-2} \\ \qquad\qquad [\text{,data-base-identifier-3}]... \end{array} \right\}$$

         [THEN THRU set-name-3 WHERE
            OWNER IDENTIFIED BY data-base-identifier-4]...]...]...

The general format of "record-entry" is:
  RECORD NAME IS record-name
      [LOCATION MODE IS CALC USING data-base-identifier-1
        [,data-base-identifier-2]...DUPLICATES ARE NOT ALLOWED]
      WITHIN area-name-1[,area-name-2...
         AREA-ID IS data-base-data-name]
      ["data-subentry"]...

The general format of "data-subentry" is:
  [level-number] data-subentry-name

$$[\text{PICTURE IS} \left\{ \begin{array}{l} \text{"character-string-picture-specification"} \\ \text{"numeric-picture-specification"} \end{array} \right\}]$$

$$[\text{TYPE IS} \left\{ \begin{array}{l} \underline{\text{BINARY}} \\ \underline{\text{DECIMAL}} \\ \underline{\text{DATA-BASE-KEY}} \end{array} \right\}]$$

$$[\underline{\text{OCCURS}} \left\{ \begin{array}{l} \text{integer} \\ \text{data-base-identifier} \end{array} \right\} \underline{\text{TIMES}}]$$

We assume the same syntactic restrictions on the schema as in the
original report.

2.2 Interpretations of the DDL

To be complete we have to specify through interpretations the
meaning which a schema has as seen from the users respectively
the implementors point of view. In this paper we do not describe
these interpretations of DDL, but we only discuss the different
abstractions of the real world to be used for the interpretation
of DDL. The interpretations may be found in /Biller 75a/.

2.2.1 The View of the Implementor

For an implementor the meaning of a schema is given in terms of
storage properties. We model the storage as a mapping from structured locations into value ranges, i.e. by a set of structured
locations for which the type of objects they can hold is specified. The elementary locations L_e are subdivided into pairwise disjoint sets A_i, each of which corresponds to an area i.

Any possible (composite) location is an element of
$$L_i = A_i + [\,|N \longrightarrow L_i\,]$$
and all locations are given by
$$L = \Sigma_{i \in I} L_i.$$
The value ranges which are assigned to the locations are constructed
from the elementary range
$$C_o = DEC + BIN + STRING + B(KEY) + B(NAME) + B(LENGTH)$$
which should be selfexplanatory.
Any range is an element of
$$C = C_o + [\,|N \longrightarrow C\,].$$
We define a **storage** as a structure preserving function from
L to C which assigns to any location a suitable range.

The implementation oriented meaning of a schema is defined by an interpretation called **realization** or **implementation** **concept** as the set of
all storages which can be used to store the states of the data base
system which are described by the schema.

2.2.2 The View of the User

At the user level a schema is seen to describe the set of all possible states of the abstract model of the world. This meaning is attached to a schema through the **standard interpretation**. The abstract

model of a CODASYL data base consists of <u>record objects</u> and <u>**set**</u>
<u>**objects**</u>. In a CODASYL world it is possible that a single object
occurs several times. Different <u>occurrences</u> of the same object are
distinguished by properties which are not intrinsic to the object,
but are provided by the system itself as data base keys. Therefore
in the abstract world model a record occurrence is given by a pair
of a natural number and a record object, so that different occurrences of the same object can be distinguished by this number.
The record objects are built up from elementary objects which
are strings and numbers. These are elements of the lattices $CHAR^*$
respectively NR. A record object may have as components items (i.e.
strings, numbers, or data base keys), vectors, or repeating groups.
So we can model any possible record object as an element of

$$RO = (CHAR^* + NR + (RO \times |N) + RO)^*.$$

The user does not deal with data base keys, i.e. internal unique
names of the record occurrences, but with the occurrences they
identify. Therefore in the user view the set of data base keys
is replaced by $RO \times |N$, the set of record occurrences. A set ob-
ject consists of an owner record object and a sequence of member
record objects and consequently is an element of

$$SO = (RO \times |N) \times (|RO \times |N)^*.$$

The model P of all possible abstract worlds now is the lattice of
all sublattices of $RO^* \times SO^*$, and the standard interpretation
I_{DDL} attaches to each possible schema an element of P.

3. Dynamic Aspects of the Data Base

The static model of the reality which is represented in a state of
the data base system will have to be adjusted to the changes appearing in this reality. These changes, i.e. data base state transitions,
can be specified in terms of the data base schema and the data mani-
ulation language DML and they will have to be interpreted for the
implementor as functions from storage states to (successor) storage
states, and for the user as functions from states of the abstract
world to (successor) states of the abstract world. The meaning of a
sentence, i.e. a program, of DML is then given by an interpretation
into the appropriate function space. To describe these interpretations we first have to add components to the abstract world and
storage models for controlling the various possible state transitions.

3.1 The General Storage Model

We assume that the reader is familiar with the architecture of a
CODASYL data base system and consequently give only descriptions
of the concepts relevant for the formal definition of the store.

A <u>state of the total store</u> ts is modelled by a quadruple
(db,oa,uwa,ps) where db is the data base state corresponding to the
storage state as explained in chapter 2.2.1, oa a function to distinguish open and closed areas, uwa is the user working area, and ps is
the host language program store. The lattice TS of the total store is
given by the product DB × OB × UWA × PS where DB is the lattice of
all data base states, OA the lattice of all functions oa, UWA the
lattice of all user working areas, and PS the lattice of all program
stores. The lattices DB, OA, and UWA are discussed in detail in the
chapters 3.1.1 through 3.1.3, whereas the program stores depend on
the host language and are not further described in this paper. In
chapter 3.1.4 we define two system functions which are needed for the
manipulation of data base keys.

3.1.1 The Set of States of the Data Base (DB)

A possible state db of the data base is modelled by a mapping from
locations as elements of L (see chapter 2.2.1) to values. Such a
mapping has been introduced in /Strachey 73/ and /Bekič 71/ for the
formalization of storage properties of programming languages.
The set of all possible states DB for a schema is developed from
the DDL storage model discussed in chapter 2.2.1, whereby the
limitations of a real storage medium must be taken into account. For
example the locations in the domain of db must be pairwise disjoint
and the values must be elements of the lattice

$$V = VO + [\,|N ---> V]$$

where
$$VO = \Sigma_{i=1}^{N1} DEC_i + \Sigma_{i=2}^{N2} BIN_i + \Sigma_{i=1}^{N3} STRING_i + KEY + NAME + LEN.$$

DEC_i and BIN_i are the flat lattices of numbers in decimal respectively binary representation with i digits. By introducing
upper bounds N1 and N2 we express that in any real implementation those bounds for the values must exist.

A data base state db fits a given realization of a schema, if the

value for each location of db is an element of the value range
which is associated with this location by the realization. According
to the realization of a schema suggested in /Biller 75a/ for every
stored record instance r a composite location exists which is structured according to the schema entry of the record type of r. We
realize the CODASYL sets using pointer arrays and therefore we add to
every record instance of a type declared as owner in a set an array
component to store the data base keys of the member record instances.
Since the set of locations which are used for storing information can
be changed by the execution of DML commands (for example STORE or
DELETE) the set DB of all data base states is a subset of all structure preserving functions from subsets of the set of locations to the
set of values. That means that the domains of different states of the
data base need not be identical.

3.1.2 The Set of States of the Open Area Function

One concept of the DBTG proposal allows to divide the stored data
into subsets which are accessible by a program and subsets which
are not accessible. This concept is modelled by a truth valued function
oa defined on the set L. For a given state db of the data base the
function oa(l) is <u>true</u> if l is a location of an area which has been
opened by the user. The component OA of the total store therefore is
defined by

$$OA = [L \text{ ---> } \{\underline{true}, \underline{false}\}]$$

3.1.3 The Set of States of the User Working Area

The user working area is that part of the system which connects the
data base to its environment. The structure of UWA is completely
determined by the schema and it is defined by

$$UWA = CI \times ER \times DBN \times RV$$

with the elements

$$uwa = (ci,er,dbn,rv)$$

where CI, ER, DBN, RV are the sets of states of the currency
indicators, the error register, the data base data names, and the
record value part respectively. Each of the components ci, er, dbn,
rv of an element uwa of UWA is a mapping from a set of locations
L' to the set of values V. The elementary locations used for the
construction of L' are taken from a set of elementary locations
L_e' which satisfies the condition $L_e \cap L_e' = \emptyset$, where L_e is the set

of elementary locations used in DB. The lattice L' is constructed
analogous to L.

We assume that all locations which are in the domain of one of the
components of an element uwa of UWA are mutually independent. We
shall now explain the components of UWA in greater detail.

3.1.3.1 The Set of States of the Currency Indicators

The first component of a state uwa is a mapping where the domain
contains four composite locations. We introduce the following names
for these locations:

   CRU (current of run-unit), CR (current of records),
   CS (current of sets), and CA (current of area).

CRU is a composite location with two component locations. The
range of the first component is KEY, the second component is
composed of N_{SET} locations, which all have the value range KEY.
N_{SET} is the length of the set section of the schema. The second
component of CRU is required since the DML allows to find the owner
of a record via a set instance from which the record has been deleted
or removed. We therefore use special locations, not to be updated
during the execution of DELETE or REMOVE commands, to identify the
owner records of the current record of the run unit in the different
set instances to which this current record belongs. We assume that
the components of the second component of CRU are ordered in the same
way as the set entries, i.e. $n \circ 2(CRU)$ corresponds to the n-th set
entry of the schema.

CR is a composite location with N_{REC} components arranged in the order
of the record entries of the schema. N_{REC} is the length of the record
section of the schema. Each of these components consists of two locations. The value range of the first location is KEY and the second
location is structured in the same way as the second component of
CRU.

CS is a composite location with N_{SET} components, the n-th of which
is assumed to correspond to the n-th set entry of the set section
of the schema. Each of the components consists of four locations,
the current record of the respective set type, the prior record with
respect to the set ordering, the next record, and the owner. The
value range of all these locations is KEY.

CA is a composite location with N_{AREA} components, where N_{AREA} is
the length of the area section of the schema. The n-th component
again is assumed to correspond to the n-th area entry of the area
section. The components of CA are composed of four locations.
The first of them designates the current record of the respective
area, the second its prior record, and the third its next record.
The fourth has N_{SET} components the m-th of which contains the owner
of the current of area record in the m-th set. The value range of
all these locations is KEY.

3.1.3.2 The Set of States of the Error Register

In the DBTG-proposal eight error-registers are introduced. We will
model this part only with one error register ERR, since the handling of the different conditions is done in the host language program and is therefore not described in this paper. The set of states
of the register ERR is modelled by

$$ER = [\{ERR\} \dashrightarrow \{\underline{true}, \underline{false}\}],$$

where er(ERR) is $\underline{true}$ if an error occurred during the execution of a
command.

3.1.3.3 The Set of States of the Data Base Data Nams

The domain of the third component of uwa is a composite location dn.
Each component of dn corresponds to one data base data name introduced in the schema. We restrict DDL such that data base data names
may only occur in the WITHIN clause of the schema and therefore the
values of the component locations are elements of the lattice
AREA-NAME.

3.1.3.4 The Set of States of the Record Value Part

The fourth component of uwa contains N_{REC} composite locations which
are elements of L' and pairwise independent. Again we introduce
names for these locations, rn-1,..., rn-N_{REC} where rn-i corresponds
to the i-th record entry of the schema. The structure of the location rn-i may change during the execution of commands. The possible
structure of the location rn-i is determined by the value range which
is assigned by the realization of the schema to the i-th record entry
since the value range of rn-i is equal to this set. In a state of the
total store the rv component of uwa is a structure preserving mapping

from the locations rn-1,..., rn-N$_{REC}$ into V.

3.1.4 System Functions

For any state ts of the data base system the functions loc$_{ts}$ and CALC$_{ts}$ are defined. The function loc$_{ts}$ yields for any data base key the location where the record instance to which the key belongs is stored. CALC$_{ts}$ computes the data base keys for those record instances for which LOCATION MODE IS CALC is specified in the schema. The first argument defines the record type and the second argument contains the values of the database identifiers needed for the calculation of the KEY.

3.2 The General Memory Model

3.2.1 The Components of the General Memory Model

To understand the transitions from one state of a data base to another which are possible at the user level it is of advantage to look at the data base as an extension of the user's memory. We take a memory model which is suitable to describe the possible transitions in terms of cognitive processes (/Rumelhart 72/). This memory consists of two parts. The storage component of the memory is called long term memory (LTM). The short term memory (STM) contains the information needed to control the memory processes and is the interface between the memory and the external world.

Except for retrieval processes there exist two possible mechanisms by which information can become part of the STM. The object can be created by a perception process of real world phenomenas or by a deduction process based on information already contained in STM.

It is important to differentiate between the erasure of an object from the LTM and the moving of an object out of the STM. The capacity of the STM is bounded and it must be possible to eliminate objects from the STM. These objects are then viewed as inaccessible for update and deduction purposes, but as long as they are still contained in the LTM they may become available again using a retrieval process.

All possible objects in the memory are classified according to certain of their properties (/Glatthaar 75/). The STM consists of two
components, the first of which, identified by O, provides for an orientation in LTM by identifying in each property class those of its
objects which are currently of interest. For orientation in LTM also
organizational concept may be used. Each of these concepts also identifies objects in LTM which are currently of interest. The second
component R stores temporary results of complex memory processes.

Of the processes which operate on the memory

Updating adapts the memory to the changes of the real world. Updating may consist of the insertion of new objects into the LTM, of
erasing objects form the LTM, and of changing objects in the LTM.
However before an update process can be applied, the affected object must be contained in the interface to the external world, i.e.
the STM.

Retrieval is the process of becoming aware of facts that are stored in the LTM, i.e. objects of the LTM are copied into STM. Objects can be retrieved either based on information contained in
themselves or by their relations to other objects wherby these
objects must already be available in the STM.

Deduction creates new information using information already contained in the STM. Deduction is based on logical rules as well as
on empirical laws. If one wants to define the semantics of self
contained data manipulation languages, i.e. languages which incorporate all the different LTM and STM manipulation processes, one
must include the deduction processes as well as update and retrieval
processes. In this paper we shall confine ourselves to host language
systems, in particular the CODASYL DML, where deduction processes
will mostly be expressed using the host language.

The structure of the memory model as it is used here is shown in
Figure 1. The reader may find a more detailed description in
/Biller 75b/.

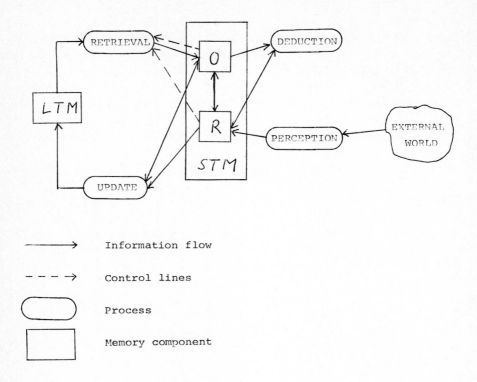

→   Information flow

- - - →   Control lines

Process

Memory component

Figure 1: The Memory Model

3.2.2 The CODASYL Memory System

To define the user semantics of the CODASYL DML (/CODASYL 71/)
we must impose some restrictions on the general memory model.
The most serious restriction of the CODASYL DML is given by the
fact that in the component O of STM record occurrences are handled
whereas in the component R only record objects are handled, i. e.
two record occurrences which are different in LTM cannot be distinguished in the temporary result component R if all their components are equal. It remains the responsibility of the user to keep
track of the different occurrences during his deduction processes.

Therefore complete set objects cannot be manipulated and for every
property class and concept only a single record object can be placed
into O and R. In a CODASYL data base the different property classes
are determined by the record type and set type definitions given in

the schema.

The component O is the semantic equivalent of the user working area registers of the CODASYL database which contain the currency indicators. But it is an extension of the CI component of the UWA since there are more property classes and concepts than currency indicators. Especially the set of concepts includes the following elements: The last handled record (TRACK), for any set type the owner of the last handled record occurrence as well as the predecessor and successor of that record occurrence with respect to the set type, and one special concept ERR indicating whether something went wrong with a memory process. The value of ERR is usually undefined, but whenever an error occurs it becomes _true_.

3.3 The Semantics of DML

A state of the data base system is a representation of a state of the memory model. This means that we must be able to set up a correspondence between states of the total store and memory states. This correspondence is given by means of the verification function V, which assigns to every element ts of TS a memory state. By the verification V the meaning of the store in the abstract user model is given. We define that a realization of a DDL is correct, if a verification function V exists, such that for every schema s the standard interpretation I(s) is equal to the set of memory states given by $\bigcup_{ts \in R(s)} V(ts)$ (see Figure 2).

If a realization of DDL is correct, in the database system only states of the store exist, which are meaningful to the user.

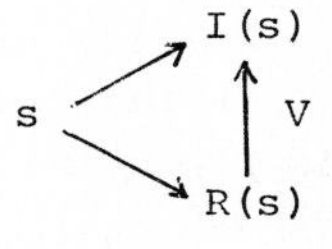

Figure 2: The verification function V

At the user level the meaning of DML commands is given by memory transitions and at the implementor level by transitions between the states of the total store. Again there must exist a correspondence between the realization R_{DML} of DML commands and the interpretation

I_{DML} of DML commands. It is expressed by a verification function V_{DML} which maps functions from TS to TS (i.e. the realization R_{DML} of commands) to functions from M to M (i.e. the interpretation I_{DML} of commands). The relationships between these functions are illustrated in Figure 3.

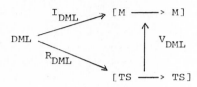

Figure 3: The verification function V_{DML}

The two verification functions V_{DML} and V are dependent on each other through the condition:
$\forall dml \in DML \ \forall ts \in TS:\ V_{DML}(R_{DML}(dml))(V(ts)) = V(R_{DML}(dml)(ts)),$
that means the function $V_{DML}(R_{DML}(dml))$ applied to the memory state m = V(ts) must yield the same state as the state which is the result of applying the function V to the storage state ts' = $R_{DML}(dml)(ts)$. (See Figure 4).

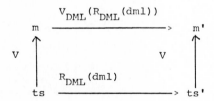

Figure 4: Correspondence between V_{DML} and V.

In this paper we shall only define the realization R_{DML} of DML commands and will not give the interpretation I_{DML}. But we shall discuss the memory transitions which arise as the consequence of the realization R_{DML} and the verification function V and we shall illustrate that on account of the concepts of data base keys and areas a DML program causes memory transitions which a user will not be able to understand. For the sake of preciseness of our arguments we first must describe the verification V in more detail. The limitations in size of this paper do not allow a complete description, and we restrict ourselves to define the realization of only four DML commands. Some more commands are described in /Biller 75b/. We have selected the STORE command, to show that by the inclusion of data base keys at the user level conflicts arise which only can be avoided if all manipulations based on this implementation oriented concept are excluded from DML. Similar arguments were given in /Engles 76/. The DELETE command together with the FIND NEXT of set name SET command is included, to illustrate how, by formal definition techniques, ambiguities in the DBTG proposal could have been avoided. The FIND VIA set-name SET command is described to show that the area concept cannot be hidden at the user level without considerable changes to the DML.

3.3.1 A Verification Function

Since an obvious correspondence between the components of a storage state ts and the parts of a memory state exists, we split up the verification function V by

$$V(ts) = (V(db,oa),V(uwa),V(ps)) \text{ where}$$

ts = (db,oa,uwa,ps) and the value of V(db,oa) is an element of LTM, and the value of V(uwa) an element of O · R. In the following we shall not discuss V(ps) since we did not introduce the structure of PS. The verification of the data base component of ts ignores all locations which are elements of closed areas. That is, V(db,oa) = V(db'), where db' is defined such that its domain is given by the set
{l; l∈domain(db) ∧ oa(l) }.

For the principal understanding of the verification function it is sufficient to discuss its most important characteristics and we can avoid many of its lengthy details. The function assigns to every location l in the domain of db' into which a record instance has been stored a unique record occurrence ro whereby the value of l, i.e. db'(l), corresponds to the record part of ro. To describe this assignment we have to define functions which map the elements of DEC_i and BIN_i to numbers, the elements of $STRING_i$ to character strings and the data base keys to those record occurrences which are identified by the verification function applied to the locations which correspond to the keys. If any of these locations is an element of a closed area, the value of the key under the verification function is undefined.

If the record instance identified by db'(1) is owner of a set instance a set occurrence of LTM is assigned to 1, whereby only data
base keys with defined values are used for the identification of the
corresponding member record occurrences. This means, that only those
member record occurrences appear in the LTM, which are stored in open
areas. If the owner record instance of a set instance is located in a
closed area, the complete set occurrence does not appear in LTM,
since the existence of a set occurrence in the abstract model depends
on the existence of the owner record occurrence.

The verification of the user working area V(uwa) maps the currency
indicators and the error register to the orientation component of the
memory whereby the correspondence between the different locations and
the property classes and concepts of the memory is established in an
obvious way using the function V for the keys kept in the different
locations. Since the area concept does not appear at the user level
the corresponding currency registers are ignored by the verification.
The record section of the user working area is mapped by the verification function V(uwa) to the component R of the STM, whereby the
verification function is defined analogous to the function for the
data base component.

3.3.2 The Representation of DML

In the following section we define for some DML commands of the
CODASYL proposal the realization R_{DML} in terms of the storage model
introduced in chapter 3.1. Henceforth we will use R instead of R_{DML}
to denote the realization of DML. Since even CODASYL specialists
sometimes cannot agree upon the semantics of some of the clauses
which we have selected for our analysis we do not claim that we
have defined the semantics of the proposal. We rather define what we
understand to be the semantics. But the following chapters will
show that a formal description of the things one is speaking of
must form the base of any critisism and that the technique we have
chosen, i.e. the mathematical semantics, is a suitable one.

For the definition of the realization R we assume that an abstract
syntax (/McCarthy 62/) is given. This means that R is defined on a
lattice DML, whose elements (dml) are the syntactically correct
sequences of DML commands. The meaning of a DML command depends on
the schema s of the data base system, which therefore forms a para-

meter of the command realization. Since the schema is not changed by
the interpretation of commands we omit the schema as an explicit
parameter of R although we sometimes must refer to it in the definition.

The realization of a sequence of commands is given by the functional
composition of the realization for the elements of the sequence and
is not further described.

Commonly used notation is given in the appendix for the reader
not familiar with the mathematical semantics.

For the abstract representation of a storage state ts we introduce
abbreviations of the form
    db= s-DB(ts), oa = s-OA(ts), uwa = s-UWA(ts), ps = s-PS(ts),
    cru = s-CI∘s-UWA(ts)(1(CRU)), etc.

We will also use the abbreviations
    rec-n = n∘s-REC-SECT(s), TSE = er[ERR/<u>true</u>], TSF = er[ERR/<u>false</u>]
    set-n = n∘s-SET-SECT(s), area-n = n∘s-AREA-SECT(s)
where all selectors refer to the abstract syntax of the schema
(see /Biller 75a/), and in addition introduce the functions
    name = $\{(1,rn-1),(2,rn-2),\ldots,(N_{REC},rn-N_{REC})\}$
    cu   = $\{(1,CRU),(2,CR),(3,CS),(4,CA)\}$

3.3.2.1 The STORE Command

The syntax of the STORE command is given by
    <u>STORE</u>   record-name

$$[SUPPRESS\ \left\{ \left\| \begin{array}{l} \underline{ALL} \\ \underline{RECORD} \\ \underline{AREA} \\ set\text{-}name\text{-}1[,set\text{-}name\text{-}2]\ldots\underline{SET} \end{array} \right\| \right\}\ CURRENCY\ UPDATES]$$

The semantics of the STORE-command for our subset DML are much
simpler than in the DBTG proposal since we only have to deal with
optional manual set membership of records. Therefore such a command
only includes a new record instance into the data base. This requires
the construction of a new composite location, the structure of which
is equal to the location in RV whose value is to be stored. We assume
that this will always be possible, i.e. we do not take into account
the limitations of the real storage medium. The creation of the

location is modelled by the function GEN_{ts}(AREA-NAME,RECORD-NAME).
The value of this function is a location l composed of elementary
locations from the area specified by the area-name. The structure of
the location is equal to the structure of the record name location in
RV. Furthermore the location l will be added to the set defined by
domain(db) whereby the restrictions given by the implementation will
be observed. We also assume that after the execution of the function
GEN the function loc_{ts} is updated to assure that the value of
loc_{ts}(ci(CRU)) is equal to l.

The abstract syntax of the command is given by

$$STS = TYP \times SUP$$
$$TYP = |N$$
$$SUP = ALL + RECORD \times AREA \times SETL$$
$$SETL = |N^*$$

where ALL, RECORD, AREA are lattices containing as their single
elements the respective key words. STS is the set of all syntactically correct abstract store commands sts.
In a top-down approach the semantics are defined by

R(sts)(ts) := (er(Rs-single)(ERR) ⊃ TSE, Rs-single).

That is, if an error would occur during the execution of the command
then only the value of the location ERR is set to <u>true</u>.
Rs-single is an abbreviation for Rs(s-TYP(sts),s-SUP(sts))(TSF).
We do not describe the semantics of the procedures specified by means
of the USE statement. As a consequence, if during the execution of a
sequence of commands $(c_1,...,c_n)$ the command c_i leads to an error,
then the command c_{i+1} nevertheless will be executed. To avoid an
incorrect error condition after the execution of the command c_{i+1},
the error register must be set to the value <u>false</u>, before the
command c_{i+1} is processed.

Rs is defined by

Rs(n,sup)(ts) :=

      (ERROR ⊃ TSE,

      length(1(acl))>1 ⊃ SUPR(n,sup) ∘Rsu(n) ∘

              GEN_{ts}(dbn(dn(2(acl))),name-n)(ts),

        SUPR(n,sup) ∘Rsu(n) ∘GEN_{ts}(1(acl),name-n)(ts))

with the abbrevation for the error condition

    ERROR = length(1(acl))>1 ∧ ¬(∃i)(dbn(dn(2(acl))) = i ∘1(acl)) ∨

        ¬oa(GEN_{ts}(dbn(dn(2(acl))),name-n)) ∨

        loc-n ≠ ⊥ ∧ $CALC_{ts}$(n,v) ≠ ⊥

where we use

    acl = s-AREA-CL(rec-n), rv = rv(name(n)) and

    v = (1(loc-n))(rv),...,(length(loc-n)(loc-n))(rv)

The error condition has to ensure that the area where the object is
to be stored is specified, that the new location which is generated by
the system is included in an open area, and that, if the location
clause is specified in the schema entry of the corresponding record
type, the data base does not already contain a record instance with
the same calc arguments. Only the third of these error conditions
can be understood by the user. Therefore he would expect that a
record object could always be stored, as long as the third condition is not violated.

We have divided the STORE command into three functions, the first,
GEN_{ts}, generating a new location, the second, Rsu, storing the
record value, and the third, SUPR, updating the currency registers.

The function GEN_{ts} has already been discussed, and we continue with
the definition

    Rsu(n)(ts) := db[loc_{ts}(cru)/rv(name(n))]

The function SUPR updates the currency registers according to the
rules specified in the SUPPRESS clause of the STORE statement.
A precise definition can be found in /Biller 75b/. After a new
record instance has been stored, the function loc_{ts} has to be
adjusted such that the data base key of the new record instance
identifies its storage location.

In the memory the semantics of the store command are defined as an
insertion of a new record occurrence into LTM and an update of
the orientation component O. But if the key used for the new instance
ri is already stored as a component of other instances ri', ri", ...
the store command has side effects which the user cannot understand.
In the new memory state into which the new storage state is mapped by
the verification function V the new record occurrence ro is inserted
into all record occurrences ro', ro", ... corresponding to ri', ri",
... respectively. To avoid these side effects, the system must always
select a data base key never used before. But it would now be very
difficult for a user of the system to create by himself a correct
unique data base key for use in a DML command.

3.3.2.2 The DELETE Command

We only discuss the DBTG DELETE command with the syntactic form
DELETE ONLY.
This command deletes the record instance which is designated by
the CRU register and changes some of the information contained in the
currency registers. In addition the owner records of all set instances of which the deleted record is a member are changed. All set instances of which the deleted record is the owner are deleted but
the member records of these sets are not touched by the command.
The abstract syntax of the command is given as DES. We define

$$R(des)(ts) :=$$
$$(er(Rd\text{-}single)(ERR) \supset TSE, Rd\text{-}single)$$

with

$$Rd\text{-}single = Rd(cru)(ci[1(CRU)/\bot], TSF)$$

Rd is a function with two parameters, a data base key and a storage
state, and it is defined by

$$Rd(key)(ts) := (ERROR \supset TSE, ts')$$

ERROR is $\underline{true}$ only if the record instance to be deleted is a
member of a set instance, the owner of which is located in a closed
area. This error condition again cannot be understood by the user
since in the memory such a set occurrence does not exist. Only those
set occurrences appear in the LTM where the corresponding owner
record instances are stored in open areas.

The state ts' is equal to ts except for the following changes:
1.) Assume l is a location in db which contains the owner record
    instance of a set instance si in which the record to be deleted
    is a member. Then l is changed to l', where l' is equal to l ex-
    cept that in that component of l which contains the keys of the
    members of si, the key of the record to be deleted is removed.
    The formal definition can be found in /Biller 75b/. Furthermore
    the functions loc_{ts} and add_{ts} are changed appropriately.
2.) The conditions
    loc_{ts}'$(key) = \bot$ and $db'(loc_{ts}(key)) = \bot$ have to be satisfied.
3.) $(\forall i)(ci \circ i(ci(CS)) = key \supset 2 \circ i(ci'(CS)) = PRIORS_{ts}(key,i))$,
    $(\forall i)(ci \circ i(ci(CS)) = key \supset 3 \circ i(ci'(CS)) = NEXTS_{ts}(key,i))$,
    $(\forall i)(ci \circ i(ci(CA)) = key \supset 2 \circ i(ci'(CA)) = PRIORA_{ts}(key,i))$,
    $(\forall i)(ci \circ i(ci(CA)) = key \supset 3 \circ i(ci'(CA)) = NEXTA_{ts}(key,i))$
where $PRIORS_{ts}$ is a function which produces the key of the record

which is the predecessor of the deleted one with respect to the ordering of the i-th set, $NEXTS_{ts}$ is a function which produces the
key of the next record, and $PRIORA_{ts}$ and $NEXTA_{ts}$ are the corresponding functions for the areas. In these functions record instances
which are stored in closed areas are also taken into account. If such
a function produces a key whose corresponding record instance is
stored in a closed area, then no corresponding record occurrence
exists in the memory and this cannot be understood by the user. He
would always expect that such a record can be found as long as,
for example in the NEXT case, the current record occurrence is not
the last member of the set occurrence.

The update of the CI-component is required since we have to keep the
keys of the PRIOR and NEXT records in the currency registers to allow
access to these records even after the current record has been deleted. The verification function associates these components of the
current of set registers with the concepts NEXT respectively PRIOR of
the last handled record occurrence of the respective set. But at the
user level this record occurrence is only defined unambiguously if no
members have been inserted into the set or have been removed from
the set since the record occurrence to which the NEXT refers has
been deleted. This might happen as a side effect of an OPEN AREA
or CLOSE AREA command but also when a DELETE or REMOVE command is
executed.

Assume for example a set occurrence $s = (o,m_1,m_2,m_3)$ of type S and
that at a certain time t m_1 would be the current record of S. Then
m_2 is the object which is denoted by the concept NEXT of set type S.
If we now remove or delete m_1 at time t', the concept NEXT of set
type S remains still defined (i.e. m_2), s' will contain (o,m_2,m_3),
and the current object of the set is undefined. But if at time t"
m_2 is also deleted, what happens to the value of the concept NEXT of
set type S? Should it be changed to m_3 or is it now undefined? The
question arises, whether the concept still has to represent the
situation at time t' when m_1 was deleted or should it reflect the
time t" if it is used by a FIND command to identify the next
member following the (already deleted) object m_1. In our realization we have decided to update the pointers in the respective registers every time a record instance is deleted. Here it is important to observe that this ambiguity of the CODASYL proposal could

not have occurred if a formal specification technique would have
been used for its production.

3.3.2.3 The FIND Command

The syntax of the FIND command is given by

FIND rse

$$
[SUPPRESS \left\{ \left| \begin{array}{l} \underline{ALL} \\ \underline{RECORD} \\ \underline{AREA} \\ set\text{-}name1[,set\text{-}name\text{-}2]...\underline{SET} \end{array} \right| \right\} CURRENCY\ UPDATES]
$$

The allowed formats for the record selection expression rse are
given below, each at the beginning of the paragraphs where its realization is described. The abstract syntax of the command is given by

FIS = FIND × RSE × SUP

SUP = ALL + RECORD × AREA × SETL

SETL = $|N^*$.

The FIND command moves the key of the record instance specified in
the rse-expression into the CRU-register. Furthermore other currency
registers may be altered depending on the suppress clause. The
realization is given by

$$R(fis)(ts) := (ERROR \ni TSE,FIND)$$

The FIND command cannot be successfully executed if the location
which corresponds to the data base key of the record instance designated by the record selection expression is an element of a closed
area or if it does not exist at all. FIND is an abbreviation for

FIND = SUPR'(s-SUP(fis)) ∘ MOVOWN ∘ If(s-RSE(fis))(TSF)

The function SUPR' updates the currency registers as specified in the
suppress clause of the find command. The function MOVOWN updates the
CRU register such that the keys of the owners of the current record
become the values of the corresponding components of the record component kept in the CRU register. The precise definitions of the error
condition ERROR and the functions SUPR and MOVOWN can be found in
/Biller 75b/ and are not given here.

We still have to describe the state transitions caused by the function If(s-RSE(fis)), which is assumed to change the uwa by including
the key of the record instance defined by rse as the value of the
CRU register.

The first form of the rse to be discussed here is given by

NEXT RECORD OF set-name SET

with the abstract syntax

$$FOR1 = DIR \times |N$$

This form allows to "navigate" within set instances whereby use is made of the insertion order of the member instances. The representation is defined by

If(next,n)(ts) :=

(UNDEF $\supset$ ci $\lceil$1(cru),2(cru)/3∘n(ci(CS)),⊥],

ci $\lceil$1(cru),2(cru)/NEXT$_{ts}$(ci(1∘n(CS)),n),⊥])

where UNDEF is true, if the record instance which is the current of the n-th set has been either removed from the set or deleted. In these cases the key of the next record instance is found in the third component of the n-th current of set register. Otherwise the function NEXT$_{ts}$ is used which has been described in section 3.3.2.2.

To simplify the semantics we suggest to introduce into DML a command FIND NEXT OF RECENT MEMBER OF set-name SET, which should be used in case the current record of the SET has been deleted or removed from the set.

If the record instance selected by using the above form is stored in a closed area, an error will occur at the implementors level, whereas the user expects an error only in case that the NEXT form is applied to the last member of the set.

The second form of the rse to be discussed is

record-name VIA [CURRENT OF] set-name

[USING data-base-identifier[,data-base-identifier]...]

with the abstract syntax

$$FOR2 = |N \times CURRENT \times |N \times IDL$$

This command is an example of a single DML command which comprises a sequence of elementary DML commands. But for reasons discussed below the command cannot be split up into an equivalent sequence of elementary commands.

For the evaluation of this rse the search path specified in the set selection clause of the member entry in the schema must be followed starting from a record instance which must be found according to the set selection clause. The specified path then has to be followed through the sets until the desired record instance is found.

The realization is defined by

If(n1,cur,n2,idl)(ts) = SEARCH(n1,idl,n2)∘SET(n1,cur,n2)(ts)

where the function SET stores the key of the owner of the set
instance specified by the set-selection-clause of the FIND command
into the CRU register and the function SEARCH calculates the key of
the record instance which is to be located.

$$SET(n1,cur,n2)(ts) :=$$
$$(cur \neq \bot \supset ci[1(CRU),2(CRU)/4\circ n2(ci(CS)),\bot],$$
$$O_{i=2}^{length(suc)} MEM(i\circ suc, 1\circ(i-1)\circ suc)\circ MEM(1\circ suc,2(s\text{-}TOP(sos)))\circ$$
$$FIN(s\text{-}TOP(sos))(ts))$$

where we use the abbreviations

sos = s-SOS(k∘s-MEMBER-CL(set-n2)), suc = s-SUC-CL(sos)

and k is the unique number where

s-REC-NAME∘k∘s-MEMBER-CL(set-n2) = s-REC-NAME(rec-n1)

The function FIN is defined as

$$FIN(spec,n)(ts) :=$$
$$(is\text{-}CURRENT(1(spec)) \supset ci[1(CRU),2(CRU)/4\circ n(ci(CS)),\bot],$$
$$is\text{-}KEY(1(spec)) \supset ci[1(CRU),2(CRU)/val1,\bot],$$
$$is\text{-}CALC(1(spec) \supset ci[1(CRU),2(CRU)/val2,\bot])$$

with
$$val1 = RV(O_{i=2}^{length(2(spec))}(i\circ 2(spec))(name(1(2(spec)))))$$

and
$$val2 = CALC_{ts}(nr,v)$$

where nr is the unique number where

s-OWNER(set-n) = s-REC-NAME(rec-nr)

and v is the tuple of values specified in the schema for the calculation of the key.

The function MEM has the definition

$$MEM((n1,tup),n2)(ts) := CI[1(CRU)/key]$$

where key is the database key of an instance of the owner record
type of the n1-th set of the schema which has the values designated
by the identifier tup and is member of the n2-th set instance whose
owners key is stored in the CRU-register of ts. The function
SEARCH(n1,idl,n2) stores the key of a record instance ri in CRU which
satisfies the following conditions:

1.) ri must be member in that set instance si of the n2-th set whose
    owner key is stored in the CRU register.
2.) ri must be the first instance in si of the n1-th record entry
    possessing the values specified in the identfier list idl.

In the evaluation of the search path through the hierarchy of sets
it is possible that set instances or record instances are used
which are stored in closed areas. As a consequence, it is not
possible to replace the search by a DML programm "FIND top owner,
Find the owner of the next set by its membership in the top set, ..."
Another consequence is given by the fact that the search path cannot
be travelled along in the STM component of the memory, since the
user does not see some of the records or sets in this path. Again
the concept of the areas can not be hidden unless the semantics
of the DML are changed in an appropriate manner.

4. Conclusions

In this paper we have shown how the semantics of a data manipulation
language can be formally defined. We have taken as an example the
CODASYL DML and illustrated, that by means of formal description
techniques ambiguities in the language can be revealed. Furthermore we have shown that a user may not be aware of the side effects
which are caused by the data base keys in the STORE command. Finally
we have concluded that the area concept cannot be hidden from the
user without changing the semantics of the DML.

Up to now we have only described a single user system. A still open
research area can be found in applying the semantic description
techniques to the synchronization problems arising in multi user
systems.

The transition from the user view to the implementor view of the data
base languages DDL and DML is clearly established by the definition
of the verification functions. The implementor view as described in
this paper still is an abstraction from a real implementation of a
CODASYL data base system. But using the same method further levels
might be introduced in which more details of a real implementation
are taken into account. The correctness of each of these descriptions
can be shown by constructing suitable verification functions. This
leads to a stepwise process which ends in a description of the
CODASYL system which directly could be coded in a suitable programming language. When applied in such a fashion the theory of mathematical semantics will become a valuable tool for the development of
complex software systems.

5. References

Bekič,H.,Walk,K.(71): Formalization of Storage Properties. In:
    Lecture Notes in Mathematics 188

Biller,H.(74),Neuhold,E.J.: Formal View on Schema-Subschema Corres-
    pondence. In: Proc. IFIP Congres 74, North Holland, Amsterdam

Biller,H.(75a),Glatthaar,W.: On the Semantics of Data Bases: The
    Semantics of Data Definition Languages. In: Lecture Notes in
    Computer Science, Vol. 34

Biller,H.(75b),Glatthaar,W.,Neuhold,E.J.: On the Semantics of Data
    Bases: The Semantics of Data Manipulation Languages - A Logical
    Data Manipulation Language. Report 06/75, Inst.f.Informatik,
    Universität Stuttgart

CODASYL (71): CODASYL Data Base Task Group Report. April 1971, ACM

CODASYL (73): CODASYL DDL, Journal of Development. June 1973, ACM

Douqué,B.C.M.(75), G.M. Nijssen (eds): Data Base Description.
    Amsterdam

Engles,R.W.(76): Currency and Concurrency in the COBOL Data Base
    Facility. In this volume

Glatthaar,W.(75): A Problem-Oriented Input Processor Supporting
    Problem Solving. Report 02/75 Institut für Informatik, Universi-
    tät Stuttgart

Lucas,P.,Walk,K.(70): On the Formal Description of PL/I. In: Annual
    Review in Automatic Programming, Vol. 6

McCarthy,J.(62): Towards a Mathematical Science of Computation. In:
    Proc.2nd IFIP Conference, Amsterdam

Rumelhart,D.E.(72): A Process Model for Long-Term-Memory. In: Tul-
    ving,E.(ed.), Organization of Memory, New York

Scott,D.(70): An Outline of a Mathematical Theory of Computation.
    In: Proc. Fourth Annual Princeton Conference on Information
    Sciences and Systems, Vol. 2, March 1970

Scott,D.(71): The Lattice of Flow Diagrams. In: Lecture Notes in
    Mathematics 188

Strachey,C.(73): The Variety of Programming Language. Oxford Uni-
    versity Computing Laboratory, Technical Monograph PRG-10

Sundgren,B.(73): An Infological Approach to Data Bases. Urval Nr.7,
    Statistika Centralbyran, Stockholm

Appendix: Notations

1. If $M = (m_i; i\epsilon I)$ is a set, then the operator B constructs the complete lattice

   $$B(M) = \quad$$

2. Let be D_i $(1 \leq i \leq n)$ a finite family of complete lattices. We define compound lattices corresponding to /Scott 70/:
   a) $\pi_{i=1}^n D_i$ as the product lattice $D_1 \times \ldots \times D_n$; by a product the concurrent occurrence of several components can be described,
   b) if the D_i's are pairwise disjoint, then $\Sigma_{i=1}^n D_i$ denotes the sum $D_1 + D_2 + \ldots + D_n$; by a sum it is described that the elements of the component domains can occur alternatively,
   c) $D_i^n = \pi_{k=1}^n D_i$; $D_i = D_i^1 + D_i^2 + \ldots$,
   d) $[D_i \dashrightarrow D_j]$ as the set of continous functions from D_i to D_j.
3. For any compound lattice we have an abstract syntax /Mc Carthy 62/ to decompose it. The names of the predicates and functions are derived from the (unique) names of the described domains as it is done in the Vienna Definition Language (/Lucas 70/):
   a) For $\Sigma_{i=1}^n D_i$ the <u>predicate</u> is-D_i(d) is true if $d\epsilon D_i$.
   b) For $d \epsilon \pi_{i=1}^n D_i$ the <u>function</u> (selector) s-D_i or the number i extracts the i-th component of d.
   c) For $d \epsilon D_i^*$ the function <u>length</u> is defined as:
      length(d) = n iff $d\epsilon D_i^n$.
   d) Some predicates and functions have self-explanatory names, e.g. first and is-first.
4. By $\supset$ we denote the conditional as it is defined in /Scott 71/.
5. If f is a function as above and a is an element of D_i and v of D_j, then f[a/v] denotes the function which results, if the value of f for the argument a is altered to v.
   $f[a_1/v_1, \ldots, a_n/v_n]$ and $f[a_1, \ldots, a_n/v_1, \ldots, v_n]$ denote both the corresponding function altered for the arguments $a_1, \ldots, a_n$.
6. $\bigcirc_{i=1}^N f_i$ is the product $f_N \circ \ldots \circ f_1$ of the functions $f_1, \ldots, f_N$. If the product of the functions f_i with $i \epsilon I$ is invariant under any permutation of the factors, we denote this unique product by $\bigcirc_{i \epsilon I}$.
7. Let a function $f: \pi_{i=1}^n D_i \dashrightarrow \pi_{i=1}^n D_i$ be representable as $f_1 \times \ldots \times f_n$ with $f_i: D_i \dashrightarrow D_i'$, i.e. f maps the D_i's collaterally but independent. Then $f' := f_i[a/v]$ denotes that f' is the result of changing the i-th component of f in the described manner.

Modelling in Data Base Management Systems, G.M. Nijssen, (ed.)
North Holland Publishing Company, 1976

A SEMANTIC MODEL OF INTEGRITY CONSTRAINTS
ON A RELATIONAL DATA BASE

Herbert Weber
Technische Universität Berlin

Abstract

To allow different users to share a common Data Base makes it necessary to define
the semantics of the data in precise terms. This paper introduces a technique to
define semantic constraints on a relational Data Base and describes the specifications of Data Base operations. The specification method is the well known
concept of "operational semantics". The paper demonstrates the technique by
defining an abstract operation 'add relation value'.

1 Introduction

In current concepts a Data Base is defined as "... a collection of data stored on
disks, drums or other secondary storage media" [3]. It contains the data of a
variety of users whose concern is just one portion of the entire Data Base.
"Different users' portions will overlap in different ways"[3].

Since data are descriptions of real entities, the definition of such portions
requires the specification of their logical consistent overlapping and sharing
among different users. In order to develop a precise notation for such a logical
consistent sharing of data we need some means to express the relationship between
real world entities as seen by different users and their representation as data.

We consider therefore in this paper a Data Base as a symbolic representation of
knowledge about some parts of the real world. In order to allow different views
on a Data Base we develop a uniform and hopefully unambiguous symbolic representation of knowledge based on the relational concept of Data Bases.

Starting from a semantic net representation of knowledge one can show the major
deficiencies of the relational concept as a representational tool. We show that
two different types of integrity constraints have to be added to the concept,
those which define new representational primitives and those which give further
specification capabilities for the primitives already existent in the model.

To model both the relational concept and the two kinds of integrity constraints
in a uniform way we introduce a graph schema - so called D-graphs.

Besides this static representation of knowledge we specify formally how the
representation of knowledge may be changed in order to reflect the real world
changes. This specification is done using operational semantics as introduced
for the specification of the programming language semantics.

2 Data Semantics

A Data Base is a symbolic representation of knowledge about some parts of the
real world. To achieve an adequate representation of this real world we need a
specification of the relationship between the real world and its representation.
This relationship, however, is determined by someone's knowledge about this real
world and his interpretation of an abstract representation.

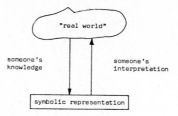

Since we can't control human beings'cognitive processes we can't specify this
relationship formally as we do in specifying the relationship between computational processes and their representation by programs.

The only way to support an adequate representation is by enforcing the users to
embed a certain type and amount of information into the Data Base so that further
interpretations of this representation are as unambiguous as possible. The specification of the kind of information which should be represented in the Data Base
in order to make the Data Base suitable for a certain purpose is called here
data semantics.

The use of any symbolic representation to model the reality is based on the
assumption, that human beings have a common understanding of the symbolic model.
This is usually true only for a symbolic representation of a natural language.
Using this natural language representation all the symbols of the natural
language encoded in a machine readable form are the data of the Data Base.
Neither is this model simple enough to allow the computations which are considered to be necessary on a Data Base nor is it sufficiently formal to serve as
an easy understandable basis to communicate precisely about the reality.

Human beings therefore tend to develop more abstract specialists'languages or
very simplified abstract representations of natural languages. The simplification
which we believe is appropriate to meet the requirements for Data Base purposes
enclose the following language elements:
(1) symbols defined on the same alphabet e.g., the english alphabet,
(2) classes of symbols *,
(3) dependencies between different symbols and between different classes of
    symbols and
(4) classes of dependencies.

The representational tool to model this simplified natural language is the
semantic net concept [1] which is introduced for natural language modelling.
This model provides a framework to analyse existing data models(e.g., relational
data model),their deficiencies and advantages.

2.1 Semantic nets

This model allows the representation of symbols and dependencies: symbols are
representations of real entities e.g., objects, attributes, characteristics etc.,
and might be words, numerals or -numeric strings. The notion of dependency is
based on the assumption that every symbol gets its meaning through its connection
to other symbols. This connection indicates that the symbols involved are in some
way dependent upon each other.

---

* The term classes as used here does not correspondend to the one defined as
  disjoint subsets of a set in mathematics.

EXAMPLE

The connection of the symbol 'SCHEDULE' with the symbols 'ACTIVITY', 'START' and 'TERMINATION' characterizes a schedule as a listing of activities and their start and termination times.

A graphical depiction used to demonstrate the model will be given in the following paragraph.

Symbols are represented as nodes, dependencies as directed arcs of a graph called the semantic net.

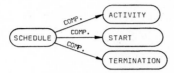

The relationship between 'SCHEDULE' and its characterizing symbols is named 'COMPONENT' to indicate that the identification of an activity and the determination of its start and termination times are the components of a schedule.

This semantic net represents a schedule in a very abstract sense. It does not indicate whether this is a schedule of a processor of a computer-system or a schedule for a transportation vehicle. In order to make the net more complete one has to add other symbols and to connect them to the existing graph.

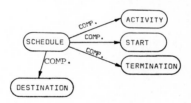

The connection of a symbol 'DESTINATION' with the previously defined semantic net indicates that it describes a vehicle schedule. This net, however, is not complete in the sense that it does not describe all the dependencies existing between the drawn symbols: e.g., there exists a dependency between 'ACTIVITY' and 'START' and between 'ACTIVITY' and 'TERMINATION' which represents the fact that one start and termination time might be associated with one activity.

The semantic net concept as introduced above is still a rather incomplete representational tool in order to model the knowledge about the reality. We will show now that the modelling of a certain type of knowledge requires the representation of classes of symbols, dependencies among classes of symbols and classes of dependencies. Before we explain what kind of knowledge may be represented by these three modelling concepts we want to stress another point of the semantic net representation.

Despite the fact that arcs and nodes represent different things (symbols and dependencies) we identify them both by symbols. This means that one type of symbols used in this depiction is a representation of an interrelationship between symbols. Thus we don't use symbols only to denote elementary entities but also to identify compositions of such entities. These kinds of symbols are therefore abstract representations for a collection of composed entities. This concept of abstraction is one of the most powerful tool to handle complexity [4] and is the underlying principle to compose classes of symbols and classes of depen-

dencies as well. We will use this technique in a very systematic way to define
the D-graph model of Data Bases in the following chapters of this paper.

Classes of symbols are collections with a common meaning of all the elements e.g.,
'JOHN', 'PAUL', 'FRITZ' is a collection of symbols usually used as person names.
Their common meaning is given by their common characteristic to identify persons.
In order to simplify the communication about this class of symbols the term
'FIRST NAME' might be introduced as an abstract representation of the entire
class of symbols used to identify persons. This class building concept is an
abstraction in the sense defined above.

Dependencies among classes of symbols are a further abstraction and they model
the characteristics of a relationship between collections of entities like those
between PERSON NUMBERS and SALARY. In order to express the fact that every person
has a unique salary but a number of persons may have the same salary we define
a functional dependency among the classes of symbols PERSONNUMBER and SALARY (a
detailed discussion of those dependencies will follow in section 2.4).

Classes of dependencies are collections with the same characteristics e.g., a
SUPERIOR / SUBORDINATE dependency might appear between EMPLOYEES, MACHINE PARTS
etc. Their abstract representation by the symbol 'SUPERIOR / SUBORDINATE'
denotes again an abstraction in the sense explained above.

Thus we represent knowledge in a symbolic form through the association of
symbols (identifiers) with real world entities and by abstractions.

The same graphical depiction as the one used to represent symbols and dependencies between symbols is than appropriate to represent classes of symbols and
classes of dependencies as well.

The semantic net representation, however, does not allow to distinguish between
symbols representing elementary entities and those which are representations for
classes of symbols and dependencies. We will show later that a further specification of the abstractions is essential in order to model the semantics of the
described real world correctly (see chapter 2.5).

The semantic net representation of knowledge lacks also with respect to a precise
notation of views. Views are subsets and compositions of subsets of the knowledge
embedded in a Data Base compatible with the defined data semantics. Thus the
definition of views requires some means to partition semantic nets into subnets
and their recomposition in a modified form. We therefore introduce in Chapter 3
and 4 a constructive approach to build a semantic net which allows the definition
of views in a very straight forward way.

2.2 The relational Data Base concept and semantic net representation of knowledge

We show in this section how the described semantic net concept relates to
existing Data Base concepts. In current existing Data Base concepts (relational
concept, network concept [5, 6]) the data model or the schema represents the knowledge about the real world. They both might be interpreted as simplified semantic
nets [7]. They are, however, less a representation of knowledge than a symbolic
representation of more or less arbitrarily selected real world entities. And the
symbolic representation in terms of a data model allows only the specification
of a very limited number of dependencies e.g., functional dependencies between
record types (in the network model) and functional dependencies between relation
domains (in the relational model).*

---
*
We expect here that the reader is familiar with this notation and the concepts
mentioned above.

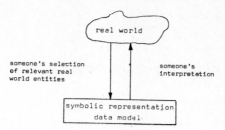

In order to explain the relational data model as a simplified semantic net we use the example introduced in chapter 2.1.

The information necessary at a certain airport to allow seatreservations, crew assignments and the scheduling of starts and landings might be represented by the following semantic net.

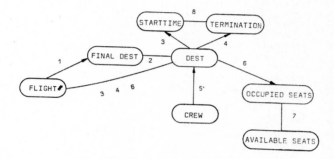

Arrows represent functional dependencies. All other types of dependencies are represented as undirected arcs. We specify now the semantics of this symbolic representation of a real situation: Therefore we specify the type of dependency connecting the different symbols displayed in this net.

(1) Unique identification of a final destination by a FLIGHT NUMBER but a number of flights can terminate at the same FINAL DESTINATION.

(2) FINAL DESTINATION is one element of the set DESTINATION.

(3) Only FLIGHT NUMBER and DESTINATION together determine a unique STARTTIME.

(4) and LANDING TIME.

(5) One CREW can go to one DESTINATION only but many CREWS can fly to the same DESTINATION.

(6) Only FLIGHT NUMBER and DESTINATION together determine the number of OCCUPIED SEATS.

(7) The number of AVAILABLE SEATS is greater than or equal to the number of occupied seats.

(8) The STARTTIME at one DESTINATION is greater than the TERMINATION time and every STARTTIME is associated with one TERMINATION time and vice versa.

Relations are considered as named components of a semantic net. Each symbol of
the component represents an abstract description of a class of symbols. A named
subset of the cartesian product over all n classes of symbols of this net component - that is a set of n-tuples - is a relation.

e.g., FLIGHTSCHEDULE: DESTINATION, TERMINATIONTIME, STARTTIME
     FLIGHT: FLIGHT#, DESTINATION, OCCUP SEATS

In these examples 'FLIGHTSCHEDULE' and 'FLIGHT' are relation names and the
symbols 'DESTINATION', 'LANDINGTIME', 'STARTTIME' etc. are attributes of these
relations. The symbols 'FLIGHTSCHEDULE' and 'FLIGHT' are abstract representations
for a set of n-tuples. The symbols 'DESTINATION', 'LANDINGTIME', 'STARTTIME' are
abstract representations for sets of symbols with common meaning.

In order to understand the semantics of a relation we describe the abstraction
underlying the definition of a relation in more detail:

For the pure relational model as described in [5] a relation can be considered
as an isolated and simplified component of a semantic net. Since a semantic net
represents the available knowledge of some part of the real world the separation
of the relation from the net has to take into account the connections which
exist between this component and the rest of the net. This connection is expressed
by a suitable relationname e.g., 'FLIGHTSCHEDULE' indicates that the symbols
'DESTINATION', 'STARTTIME' and 'TERMINATIONTIME' are components of a flight
schedule as indicated by the semantic net and are not components of a travelling
salesmen time table. We say therefore the relationname is a specification - at
least to some extent - of the context in which certain attributs are interrelated
in a relation.

Besides this it is assumed that a relation name specifies the subset of the
cartesian product - the set of n-tuples - which is permissible in the context
defined by the relation name e.g., the relationname 'FLIGHTSCHEDULE' indicates
that no more than one activity can take place at the same time at the same airport to avoid crashes. This restriction excludes a number of tuples which might
be permitted in a trainschedule. In a relation 'TRAINSCHEDULE', however, more
starts and terminations of trains at the same time at one station are allowed
depending on the number of platforms in this station.

A relation in the pure relational model does not express the dependencies between the different attributs of this relation as they are displayed in the
semantic net. We therefore expect that the relation name and the attribute names
indicate of what nature these dependencies are.

e.g., The relationname 'FLIGHT' indicates that the attribute 'FINAL DESTINATION'
      is functional dependent on the attribute 'FLIGHT#' in the 'FLIGHT' relation.

Thus the relational model introduces a new kind of abstraction. We find therefore
in the model abstract representations for (1) classes of symbols (2) dependencies
between classes of symbols and (3) relations as compositions of dependencies.

2.3 Integrity constraints

We have learned from the semantic net concept that the symbolic representation of
knowledge in terms of the relational data model is a very restricted description
of the reality since it does not allow the explicit representation of arbitrary
dependencies and validity sets.

This incompleteness causes the necessity to avoid manipulation of the Data Base
by persons who don't know the complete intrinsic dependency structure of the
Data Base. This requirement, however, is opposed to the idea of integrated Data
Bases and views. To overcome this disadvantage of the described data model repre-

sentations of knowledge a new level of description of the data is proposed. This level on top of the data model is introduced to represent <u>integrity constraints</u> [8, 9].

These integrity constraints are specified in current concepts in terms of manipulation restrictions: The manipulation of one Data Base object dependent on another object requires to check that the manipulation of this object is compatible with the existing dependency or that both objects connected by this dependency may be manipulated in a corresponding way.

The insertion of integrity constraints is even more important with respect to views where objects "visible" via one view are dependent on objects "visible" via another view. A Manipulation of such objects via one view requires to check whether this manipulation is compatible with the existing dependency or whether a corresponding manipulation can be performed on the object "visible" through the other view in order to keep the Data Base consistent.

As we have seen the notion of completeness of a symbolic representation is important with respect to descriptions of the reality and for the introduction of integrity constraints.

There is certainly no way to specify the completeness of a symbolic representation in an absolute sense but rather relativ to (1) the ability of the human beings who create the representations and (2) with respect to the purpose the representation serves for.

With this restriction in mind and considering the examples given in the previous section we can ask two different questions about the completeness of a representational model:

(1) Can we embed all the knowledge a human being wants to represent for a certain purpose? If not the model is incomplete with respect to the available representational capabilities and we have to introduce new primitives into the representational model.

    EXAMPLE:
    For the relational data model we need some additional representational capabilities in order to represent other than functional dependencies.

(2) Can we represent the knowledge completely or do we need further specification capabilities for the primitives of the representational model?

    EXAMPLE:
    For the complete specification of a relation we would need means to specify the set of valid tuples of a relation.

We thus define two types of integrity constraints in order to achieve sufficiently complete symbolic representations. We are going to introduce a classification of integrity constraints of the first type for the relational data model in the following chapter and discuss the nature of the constraints of second type thereafter.

2.4 Dependencies

In the previous sections of this chapter we have shown that dependencies are an essential part of the symbolic representation of knowledge. In both the semantic net model and the data model representations the explizit specification of dependencies is necessary either to characterize the arcs in the semantic net or to denote integrity constraints on the data model representations. In either case dependencies serve as a tool to establish and complete a symbolic representation of knowledge.

The other advantage of a notation for dependencies is that they are a direct representation of the semantic facts a user wants to incorporate into the Data Base.
Considering semantic facts rather than data elements as the primitives of the Data
Base is the reason why the relational concept is much closer to the needs of a
nonprofessional user of the Data Base than the network oriented concepts. We
therefore follow this line and incorporate a concept to represent arbitrary interrelationships in the relational concept. Thereby we provide the opportunity to
express the manipulation of semantic facts directly.

Since we are interested to model complex interrelationships (e.g., complex semantic facts) we propose here a very constructive and structural approach: we introduce simple dependencies which might be composed into more complex ones. This
constructive approach is also choosen in order to simplify the correctness prove
of the specifications of the dependencies in a structural way. We therefore introduce a classification of dependencies.

We distinguish roughly the following types of dependencies: (1) dependencies among
symbols,(2) dependencies among classes of symbols e.g., domains,(3) intrarelational dependencies (binare relations between symbols and classes of symbols e.g.,
attribute values, attributes and their composition within a relation),(4) interrelational dependencies (among different relations).

2.4.1. Dependencies among symbols

A dependency among symbols denotes any kind of relationship between symbols
contained in the Data Base.

EXAMPLE:

The alphabetic ordering of literals establishes a dependency PREDECESSOR/
SUCCESSOR

a < c / e > c
or the dependency IMMEDIATE PREDECESSOR/IMMEDIATE SUCCESSOR
a << b / c >> b

Other dependencies among symbols might be EQUAL, NONEQUAL, LESS, GREATER etc.

2.4.2. Dependencies among classes of symbols

We defined classes of symbols as not necessarily disjoint sets. The kind of
dependencies which might exist between these sets in a Data Base are:

subset dependency

A subset dependency denotes that a class A of symbols is the subset of a class B
of symbols

A $\subseteq$ B

EXAMPLE:

The class of symbols representing MANAGERS is a subset of the class of symbols
representing EMPLOYEES

MANAGER $\subseteq$ EMPLOYEE

disjoint dependency

A disjoint dependency denotes that a class A of symbols has no common elements
with a class B of symbols

A $\vee$ B = $\emptyset$

EXAMPLE:

The class of symbols representing PERSON ≢ can't represent MACHINEPART ≢ at the
same time in order to avoid misunderstandings: PERSON ≢ v MACHINEPART ≢ = ∅.

This were just very simple dependencies among symbols and classes of symbols.
Other more complex relationships among arbitrary abstractions are easy to construct. In this paper, however, we want to establish a notion of dependencies
within the relational framework. The dependencies identifyable there are also
those between symbols and classes of symbols and between more complex abstractions. But we have to be aware of the fact that relations are isolated parts of
the entire knowledge one wants to represent (parts of the entire semantic net).
And relations define a certain context in which a dependency might exist which
does not exist in another context. We therefore have to distinguish between intrarelational dependencies (in a certain context) and interrelational dependencies
(they exist independent of certain relations in the entire Data Base).

2.4.3. Simple intrarelational dependencies

Contexts

These primitives express the relationship between two attributes in a relation.
These intrarelational dependencies are defined only within a relation e.g., in a
certain context defined by this relation. They don't necessarily exist in another
relation which contains the same attributes.

EXAMPLE:

In a relation AIRLINE SCHEDULE the attribute NUMBER OF PASSENGERS is less or
equal the NUMBER OF SEATS

AIRLINE SCHEDULE: NUMBER OF PASSENGERS ≤ NUMBER OF SEATS

This dependency does not exist in a relation TRAINSCHEDULE since trains allow
passengers to stand in the train. Thus we introduce here context dependend
dependencies.

Correspondence

Correspondence denotes the fact that an n to n mapping between two attributes
(classes of symbols) exist. The set of all valid value pairs of this correspondence is defined by the cartesian product between the two sets of symbols*. Since
we talk about dependencies in a relation we understand by correspondence the un-
ristricted combination of values of the two classes of symbols within the relation.

Subset dependency

If the set of values of one attribute is a subset of the set of values of the
second attribute these two attributes are said to be in a subset dependency. To denote a subset dependency we use the following notation:

RN: A ⊆ B

EXAMPLE:

SCHEDULE: FLIGHT≢, CREW, DESTINATION ⊆ FINAL DESTINATION

---

*
The difference between correspondence and a binary relation is that a relation
is a named (by the relationname) correspondence.

Functional dependency

A functional dependency between two attributes of a relation denotes an n to l mapping between the value sets of these two attributes

RN: A → B

EXAMPLE:

SCHEDULE: FLIGHT#, CREW → DESTINATION

θ-dependency

If the corresponding values of two attributes of a relation (values in the same tuple) are in the same θ-relationship, the two attributes are said to form a θ-dependency.

RN: A θ B

EXAMPLE:

FLIGHT: FLIGHT#, SEATS $\geq$ OCCUPANCY

2.4.4. Compound dependencies

In the previous sections of this paragraph we considered simple dependencies between two attributes. To reflect real situations in a relational Data Base we have to treat compositions of these simple dependencies.* We will distinguish between a number of different types of compositions.

Dependencies between compound attributes

This simple type of composition is well understood for functional dependencies between compound attributes. They are the primitive objects in a Third Normal Form Data Base and the manipulation of such a Data Base is formally described in the literature [11].

Compound attributes are concatenations of simple attributes of a relation. Dependencies between compound attributes indicate that a relationship exists only between concatenations of symbols. We refer here again to the example introduced in chapter 2.2 and show now an example of a compound dependency.

EXAMPLES:

(F#, DEST → START), (F#, DEST → TERM), (F#, DEST → OCCUP)

Dependency concatanations

A number of concatanated dependencies of a relation could be established if some attributes of this relation participate in two different dependencies e.g.,

R: A θ B → C θ D

EXAMPLE:

Supposed we define a relation
CREWSCHEDULE: CREW, DESTINATION, STARTTIME
the following dependency concatenation exist:

CREW → DESTINATION → STARTTIME

---

* That means we consider now dependencies among more complex abstractions.

The attribute DESTINATION participates in the two functional dependencies

CREW → DESTINATION and
DESTINATION → STARTTIME

indicating that one crew can go to one destination only and that this crew can start to this destination at one time only.

Multiple dependencies

If attributes of a relation are dependent in more than one way we call them multiple dependent e.g.,

R: (A B) (→, Θ) (C D)

EXAMPLE:

Supposed we define a relation

AIRPORT TIMETABLE: (F#, STARTTIME) (→,≠) (F#, TERMINATIONTIME)

the two compound attributes (F#, STARTTIME) and (F#, TERMINATIONTIME) are in a functional dependency and in a not equal dependency as well. This two simultaneous existing dependencies indicate that for one starttime of a certain flight only one terminationtime exists and that the starttime is not equal to the terminationtime.

Note that an equal dependence is always functional and a subset dependence can never be functional.

Another kind of multiple dependency exists if one attribut participates in a number of different dependencies with other attributes of this relation e.g,

(A B) :: (→ C) , (Θ D), ((→, Θ) E)

The compound attribute (A B) participates in the functional dependency (A B) → C, the Θ-dependency (A B) Θ D and the multiple dependency (A B) (→, Θ) E as well.

EXAMPLE:

Supposed we define a relation

SECURITY CONTROL: (F#, DEST), START, OCCUP

the attribute destination participates in the multiple functional dependency

$$(F\#, DEST) \quad \begin{array}{c} \longrightarrow \quad START \\ \longrightarrow \quad OCCUP \end{array}$$

indicating that for one flight to a certain destination only one starttime and only one number of occupied seats can exist. (This kind of multiple dependencies is already discussed in the literature [3, 10] at lenght.)

2.4.5. Composite dependencies

The most complex kind of abstraction which might be constructed within a relation are composite dependencies: they represent dependencies between dependencies.

EXAMPLE:

Supposed we define a relation

UN-CITIZEN: SOCSEC#, NAME, CITY, COUNTRY

we can define the following dependency structure (the complexity of the dependency considered here forces us to depart from our standard example and to choose one of international dimension).

(SOCSEC# → NAME) → (CITY → COUNTRY)

The semantics of this dependency structure is described below

(1) Every person with a certain name A has only one social security number
(2) Every city is only in one country
(3) Every social security number exists only once in a city of a certain country
    it might, however, exist a number of times in different countries
(4) Every social security number exists only once in a country
(5) Every person with a certain social security number lives in only one city of
    one particular country (at least at a certain time)

2.4.6. Relations

Relations are arbitrary concatenations of

(1) simple dependencies and/or
(2) compound dependencies and/or
(3) composite dependencies
e.g.,

R: A, B, C → [(C ⊖ B) → (E ⊖ F)].

2.4.7. Interrelational dependencies

We want to show now that we don't model the reality by relations and their
internal structure completely. That means that connections between relations
are of great importance too. We can distinguish two different types of interrelational dependencies:

(1) Those which depend upon the existence of common components (e. g. attributes)
    in different relations and
(2) Those which exist independent of the relational structure of the Data Base
    (e.g., among different attributes of different relations)

We are going to explain this two dependency types with a few examples only.

(1) Suppose the Data Base contains the two relations

    FLIGHT: FLIGHT#, DESTINATION, OCCUP
    FLIGHT SCHEDULE: FLIGHT#, START, TERM, DEST

    The second relation might be considered as a characterization of the objects
    described in the first one. Thus tuples in the second one need not to be
    kept in the Data Base if the corresponding tuple in the first one is deleted.
    We can refer to that fact by defining it as a GOVERNOR/DEPENDENT dependency
    among these two relations.

    A number of papers have been published recently in which this kind of
    connection is described in very detail [13, 14, 15] which should not be
    repeated here.

(2) Suppose the Data Base contains the domains SOCIAL SECURITY# and EMPLOYEE#

    These two domains are in a functional dependency independent of the relatio-
    nal structure of the Data Base. And in every relation in which subsets of
    these domains appear as attributes, the attributes are in a functional de-
    pendency SOCSEC# → EMPLOYEE#.

A more detailed explanation of these two types of interrelational dependencies
may be found in [7].

2.4.8. Connections and couples

Since there exist dependencies in a certain context only (in a certain relation)
we have to be aware of another kind of (potential) dependencies. The relational
concept provides compositions of relations by joins and their decomposition by

projections. Suppose we perform a projection seperating the two components of an intrarelational dependency we would loose some information. In order to perform a recomposition at a later time we would need this information again since this information represents a join restriction. Therefore we need some means to keep this information in the meantime. We propose a particular kind of dependency too - so called connections between domains and couples between simple dependencies - to treat this problem [12]. A detailed description of this concept is beyond the scope of this paper.

This is of course not a complete set of dependency types existing in the real world nor do we believe it is possible to specify all the dependencies existing between certain value sets. This is caused by the fact that a human being has always a limited knowledge about the real world. Though we don't expect to be able to define the integrity of a Data Base in an absolute sense but as a measure relative to the recognized dependencies.

2.5. Abstractions

We introduced the term abstraction and the concept underlying this notation in chapter 2.1 of this paper in a very informal way. We therefore precise this concept in the following paragraphs.

By abstraction we understand a mechanism to gather simple components into a complex system and the representation of this system by a more abstract description - the abstract object. The abstract description serves as a tool to express relevant details and to suppress irrelevant details of the components description.

Applied to the concept of representing knowledge this mechanism specifies the combination of elementary information entities into a complex one and its representation by an abstract object. The abstract description should <u>express what</u> the meaning of this abstract entity is rather than <u>specifying how</u> this meaning is established in terms of lower level abstract objects (e.g., how this abstraction is implemented).

As we have shown in chapter 2.3 for a complete representation of knowledge it is insufficient to specify an abstract object just by the set of components currently associated with the abstract object. We must define for the abstract object the entire set of all valid components in order to prevent the Data Base from invalid components after its manipulation.

As a large number of investigations have shown (see for example [17]) a static representation of knowledge as demonstrated so far is insufficient to model the real world correctly. It is widely accepted that the use one can make of information entities determines its meaning to a great extent. Thus a complete specification of an abstract object has to consider its dynamic characteristics too.

EXAMPLE:

Supposed a class of symbols COINVALUE contains the symbols '0.01', '0.05', '0.10', '0.50', '1.00'. In order to model the semantics of this abstract object one might allow the following operations: (1) compare of equality (2) add (3) substract but not the operations (1) update (leads to an undefined type of coin) (2) multiply (the multiplication of money values is senseless). The operation insert might be allowed if one inserts a symbol '0.25' in order to express that the class should contain the series of american coins and not coins of german currency.

We thus associate with every abstract object a piece of code describing all the operations which might be applied to this object. This is the concept of abstract data types [2] where each abstract data type is characterized by all the operations applicable to it.

Since this concept is suitable to model the static properties of abstract data objects (the composition by which it is defined) and the behavioural properties too we have found a method to specify the second kind of integrity constraints in a systematic manner.

A more detailed description of the concept can be found in [18]. It represents a combination of static and procedural embedding of knowledge in a Data Base.

3   The D-graph model

We introduce now a modified semantic net concept which is suitable to represent the relational data model, the two types of integrity constraints and therefore the specification of Data Base changes in precise terms. We call this uniform concept a semantic model of integrity constraints.

The model which we will introduce here briefly is supposed to have the following characteristics:

(1) We expect to be able to represent and specify every kind of abstraction e.g., we will model arbitrary classes of symbols and arbitrary dependencies in a clear way. (It also means that we are able to model any kind of integrity constraints).

(2) The model should provide means to represent any abstraction as an independent entity on which we can perform the usual Data Base operations e.g., retrievals and manipulations. This gives us the opportunity to represent semantic facts rather than machine oriented data items like records and fields in the Data Base.

(3) The model should also allow to express the separation of parts of the Data Base in order to define views compatible with the semantics of the entire Data Base.

(4) The sharing of objects among various abstractions is an intrinsic property of the relational model (the same domain might be a component of various relations, a dependency might be shared between a number of relations [7]) and is also important with respect to views if different views "contain" the same data objects. The model must therefore provide a mechanism to express the sharing of objects.

The model which we propose here meets these requirements. In this model the content of the Data Base is represented by a D-graph (directed acyclic graph or dependency graph). The graph is composed of two kinds of nodes: terminal nodes which represent atomic (nondecomposable) objects of the Data Base and nonterminal nodes representing abstractions. With the directed arcs of this graph we associate the relationship "contains". Common subcomponents of different abstractions are represented as nodes to which a number of arcs point and the number of components of an abstract object is depicted by the number of emanating arcs from the node representing this abstraction (the arcs are supposed to point downward). Every arc label identifies only one node but one node might be identified by a number of labels.

EXAMPLE:

To illustrate the concept we represent elements of the relation FLIGHTSCHEDULE of Chapter 2 as a D-graph. We assume here attributes to be atomic.

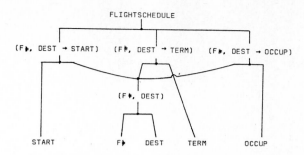

The relation FLIGHTSCHEDULE is composed of three functional dependencies

F#, DEST → START
F#, DEST → TERM
F#, DEST → OCCUP

Each of them contains the compound attribute (F#, DEST) e.g., they share this component. They are defined as composed of simple attributes and the compound attribute mentioned above. The atomic Data Base objects are the attributes START, F#, DEST, TERM, OCCUP. Every node in this graph represents an independent Data Base object.

The complete picture of a D-graph would have to enclose a piece of code associated with every node in the graph specifying all the operations applicable to the objects represented by the nodes. The model indicates that there is no basic difference between relationsand the integrity constraints of the first type. They all are just a dependency schema defined for a collection of atomic objects.

4 Views on a relational Data Base

The idea of views is first exhibited in CODASYL's network concept of a Data Base [6]. The content of the entire Data Base is described by a schema in terms of a Data Model. The information contained in the schema should grant a user to interpret the data in a reasonable way and the program system to manipulate the Data Base correctly. A part of the Data Base is represented by a subschema and is considered to be the appropriate picture of the Data Base of one user. As Date [19] points out this concept in fact provides a mapping between different descriptions of the same data. Thus programs using data as defined in a subschema have to be transformed into 'equivalent' programs which use schema terms as primitives [20]. A number of anomalies caused by propagations of operations from the subschema level down to the schema level are described in the literature [8, 22] and will not be repeated here.

Instead of using this schema-subschema approach we propose here a different philosophy to establish views: views are considered to be different abstractions of the same elementary data.

To define our approach we recall our explanation of the relationship between the reality and its symbolic representation. We assume that every symbolic representation is incomplete.and therefore to some extent ambiguous. Thus every symbolic representation allows different interpretations of its content.

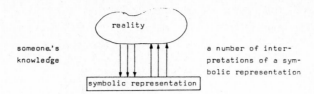

These different interpretations however "share" a number of Data Base objects. The concept we define here provides the sharing of parts among different views only if their meaning is the same in every view. And as we know the meaning of a component is the same if it is composed in the same way and its characterizing operations are identical. As we can see now it is the advantage of the D-graph model which is based on the concept of abstract data types to provide a precise model of views.

We would represent a Data Base seen by different views in the following way

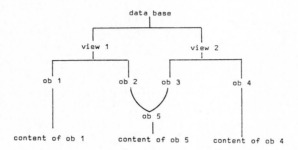

For a more detailed description of the concept we must refer again to [18].

5   Formal Semantics of Data Base Systems

So far we have just developed a static description of the Data Base - a dependency schema associated with information which operations may be performed on different Data Base constituents. But we don't have a description of the execution of operations on the Data Base. A solution to this problem is essential for a complete semantic specification of integrity constraints since they establish a variety of restrictions for the execution of operations. The problem is very well known from work on programming languages and is called there the formal specification of the semantics.

One specification technique introduced to specify the semantics of programming languages is called operational semantics [22] and will be used here to specify a programming system which supports semantic constraints on a relational Data Base. This method provides the specification of a programming system by defining an abstract interpreter of this system. This interpreter itself is defined in terms of an abstract language. The best known language to specify an abstract interpreter is the VDL concept [23] which provides means to represent tree structures and tree manipulation functions to define the interpreter. Following this concept the specification of a programming system requires its translation into an abstract tree oriented representation and the specification of the source program execution in terms of tree manipulations.

For our purposes we propose the usage of Common Base Language [24] as an interpreter specification language which allows the definition of acyclic directed
graphs and their manipulation. This concept thus provides a means to express
the sharing of objects and is therefore suitable to define different views of
the Data Base.

The same graph model was introduced in chapter 3 to represent arbitrary abstractions. The model will be used now to describe the state of the relational Data
Base.

The complete specification of a programming system requires the representation
of all the information about data, programs which act upon this data and control
information. The data on which the programming system operates is the entire
Data Base. Using this specification method therefore requires the description of
the components of the Data Base, the specification of abstract instructions whose
execution change this description of the Data Base and the description of the
necessary control information as an acyclic directed graph.

The information represented by abstract objects of the type described above thus
specifies the state of the abstract interpreter and the execution of instructions
causes state transitions by corresponding graph manipulations.

In order to describe modifications of the state of the Data Base we have to
define the operations with which we are able to express the access to components
of the graph and the manipulation of this graph:

SELECT(P, x)   This operation selects a component object if there is a branch
                labeled with x and emenating from a node to which P refers.

DELETE(P, x)   This operation deletes a component object which is selected by
                the previously defined SELECT operation.

This is of course an incomplete set of the possible graph manipulations to represent transitions of the Data Base state. Those manipulations compatible with a
state specification representing semantic constraints are considered in the
following sections of the paper.

A description of the state of a pure relational Data Base system and its state
transitions by abstract retrieval, update, delete, and create operations is already described in the literature [25] and serves as a basis for our considerations about the representation of semantic constraints in the following paragraph.
In this paper we are going to restrict ourself to the representation of the data
component of the state representation of the interpreter.

5.1. Formal Specification of the State of a Relational Data Base Considering Semantic Constraints

This section provides the specification of a Data Base system in order to represent semantic constraints on a relational Data Base.

We therefore represent first an abstract object describing a part of the Data
Base state specification in order to explain the used technique.

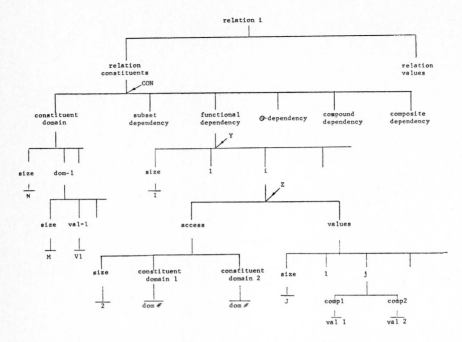

This abstract object represents a relation and is therefore a part of the representation of the state of the Data Base. A relation is specified in this depiction by the relation constituents and the relation values.

Definition

A branch of the state defining graph emenating from the "relation node" and terminating on the "relation constituent node" represents the constituents of this relation. These constituents are objects which represent: functional dependencies, Θ-dependencies, subset dependencies, compound dependencies, composite dependencies and constituent domains.

The further specification of this part of the Data Base state is depicted in our representation for the component "functional dependency". A similar specification would be necessary for all the dependencies recognized in this relation.

Definition

A branch emenating from the "functional dependency node" terminates on a "fd-i" node denoting the ith functional dependency defined in this relation. Each functional dependency is specified by a set of "functional dependency values". And each "functional dependency value" in turn is specified as a composition of two components which are "domain values" of different domains.

Now we have to specify the second component of a relation - the relation values - in a similar way. Relation values are the tuples which might be associated with a relation. The specification has to show how these tuples are composed of domain values and how they reflect the semantic constraints defined on this relation.

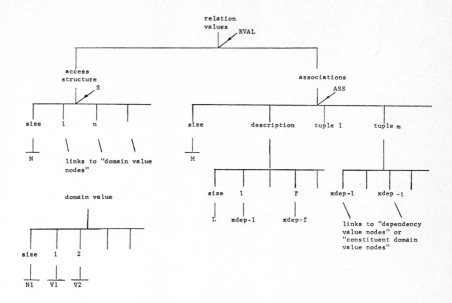

Defintion

A branch emenating from the "relation   value node" and terminating on the "access structure node" depicts an abstract object which represents the constituent domains of this relation and the degree of this relation (numbers of domains in this relation). A branch which emenates from the "access structure node" is named size and points to a terminal node containing an integer which represents the degree of this relation. Branches emenating from the "access structure node" named by integers are linked to "domain value nodes" indicating that each component of a tuple must be an element of a certain domain. (The specification of domains is not included in this description of the state of the Data Base.)

The second component of a relation value is called its association and reflects the semantic constraints defined in this relation.

Definition

One branch emenating from the "association node" is named "size" and terminates on a terminal node containing an integer which represents the number of tuples contained in this relation. Another branch emenating from the "association node" terminates on a node named "description". The description component represents the decomposition of all relation values. Each branch emenating from the "description node" denotes one of the constituents of this relation defined in the "constituents" component of the state representation. The "description" component, however, contains only independent constituents - those which are not itself constituents of higher order dependencies.

Definition .

Branches emenating from the "association node" named "tuple i" terminate on objects which represent the components of a tuple as described in the "description" component of this graph. Components of tuples might be   arbitrary collectionsof dependency values or domain values which is indicated by links pointing to these objects in the description of the abstract state.

5.2. Formal Specification of State Transitions

To be able to describe manipulations of the state representing graph we first
have to define means by which we can identify substructures in this graph.

To select components of an object we allow pointer expressions to be assigned to
pointer variables. Pointer expressions itself are pointer variables followed by
a dot and an arbitrary number of selectors, e.g., if pointer variable P points
to the data base node a pointer variable

$$Q = P.\text{'relations'}$$

points to the relation node of the state representing graph.

The formal description of state transitions is now expressed in terms of a graph
manipulation language. The syntax of this language is ALGOL-like and requires no
definition. To explain the method we define here a semantic procedure 'addrv'
which specifies the adding of a relation value (a tuple) into the Data Base. The
definition of this semantic procedure refers to the state representation in the
preceding figures. The insertion of a new value corresponds to an insertion of
a value representing graph of the following form:

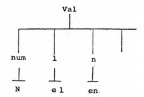

into the state representing graph. The main procedure calls a number of sub-
procedures to perform different tasks, and its decomposition is shown in the
following picture:

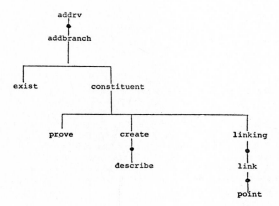

A rough description of the semantic procedure using the graph manipulation
language mentioned above will be found in the sequel.

Semantic Procedure 'add relation value'

Assume that the pointer variable P refers to the Data Base node, then the procedure takes the following form:

```
procedure addrv(relationi,VAL)              (1)
     R = P·'relations';                     (2)
     if select (R·'relationi') = FALSE then (3)
     return F
     else Q = R·'relationi';                (4)
     CON = Q·'relation constituents';
     RVAL = Q·'relation values';
     adbranch (CON, RVAL, VAL);             (5)
     return T;                              (6)
     end;

procedure adbranch (CON, RVAL, VAL)         (7)
     if select (RVAL) = TRUE then           (8)
     exist(RVAL,VAL);                       (9)
     else return F;
     if select(CON) = TRUE then             (10)
     constituent(CON,VAL,RVAL);             (11)
     return;
     end;
```

A short description of these two procedures is given in the following section: line numbers in the procedure code correspond to the paragraph numbers in this section.

1. The semantic procedure is defined by the term procedure and its name is 'addrv' (add relation value). This procedure is defined for the two parameters 'relationi' and VAL indicating that the execution of this procedure inserts the relation value VAL into the relation named 'relationi'.

2. Definition of a pointer variable R to which the result of the evaluation of the pointer expression (P.'relations') is assigned. (The pointer variable P is assumed to refer to the entry point of this graph: the data base node.)

3. This statement represents a check whether a relation with the identifier 'relationi' exists.(The used semantic procedure 'select' is assumed to be a primitive of our specification language.)

4. Definition of a pointer variable Q to which the result of the evaluation of the pointer expression (R.'relationi') is assigned. Similar definitions for CON and RVAL follow.

5. The call of the semantic procedure 'adbranch' performs the insertion of a new tuple into the relation and will be specified below.

6. This command represents a return to the caller of the procedure.

7. Definition of the semantic procedure 'adbranch'.

8. Definition of a check whether there already exists a value of this relation. If there exist one the following statement defines a pointer variable which refers to the component 'access structure' of the 'relation value' component of the graph.

9. This procedure checks whether the number of elements of the relation value defined in the 'access structure' corresponds to the number of elements of the new relation value. It also checks whether each of the elements of the new relation value is also an element of the corresponding domain.

10. This statement checks whether semantic constraints are defined for this relation and whether they are represented as constituent objects of this re-

lation in the state representing graph.

11. This procedure determines the domains on which a semantic constraint is defined and checks whether the corresponding elements of the new value are already stored as a value of this constraint representing object. If not the procedure creates a new branch in the 'values' representing object. A detailed description of the insertion of new values of relation constituents and their connection with a new inserted object representing a new tuple of this relation is given in [26].

6 Conclusion

This paper shows that the relational model of Data Bases does not provide all the necessary representational capabilities to (1) allow a complete representation of knowledge and to (2) allow a semantically correct sharing of the Data Base among various user views. It introduces therefore two types of integrity constraints to overcome this deficiencies. The model introduced to represent both the relational model and integrity constraints takes the semantics of Data Base changes into account in order to model the dynamics of the reality too. The dynamic behaviour of the Data Base is specified with operational semantics. Thus the entire concept gives a notation for data semantics and formal semantics of Data Base Systems.

Acknowledgement

This paper benefits from discussions with Sheldon Borkin (MIT) and from very helpful corrections of earlier version by Jim Gray (IBM San Jose) and H. A. Schmid (University Stuttgart).

Literature

[1] R. C. Schank, K. M. Colby eds.: "Computer Models of Thought and Language",
W. H. Freeman & Company, San Francisco 1973, in particular p. 63 - 113.

R. F. Simmons: " Semantic Networks: Their Computation and Use for Understanding English Sentences in ⌐1⌐.

[2] B. Liskov, S. Zilles: "Programming with Abstract Data Types" SIGPLAN Notices
9/4 April 74.

[3] C. J. Date: "An Introduction to Data Base Systems", Addison Wesley 1975.

[4] E. W. Dijkstra: "Notes on Structured Programming in Structured Programming"
by Dahl, Dijkstra, Hoare, Academic Press 1972.

[5] Codd, E. F.: "A Relational Model of Data for Large Shared Data Banks",
CACM, Vol. 13, No. 6, June 1970.

[6] CODASYL / DBTG Report April 1971, Available from ACM.

[7] H. Weber: "On the Semantics of Data Base Systems", Technical Report No. 76-03
of the Technical University of Berlin, February 1976.

[8] K. P. Eswaran, D. D. Chamberlin: "Functional Specification of a Subsystem
for Data Base Integrity", IBM Research Laboratory San Jose 1975.

[9] M. Stonebreaker: "High Level Integrity Assurance in Relational Data Base
Management Systems", Memo ≠ ERL - M473 August 1974.

[10] E. F. Codd: "A Data Base Sublanguage foundet on the Relational Calculus" and

[11] E. F. Codd: "Further Normalization of the Data Base Relational Model", in
Data Base Systems, Randall Rustin, Editor, Prentice Hall, 1972.

[12] H. Weber: "Data Description of Large Shared Heterogeneous Data Bases",
MIT/Project MAC Working Paper, June 1975.

[13] C. Deheneffe, H. Hennebert, W. Paulus: "Relational Model for a Data Base",
Proceedings for the IFIP Congress North Holland 1974.

[14] H. A. Schmid, J. R. Swenson: "On the Semantics of the Relational Data Model",
ACM SIGMOD, Conference Proceedings May 1975.

[15] P. P. Chen: "The Entity-Relationship Model - Towards a Unified View of Data",
MIT/Sloan School of Management to be published.

[16] R. C. Schenk: "Identification of Conceptualization Underlying Natural
Language" in [1].

[17] T. Winograd: "A Procedural Model of Language Understanding in [1].

[18] H. Weber: "The D-graph Model of Large Shared Data Bases: A Representation
of Integrity Constraints and Views as Multiple Data Abstractions" to be
published.

[19] C. J. Date, P. Hopewell: "File definition and Logical Data Independence",
Proceedings SIGFIDET 1971, Available from ACM.

[20] H. Biller, E. J. Neuhold: "Formal View on Schema - Subschema Correspondence",
Proceedings IFIP Congress, North Holland 1974.

[21] E. F. Codd: "Recent Investigations in Relational Data Base Systems",
     Proceedings IFIP Congress, North Holland 1974.

[22] Wegener, P.: "Data Structure Models for Programming Languages", SIGPLAN
     NOTICES, Vol. 6 No. 2, February 1971.

[23] Neuhold, E. J.: "The Formal Description of Programming Languages", IBM
     Systems Journal, No. 2, 1971.

[24] Dennis, J. B.: "On the Design and Specification of a Common Base Language",
     Computation Structure Group Memo 60, MIT, Project MAC, July 1974.

[25] Hawryszkiewycz, I. T.: "Semantics of Data Base Systems", MAC TR 112, MIT,
     Project MAC, December 1973.

[26] H. Weber: "A Semantic Model of Integrity Constraints on a Relational Data
     Base" Technical Report No. 76-06 of the Technical University of Berlin.

Modelling in Data Base Management Systems, G.M. Nijssen, (ed.)
North Holland Publishing Company, 1976

A PROCEDURAL LANGUAGE FOR EXPRESSING INTEGRITY
CONSTRAINTS IN THE COEXISTENCE MODEL

Claude MACHGEELS
Université Libre de Bruxelles
Campus Plaine C.P.212
Boulevard du Triomphe
B-1050   Bruxelles
Belgium

The need for a centralized control model for a Data Base is now
well recognized. The Coexistence Model described in ref [7] and
[8] is a simple well-structured example of that kind of models.
To avoid duplication of effort and inconsistency, the best place
for the expression of the Integrity Constraints appears to be at
the level of the Conceptual Schema. A Conceptual Schema is briefly
described, where each data-item can be accessed logically,
together with its description. A procedural language, PLIC, is
then defined which allows to express integrity constraints. PLIC
treats static and dynamic aspects of the values in the Data Base.
Changes in integrity constraints are also complied with using
the same language. Examples are given, using PLIC, of the
different types of Integrity Constraints.

CONTENTS

1. INTRODUCTION

For the last five years or so, much effort has been paid to try to define
standardized requirements for Data Base Management Systems.
The best known reports in that field are no doubts those issued by the CODASYL in
1971 [4] and 1973 [5] as well as the report issued by the ANSI/DBMS Committee in
1975 [2].

In a working paper prepared for the IFIP WG 2.6 May 1975 meeting [7],
G.M. Nijssen presented the Coexistence Model, based partly on a paper by
G. Bracchi et al [3]. Using the same idea of an overall, common conceptual view of
the Data Base as the ANSI Model, the Coexistence Model is simpler in the interdependence of the different personal views that can exist. Also, it does not
enforce any restricting concept at any level.

The existence of those two models, where all kind of views can co-exist, should without any doubt damp the long discussions about which view is the universal and only one: n-relational view and network view can from now on co-exist with binary relational view for the same Data Base.

It is now time to analyze what is needed in that common Conceptual Schema and to design the tools to meet those requirements. Among other things, integrity constraints must be introduced and the language to express and check them must be designed.

The purpose of this paper is to investigate what kinds of integrity constraints are needed and to define the elements of one language (PLIC) that takes them into account.

The Coexistence Model is used and a simple model is defined at the Conceptual Schema level.

After a short reminder of the relevant facts of the Coexistence Model, the question of the place of the integrity constraints is examined. The model used in the Conceptual Schema is then described; thereafter, the different kinds of integrity constraints are reviewed and examples are given using PLIC to express them.

2. THE COEXISTENCE MODEL

A description of the Coexistence Model is given in the paper by G.M. Nijssen in ref [7] and [8]. Figure 1 shows the architecture of the model. For the sake of completeness, let us briefly describe it.

Going down from the Data Base to the users, there is a first description of the physical organization of the data, in a module called Storage Schema. There is then a mapping between that physical view and the complete logical view of the information, which is described in the Conceptual Schema. From the Conceptual Schema, there are different mappings to partial or complete views of the Data Base, which are expressed using different models (network, n-ary relational, binary relational, hierarchical, ...) in User Schemas.

From figure 1, it is now easily understood how the Coexistence Model allows for the coexistence of different kinds of view of the Data Base and how it provides independence between the users and the physical implementation of the datas.

3. PLACE OF THE INTEGRITY CONSTRAINTS

Referring to figure 1, it is seen that all the informations put in or got from the Data Base are under control of both the Conceptual Schema and the Storage Schema. Therefore, integrity constraints should be placed in either of those schemas: there remains to choose in which one.

Most changes in the Conceptual Schema will result in changes in the Storage Schema, while changes in the Storage Schema may not induce any change in the Conceptual Schema. Moreover, integrity constraints express users'views, and do not at all pertain to the physical aspects of the Data Base (for these, the concepts related to "recovery" are invoked: see e.g. ref [2]). The best place of the expression of the integrity constraints appears thus to be the Conceptual Schema.

All the datas introduced by any user will then be checked against those integrity constraints. If some data is rejected, a mechanism has to inform the user of the reason for the rejection, e.g. via a code. All the users should be informed of the various integrity constraints maintained in the Data Base. For some reason, privacy for example, some integrity constraints could be kept hidden from some or all users: this can be achieved by the mappings by sending a very neutral message

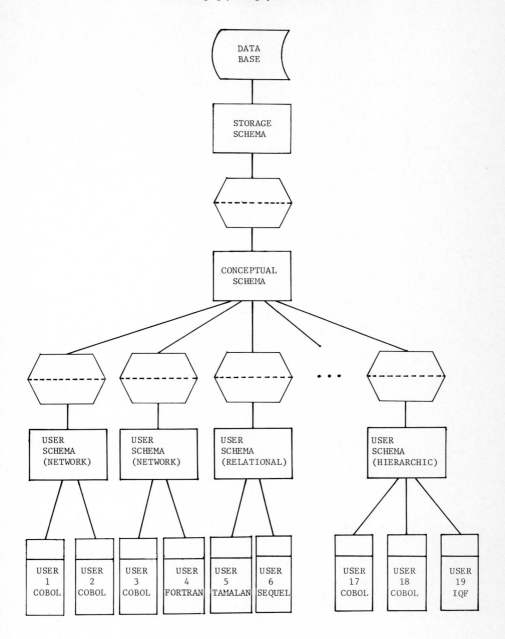

Figure 1: Coexistence Model

to the user while a very detailed one is sent to the Data Base Administrator.

Some users might want to introduce integrity constraints not supported by the Data Base for all users. Therefore, it may be worth designing tools to allow such descriptions at the User Schema level. Nevertheless, it must be recognized that this is not very appealing from the homogeneity point of view. Those tools will probably be different for each kind of view supported in the Data Base.

Of course, the integrity constraints introduced in the User Schema or in the programs are additions to the ones declared at the Conceptual Schema level: they are no substitutes for them but appear to be refinements to them needed by a class of users. Moreover, it remains the responsability of the users of the integrity constraints described at a lower level to check if datas are not violating those constraints, both at the input and at the retrieval: effectively, datas could have been introduced by users using other routes.

To summarize, it is not too clear if one should accept to declare integrity constraints at another level than the Conceptual Schema.

4. DESCRIPTION OF THE CONCEPTUAL SCHEMA

As already emphasized in the introduction, all the requirements for the Conceptual Schema are not yet fixed. To study the problem of the integrity constraints, it was not deemed necessary to define entirely a model. We only chose some specifications that a viable implementation could fit.

The hypothesis was made that every data-item used is supplied with its complete descriptions. For instance, it is possible to check if a data-item comes from the Data Base or from the user. It is also possible to get any data-item needed from the Data Base, just by naming it: no mechanism of access has to be provided as this is the role of the Storage Schema and associated processes.

5. TYPES OF INTEGRITY CONSTRAINTS

At the Conceptual Schema level, the integrity constraints can be subdivided into two classes. The first class concerns the putting of data-items in, either by replacing the old value of an existing data-item by a new one, or by adding a new data-item to the population. The second class concerns the deleting of an existing data-item.

In each class, a further classification can be made, using the number and the source of the data-items involved.

5.1. Putting Data-Items in

Integrity constraints can affect one data-item supplied by the user, without any reference to any other data-item. Simple examples of that kind are: length, type, set of acceptable or forbidden values (range is a special case).

Integrity constraints can also affect n user-supplied data-items at a time. For example, the sum of a certain number of successively supplied data-items should be equal to a last one.

Integrity constraints can also relate one user-supplied data-item to one or more data-items already stored in the Data Base. For example, there could be a stored data-item which is the sum of all data-items of a certain kind: everytime a new data-item of that kind is stored, the sum shall be updated.

Finally, integrity constraints can relate n user-supplied data-items to one or more already stored data-items. For example, the set of data-items describing an order may not be accepted if there are no stored data-items identifying the purchaser as a customer.

5.2. Deleting Data-Items

Integrity constraints can prohibit permanently the deletion of one stored data-item. Also, the deletion of one data-item can be prohibited, depending on its value. A trivial example could be to prohibit the deletion of the name of the firm owning the Data Base. The deletion of a debt that is positive could also be rejected.

Integrity Constraints can also affect the deletion of n stored data-items. For example, all data-items pertaining to an order should be deleted at the same time and not separately.

Integrity Constraints can also relate one data-item to be deleted to one or more other data-items. For example, one should update the value of a data-item that is the sum of the values of other data-items when one of these is deleted.

Finally, Integrity Constraints can relate n data-items to be deleted to one or more other data-items. For example, one should prohibit the deletion of the data-items describing the name and address of a person who is still hiring books from the library described by the Data Base.

6. PLIC: A PROCEDURAL LANGUAGE FOR INTEGRITY CONSTRAINTS

6.1. Elements of the Language

A procedural form was choosen because it seems more flexible and more suited to our present way of thinking. For very convincing arguments, the reader is referred to [6]. It is however clear that some integrity constraints are expressed very well using a structural manner.

The operands in the expressions that can be formed are of four kinds: constants (denoted by c_1, c_2, ...), user-supplied data-items (u_1, u_2, ...), data-items to be deleted (d_1, d_2, ...) and stored data-items (s_1, s_2, ...).

The operators are arithmetical (e.g. +, -, *), relational (e.g. =, $\neq$, $\leqslant$, $\in$), logical (e.g. $\vee$, $\neg$, $\exists$, $\forall$).

Certain words have a special function. For example, DECLARE SET allows for the description of a set of values to which expressions can refer; BIT(K) takes the Kth bit of the following operand, while CHAR(K) takes its Kth character; NUMERIC can be used to check if an expression or a data-item is a number.

The detailed description of PLIC does not seem to be very useful here. Rather, we shall give some examples of each type of integrity constraint described in the previous paragraph, showing the main features of the language.

6.2. Examples of Expression of Integrity Constraints

6.2.1. Integrity Constraints on u_1

A simple example of that kind of integrity constraints is to check the type of a value supplied. The following expression will accept the storing of a data-item if it is a number but will reject it and send back a message otherwise.

<u>if</u> u_1 $\in$ <u>numeric</u> <u>then</u> <u>accept</u> u_1
<u>else</u> <u>reject</u> code$_1$;

A second example shows how to check a number representing a jobcode. The values
that the jobcode may take on are first given as elements of a set; at run time,
those values are checked against the value supplied by the user.

> <u>declare</u> <u>set</u> S4 = {1020 <u>to</u> 1030, 1045, 1300 <u>to</u> 1400};
>
> <u>if</u> u_1 $\in$ S4 <u>then</u> <u>accept</u> u_1
>
>   <u>else</u> <u>reject</u> code$_1$;

The last expression is another example of checking a value against a set of
admitted values. Here, the admitted values are known using an algorithm: the
number has 9 digits (this is checked outside the expression shown) and the two
last digits represent the value of the sum of the first 7 digits, taken modulo 11.

> <u>if</u> <u>mod</u> (<u>sum</u> (<u>char</u> (i) u_1, i=1 <u>to</u> 7), 11)
>
>   = <u>con</u> (<u>char</u> (8) u_1, <u>char</u> (9) u_1)
>
>   <u>then</u> <u>accept</u> u_1
>
>   <u>else</u> <u>reject</u> code$_1$;

6.2.2. Integrity Constraints on a set of u_i

Suppose we want to check if the value given for the total in a bill is equal to
the sum of the prices of each part, which are given first. The expression will
read as follows:

> <u>if</u> <u>sum</u> (u_i, i=1 <u>to</u> n) = u_{n+1}
>
>   <u>then</u> <u>accept</u> (u_i, i=1 <u>to</u> n+1)
>
>   <u>else</u> <u>reject</u> code$_1$;

6.2.3. Integrity Constraints on u_1 versus one or more s_i

This kind of integrity constraints is related to both the static and the dynamic
aspects of the values in the Data Base. For example, if the value of a data-item
is the sum of the values of other data-items in the Data Base, then its value
must be updated automatically each time the value of one of the terms is changed.
The expression will read as follows:

> s_1 $\leftarrow$ s_1 - s_2 + u_1;

where s_1 stands for the sum data-item

     u_1 stands for the new value of the updated term

     s_2 stands for the old value of the updated term.

The following statement shows how to treat an example given by J. Abrial in
ref [1], which handled the allowed and forbidden transitions between 4 states:
single, married, widowed and divorced. It expresses how to treat the transitions
from married to the other states. To treat the whole example, one needs three
more similar statements.

> <u>if</u> s_1 = married <u>then</u>
>
>   <u>if</u> u_1 = single <u>then</u> <u>reject</u> code$_1$ <u>else</u>
>
>   <u>if</u> u_1 = married <u>then</u> <u>reject</u> code$_1$ <u>else</u>
>
>   <u>if</u> u_1 = widowed <u>then</u> s_1 $\leftarrow$ u_1 <u>else</u>
>
>   <u>if</u> u_1 = divorced <u>then</u> s_1 $\leftarrow$ u_1
>
>   <u>else</u> <u>reject</u> code$_2$;

It is also possible to express all the cases using a single expression [9], which demonstrate the structuring capabilities:

<u>if</u> u_1 = single <u>then</u> <u>reject</u> code$_1$ <u>else</u>

<u>if</u> u_1 = married <u>then</u> <u>if</u> s_1 = married <u>then</u> <u>reject</u> code$_2$

                                    <u>else</u> $s_1 \leftarrow u_1$ <u>else</u>

   <u>if</u> u_1 = divorced **v** widowed

                <u>then</u> <u>if</u> s_1 = married <u>then</u> $s_1 \leftarrow u_1$

                               <u>else</u> <u>reject</u> code$_3$

        <u>else</u> <u>reject</u> code$_4$;

6.2.4. Integrity Constraints on a set of u_i versus one or more s_i

As the previous one, this kind of integrity constraints is related to both the static and the dynamic aspects of the values in the Data Base. Suppose we want to check that we know a person as an accepted customer (data-items s_1, s_2 and s_3 must exist) before placing an order for him (data-items u_1 and u_2).

A first way to express that is:

<u>if</u> $s_1 \neg \exists$ **v** $s_2 \neg \exists$ **v** $s_3 \neg \exists$ <u>then</u> <u>reject</u> code$_1$

                                      <u>else</u> <u>accept</u> u_1, u_2;

Another way of expressing the same condition reads as follows:

<u>if</u> $s_1 \exists$ $\wedge$ $s_2 \exists$ $\wedge$ $s_3 \exists$ <u>then</u> <u>accept</u> u_1, u_2

                                      <u>else</u> <u>reject</u> code$_1$;

Still another expression can be:

<u>if</u> $s_1 \neg \exists$ <u>then</u> <u>reject</u> code$_1$ <u>else</u>

<u>if</u> $s_2 \neg \exists$ <u>then</u> <u>reject</u> code$_1$ <u>else</u>

<u>if</u> $s_3 \neg \exists$ <u>then</u> <u>reject</u> code$_1$

         <u>else</u> <u>accept</u> u_1, u_2;

6.2.5. Integrity Constraints on d_1

Some data-items may never be deleted from the Data Base, such as the name of the firm described, its address, etc. All those data-items could be members of a set S1; at run time, a check is first made against that set before any deletion can be executed. The expression reads

   <u>if</u> $d_1 \in$ S1 <u>then</u> <u>reject</u> code$_1$;

One could also require that a debt should be first set to zero before **all**owing to delete it. This could be checked by

   <u>if</u> $d_1 \neq 0$ <u>then</u> <u>reject</u> code$_1$;

6.2.6. Integrity Constraints on a set of d_i

To prevent some irrelevant data-items from remaining in the Data Base, one could impose e.g. to delete at the same time all data-items describing the same customer. For a customer described by two data-items, we could write

   <u>if</u> $d_1 \exists$ $\wedge$ $d_2 \exists$ <u>then</u> <u>delete</u> d_1, d_2 ;

If logical redundancy is accepted in the Data Base, one could reject the deletion of some data-items if two of them are not equal. One could have:

$$\underline{if} \ d_1 \neq d_3 \ \underline{then} \ \underline{reject} \ code_1$$
$$\underline{else} \ \underline{delete} \ d_1, \ d_2, \ d_3, \ d_4;$$

6.2.7. Integrity Constraints on d_1 versus one or more s_i

As in points 6.2.3. and 6.2.4., this kind of Integrity Constraints is related to both the static and the dynamic aspects of the values in the Data Base. Taking an example close to the first one in point 6.2.3., one should update the value of a data-item that is the sum of other ones each time one of the term is deleted. This is expressed by

$$s_1 \leftarrow s_1 - d_1 \ ;$$

6.2.8. Integrity Constraints on a set of d_i versus one or more s_i

This last kind of integrity constraints in our classification is also related to both the static and the dynamic aspects of the values of the data-items in the Data Base.

Suppose we want to reject the deletion of the information (d_1, d_2 and d_3) about a customer of a library if he is still hiring a book (s_1 and s_2 describe a book). The first formulation we could think of is

$$\underline{if} \ s_1 \exists \ \vee \ s_2 \exists \ \underline{then} \ \underline{reject} \ code_1$$
$$\underline{else} \ \underline{delete} \ d_1, \ d_2, \ d_3 \ ;$$

A better way seems to use an integrity constraint of the type described in point 6.2.6.: s_1 might never been deleted without deleting s_2 at the same time. At the time of the deletion of d_1 to d_3, one has only to check for the existence of s_1 or of s_2. One has thus

$$\underline{if} \ s_1 \exists \ \underline{then} \ \underline{reject} \ code_1$$
$$\underline{else} \ \underline{delete} \ d_1, \ d_2, \ d_3 \ ;$$

7. CHANGES IN INTEGRITY CONSTRAINTS

The Data Base is a part of a model of the real world, which is dynamic. This implies that every constituent of the Data Base has to be dynamic too, including the integrity constraints.

Three cases are to be considered. First, an integrity constraint can be canceled: this simply means we have to remove its expression (including perhaps some "declare" statement) from the set of the integrity constraints. A recompilation is also required if integrity constraints are not purely interpreted.

If a new integrity constraint is introduced, its expression is added to the existing set and, if needed,. recompilation will occur. A special program has then to be run to check if all the already existing datas comply with the new set of constraints. As the Data Base is shared by many users through many programs or other routes, the messages fed back to the users should be designed clearly enough to be understood by those unaware of the new integrity constraints.

The last case in when an integrity constraint is changed. This can be decomposed in two steps: a delection and the introduction of a new integrity constraint. There is of course a unique possible recompilation and the rest is the same as in the previous case.

It is thus seen that changes in integrity constraints induce no further tools than the language already described, plus a special run to check if new constraints are complied with by the existing datas.

8. CONCLUSION

In a Data Base organized on the scheme proposed by ANSI in ref [2] or by Nijssen in ref [7] and [8], it is possible to express all the integrity constraints at the level of the conceptual schema. A procedural language can be defined, e.g. PLIC, which allows to take into account integrity constraints to be used when adding, updating or deleting datas.

The same language can treat the static aspects of the values in the Data Base and also their dynamic aspects, by updating automatically values of data-items already stored.

The language defined for expressing the integrity constraints need not contain any special features to handle changes in integrity constraints.

REFERENCES

[1] ABRIAL J.R., "Data Semantics" in: Data Base Management, Proc. of the IFIP Working Conference on Data Base Management, Cargese, North-Holland Publ. Cy, Amsterdam (1974).

[2] ANSI, "Interim Report ANSI/X3/SPARC Study Group on Data Base Management Systems", ANSI, Washington DC (1975).

[3] BRACCHI G., FEDELI A. and PAOLINI P., "A Multilevel Relational Model for Data Base Management Systems" in: Data Base Management, Proc. of the IFIP Working Conference on Data Base Management, Cargese, North-Holland Publ. Cy, Amsterdam (1974).

[4] CODASYL, "Data Base Task Group 1971 Report", ACM, New York (1971).

[5] CODASYL, "DDL Journal of Development, June 1973 Report", ACM, New York (1973).

[6] HUITS M., "Requirements for Languages in Data Base Systems" in Proc. of the IFIP-TC-2 Special Working Conference "A Technical in-Depth Evaluation of the DDL", Namur, North-Holland Publ. Cy, Amsterdam (1975).

[7] NIJSSEN G.M., "An Evaluation of the ANSI DBMS Architecture and Conceptual Schema as in the February 1975 Report", working paper presented at the IFIP WG 2.6 May 1975 meeting.

[8] NIJSSEN G.M., "A Gross Architecture for the Next Generation DBMS", these Proceedings.

[9] REMMEN F., private communication (1976).

Modelling in Data Base Management Systems, G.M. Nijssen, (ed.)
North Holland Publishing Company, 1976

RELATIONAL-NETWORK DATA STRUCTURE MAPPING

L. A. Kalinichenko
Complex Computer Control Institute
Vavilova 24, Moscow, GSP 312, USSR

INTRODUCTION

The process of data base design consists in multilevel model construction. Here it will be sufficient to distinguish between four levels of such model: (1) system of real world objects, (2) information structures describing such system, (3) data structures used for representation of information structure in data base and application programms, (4) storage structures used for data structures memorizing. Data base management system (DBMS) should resolve mapping (1)———(4) by means of chain of mappings (1)———(2), (2)——— (3), (3)———(4).

In this paper the (2)———(3) mapping is considered, n-ary relations being used as information structures, and network model being used for data structures representation. Network data correspond to DDL-73 CODASYL /1/, relational schema is in accordance with E.F. Codd approach /2/. Several proposals devoted to such mapping are wellknown /3, 4, 5/. Method of establishing relational to network data base schema correspondence proposed here gives possibility of usage of the main schema description features defined in the DDL-73.

NETWORK SCHEMA REPRESENTATION BY ORIENTED GRAPH

Several network data base schema representations in frame of DDL-73 will be chosen here so that application of relational model at higher level of abstraction be possible. For convenience reason network data base schema will be expressed by means of oriented graph $S = < \rho, \sigma >$ (mentioned below as S-graph) where ρ is the set of graph nodes which is equal to the set of all different record types declared in the schema, σ is the set of ordered pairs < ow, mem > representing arcs corresponding to all different pairs of "owner-member" record types in all sets of data base schema. If $r \in \rho$ and there is no ow $\in \rho$ and mem $\in \rho$ such that < ow, r >$\in \sigma$ or < r, mem >$\in \sigma$ then record type r is not included into any set type and represents an isolated node of S-graph. sys $\in \rho$ is a special node of S-graph which corresponds to the system – owner of singular sets. It's obvious that < r, r >$\notin \sigma$ because of the DDL restrictions.

It is assumed further that to each record type $r \in \rho$ primary key K_r corresponds being an unredundant set of the record type r data items, values of which identify an occurence of record r among other occurences of this record type.

The set of S-graph nodes is considered consisting of two distinct subsets: ρ = E U I. Record type r belongs to E – the subset of external nodes of S-graph if location mode CALC for r in data base schema is declared (CALC keys coinciding with primary key K_r of the record type r) or if record type r is declared as a member of at least one of singular sets, i.e. $< sys, r> \in \sigma$. All other record types belong to I – subset of internal nodes of S-graph.

Two different canonical representations of set type schemas (bearing essential information or used as additional access paths to data base records) which allow to construct the corresponding relational schema will be considered further. Every path $\mu = < r_1, r_2, \ldots, r_n>$ in the S-graph corresponds to the sequence of record types in which every predecessor record type plays role of an owner in some set in which its successor in the sequence is a member. It is assumed that two different type of paths are allowed in the S-graph: – path in which relations between records hold automatically (μ_A type of path), – path with manually established relations (μ_m type of path).

Definition 1. Cycleless path $\mu = < r_1, r_2, \ldots, r_n>$, $r_1 \in$ E in the S-graph belongs to μ_A type if for each set type arc of the μ path, defined by the pair $s_{i-1} = < r_{i-1}, r_i>$, $i = 2, 3, \ldots, n$, schema of s_{i-1} set type has the following format (DDL subentries of set type description which are invariant to the requirements of μ_A path definition are not included in the format):

SET s_{i-1}

OWNER IS $\left\{ \begin{array}{l} r_{i-1} \\ \text{SYSTEM} \end{array} \right\}$

[SET IS PRIOR PROCESSABLE]

ORDER IS PERMANENT

MEMBER IS r_i MANDATORY AUTOMATIC [LINKED TO OWNER]

DUPLICATES ARE NOR ALLOWED FOR e_{r_i} [, e_{r_i}] $\ldots$

SET SELECTION IS THRU s_1 OWNER

IDENTIFIED BY $\left\{ \begin{array}{l} \text{SYSTEM} \\ \text{CALC-KEY EQUAL TO } v_{r_i}^{r_1} \left[, v_{r_i}^{r_1}\right] \ldots \end{array} \right\}$

THEN THRU s_2 $\left\{ \text{WHERE OWNER IDENTIFIED BY } e_{r_2} \text{ EQUAL TO } v_{r_i}^{r_2} \right\}$ $\ldots$

.
.
.

THEN THRU s_{i-1} $\left\{ \text{WHERE OWNER IDENTIFIED BY } e_{r_{i-1}} \text{ EQUAL TO } v_{r_i}^{r_{i-1}} \right\} \ldots$

Here e_{r_i} identifies data item included in K_{r_i}; $v_{r_i}^{r_j}$ is data item in r_i record type the value of which is keeped equal to the value of data item e_{r_j} in K_{r_j} of r_j record type. r_i, r_j are record types which belong to μ_A path, $j = 1, 2, \ldots, i-1$. In such case in the sequence of record types $r_1, r_2, \ldots, r_i$ it is convenient to use the sequence of virtual source data items $v_{r_2}^{r_1}$,

$v_{r_3}^{r_2}$, $v_{r_3}^{r_2}$, . . . , $v_{r_{i-1}}^{r_{i-2}}$, $v_{r_i}^{r_{i-1}}$. Thus every record r_i which belongs to $J^\mu{}_A$ path contains in virtual source data items sufficient amount of information for anambiguous identification of all records r_1, r_2, . . . , r_{i-1} belonging to one particular occurence of $J^\mu{}_A$ path.

Definition 2. Path $J^M = \langle r_1, r_2, \ldots r_n \rangle$, r_1, r_2, . . . , $r_n \in E$ in the S-graph represents path of $J^\mu{}_m$ type if to each arc of the path defined by the pair $s_{i-1} = \langle r_{i-1}, r_i \rangle$, $i = 2,3,$ . . . , n set type s_{i-1} corresponds with the following schema format:

SET s_{i-1}

OWNER IS $\left\{ \begin{array}{l} r_{i-1} \\ \text{SYSTEM} \end{array} \right\}$

[SET IS PRIOR PROCESSABLE]

ORDER IS PERMANENT

MEMBER IS r_i MANDATORY MANUAL [LINKED TO OWNER]

DUPLICATES ARE NOT ALLOWED FOR e_{r_i} [, e_{r_i}] . . .

SET SELECTION IS THRU s_1 OWNER

IDENTIFIED BY $\left\{ \begin{array}{l} \text{SYSTEM} \\ \text{CALC-KEY} \end{array} \right\}$

THEN THRU s_2 {WHERE OWNER IDENTIFIED BY e_{r_2}} . . .

THEN THRU s_{i-1} {WHERE OWNER IDENTIFIED BY $e_{r_{i-1}}$} . . .

It is important to note that $J^\mu{}_m$ path may contain cycles but one and the same arc of the S-graph cannot be represented in $J^\mu{}_m$ more then once.

$J^M{}_A$ path in the S-graph may be used as a continuation of $J^M{}_m$ path (and vice versa). The important thing to notice that any node r_i ($r_i \neq$ sys) which belongs to any $J^M{}_A$ or $J^\mu{}_m$ path may belong also to any number of other $J^M{}_A$ or $J^M{}_m$ paths of the S-graph.

S-GRAPH-RELATIONAL SCHEMA CORRESPONDENCE

In frame of this paper for the sake of simplicity it is assumed that all record types in data base schema have linear structure and do not contain data aggregates.

Simple procedure for mapping of network data base schema interpretable by S-graph into relational data base schema will be defined now.

1. For representation of each path of $J^\mu{}_A$ type in relational schema it is sufficient to put into correspondence to each record type $r_i \in J^\mu{}_A$ ($r_i \neq$ sys) normal relation R_{r_i}, primary key of R_{r_i}

being primary key of record type r_i. All virtual source data items
in record type r_i which appeared as $v_{r_i}^{r_1}$, $v_{r_i}^{r_2}$, . . . , $v_{r_i}^{r_{i-1}}$ in
each path $\mathcal{J}^{\mu}{}_A$ to which record type r_i belongs should become domains of R_{r_i}.

2. Path of $\mathcal{J}^{\mu}{}_m$ type is represented in relational schema by
means of relations R_{r_i} one for each $r_i \in \mathcal{J}^{\mu}{}_m$, $i = 1, 2, . . . , n$,
and by means of relation R_m domain set of which includes
only primary keys K_{r_1}, K_{r_2}, . . . , K_{r_n} of all record types $r_i \in \mathcal{J}^{\mu}{}_m$.
The set of R_m tuples coincides with the set of different collect-
ions of primary key values in the occurences of record types
$r_i \in \mathcal{J}^{\mu}{}_m$ belonging to the same occurence of $\mathcal{J}^{\mu}{}_m$ path.

The procedure defined above makes it possible to implement in
frame of relational model the functions of:
- retrieving of relation tuples satisfying the retrieval
criteria,
- updating of tuple data item values not included into the
primary key,
- inserting (removing) of relation tuples (to update the primary key values it's necessary to apply pair of insertion-removal
functions to the appropriate tuples).

It is important to note that practical implementation of the
updating functions mentioned above will require proper discipline
to be imposed on the sequence of application programmer actions:
new tuple T of relation R domain set of which includes primary
keys of another relations R_1, R_2, . . . may be inserted into the
data base only after insertion of tuples R_1, R_2, . . . referenced
by primary key values presented in the new tuple T of R.

RELATIONAL TO NETWORK DATA BASE SCHEMA MAPPING

The procedure which puts into correspondence to relational
data base schema the network schema interpretable by S-graph is
defined in the following way.

Three different categories of normalized relations will be distinguished in the relational data base schema:
1) relations domains of which do not constitute primary key
of any another relation in the schema,
2) relations domains of which constitutes their own primary
key, primary keys of another relations and data items which does
not constitute primary key of any another relation in the schema,
3) relations domain of which constitutes only primary keys of
another relations, their own primary keys being the set of all such
domains.

Every relation belonging to the first and second category is
mapped into the record type $r \in \rho$ in the network schema.
Every sequence of schemas of relations R_a, R_b, R_c,..., R_p, R_q
belonging to the first or the second category and such that domain
set of R_b includes primary key of R_a, domain set of R_c includes
primary keys of R_a and R_b,..., domain set of R_q includes primary
keys of R_a, R_b, R_c,..., R_p is mapped into the $\mathcal{M}^q{}_A$ path in the network schema.

Every relation belonging to the third category is mapped into the $\int^{\mu}$ m path in the network schema.

The important thing to notice that the procedure proposed above allows to define anambiguously all record types and main $\int^{\mu}$ A and $\int^{\mu}$ m paths in the S-graph. The choice of way of the owner of the first set in $\int^{\mu}$ A or of the owners of the sets in $\int^{\mu}$ m identification (BY SYSTEM or BY CALC-KEY) and the choice of additional $\int^{\mu}$ A paths which may be represented by means of arbitrary number of additional singular sets is beyond the scope of this procedure and may be considered as the function of Data Administrator.

EXAMPLES OF RELATIONAL TO NETWORK DATA BASE SHCEMA MAPPING

Fig. 1 shows several classes of real objects and their relations.

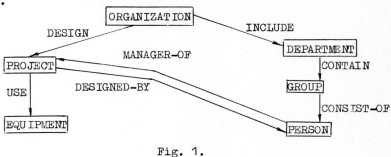

Fig. 1.

Several different relational schemas for the set of object classes in Fig. 1 and corresponding to them network schemas are considered below.

Schema 1

```
ORGANIZATION (ORG-NAME, ADDRESS)
PROJECT (PROJ-NUMB, PROJ-NAME, TERM-DATE)
EQUIPMENT (EQUIP-NUMB, EQUIP-NAME, QTY)
DEPARTMENT (DEP-NUMBER, DEP-MANAGER)
GROUP (GR-NUMB, GR-NAME, GR-MANAGER)
PERSON (MANNUMB, NAME, POSITION)
ORG-PROJECT (ORG-NAME, PROJ-NUMB)
PROJECT-EQUIP (PROJ-NUMB, EQUIP-NUMB)
ORG-DEPARTMENT (ORG-NAME, DEP-NUMB)
DEP-GROUP (DEP-NUMB, GR-NUMB)
GROUP-PERSON (GR-NUMB, MANNUMB)
PERSON-PROJ (MANNUMB, PROJ-NUMB)
PROJ-PERSON (PROJ-NUMB, MANNUMB)
```

Every relation from the first six schemas corresponds to some class of objects in Fig. 1. Primary keys of relations are underlined. Next seven relation schemas correspond to relations between objects denoted in Fig. 1 by arrows.

The network schema (S-graph) will contain six record types corresponding to the first six relations and seven $\int^{\mu}$ m paths corresponding to the last seven relations of the relational shema. Notice that each $\int^{\mu}$ m path has length equal to one.

Schema 2

First six relation schemas in schema 2 coincide with the first six relation schemas in relational schema 1. The rest relations are the following:

ORG-PROJ-EQUIP (ORG-NAME, PROJ-NUMB, EQUIP-NUMB)
ORG-PERSON-PROJ (ORG-NAME, DEP-NUMB, GR-NUMB, MANNUMB, PROJ-NUMB)
ORG-PROJ-PERSON (ORG-NAME, PROJ-NUMB, MANNUMB)

This relational schema is mapped into the network schema which contains six record types corresponding to the first six relations and $\int^\mu{}_m$ paths corresponding to the first six relations given above:

- path ORGANIZATION-PROJECT - EQUIPMENT
- path ORGANIZATION - DEPARTMENT - GROUP - PERSON - PROJECT,
- path ORGANIZATION - PROJECT - PERSON.

Schema 3

ORGANIZATION (ORG-NAME, ADDRESS)
PROJECT (PROJ-NUMB, ORG-NAME, MANNUMB, PROJ-NAME, TERM-DATE)
EQUIPMENT (EQUIP-NUMB, PROJ-NUMB, EQUIP-NAME, QTY)
DEPARTMENT (DEP-NUMB, ORG-NAME, DEP-MANAGER)
GROUP (GR-NUMB, DEP-NUMB, GR-NAME, GR-MANAGER)
PERSON (MANNUMB, GR-NUMB, PROJ-NUMB, NAME, POSITION)
PROJ-PERSON (PROJ-NUMB, MANNUMB)

In schema 3 the relations corresponding to different classes of objects in Fig. 1 contain also information on relationship between the classes of objects. E.G., the relation PERSON contains information on the group to which particular person belongs and information on the project managed by this person. Domains of relations used for stating of such relationships are underlined by dotted line.

The network schema will contain six record types corresponding to the first six relations of schema 3 (data items corresponding to domains of relations underlined by dotted lines are virtual source items), $\int^\mu{}_A$ paths:

ORGANIZATION-PROJECT, PROJECT - EQUIPMENT,
ORGANIZATION-DEPARTMENT, DEPARTMENT - GROUP,
GROUP - PERSON, PERSON - PROJECT, and
$\int^\mu{}_m$ path PROJECT - PERSON. All paths in the schema has length equal to one.

Schema 4

ORGANIZATION (ORG-NAME, ADDRESS)
PROJECT (PROJ-NUMB, ORG-NAME, DEP-NUMB, GR-NUMB, MANNUMB, PROJ-NAME, TERM - DATE)
EQUIPMENT (EQUIP-NUMB, ORG-NAME, PROJ-NUMB, EQUIP-NAME, QTY)
DEPARTMENT (DEP-NUMB, ORG-NAME, DEP-MANAGER)

GROUP (<u>GR-NUMB</u>, O̱ṞG̱-̱ṈA̱M̱E̱, ḎE̱P̱-̱ṈU̱M̱Ḇ, GR-NAME)

PERSON (<u>MANNUMB</u>, O̱ṞG̱-̱ṈA̱M̱E̱, ḎE̱P̱-̱ṈU̱M̱Ḇ, G̱Ṟ-̱ṈU̱M̱Ḇ, NAME, POSITION)

PROJ-PERSON (<u>PROJ-NUMB</u>, <u>MANNUMB</u>)

This variant is schema 3 alike, but some relations now express more connections between the classes of objects.

The network schema will contain six record types corresponding to the first six relations, $\mathcal{J}^{\mu}_{A}$ paths: ORGANIZATION-PROJECT-EQUIP-MENT, ORGANIZATION-DEPARTMENT-GROUP-PERSON-PROJECT, $\mathcal{J}^{\mu}_{m}$ path PROJECT- PERSON.

Comparison of the data base schemas given above shows that the main difference between them consists in:

- the number of relations in relational schema and the number of their domains,
- the number and length of $\mathcal{J}^{\mu}_{A}$ and $\mathcal{J}^{\mu}_{m}$ paths in the network schema,
- the record types in S-graph which should belong to E class of nodes,
- the number of virtual source data items in the record types belonging to $\mathcal{J}^{\mu}_{A}$ paths.

CONCLUSION

The proposed method of relational to network schema mapping may be helpful in
- design of multilevel data model of real objects,
- design of methods of interpretation of relational data manipulation languages,
- design of relational and network data base schema by Data Administrator.

Simple procedures of relational to network schema mapping should stimulate inclusion of owner set types into the network schema in multilevel data model (notice that in all examples given above relations could be interpreted solely by means of record types in corresponding network schema without any owner set types). Reasonable inclusion of owner set types leads to the organization of additional useful access paths to data and to increased efficiency of the data base.

REFERENCES

Codasyl Data Description Language Journal of Development, June, 1973.

Codd E.F., A Relational Model of Data for Large Shared Data Banks, CACM, June 1970.

Codd E.F., C.J. Date, Interactive Support for Non-programmers: the Relational and Network Approaches, IBM Research, June 6, 1974.

Nijssen G.N., Data Structuring in the DDL and Relational Data Model, IEIP TC-2 Working Conference, April 1974.

Kay M.H. An Assessment of the Codasyl DDL for Use with a Relational Subschema, IFIP TC-2 Working Conference, January 1975.

Modelling in Data Base Management Systems, G.M. Nijssen, (ed.)
North Holland Publishing Company, 1976

A UNIFIED APPROACH FOR MODELLING DATA
IN LOGICAL DATA BASE DESIGN

M. Adiba, C. Delobel, M. Léonard
Laboratoire d'Informatique de l'Université I de GRENOBLE
B.P. 53 / 38041 GRENOBLE Cedex (France)

Data Base Management systems can be categorized and discussed
according to three points of view :
- hierarchical,
- network,
- relational.

These approaches have been discussed and compared in the past
and tentatives have been made to convert one point of view to
an other. Here we examine how this conversion can be made (in
both ways) between network and relational concepts, using the
DBTG-CODASYL and SOCRATE systems as examples.

In the relational model proposed by CODD, the construction of
relations is directly influenced by the functional relations
over a set of attributes. For integrity and for maintenance
purposes it is important to eliminate inherent redundancy within
a relation due to   functional relations between attributes.
The normalization process leads to these goals by introducing the
concept of third Codd's normal form.

After the presentation of the main concepts of the relational
model (§ 2), we shall study in the first part (§ 3) how it is
possible to detect in the logical definition of the data of
CODASYL and SOCRATE' systems the functional relations.

Then (§ 4), we shall discuss how the use of functional relations
leads to a rigorous and clear description of complex data relationships. More specifically, we shall state an algorithm which
produces third normal form relations under some conditions.

At last (§ 5), we shall outline with a complete example how it is
possible to express the relations obtained by the normalization
process in terms of SOCRATE and CODASYL'DDL.

CHAPTER 1 - INTRODUCTION

Up to this time the data-base design methodology has been more the result of
trials than a rational approach to the problem. This lack of strictness has led
to systems which do not meet the prescribed requirements. One of the most important
requirements is the ability to modify the organization of data as the user's
requirements change.

In this paper, we shall look into only one fundamental aspect in the use of Data
Base Management System : the data modelling process which leads to the construction of a data structure common to all users. This data structure is called in
the current terminology the conceptual schema [1][2].

The choice of one conceptual schema depends on the capabilities of Data Base Management Systems. These systems may be categorized and discussed according to three main models :
- hierarchical,
- network,
- relational.

Our purpose is neither to discuss the advantages or the disadvantages of these models nor to adopt a definite position regarding one of these models and systems, but to analyse on one hand,how the basic concepts of each system can be interpreted in another system, and on the other hand how these interpretations can be useful in the data modelling process.

More precisely our work could be divided into three main parts according to the figure 1.1 :
- in the first part we shall attempt to look into the basic concepts which are necessary in the conversion from hierarchical or network view to a relational view. More precisely we examine this point on two systems : CODASYL [3] and SOCRATE [4] (chapters 2 and 3).
- in the second part we analyse the possibility of removing redundancy in relational schema by means of algorithmic processes (chapter 4).
- in the third part we study how it is possible to express a relational view from a network viewpoint (chapters 3 and 5).

A full example illustrating the whole process is given in chapter 5.

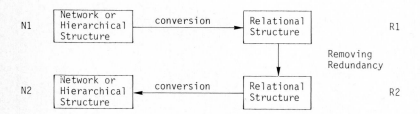

Figure 1.1

CHAPTER 2 - RELATIONAL CONCEPTS

The concepts introduced in CODD's [5] relational model and discussed again by J.R. ABRIAL in [6] are in the center of the transformation process. For this reason, it seems to us very important to summarize these main concepts.

2.1. Binary Relation

For ABRIAL, a binary relation is an association between two categories of objects characterized by the two access functions which can be used to go from one category to the other.

Each of these access functions is defined by its name and two parameters, respectively representing the maximum and minimum number of elements which can be reached from an object of the category. For instance, between the categories : 'AUTHOR' and 'BOOK' we can define a binary relation r1 characterized by the two access functions : 'author of book' and 'book written' :

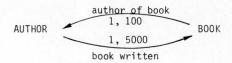

This will be written :
r1 = <u>rel</u> (AUTHOR, BOOK, book written = <u>afn</u> [1,5000], author of book = <u>afn</u>[1,100])

The parameters [1,100] and [1,5000] characterize the access functions as follows :
- a book has one author at least and 100 at most
- an author has written one book at least and 5000 at most.

2.2. N-ary Relations - Functional Relations

From the basic model of binary relations, it is possible to represent the associations between n objects. For instance an ORDER could be represented by the
following diagram :

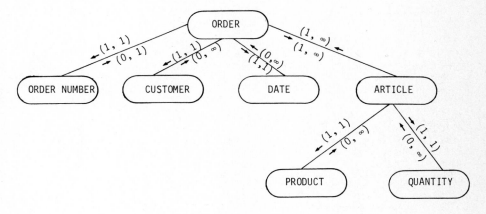

In this diagram, we have not mentionned the name of the access functions, but
only their parameters.

In CODD's model there corresponds to this diagram an n-ary relation named ORDER
between the attributes CUSTOMER, DATE-OF-ORDER, PRODUCT, QUANTITY, ORDER-NUMBER.

A representation of this relation is a table in which each column represents one
attribute and each row one element (one tuple) of the relation. In such a representation the constructed relations may have some undesirable properties which
make them unsuitable for use. For this reason, CODD introduced the normal form
concept for a relation [7, 8]. This notion depends upon the interrelationships[*]
which may exist between attributes of a relation. These interrelationships are
named <u>functional relations</u> (FR).

---

[*] They correspond in some degree to classes of access functions which have as parameters : [0,1] or [1,1].

For instance in the relation :
    ORDER (ORDER-NUMBER, CUSTOMER, DATE-OF-ORDER, PRODUCT, QUANTITY)
we have the following functional relations
    ORDER-NUMBER → CUSTOMER, DATE-OF-ORDER
    ORDER-NUMBER, PRODUCT → QUANTITY

Generally speaking if a relation R is built upon the attributes A_1, A_2, ..., A_n
we shall write it : $R(A_1, A_2, ..., A_n)$ and $f : E → F$ denotes a FR such as :

    . E and F are parts of $\{A_1, A_2, ..., A_n\}$
    . E is the left-hand part of f and will be denoted by $\ell(f)$
    . F is the right-hand part of f and will be denoted by $r(f)$

if, for a given E and F the above relation holds, and if, in addition, for every
proper subset E' in E it is false that E' → F, then we shall say that E → F is an
elementary functional relation (EFR).

The properties of the FR's have been studied in [9] [10] [11] and a brief summary
is given in the following section.

The analysis of FR's allows us to know precisely one part of the integrity constraints and at the same time to study how to regroup the attributes to form suitable relations.

This process, initially proposed by Codd with the name of normalization process
is in fact a decomposition process. In particular, we have pointed out the part
played by the boolean algebra in this process [12], and we have proved in that the
decomposition process is not based only upon the FR's but also upon other effects
[13].

Example 1

Let R1 be a relation between projects, products implied in these projects and
suppliers of the products.

    M1 : project-number
    M2 : product-number
    M3 : product-price
    M4 : supplier-name.

We have the functional relations :
    f1 : M1 M2 → M4
    f2 : M2 → M3

Figure 1.2 gives an instance of R1.

Project M1	Product M2	Price M3	Supplier M4
1	a	5	α
1	b	10	α
1	c	5	β
2	b	10	γ
2	d	6	α
2	e	5	α
2	c	5	δ

Figure 2.1 - Example of R1

2.3. Properties of functional relations and normal forms

Taking the FR's as a basic concept to modelize a data base management system it is necessary to propose a method to produce relational schemas. This method, using the normalization concept, requires the knowledge of the properties of a FR's set. Indeed, a set of FR's may be redundant and this will give undesirable relations.

Let us summarize the properties of the FR's and their links with Codd's normal forms.

We express by R(A) an n-ary relation built upon a set of attributes $A = \{M_1, M_2, ..., M_n\}$ and by $\mathcal{F}(R)$ or simply $\mathcal{F}$, a set of FR's. This set has the following properties :

let, E, F, G and H be parts of A :

P1. Reflexivity : $E \rightarrow E$
P2. Projection : if $E \rightarrow G,F$ then $E \rightarrow G$ and $E \rightarrow F$
P3. Augmentation : if $E \rightarrow F$ then $\forall G \quad E,G \rightarrow F$
P4. Additivity : if $E \rightarrow F$ and $E \rightarrow G$ then $E \rightarrow F,G$
P5. Transitivity : if $E \rightarrow F$ and $F \rightarrow G$ then $E \rightarrow G$
P6. Pseudo-transitivity : if $E \rightarrow F$ and $F,G \rightarrow H$ then $E,G \rightarrow H$.

The concept of FR is similar in nature to that of a key attribute. E is a candidate key of a relation R(A) if f :

. $E \rightarrow A$
. $\not\exists E' \subset E : E' \rightarrow A$

For each relation R one of its candidate keys is arbitrarily designated as the primary key of R. The usual operational distinction between the primary key and other candidate keys (if any) is that no tuple is allowed to have an undefined value for any of the primary key components, whereas any other component may have an undefined value.

The keys of a relation play a very important part, especially concerning the redundancy the relation may contain.

2.3.1. First normal form

Let $R_1(M_1, M_2, ..., M_n)$ be a relation where M_1M_2 is a key and suppose the existence of M_3 such as :

$M_2 \rightarrow M_3$ (see example 1).

Such a relation presents two main imperfections :

1) Some occurrences of M_2M_3 can be destroyed, and the corresponding information will be lost.
For instance, in R_1 if we delete the first tuple, we lose the information : "the price of product a is 5" (see Fig. 2.1).

2) There will be some redundancy on the occurrences of (M_2,M_3) and this will make the updating more complicated.

If we write $n(m_1|m_2)$ the average number of occurrences of M_1 corresponding to an occurrence of M_2 and if $n(m_2)$ is the total number of occurrences of M_2, an estimation of this redundancy is given by :

$[n(m_1|m_2) - 1] \, n(m_2)$

Such an n-ary relation is said to be in first normal form (FNF).

2.3.2. Second Normal Form

Let $R_2(M_1, M_2, \ldots, M_n)$ be a relation where M_1M_2 is a key such as :

$$\forall M_i \in R_2 : M_1 \to M_i \text{ or } M_2 \to M_i$$
$$\exists M_3 \in R_2 : M_1M_2 \to M_3 \text{ and } M_3 \to M_4$$

Example 2

Let $R_2 (M_1, M_2, M_3, M_4)$ be the relation between :

    M1 : project-number
    M2 : product-number
    M3 : supplier-name
    M4 : supplier-city.

We have : f1 : $M_1, M_2 \to M_3$
           f2 : $M_1, M_2 \to M_4$
    and   f3 : $M_3 \to M_4$.

Figure 2.2 shows an example of R_2.

M_1	M_2	M_3	M_4
1	a	α	r1
1	b	α	r1
1	c	β	r3
2	b	γ	r2
2	d	α	r1
2	e	α	r1
2	c	δ	r2

Figure 2.2 - R_2

Such a relation has two imperfections :
such that :
1) Some occurrences of M_3M_4 can be destroyed and corresponding information will be lost.
For instance, we can lose the information : supplier β is in the town r3, if the third row is deleted (see example 2).

2) There will be some redundancy on the occurrences of M_4 compared to the decomposition of R_2 in two relations namely $R_{21}(M_3M_4)$ and $R_{22}(M_1, M_2, M_3)$, and then updating of R_2 will be more complicated.

An estimation of this redundancy is given by :
$$[n(m_1m_2|m_3)-1)] \, n(m_3)$$

The decomposition of R_2 into R_{21} and R_{22} eliminates these two imperfections. R_2 is said to be in second normal form (SNF).

2.3.3. Third Normal Form

Let $R_3 = (M_1, M_2, M_3, \ldots, M_n)$ be a relation where $M_1 M_2$ is a key such that :

$\not\exists \, M_i : M_1 \rightarrow M_i$ or $M_2 \rightarrow M_i$

$\not\exists \, M_i, M_j \quad M_1 M_2 \rightarrow M_i$ and $M_i \rightarrow M_j$

This relation is said to be in third normal form (TNF).

One of its particularities is to have only one key and one of its fondamental properties is to <u>create</u> no redundancy.

In fact the relation R_2 in section 2.3.2. could be decomposed **into** two relations in TNF and that is why the redundancy has been eliminated (see fig. 2.3).

M_1	M_2	M_3
1	a	α
1	b	α
1	c	β
2	b	γ
2	d	α
2	c	α
2	c	δ

M_3	M_4
α	r1
β	r3
γ	r2
δ	r2

Figure 2.3 - Relations in TNF

This leads to a more general problem :
 - how to decompose a set of relations in first, second and third form into a set of relations in TNF ?

In chapter 4, we give some indications to solve this problem.

CHAPTER 3 - CONVERSION OF HIERARCHICAL OR NETWORK DATA STRUCTURE INTO A RELATIONAL SCHEMA

The first step in data modelling is to identify the elements of the real word which may be needed to be represented in the data base system. These basic elements of the real word according to Abrial's concepts [6] can be considered as objects belonging to some categories, and these objects may be related to other objects (see figure in section 2.2). Furthermore each object can be characterized by attributes. In this representation, the access functions and their parameters between the two categories play an important role in the design process for the following reason : if two categories are related to each other by access functions with their parameters, how is it possible to implement this association with the capabilities of a given data base system ? Here we want to consider only two systems : CODASYL [3] and SOCRATE [4] for an illustrating purpose. Conversely if a CODASYL or SOCRATE data structure is given how is it possible to deduce categories of objects and their links between them ? Then, we can obtain quite easily a relational schema.

Both CODASYL and SOCRATE have no concept of category of objects but they use something equivalent in some ways which is the notion of block of attributes. This notion is similar to the notion of Singular Class of $\overline{\text{Attri}}$butes developed in [18]. Block is called RECORD in CODASYL and ENTITY in SOCRATE. A block may contain sub-blocks called repeating groups in CODASYL and included entity in SOCRATE.

Roughly speaking, to each block or sub-block, we associate an n-ary relation which we called a <u>main relation</u> (MR).

This statement will be explained in the section 3.1.2.

Between these blocks the two systems provide different possible links : these links are in fact binary relations which we shall call <u>linking relations</u> (LR). These links permit the construction of network structures.

In the first part of this chapter, we shall study the different possibilities of linking two blocks according to the value of the access function parameters, with the data structure proposed by SOCRATE and CODASYL.

In the second part we present, using the same approach, the possibility of deducing a relational schema.

3.1. Binary Relations between blocks

In a data structure written in one of the two systems the binary relations correspond to existing links between two blocks of attributes.

Frequently these links provide an access path from one block to another.

Let A and B be two blocks with respective keys K(A) and K(B) and suppose the existence of a link <u>between A and B</u>. Let us study the nature of this link, according to :
   - the system (SOCRATE or CODASYL)
   - the binary relation existing between A and B.

3.1.1.

$r1 = rel(K(A), K(B), AB = \underline{afn} (1,1), BA = \underline{afn} (x,y))$ where x and y are any integers.
In this case, there is a FR :
$$K(A) \rightarrow K(B)$$

   a) A first possible link between A and B can be realized by including K(B) in A. Such a link can be implemented in the two systems.

Example 3.1

Block A : <u>part-number</u>, machine-type, supplier-name
(we underline part-number to indicate that this attribute is the key of block A).

Block B : <u>supplier-name</u>, city.

Here the attribute "supplier-name" which is the key of B also appearing in A.

| SOCRATE | CODASYL |
| | |

```
          SOCRATE                              CODASYL

entity A                             record name A
begin                                         location mode is ...
│       PART-NUMBER                            ...
│       MACHINE-TYPE                           PART-NUMBER
│       SUPPLIER-NAME                          MACHINE-TYPE
│                                              SUPPLIER-NAME
│         :
│         :                                      :
end                                              :
```

SOCRATE

```
entity B
begin
        SUPPLIER-NAME
        CITY
        :
end
```

CODASYL

```
record name B
        location mode ...
        SUPPLIER-NAME
        CITY
        :
```

b) A second possibility uses particular features of each system :

CODASYL

A set can link a member record type to an owner record type if (from [3] p. 44-45) the propositions P1 and P2 are true :

P1 : A record occurrence cannot appear in more than one occurrence of the same set.

P2 : Each set occurrence has only one occurrence of the owner.

There exists a FR :
    MEMBER → OWNER

The link between A and B is established by a set with B as owner and A as member.

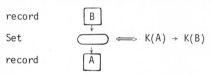

SOCRATE

The specific link in this case is called <u>reference</u> (REF)

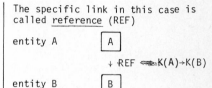

For instance, in the last example we modify A in the following manner :

A : <u>part-number</u>, machine-type

and we consider the link between A and B :

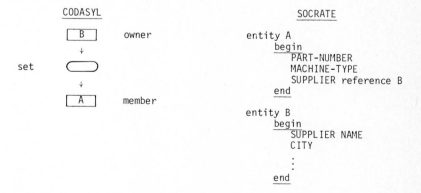

c) A third possibility is to make K(B) be a part of K(A), the functional relation is then trivial.

The block A can then be considered as an included entity for SOCRATE or, for CODASYL, as a repeating group of B or as a member mandatory automatic of a set, the parent of which is B ([3], [16]).

3.1.2.

$r2 = \underline{rel}\ (K(A),\ K(B),\ AB = \underline{afn}\ (x,\ y),\ BA = \underline{afn}\ (1,\ 1))$

where x and y are any integers.
Here the FR is : $K(B) \rightarrow K(A)$

The set of CODASYL as the reference in SOCRATE between two blocks A and B such as $K(B) \rightarrow K(A)$ provides not only the access path B to A but also A to B.
So, this case is the same as the previous one, exchanging the roles of A and B.

3.1.3.

$r3 = \underline{rel}\ (K(A),\ K(B),\ AB = \underline{afn}\ (x,\ y),\ BA = \underline{afn}\ (x',\ y'))$

where $(x,\ y)$ and $(x',\ y')$ are couples of integers not equal to $(0,\ 1)$, $(1,\ 1)$.

Example 3.4

A : Courses
B : Students

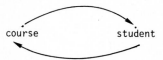

course   student

To a given course there corresponds any number of students and one student may take any number of courses.

SOCRATE

In SOCRATE we have the choice between two links :
- INVERSE (INV)
- ENTITE-REFERENCE (EREF) i.e. an entity which contains only a reference.

The choice between these two links depends upon the ratio between the maximum number of occurrences of B corresponding to an occurrence of A (here y) and the total number of occurrences of B. If this last number is not very important it is better to use EREF, otherwise INV.

CODASYL

The link between A and B is implemented by a third record in which we can put K(A) and K(B) as virtual.
This third record is linked to record A and record B by two different sets as follows :

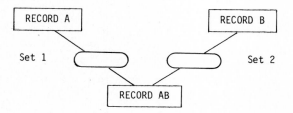

3.1.4. Summary

These different cases can be summarized in the table of the figure 3.1. The table can be read in two ways ; i.e., from a CODASYL or SOCRATE data structure we can find if we can generate :

(a) a FR
(b) a linking relation over the attributes K(A) and K(B).

In a same way we can use this table to find what is the possible representation in CODASYL or SOCRATE data description language of a binary relation between two blocks. This utilisation is the basis of the process described in chapter 5.

TYPE OF BINARY RELATION BETWEEN BLOCKS	CODASYL	SOCRATE
1 $\underline{rel}(K(A),K(B),AB=afn(1,1),$ $BA=afn(x,y))$ or $\underline{rel}(K(A),K(B),AB=afn(0,1),$ $BA=afn(x,y))$ 2 $K(A) \rightarrow K(B)$	- K(B) in record A or - Set with owner B member A or - A repeating group of B	- K(B) in entity A or - REF from entity A to entity B or - entity A included in entity B
3 $\underline{rel}(K(A),K(B),AB=afn(x,y),$ $BA = afn(x',y'))$	Third record for the link	INV or EREF from A to B and from B to A

Figure 3.1

3.2. N-ary relations corresponding to blocks

To each block or sub-block of a data structure written in any of the two systems corresponds an n-ary relation called main relation (MR).

In the data structure, each block has, at least, one key which allows us to distinguish one occurrence from all others. The set of these keys is called the conceptual key of the associated n-ary relation (see section 2.3).

This relation must be composed with :
- the conceptual key
- all the others attributes of the block.

However, in Codasyl or in Socrate, it may occur that all the components of the conceptual key doesn't appear explicitly in the given block.

The consequence is that to form the n-ary relation, it is necessary to look for the lacking components in the remaining of the data-structure.

Let us look at three important cases where such a situation occurs.

3.2.1. Case of sub-blocks

To associate a sub-block to an n-ary relation, it is necessary to determine its conceptual key which generally depends upon the conceptual key of the including block (see example 6).

Example 6 (Socrate)

```
entity PERSON
      begin
      |    NAME
      |    :
      |    :
      |    entity CHILD
      |    begin
      |    |    FIRST-NAME
      |    |    AGE
      |    end
      end
```

The key of the sub-block "child" must be formed with :

    1) the key of the including block, "person", namely "name"
    2) the key of the sub-block "child", namely "first-name",

then, the corresponding n-ary relations are :

    person (name, address ...)
    child (name, first-name, age, school).

3.2.2. Case of links between blocks

Given two blocks A and B with respective conceptual keys K(A) and K(B) such that :

    - K(A) contains K(B)
    - A and B are linked by :

        . either, in Codasyl, a set with B as owner
        . either, in Socrate, a reference from A to B.

In this case, one part of the key of A is in B.

Example 7

```
entity PERSON                      entity CHILD
begin                              begin
|    NAME                          |    FIRST-NAME
|    JOB                           |    AGE
|    SALARY                        |    FATHER reference CHILDREN OF PERSON
|    :                             end
|    :
|    CHILDREN RING
end
```

Here again, we have to extract "name" from the entity "person" to generate the n-ary relation corresponding to "child".

3.2.3. Particular case of Codasyl

It corresponds to a particular definition of an access path to a record through sets.

Let us write the LOCATION MODE of a RECORD A:RAM (A) (= Record Access Method) and the SET OCCURRENCE SELECTION of a SET S for the MEMBER (M) : SAM (S|M) (= Set Access Method) ;

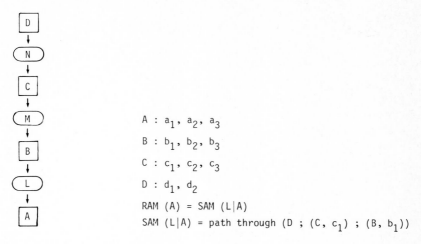

$A : a_1, a_2, a_3$

$B : b_1, b_2, b_3$

$C : c_1, c_2, c_3$

$D : d_1, d_2$

RAM (A) = SAM (L|A)

SAM (L|A) = path through $(D ; (C, c_1) ; (B, b_1))$

Thus, one key of A is composed of :
- the key of D
- the attributes c_1 and b_1
- one or more attributes of A.

3.2.4. In summary

As we have just seen, from blocks and sub-blocks of a data structure in Codasyl or Socrate, we can generate n-ary relations including :
- the attributes of the corresponding blocks or sub-blocks
- the keys.

The keys cannot always be determined by a simple view of the structure but it is possible, under some conditions, to lead the search.

Indeed, the keys can only be found in :
- nested blocks
- blocks to which the given block refers (Socrate)
- owner blocks of sets, the given block of which is a member (Codasyl).

Once all the keys have been found, we can constitute all the FR's which link each key to the others attributes.

If in the same relation, we have more than one key, i.e. A, B, C, ..., this set of keys constitutes the conceptual key of the relation and in Socrate as in Codasyl we have the following functional relations

$A \rightarrow B$

$B \rightarrow C$

$C \rightarrow A.$

3.3. Finding the relational schema

All these results come from an atomic view of the data structure. Now our purpose is to convert a complete SOCRATE or CODASYL data structure into a relational schema.

For this it is necessary to built a graph which is anunified representation
of the CODASYL and SOCRATE data structure. Furthermore this graph will also be used
in the chapter 5.

3.3.1. Graph_of_blocks

Let $G(\mathcal{B}, \mathcal{L}, \mathbb{N}, \gamma, \mu)$ be a graph where :
- $\mathcal{B}$ is the set of block names determined by scanning the data structure (remember
  that we consider henceforth sub-blocks as blocks).
- $\mathcal{L}$ is a set of names which correspond to the names of links between blocks (i.e.
  in SOCRATE : reference, inverse, ring, in CODASYL : set). The set $\mathcal{L}$ contains the
  element H to denote hierarchical link, and the element K to denote implicit link.
- $\mathbb{N}$ is the integer set.
- γ and μ are partial functions

$$\gamma : \mathcal{B} \times \mathcal{L} \longrightarrow \mathcal{B}$$
$$\mu : \mathcal{B} \times \mathcal{B} \times \mathcal{L} \longrightarrow \mathbb{N}$$

which are defined by table 3.2.

Case	SOCRATE		CODASYL		
		γ		γ	μ
1	Entity A contains a reference of name L to entity B	$\gamma(A,L) = B$	There exist a set name L between the records A and B (owner B, member A)	$\gamma(A,L) = B$	1
2	Key of B belongs to A	$\gamma(A,K) = B$	Key of B is in A	$\gamma(A,K) = B$	1
3	A is entity included in B	$\gamma(A,H) = B$	- A is a repeating group of B - A is MEMBER MANDATORY AUTOMATIC of a SET, the PARENT of which is B	$\gamma(A,H) = B$	2
4	There exists an INV or EREF of name I from A to B	$\gamma(A,I) = B$			3

Table 3.2

Certains connections between blocks of a given structure have to be modified for
semantic reasons. In particular, it is the case when between two blocks we have two
different edges. How to determine meaning is currently not a well understood area ;
nevertheless we make the assumption that it is possible to break the terminal node
in several parts according to their specific meanings.

For instance, we consider two blocks PLANE and PERSON and two relations between
them :

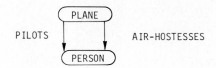

PILOTS   AIR-HOSTESSES

This will be broken into :

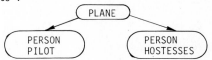

Now we consider only data structures to which the process described above have been applied. Thus, we obtain data structures to which corresponds a simplified graph where there is only one link between two blocks.

Furthermore we assume that the reflexive loops between blocks are deleted in the data-structure.

3.3.2. Components of the relational schema

A relational schema is composed of :
- a set of relations of two types : main relations issued from blocks, linking relations issued from links between blocks ;
- a set of FR's which are automatically deduced from the nature of the link between two blocks (see table 3.1) and from the knowledge of the keys

There are two steps to determine the relational schema corresponding to a given network data structure :

Step 1 : Determination of the keys of each blocks. If the keys are not explicitly defined in the data structure, for instance, called foreign keys [7], we have to search for them through a path in the graph, by following an edge where $\mu = 1$ or 2. Then it is possible to determine the key for each block.

Step 2 : For each block A generated : a main relation R composed of the key K(A) and the other attributes M, and the FR : $K(A) \to M$.

For each pair of blocks A and B with label L such that :
- if $\mu(A, B, L) = 1$ we generate a linking relation R(K(A), K(B)) and a FR $K(A) \to K(B)$
- if $\mu(A, B, L) = 2$ we could generate a relation R(K(A))
- if $\mu(A, B, L) = 3$ we generate a linking relation R(K(A), K(B)).

Up to now, the design process is based upon only the information which can be automatically deduced from the data structure. However SOCRATE or CODASYL data structure cannot express all the integrity constraints that the user may want to specify. Some of these constraints can be very useful in the design process and they could be taken into account only if they are desired and given by the user. Such could be the case for additional FR's.

CHAPTER 4 - PRELIMINARY NOTIONS

In chapter 3, we have shown that is possible to convert a CODASYL or SOCRATE's conceptual schema in a relational schema which is composed of :

- a set of relations

$$\{R_1(A^1), R_2(A^2), \ldots, R_k(A^k)\}$$

where R_i denotes the name of the relation and A^i the set of attributes ;

- a set $\mathcal{F}$ of FR's defined over the attribute set $A = \bigcup_i A^i$.

Any relations can be represented by tables such as in example 2.1. Such tables would be, in most cases, highly redundant and inefficient to maintain. The goal of this chapter is to study how the knowledge of the set $\mathcal{F}$ allows one of substitute into each relation R_i a set of relations $\{R_{i1}, R_{i2}, \ldots, R_{in(i)}\}$ such that :

- $R_i = R_{i1} * R_{i1} * \ldots * R_{in(i)}$, where the $*$ operation denotes the join operation, this equation means that the relation R_i can be regenerated by means of the join operation,
- R_{ij}, $j=1,\ldots,n(i)$ is a projection of R_i.

Then it is possible to replace the relational schema $\{R_1, R_2, \ldots, R_k\}$ by another schema $\{R_{11}, \ldots, R_{1n(1)}, \ldots, R_{k1}, \ldots, R_{kn(k)}\}$ which we consider as equivalent to the first one.

The research of equivalent relational schemas depends upon the two concepts introduced by C. DELOBEL and D. CASEY in [12] :

- eliminating redundancy in relation is equivalent to eliminate redundancy between the FR's ;
- replacing, if possible, each relation R_i by relations in Codd's third normal form (TNF).

Different algorithms have been proposed by P.A. BERNSTEIN and al [14], C.P. WANG, H.H. WEDEKING [15]. The main aspect of our work is that we give a condition on the FR's set to produce relations in TNF and we built an algorithm which determines both the closure and the minimum covering of the set of FR's in one step.

4.2. Definitions

4.2.1. Closure and Coverings

Reconsider properties P1, P2, P3, P4, P5, P6 now as a set of rules for obtaining new FR's from a given set $\mathcal{F}$. The closure of $\mathcal{F}$, denoted $\mathcal{F}^+$, is defined as the set of all FR's that are obtainable by successive application of properties P1-P6 on the FR's of the set $\mathcal{F}$. The elementary closure of $\mathcal{F}$, denoted $\mathcal{F}^\oplus$ is a part of $\mathcal{F}^+$ such every FR is an EFR. The minimum covering of $\mathcal{F}$, denoted $\mathcal{F}^*$, is a part of $\mathcal{F}^\oplus$ such that :

(a) $(\mathcal{F}^*)^+ = \mathcal{F}^+$

(b) $\forall \mathcal{K} \subset \mathcal{F}^* : \mathcal{K}^+ \neq \mathcal{F}^+$

4.2.2. Graphical representation of a set of FR's

Let $\mathcal{F}$, be a set of FR's $\{f_1, f_2, \ldots, f_n\}$ over an attribute set $A = \{A_1, A_2, \ldots, A_k\}$. We define a graph, denoted $G(\mathcal{F})$, as follows. In the graph, there are two types of nodes ; the round nodes representing the attribute nodes, the square nodes representing the FR's.

An edge is oriented from a round node A_i to a square node f_j if $A_i \in \ell(f_j)$.
An edge is oriented from a square node f_j to a round node A_m if $A_m \in r(f_j)$.

Example

Let $\mathcal{F}$ be the set of FR's over the attributes $\{A,B,C,D,E,F,G\}$
$\mathcal{F}$ = {f1, f2, f3, f4, f5}
f1 : ACG → E, f2 : F → E, f3 : AD → F, f4 : BC → D, f5 : AC → B.

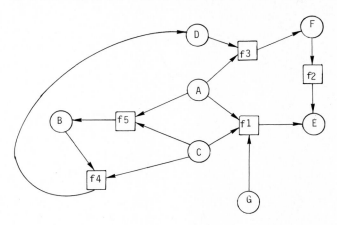

Figure 4.1

The traditional notion of <u>path</u> and <u>cycle</u> in a graph can be applied to the graph $G(\mathcal{F})$.

To the notion of path we can associate the notion of <u>chain</u> of FR's defined as follows :
the ordered set $(E \to E_1, E_2 \to E_3, \ldots, E_{i+1} \to F)$ is a <u>chain</u> if and only if
$E_1 \subseteq E_2, E_3 \subseteq E_4, \ldots, E_i \subseteq E_{i+1}$ $F \not\subseteq E$.

Similarly to a cycle we associate the notion of <u>closed-chain</u>. A closed-chain is a chain such $F \subseteq E$.

4.2.3. <u>Pseudo-transitivity operation on FR's</u>

To the property of pseudo-transitivity, we can associate a formal binary operation denoted +> between FR's. If the FR, f_1 can be deduced from f_2 and f_3 by the pseudo-transitivity law we write :

$$f_1 = f_2 \;+\!\!> f_3$$

This formal operation is non-commutative and non-associative as shown by the following example.

Example

Let f_1, f_2, f_3 be three FR's such :

$$f_1 : A,B \to C \quad f_2 : C,D \to E \quad f_3 : E,C \to G$$
$$f_1 \twoheadrightarrow (f_2 \twoheadrightarrow f_3) = (AB \to C) \twoheadrightarrow (CD \to G) = ABD \to G$$
$$(f_1 \twoheadrightarrow f_2) \twoheadrightarrow f_3 = (ABD \to E) \twoheadrightarrow (EC \to G) = ABDC \to G$$

4.2.4. Properties of a minimal covering of a given set of FR's

Let $\mathcal{F}$ be a set of FR's over an attribute set A such $G(\mathcal{F})$ is without a cycle, then the unicity of the minimum covering $\mathcal{F}^*$ is proved in [17].

Theorem[*] :

If $\mathcal{F}^*$ is the minimum covering of a set F of functional relations, and if the graph of $\mathcal{F}^*$ is acyclic, then there is no attribute $X \neq \phi$ such that the following statements are true.

$$S_1 : A_1 \to X \in \mathcal{F}^\oplus$$
$$S_2 : A_2 X \to C \in \mathcal{F}^\oplus$$
$$S_3 : A_1 A_2 \to C \in \mathcal{F}^*$$

where A_1, A_2 and C are attributes (or attribute sets) such that

$$X \cap A_2 = \phi$$

Proof :

Assume the contrary, i.e., there is such an X. We shall shown that S_1, S_2, S_3 then imply either that the graph contains a cycle ; or else that $\mathcal{F}^*$ is not a minimum cover. This constitues proof by contradiction.

The following four cases will be examined :

    (1) $S_1, S_2 \in \mathcal{F}^*$

    (2) $S_1 \notin \mathcal{F}^*, S_2 \in \mathcal{F}^*$

    (3) $S_1 \in \mathcal{F}^*, S_2 \notin \mathcal{F}^*$

    (4) $S_1, S_2 \notin \mathcal{F}^*$

[*] This result has been obtained conjointly with D. CASEY (IBM Research Laboratory San Jose) and P. BERNSTEIN (University of Toronto).

Case (1) : the FR's S_1-S_3 are not independent : $S_3 = S_1 \text{ +> } S_2$. Thus all three can not belong to the same minimum cover, so this case leads to an immediate contradiction.

Case (2) : since S_1 belongs to $\mathcal{F}^\oplus$ it must be derivable from the FR's of the minimum cover.

$$S_1 = f(V_1, V_2, \ldots, V_n) \text{ where } V_i \in \mathcal{F}^*$$

where f is an expression using only the +> operator (for example

$$S_1 = (V_2 \text{ +> } V_3) \text{ +> } (V_4 \text{ +> } V_5))$$

and because the closure $\mathcal{F}^\oplus$ can be obtained by successive application of +> to members of $\mathcal{F}^*$. The function f defined above is an instance of such an application. Suppose that $S_3 \neq V_i$ for any i.

Then $S_3 = f[V_1, V_2, \ldots, V_n] \text{ +> } S_2$ which shows that S_3 can be derived from members of $\mathcal{F}^*$ and thus cannot belong to $\mathcal{F}^*$ itself, a contradiction.

On the other hand, consider $S_3 = V_i$ for some i.

Since $S_2 \in \mathcal{F}^*$ there is a path from X to C in the graph of $\mathcal{F}^*$. But since $S_1 = f[V_1, V_2, \ldots, V_{i-1}, S_3, V_{i+1}, \ldots, V_n]$ then if we assume that there is a path from C the right hand part of S_3 to X the right hand part of S_1, then we obtain a cycle and so a contradiction.

Cases (3) and (4) are proved the same way.

We have just to prove that the here above assumption is true on any f expression :

Lemma :

    Let $f(V_1, V_2, \ldots, V_n)$ be an f-expression obtained by the following syntaxic rules :

<f-expression> ::= <chain> | (<f-expression>) +> (<f-expression>)

<chain> ::= <EFR> | <EFR> +> (<chain>)
where EFR is an elementary functional relation.
An f-expression expresses all the different possibilities to derive functional relation form given a set of EFR.

    Let $S = f(V_1, V_2, \ldots, V_n)$ then for any attribute A in f there exist a path from A to r(f) where r(f) denotes the right hand part of the functional relation S. The proof is by induction on the definition of an <f-expression> :

(a) If f is a chain the proposition is true, it is evident.

(b) Let f_1, f_2 be two f-expressions such that the path property is true, then the path property is true for $f = (f_1) \text{ +> } (f_2)$.

   (1) if the attribute A belongs to f_2 then there exists a path from A to $r(f_2)$, but as the operation $(f_1) \text{ +> } (f_2)$ is possible $r(f) = r(f_2)$, then there exists a path from A to $r(f)$.

   (2) if the attribute A belongs to f_1, then there exists a path from A to $r(f_1)$, but as $(f_1) \text{ +> } (f_2)$ is possible $r(f_1)$ is an attribute of f_2, then by transitivity there exists a path from A to $r(f)$.

4.2.5. Consequence_of_this_properties

Let R be an n-ary relation and $\mathcal{F}$ the acyclic set of FR's which is associated with R ; an important conclusion of this theorem is that for each FR f_i belonging to $\mathcal{F}^*$ we can associate a relation R_i in TNF ($i \in [1,n]$).

So, since it is proved in [12], R can be replaced by

. $R = R_1 * R_2 \ldots * R_i \ldots * R_n$ if the key K of R is included in one relation R_i ;

. $R = K * R_1 * R_2 \ldots * R_n$ if not.

The properties of $\mathcal{F}^*$ are fundamental in the analysis of the algorithms given in the next section. These algorithms are based upon the condition that $G(\mathcal{F})$ is without cycles. This condition may seen restrictive because in some cases $G(\mathcal{F})$ possesses cycles. In practice such cycles are perhaps unlikely to occur. Nevertheless, it is the case when there are several candidate keys for a relation. These cases can be handled by breaking the cycle, but details of this procedure will not be given in this paper.

4.3. Algorithms to solve the closure and the minimum covering problems

For explanation purposes we proceed in two steps. In the first step, we give an algorithm for the closure problem, and in the second step we explain how to modify the first algorithm to take in account the minimum covering problem. We cannot separate these two problems because they are both of equal importance. The closure problem allows us to determine the candidate keys, and the minimum covering problem produces a set of relations.

4.3.1. Closure_algorithm

The trivial algorithm to find the closure of $\mathcal{F}$, processes by combining all pairs of FR's for producing new FR's and then recursively. Obviously such an algorithm is unfeasible for even small values of the number of FR's in $\mathcal{F}$.

Our algorithm is based upon two considerations :

- we produce new FR's only by grouping FR's in the following way

$$f_1 \leftrightarrow (f_2 \leftrightarrow f_3)$$

according to the property shown in section 4.2.3.

- by defining a linear ordering on FR's of $\mathcal{F}$, it is possible to scan successively each FR of $\mathcal{F}$ without loops.
  The linear ordering on FR's is defined as follows :

   (a) we label each attribute with a level number called the attribute level number (ALN).
       The ALN zero is given for an attribute which does not belong to a left hand part of a FR.

   (b) The ALN of an attribute A is equal to j ($j > 1$) :
       . if there exists at least one attribute B with ALN = j-1 and A,X → B (where X could be empty)
       and
       . there exists no attribute C with ALN > j and A,X → C (where X could be empty).

   (c) We order attributes according to their ALN and, inside an ALN we ordered the attribute in an arbitrary way.

   (d) For every attribute A we associate all the FR's f such as r(f) = A which are ordered in an arbitrary way.

At the end we obtain a linear ordering of the FR's. One can notice that this linear ordering is made only with the initial FR's belonging to $\mathscr{F}$.

The figure 4.2 gives the algorithm where $\mathscr{F}$ is the initial set of FR's.

$\mathscr{G} := \mathscr{F}$
Do for each attribute A
$\quad \mathscr{D} := \phi$
$\quad$ Do for each FR f in $\mathscr{F}$ such r(f) = A
$\qquad \mathscr{G}_1 := f \mathrel{+>} \mathscr{G}$
$\qquad$ if $\mathscr{G}_1 \neq \phi$ then
$\qquad \begin{bmatrix} \mathscr{G}_1 := \mathscr{G}_1 - (\mathscr{G}_1 \cap \mathscr{G}) \\ \text{delete in } \mathscr{G}_1, \mathscr{F} \text{ and } \mathscr{G} \text{ all the FR's which are contained in} \\ \text{each other} \\ \mathscr{D} := \mathscr{G}_1 \cup \mathscr{D} \\ \mathscr{G}_1 := \phi \end{bmatrix}$
$\quad$ end
$\qquad \mathscr{G} := \mathscr{G} \cup \mathscr{D}$
end
$\mathscr{F}^* := \mathscr{F} \cup \mathscr{G}$

Figure 4.2 : Closure algorithm

There are a number of improvements that can be made to the above procedure 16 , but their details and justifications are beyond the scope of this paper.

4.3.2. Minimum covering-closure algorithm

As shown in section 4.2.4, an EFR of the minimum covering cannot be obtained by the composition +> of two EFR of the closure. This is an interpretation of the theorem of section 4.2.4.

The procedure is the following :

(a) at the beginning the minimum covering $\mathscr{F}^*$ is equal to $\mathscr{F}$

(b) for each FR f generated by the closure algorithm such f = g +> h, then :

. f $\notin \mathscr{F}^*$ if f $\not\subseteq$ h or if f $\subseteq$ h then f is not contained in any FR's belonging to $\mathscr{F}^*$.

. f $\in \mathscr{F}^*$ in the contrary.

Example

Let R(A,B,C,D,E,F,G) a n-ary relation associated with a set $\mathscr{F}$ of FR's.

$$\mathscr{F}^* \begin{cases} 1 : \text{ACG} \rightarrow \text{E} \\ 2 : \text{F} \quad\rightarrow \text{E} \\ 3 : \text{AD} \quad\rightarrow \text{F} \\ 4 : \text{BC} \quad\rightarrow \text{D} \\ 5 : \text{AC} \quad\rightarrow \text{B} \end{cases}$$

The computing of the ALN gives the table

ALN	Attributes
0	E
1	F,G
2	D
3	B
4	A,C

The algorithm will generate the FR's in the following order :

			Observations
6	3 +> 2	AD → E	6 does not contain 2, then $6 \notin \mathscr{F}^*$
7	4 +> 3	ABC → F	$7 \notin \mathscr{F}^*$
8	4 +> 6	ABC → E	$8 \notin \mathscr{F}^*$
9	5 +> 4	AC → D	9 does not contain 4, then $9 \notin \mathscr{F}^*$, but we must be careful because 9 +> 6 satisfies the condition : (5 +> 4) +> 6 = 5 +> (4 +> 6), also the FR (5 +> 4) + 6 does not delete 6, so we store this result in a working table where AC → E = (5 +> 4) +> 6 cannot belong to $\mathscr{F}^*$
10	5 +> 7	AC → F	10 contains 7 which does not belong to $\mathscr{F}^*$, further 10 does not delete any FR in $\mathscr{F}^*$, then $10 \notin \mathscr{F}^*$
11	5 +> 8	AC → E	11 contains 8 and also 1 which belongs to $\mathscr{F}^*$, as 11 is in working table, $11 \notin \mathscr{F}^*$

The minimum covering set is composed of :

$$\mathscr{F}^* \begin{cases} F \to E \\ AD \to F \\ BC \to D \\ AC \to B \end{cases}$$

Since the key of R (A,C,G) does not belong to any relation of $\mathscr{F}^*$, we can write :
R = (A,C,G) ⋆ (F,E) ⋆ (A,D,F) ⋆ (B,C,D) ⋆ (A,C,B).

CHAPTER 5 - A COMPLETE EXAMPLE ON THE CONVERSION PROCESS

To illustrate the applicability of this synthesis to a realistic application problem, we consider a room reservation system for hotel in skiing resort.

A prospective customer telephones to the reservation system to indicate an intention to make a room reservation. The reservation clerk responds to the call and obtains, through a series of questions and answers, the name of the customer, the home address and telephone number and the characteristics of the request, the period of the season, the desired class of hotel, the number of persons, the number of rooms, the resort.

The task of the reservation clerk is to verify that there is a possibility corresponding to the request. If no possibility as requested can be found the clerk must advise the customer and define a new request. Once the confirmation of the request is done it is possible to generate a reservation order which contains all the information necessary to prepare a bill.

The reference information in the model consists of five major categories of objects. CUSTOMER, REQUEST, RESERVATION-ORDER, RESORT, HOTEL.

Referring to our process, we make the assumption that a system analyst has proposed in SOCRATE the following data structure figure 5.1.

```
entity RESORT (S)
      begin
            NAME key (s)
            ALTITUDE        }  (s₁)
            DEPARTMENT      }
            HOTEL inverse all HOTEL
      end

entity HOTEL (H)
      begin
            NAME (h₁)

            RESORT-NAME (s)
            CLASS           }(h₂)
            NB-OF-ROOMS     }
            entity STATUS (T)
                  begin
                        PERIOD (p)
                        NB-OF-FREE-ROOMS  }  (t₁)
                        PRICE             }
                  end
      end

entity RESERVATION-ORDER (R)
      begin
            HOTEL reference one HOTEL
            CUSTOMER reference one CUSTOMER
            PERIOD reference one STATUS of one HOTEL
            NB-OF-ROOMS
            TOTAL-PRICE      }  (r₁)
            NB-OF-PERSONS    }
      end
```

```
entity CUSTOMER (C)
      begin
      |       NAME key (c)
      |       HOME-ADDRESS  } (c₁)
      |       PHONE-NB      }
      end

entity REQUEST (N)
      begin
      |       CUSTOMER reference one CUSTOMER
      |       PERIOD (p)
      |       RESERVATION-ORDER reference one RESERVATION-ORDER
      |       RESORT reference one RESORT
      |       CLASS-OF-HOTEL } (n₁)
      |       NB-OF-ROOMS    }
      end
```

Figure 5.1 - SOCRATE data Structure

The names in figure 5.1 have been chosen to correspond as closely as possible with the meaning of each entity, in parenthesis we denote a symbol for the name.

From this data structure and according to the elements developped in chapter 3, we built the following graph (figure 5.2), where N, C, R, S, H and T are blocks.

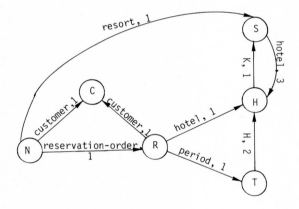

Figure 5.2

For each block, we have to determine the keys. Some keys are automatically deduced from the data structure, for example : the key of RESORT (S) is NAME (s), further-more we make the assumption that the user by analyzing the structure proposes also CUSTOMER (c), NAME-OF-HOTEL (h), PERIOD (p), NAME-OF-RESORT (s) as the key of RESERVATION-ORDER (R). All this information is collected in figure 5.3.

Block	Keys
S	s
C	c
H	(h_1,s)
N	(c,p)
T	(h_1,p,s)
R	(c,h_1,p,s)

Figure 5.3

According to step 2 in section 3.3.2, we obtain a relational schema composed of :
- main relations
  - block S $\Longrightarrow$ relation $S(s,s_1)$
  - block H $\Longrightarrow$ relation $H(h_1,s,h_2)$
  - block T $\Longrightarrow$ relation $T(h_1,s,p,t_1)$
  - block R $\Longrightarrow$ relation $R(c,h_1,s,p,r_1)$
  - block N $\Longrightarrow$ relation $N(c,p,n_1)$
  - block C $\Longrightarrow$ relation $C(c,c_1)$
- linking relations
  - relation $NC(p,c)$ which is absorbed by relation N
  - relation $NR(c,p,h_1,s)$ which is absorbed by relation R
  - relation $RH(h_1,s,c,p)$ which is absorbed by relation R
  - relation $RT(c,p,h_1,s)$ which is absorbed by relation R
  - relation $RC(c,h_1,s,p)$ which is absorbed by relation R
  - relation $HS(h_1,h_2,s)$ which is absorbed by relation R
  - relation $SH(h_1,s)$ which is absorbed by relation H
  - relation $NS(c,p,s)$ which is absorbed by relation R.
- functional relations

  $$\left. \begin{array}{ll} S & f_1 : s \to s_1 \\ C & f_2 : c \to c_1 \\ N & f_3 : c,p \to n_1 \\ R & f_4 : c,h_1,p,s \to r_1 \\ T & f_5 : h_1,p,s \to t_1 \\ H & f_6 : h_1,s \to h_2 \end{array} \right\}$$ FR's associated with the key of each block

  $$\left. \begin{array}{ll} NR & f_7 : c,p \to h_1 \\ NS & f_8 : c,p \to s \end{array} \right\}$$ FR's associated with the links between blocks

The minimum covering given by the procedure explained in chapter 4 is made up of the set of FR's listed above with the exception that the FR $f_4 : c,h_1,p,s \to r_1$ is replaced by $f_4' : c,p \to r_1$, since :

$$(c,p \to s \,+\!> (c,p \to h_1 \,+\!> c,h_1,p,s \to r_1)) = c,p \to s \,+\!> c,p,s \to r_1$$
$$= c,p \to r_1$$

It is not difficult to show that the set of FR's listed in the minimum covering gives us a set of relations in TNF :

$S(\underline{s}, s_1)$

$H(\underline{h_1, s}, h_2)$

$T(\underline{h_1, s, p}, t_1)$

$R_1(\underline{c, p}, s)$

$R_2(\underline{c, p}, h_1)$

$R_3(\underline{c, p}, r_1)$

$N(\underline{c, p}, n_1)$

$C(\underline{c}, c_1)$

This process of minimum covering and normalization of relations points out the decomposition of relation R in 3 relations R_1, R_2 and R_3. Furthermore we have now the possibility of making any appropriate combination between the relations R_1, R_2, R_3 and N because they have the same key. We decide to make the combinaison

$RN(\underline{c, p}, s, h_1, r_1, n_1)$.

Now, we are going to construct from the set of relations in TNF with their associated FR's a graph of blocks as defined in section 3.3, and then to propose a possible 'SOCRATE' structure.

In the figure 5.4, we have five blocks corresponding to the five relations, namely : S, H, T, C, RN. A directed edge between two blocks R_1, R_2 means that for one occurrence of a tuple r_1 of R_1 it could be associated with only one occurrence of a tuple r_2 of R_2. This association is equivalent to the notion of FR. For example, there is a directed edge from RN to T because the key of RN c,p determines the key of T, h_1, s, p, since $c,p \rightarrow h_1, s, p$ (see FR's f_7 and f_8).

According to table 3.2 given in section 3.3.1, we can label the edges with the parameters μ taking the values 1 or 2, and we can generate different SOCRATE's data structures since for each value of μ there are many different possibilities.

The choice between these possibilities may be considered as performance oriented considerations.

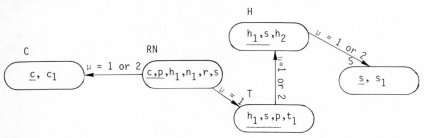

Figure 5.4

In figure 5.5, we give a possible solution :

```
entity RESORT
      begin
      |       NAME
      |       ALTITUDE
      |       DEPARTMENT
      |       entity HOTEL
      |             begin
      |             |       NAME
      |             |       CLASS
      |             |       NB-OF-ROOM
      |             |       entity STATUS
      |             |             begin
      |             |             |       PERIOD
      |             |             |       NB-OF-FREE-ROOMS
      |             |             |       PRICE
      |             |             end
      |             end
      end

entity RESERVATION-REQUEST
      begin
      |       CUSTOMER reference one CUSTOMER
      |       PERIOD reference one STATUS of HOTEL of RESORT
      |       CLASS-OF-HOTEL
      |       NB-OF-ROOMS
      |       NB-OF-PERSONS
      |       TOTAL-PRICE
      end

entity CUSTOMER
      begin
      |       NAME
      |       HOME-ADDRESS
      |       PHONE-NB
      end
```

Figure 5.5

CHAPTER 6 - SUMMARY

Conceptual schemas are defined traditionally such that logical representations and other performance-oriented considerations are intermixed. To avoid this problem we have proposed a solution which converts a traditionnal data structure into a relational schema, and conversely. From the relational schema we remove redundant relations and we reduce the number of relations necessary to derive an optimal set of relations in TNF.
Therefore this approach is more efficient in designing the data base completely and accurately.

In our approach some semantic problems have not been completely resolved as yet. These problems, for the most part, are due to the following :

- having many paths between two blocks,
- cases in which there exists more than one key per relation.

These problems are presently under investigation.

REFERENCES

[1]   Nijssen, G.M. (January 1975). DDL illustrated with Data Structure Diagrams,
       IFIP-TC-2, Namur.

[2]   Nijssen, G.M. (May 1975). An evaluation of the Ansi-DBMS architecture and
       conceptual Schema as in the February 1975 Report, Working Paper, IFIP,
       WG, 2-6.

[3]   CODASYL (1971). Data Base task group report, ACM, New-York.

[4]   Abrial, J.R., and al (1972). Projet Socrate, Université de Grenoble.

[5]   Codd, E. (June 1970). A relational model of Data for Large Shared Data Banks,
       CACM, 13, 6.

[6]   Abrial, J.R. (April 1974). Data Semantics, IFIP, Working Conference,
       Cargèse, Corsica.

[7]   Codd, E. (November 1971). Normalized data base structure : a brief tutorial,
       Proc. 1971, ACM-SIGFIDET Workshop on data description access and control,
       San Diego, Cal.

[8]   Codd, E. (May 1971). Further normalization of the relational data base
       model, Courant Computer Science Symposium, New-York.

[9]   Boittieaux,J. (Juillet 1967). Etude mathématique des relations d'un en-
       semble de notions, Contrat DGRST 65 FR 201.

[10]   Delobel, C. (Octobre 1973). Contributions théoriques à la conception et à
       l'évaluation d'un système d'informations appliqué à la gestion. Thèse
       d'Etat, Université de Grenoble.

[11]   Armstrong, W.W. (1974). Depending structure of data base relationship,
       IFIP.

[12]   Delobel, C., and Casey, D. (September 1973). Decomposition of a data base
       and the theory of boolean switching functions, IBM Journal of Research
       and Development.

[13]   Delobel, C., and Léonard, M. (May 1975). The decomposition process in a
       relational model, IRIA Workshop on Data Structures, Namur.

[14]   Bernstein, P.A., and al (May 1975). A unified approach to functional depen-
       dencies and relations. Proc. 1975 ACM-SIGMOD Workshop on Management of
       Data, San José, Cal.

[15]   Wang, C.P., and Wederking, H. (January 1975). An approach for segment
       synthesis in logical data base design, IBM Journal of Research and Deve-
       lopment, Vol. 19, N° 1.

[16]   Adiba, M., and Léonard, M. (Juin 1975). Approche algorithmique de la concep-
       tion d'un système de base de données, rapports de recherche TS0, TS1, TS2,
       Laboratoire d'Informatique, Université de Grenoble.

[17]   Delobel, C., and Portal, D. (Mai 1975). Aide algorithmique à l'organisation
       logique d'un fichier, Colloque INFORSID-IRIA, Aix-en-Provence.

[18]   Mijares, I., and Peebles, R. (January 1976). Structural Semantics of Data
       Bases, IFIP-TC-2, Working Conference, Freudenstadt.

Modelling in Data Base Management Systems, G.M. Nijssen, (ed.)
North Holland Publishing Company, 1976

CURRENCY AND CONCURRENCY
IN THE
COBOL DATA BASE FACILITY

Robert W. Engles
IBM Corporation
Palo Alto, California

INTRODUCTION
─────────────

The COBOL Data Base Facility is a language specification based on
the Subschema and Data Manipulation Language sections of the 1971
DBTG Report [1]. The objects called Area, Set, and
Set-Occurrence are now called Realm, Set-Type, and Set,
respectively. The operations OPEN, CLOSE, INSERT, and REMOVE
are now called READY, FINISH, CONNECT, and DISCONNECT. For the
purposes of this paper there are no significant semantic
differences between the 1971 DBTG Report and the COBOL Data Base
Facility specified in the COBOL Journal of Development [2].

The COBOL Data Base Facility has been recommended as the basis of
an American National Standard. As a candidate for
standardization, the COBOL Data Base Facility is properly subject
to constructive criticism. The purpose of this paper is to
explain the need for changes to the specifications concerning
currency indicators, concurrency, and the data base key. The
most important issue is concurrency; that is, the problem of
maintaining integrity while allowing the concurrent use of shared
data. The most important source of requirements is the Interim
Report of the SPARC Data Base Study Group [3].

The next three sections of this paper are an analysis of the data
base key, concurrency, and currency indicators, respectively.
The paper concludes with a proposal for changes to the
specifications. Although the analysis and proposed changes are
specific to the COBOL Data Base Facility, the principles involved
are applicable to other data base manipulation languages.

THE DATA BASE KEY

Currency indicators are part of the interface between a COBOL program and a Data Base Control System (DBCS). The content of a currency indicator is a data base key value. A COBOL program can copy the content of a currency indicator into a DB-KEY data item and subsequently use the data base key value to select a record.

It was clear in the 1969 DBTG Report [4] that data base key values were relative addresses within an Area. Subsequent reports do not explicitly state that data base key values are address-based. The COBOL Journal of Development reads: "A data base key is a conceptual entity whose value uniquely identifies a data base record. A data base key is not part of any data base record, but its value may be accessed by a COBOL program. When a record is initially stored in the data base, the DBCS assigns a unique data base key value to the record. The value thus assigned remains invariable for that record until the record is removed from the data base. After that time, the DBCS can reassign that data base key value to a new record."

The COBOL Journal of Development further states: "There is no inherent relationship between a record's data base key value and its physical location, realm, or set membership." This can be interpreted to mean that the data base key is an arbitrary identifier, rather than an address-based identifier. A more astute interpretation is that the inherent relationship between a record's data base key value and its physical location and realm is not defined in the COBOL Journal of Development. "The mapping of data base key values to physical storage locations in the data base is implementor-defined."

The values of an address-based identifier are specifically designed to facilitate an efficient mapping to storage locations. Henceforth, we will call such a value a "pointer". The observation that an implementor could define a data base key that is not a pointer data-item, neither clarifies nor justifies the concept of the data base key. The observation can be ignored because the COBOL Journal of Development provides no motivation for such an implementation. On the contrary, such an implementation would not be consistent with the specifications concerning the assignment of a data base key value to a new record as a function of its Location Mode.

Our thesis is that the data base key, as a pointer data-item, is not consistent with the requirements for an effective data base management system as expressed in the SPARC DBSG Report, and, since the data base key is unnecessary, the concept should simply be eliminated from the COBOL Data Base Facility.

Data Base Reorganization

Our objection to the data base key is not an objection to a system of inter-record pointers in an internal schema. The objection is to the capability of a COBOL program to access the value of a data base key. Indeed, the importance of a system of internal record pointers is one of the reasons why such pointers should not be accessed by COBOL programs. A system of internal pointers is certainly most efficient if based on physical addresses, but the value of a data base key is required to remain constant for the life of the record. Therefore, the concept of the data base key imposes a severe and permanent limit on the physical reorganization of a data base.

The introduction to the SPARC DBSG Report reads: "Within the limits imposed by this requirement of consistency with the conceptual schema, the data base administrator is free to alter the internal schema in any way appropriate to optimization of the data base management system operation. Indeed, by use of suitable interpreters it may be possible to reorganize the internal data base dynamically while normal operations continue. In view of the massive size of some data bases currently contemplated, this is an essential requirement...". The CODASYL Data Description Language Journal of Development [5] reads: "The permanence of data base keys must be guaranteed because data base keys may be made available and be saved by run units and may be ... re-input to a subsequent run unit in which they are referenced." Clearly, the invariability of the data base key is in direct conflict with an "essential requirement", the ability to reorganize a data base.

In a paper entitled "The DDL as an Industry Standard?" [6], W.J. Waghorn expresses a similar view of the data base key. The conflict with data base reorganization is one of the reasons why he concludes that "...there can be little doubt that data base keys serve no useful purpose whatsoever. They are therefore totally redundant and a source of potential confusion. Consequently all references to data base keys should be deleted from all Codasyl proposals as soon as possible."

Tape Storage

Another question raised by Waghorn is the inconsistency between the requirement for all records to have a data base key value and the following statement in the DDL Journal of Development: "Some devices, such as magnetic tape, because of their sequential nature, may not allow full advantage to be taken of the facilities included in the DDL. Such devices are not precluded, however, and may be perfectly adequate for some of the data." Waghorn believes that a standard, general-purpose, data base management system should provide for the storage of data base records on tape. Thus, he writes:

"One of the supplementary benefits of discarding data base keys is that this relieves implementors of the chore of maintaining them for data base records which are held on magnetic tape. It is clearly impossible for data base keys within a sequential tape file to correspond to record addresses, and hence it is clearly

impractical for anyone to use them extensively for record access
purposes. But despite the fact that nobody could reasonably want
to use them the system is required to allocate data base keys to
all records on a magnetic tape and store them somewhere (probably
in the records themselves). There is, of course, no technical
difficulty in doing this, but its absurdity is calculated to
persuade implementors that data base records do not belong on
magnetic tape."

If data base reorganization and tape storage were our only
objections to the data base key, we would propose, as an
alternative to its elimination, that the correspondence between a
record and a data base key value be defined to be invariant only
when the realm is in ready mode. This would allow a record to be
safely and swiftly reselected provided the data base key value
was acquired after the realm was placed in ready mode. Fast
selection of a record previously selected within a run unit is a
reasonable requirement and reselection is not uncommon with the
COBOL Data Base Facility because of the inability to maintain
more than one current record in each realm and set-type.
However, we do have other objections to the data base key and, as
we will show later, the "fast reselection" requirement can be
satisfied without the data base key.

Implementor-Defined

"The size, format, and characteristics of a data base key are
implementor-defined."   Therefore,   the   size,   format,   and
characteristics of the data base key will probably be different
for each implementation and neither programs nor data will be
transferable   from   one   implementation   to   another.
Implementor-defined constructs contradict the very idea of a
standard.   However, such constructs are sometimes necessary
although they are usually optional or have a standard external
form. But the data base key is not necessary, not optional, and
does not have a standard external form. The data base key is not
an appropriate concept for an industry standard.

Source of Error

The capability of COBOL programs to manipulate data base key
values is also a potential source of error. As Waghorn states,
"...it is unnecessary and unsafe to allow users to create
pointers for themselves, and it is unsafe to allow them to store
pointers in locations outside the control of the system."

Even if programs do not create or modify data base key values,
the reusability of data base key values is a potential source of
error. When a data base key value is accessed and subsequently
used to reselect a record, the program must verify that the
selected record is in fact the same record originally selected
because the original record may have been erased and the data
base key value assigned to a new record. The temptation to omit
the verification is particularly strong when there is no other

reason to retrieve the record, as in the situation where the data
base key value is used to identify a set in a STORE operation.
Unfortunately, the result in this situation can be an undetected
erroneous update of the data base.

Unnecessary Dependency

The capability of COBOL programs to manipulate data base key
values is an unnecessary dependency between COBOL programs and a
DBCS. A COBOL program is dependent on the size of the data base
key and it is not difficult to circumvent the syntactical
restrictions and write a program that is further dependent on the
representation of data base key values. This dependency is
undesirable because of the possibility of changes to the design
of the data base key. For example, to add new features to his
product such as another storage organization or more complex
mapping between internal and external records, an implementor
might have to provide additional types of data base keys.

It is not clear whether COBOL provides for more than one type of
data base key. If not, then the data base key is designed to
discourage implementors from supporting a variety of storage
organizations and mappings. Consider the implementor who wants
to provide two types of storage organizations. The first type of
storage organization restricts the movement of records so that
relationships can be efficiently represented by pointers. The
second type uses a space management technique that moves records
to maintain efficient sequential processing. The need for both
types of organizations is well-established and data base
management systems exist which support both types of
organizations and in such a way that application programs are
independent of the storage organization. There are difficulties
involved in doing this with the COBOL Data Base Facility because
the data base keys are inherently different. Unlike the data
base key values of records in the first type of organization, the
data base key values of records in the second type of
organization cannot be pointers. Unique identifiers usually
exist with this type of organization, but they are the values of
a field, the size and format of which are user-defined.

Similar difficulties arise if an implementor wants to provide a
variety of mappings between internal and external records.
Consider, for example, an external record composed of fields from
more than one internal record. Is the data base key a list of
pointers or a pointer to a list of pointers? There are problems
either way. The best solution is not to have multiple types of
data base keys, but rather to have no type of data base key.

The concept of the data base key implies a direct mapping between
internal and external schema such that the external record is a
subset of an internal record and the storage organization is the
type that restricts the movement of records. This is in sharp
contrast to the SPARC DBSG system model which allows for various
mappings and storage organizations plus the capability to change

the mappings and organizations without impacting application
programs.

The SPARC DBSG Report does not include the concept of a data base
key. Pointers are mentioned as a type of object in an internal
schema, but there is no object in an external schema that
corresponds to the data base key. This is not surprising in view
of the separation of the internal and external schema by the
interposition of the conceptual schema. The data base key is not
consistent with this model of a data base management system.
Indeed, for all the reasons we have given, it is destructive of
the very purpose of the three-level approach to modelling a data
base.

CONCURRENCY

The COBOL Journal of Development states that a data base "...must
be simultaneously accessible to all executing run units" and
"...data integrity must be protected from untoward results that
could occur during simultaneous access by different run units."

Lost Updates

A well-known problem of simultaneous access to shared data is
that the concurrent updating of the same record can produce
erroneous results. One approach to this problem of "lost
updates" is a locking mechanism that prevents simultaneous access
to the same record.

Instead of record locking, the COBOL Data Base Facility has a
conflict notification scheme called monitored mode. If all
programs cooperate, execute correctly, and do not abuse the
override capability, then monitored mode can be a solution to the
problem of lost updates. It can be argued that monitored mode is
a defective solution to the problem of lost updates. However, a
more fundamental defect of monitored mode is that it does not
provide any solution to the other problems of concurrency.

Inconsistent Analysis

One of the problems not solved by monitored mode is mentioned by
Waghorn. He calls it the problem of inconsistent analysis: "If
a run unit attempts to produce an analysis of part of a data base
the contents of which are constantly changing as it works, then
in general the consistency and meaningfulness of its results
cannot be guaranteed. Suppose, for example, that a run unit is
required to compute the total balance of a number of bank
accounts. It will, of course, do this by reading the relevant
records one at a time and accumulating the required total.
Suppose, then, that while it is doing this a second run unit
transfers an amount from an account whose balance has been
included in the total to one which the first run unit has not yet
read. The result is that the total produced is meaningless,

since it does not represent any state either of the real world or of the data base at any definable point in time; and if the run unit goes on to produce a report showing each balance as a percentage of this total, then the figures produced will be inconsistent."

Inconsistent analysis is caused by an inconsistent state of the data base or by the processing of data from different consistent states. Given a data base in a consistent state, a correct updating program transforms it into another consistent state. During the updating process the data base may be in a temporarily inconsistent state. Let R denote the set of records or relationships that are created, changed, or deleted by an updating run unit to perform the transformation from consistent state S to consistent state S'. Then we can say that inconsistent analysis may occur when a concurrent run unit references elements of R and the references are not entirely within S or S'. Some programs do not have the problem. Programs that do have the problem are not helped by monitored mode.

Currency Confusion

Another problem not solved by monitored mode is currency confusion. The problem is that any run unit performing updating operations can potentially confuse the significance of the currency indicators of concurrent run units. For example, suppose that a run unit has executed a series of FIND statements to select a record which satisfies certain criteria and that another run unit then modifies the record. When the first run unit retrieves the record it may no longer satisfy the selection criteria. Furthermore, there is no notification to the run unit that this has happened. Or suppose that between the time a run unit selected and retrieved a record, another run unit erased the record and then stored a new record which was assigned the same data base key value as the erased record. Again, the record retrieved is not the record selected and there is no notification of the anomaly.

Apparently, to use the COBOL Data Base Facility, programs must verify that each record retrieved is in fact the record sought. This is not right. Not only should such verification be unnecessary, it is not always possible unless all the selection criteria are reflected in the contents of the record. If any of the information is represented solely by structure or ordering, then the path following used to select the record must also be verified. But this cannot be done without doing more path following which, of course, is subject to more currency confusion.

Furthermore, verification can only determine whether a conflict has occurred between selection and retrieval. Verification cannot determine if a conflict occurs between selection and the subsequent use of the currency indicator to specify relative selection of another record or to specify the set membership of a

record. For example, consider a run unit that is generating a
report of employees by department. A statement in the inner loop
is FIND NEXT EMP-REC WITHIN DEPT-EMP. As the run unit is
traversing a set of the DEPT-EMP set-type, a second run unit is
processing employee transfers. Suppose that these run units
simultaneously select the same occurrence of EMP-REC and the
second run unit executes a MODIFY statement which reconnects that
record from one set to another within the DEPT-EMP set-type. The
first run unit then executes its FIND statement thereby selecting
a record from a different set than the one it was traversing.
Thus, even the simplest path following procedure can go wrong and
there is no notification that it has gone wrong.

Incredibly, the COBOL Journal of Development insists that
"records are locked and made unavailable to concurrent run units
only during the time that the DBCS is altering them or their
record relationships" and conflict notification is provided only
"if a record is in monitored mode or extended monitored mode
during the execution of a MODIFY statement, CONNECT statement,
DISCONNECT statement, or ERASE statement that affects that
record."

The only way that a run unit can avoid the possibility of
inconsistent analysis or currency confusion is to use the
EXCLUSIVE or PROTECTED option of the READY statement. With the
exception of concurrent run units using PROTECTED RETRIEVAL on
all realms, this is the same as saying that the only way to have
integrity with the COBOL Data Base Facility is not to have
concurrency.

Requirements for both integrity and concurrency are perfectly
reasonable because they are already satisfied by existing data
base management systems. These systems, such as IBM's IMS/VS
(with the program isolation feature) and Univac's DMS1100, meet
these requirements by means of locking. It is significant to
note that DMS1100, although based on the DBTG Report, implements
locking, rather than monitored mode [7]. It is also significant
to note that these systems provide for recovery.

On the grounds that something can always go wrong to compromise
data integrity, the SPARC DBSG Report states that "a systematic
method of recovering integrity must exist." The report applies
the concept of "sphere of control" to in-process and post-process
recovery. We will use the word "transaction" to mean a sphere of
control for in-process recovery and we will assume that
concurrent run units do not process within the same transaction.
This assumption is consistent with existing data base management
systems and cannot be inconsistent with the COBOL Data Base
Facility because it does not mention the subject.

Dependency On Uncommitted Changes

A data base management system can provide in-process recovery by
logging all changes to the data base made within each

transaction. Then, if an error is detected within a transaction, that part of the data base affected by the transaction can be restored to the state that existed at the start of the transaction. This capability raises another problem of the concurrent use of shared data. We call it the problem of dependency on uncommitted changes. If transaction B uses any data which has been changed by transaction A prior to the completion of transaction A, then the successful completion of B is dependent on the successful completion of A. If A is backed-out, then B must also be backed-out. Tracking such dependencies and providing cascade backout is currently not within the state of the art of generalized data base management systems. The alternative is to ensure that such dependencies do not occur. Any changes made within transaction A must not be seen by other transactions until A completes. This isolation of transactions can be accomplished by locking.

The SPARC DBSG Report specifically requires locking and queueing of requests when a conflict occurs: "The system must prevent more than one using program from accessing a data item for update purposes at the same time. The system must be capable of recognizing the intent of the using program at the time that it requests the data item and accumulating the request for the data item by second, third users, and so on..." Of course, the system must also provide a solution to the problem of deadlock. While conventions for avoiding deadlock can be useful, the restrictions involved are too severe to be mandatory. Deadlock detection is within the state of the art and, in a system that provides recovery, deadlock can be resolved by treating it as another type of error that causes the backout and rescheduling of a transaction.

The problems of lost updates, currency confusion, and dependency on uncommitted changes can all be solved by locking. When a record is selected, it must be locked and if the record is updated, it must remain locked until the transaction terminates. Many programs can also use record locking to prevent inconsistent analysis. Some form of record locking is absolutely necessary to achieve both concurrency and integrity. There is no way that the concept of monitored mode can be patched up to solve the four problems of concurrency. The COBOL Data Base Facility must therefore be changed such that monitored mode is replaced by record locking specifications.

CURRENCY INDICATORS

The COBOL Journal of Development reads: "Currency indicators are conceptual entities that are maintained by the DBCS to keep track of record retrieval and storage. There is one currency indicator for each run unit, for each realm available to that run unit, for each set type available to that run unit, and for each record type avaiable to that run unit. Unless the action is specifically suppressed, the DBCS automatically updates its

currency indicators when a record of a given type is retrieved
[sic] from a set of a given type from a given realm.   The
contents of a currency indicator consist of a data base key value
that identifies the record."

One of the basic concepts of the COBOL Data Base Facility is the
separation of selection (FIND) from retrieval (GET).   This is a
useful concept because there are many reasons why a program might
select a record and not retrieve it.   A basic purpose of a
currency indicator is to remember a selected record; then, as the
implicit or explicit operand of a subsequent COBOL statement, it
identifies the record to be retrieved, modified, erased, etc.

The independence of the selection operation is total; there is
nothing in the FIND statement to indicate what the COBOL program
will do with the selected record.   One of the possibilities is
that the program will not do anything with the selected record;
rather, it will, for example, refer to the currency indicator of
a set-type in which the record is a tenant and FIND the NEXT
record in that set. Thus, by identifying a record, a currency
indicator which is associated with an ordered collection of
records (a realm or set), also specifies a position within that
collection and can therefore be used as a cursor for that
collection.

There are some problems with currency indicators.   Compared to
currency confusion, none of them can be considered a serious
defect. However, taken as a whole, these minor problems justify
a fresh approach to the concept of currency.

Maintaining Position

"At the completion of the execution of an ERASE statement, the
value of the run unit currency indicator is null. Other currency
indicators are not affected."   Therefore, a currency indicator
can identify a record which is logically non-existent. "Currency
indicators are not affected by the execution of a DISCONNECT
statement."   Therefore, a set-type currency indicator can
identify a record which is not a member of the set-type.

Apparently, these currency curiosities are an attempt to make the
cursor function of a currency indicator less cumbersome. Thus,
for example, a run unit can presumably ERASE or DISCONNECT the
current record of a set-type and still be able to select the NEXT
record in that set-type. Maintaining position is important, but
the special status of the currency indicator should be recognized
so that appropriate restrictions can be placed on its use. For
example, if a currency indicator pointing to an erased record
were implicitly used to identify a set in a STORE operation, the
operation could be allowed except if the non-existent record had
been the owner of the set or unless its data base key value has
been reused. But this is only complicating matters for both
users and implementors and not solving the general problem of
maintaining position within an ordered collection of records

while performing updating operations.

The rules that apparently maintain position for ERASE and
DISCONNECT do not apply to MODIFY. "After successful execution
of a MODIFY statement, the current record of the run unit becomes
the current record of the set types specified." Thus, if a COBOL
program is traversing a set and uses the MODIFY statement to
reconnect a record from one set to another, position is not
maintained within the original set. Also, position is apparently
not maintained if the MODIFY changes the value of a sort control
field and causes the record to be repositioned within the same
set. It is possible to program around these problems, but the
point is that currency indicators are awkward to use and their
behaviour is conducive to programming error.

Currency Suppression

The execution of certain COBOL statements has side-effects in the
form of changes to the contents of currency indicators. These
side-effects are a function of the particular operation and the
realm and sets in which the object record appears. The COBOL
programmer must follow these side-effects in detail to correctly
execute subsequent COBOL statements.

To correctly perform certain procedures, the programmer must
selectively suppress the updating of currency indicators.
Consider, for example, the coding that precedes the STORE of a
relationship record that is an automatic member of two sets where
SET SELECTION IS CURRENT OF SET. Furthermore, assume that the
owner records are of the same type as in a bill of materials and
where-used parts structure. Having selected the owner record of
the first set, the programmer must suppress the update of that
set-type currency indicator in the statements used to select the
owner record of the second set. If this is not done properly,
the chances are that the result will be an erroneous update that
is not immediately detected. Therefore, it is important that the
behavior of currency indicators be defined to minimize the
possibility of such errors. Would it not be safer if currency
indicators behaved like normal program variables in the sense
that their contents change by explicit command of the program?

Multiple Positioning

In a paper entitled "Data Description for Computer-Aided Design"
[8], Bandurski and Jefferson explain the need for a homogeneous
set-type; that is, a set-type in which owner and member records
are of the same type. In contrast to a heterogeneous set-type
which always has disjoint sets, a homogeneous set-type allows a
recursive structure.

After showing how currency considerations complicate the
processing of a homogeneous set, Bandurski and Jefferson conclude
that the language is too cumbersome to be reasonable. Following
our suggestion in "An Analysis of the 1971 Data Base Task Group

Report [9], they advocate that the result of a FIND statement be
assigned a name so that a programmer could manipulate two or more
records or sets of the same type. They claim that this would
solve the basic problem involved in the processing of homogeneous
sets. We claim that this would also facilitate the processing of
heterogeneous sets.

As stated in the COBOL Journal of Development, "...there can be
several simultaneous current records during the execution of a
run unit..." That is clear. What is not clear is why every run
unit has exactly one current record of each set-type, one current
record of each record-type, and one current record of each realm,
plus one record that is more current than the others. There is
nothing unusual . about a program keeping track of more than one
record in the same realm or set-type. Just as a COBOL program
can associate none, one, or more index-names with the same table,
why can't a program associate none, one, or more currency
indicators with the same realm or set-type? Without such a
capability, the COBOL programmer is forced to access the data
base key value from a currency indicator by means of the ACCEPT
statement and subsequently restore it by using format 1 of the
FIND statement. In the meantime, the DBCS is constantly updating
currency indicators that are probably not being used by the COBOL
program. Would it not be more convenient and more efficient if
each run unit could have as many or as few currency indicators as
were required by the application?

The notion of an arbitrary number of currency indicators is
consistent with the elimination of the data base key. If a run
unit could have as many currency indicators as it required, there
would be no need to save and restore their contents. Thus, the
"fast reselect" requirement can be satisfied without the data
base key. Once a record is selected, it can simply remain
selected for as long as it is of interest to the run unit. The
notion of an arbitrary number of currency indicators is also
consistent with the suggestion that their contents should change
by explicit command of the program. This approach would provide
a more tractable method of maintaining currency. The details of
this approach are part of the following proposal.

A PROPOSAL

The purpose of this proposal is to suggest a unified solution to
the problems of currency indicators, concurrency, and the data
base key.

First, we propose that all references to the data base key and
monitored mode be eliminated. The COBOL language involved is the
DB-KEY data-type, the DB-CONFLICT special register, the KEEP,
REMONITOR, and FREE statements, format 1 of the FIND statement,
formats 4 and 5 of ACCEPT, and format 5 of the SET statement.

Since a realm is defined as "...that portion of the data base that contains all records having specified data base key values", elimination of the data base key would force reconsideration of the concept of the realm. If the data base key is inconsistent with the requirements of the SPARC DBSG Report, then so is the realm, but the issues are separable and the realm is not within the scope of this paper. We mention the realm because some object is necessary to provide a scope against which processing intent can be specified in a READY statement. For the purposes of this proposal, it is sufficient to assume that a realm is an ordered collection of records of multiple types.

The Cursor Concept

We propose that the concept of the currency indicator be replaced by the "cursor". A cursor is a programmer-named, implementor-defined object which is local to a run unit and is used to remember a selected record and/or a position within a data base. A cursor is similar to a currency indicator, but the language involved is in some ways more like COBOL indexing. Just as one or more index names may be associated with each table in a COBOL program, one or more cursor names may be associated with each realm and set-type. (A record-type cursor is unnecessary.) Like an index, the content of a cursor is changed by explicit command of the program using the SET statement. (Unlike an index, the content of a cursor cannot be incremented, decremented, or assigned to a data item.) Conceptually, the content of a cursor is a pointer.

With the COBOL Data Base Facility, the object record of a GET, ERASE, MODIFY, CONNECT, or DISCONNECT statement is identified by an implicit currency indicator known as the "current record of the run unit". With the cursor concept, the object record is identified by an explicitly specified cursor. Thus, the syntax of GET is changed to:

GET cursor-name [identifier]...

The record retrieved is the "current record" of the specified cursor. A similar change is made to the ERASE, MODIFY, CONNECT, and DISCONNECT statements. MODIFY and CONNECT are also changed so that set-type cursors can be used to identify sets.

The FIND statement is replaced by a new format of the SET statement. The basic syntax is:

SET cursor-name [,cursor-name]... TO selection-expression

The pointer that results from the evaluation of the selection expression is assigned to the specified cursor(s). Thus, just as the table-handling formats of the SET statement are used to set one or more named indexes to an element of a table, this proposed data base format of the SET statement is used to set one or more named cursors to a record of a data base. A detailed definition of the SET statement appears later in this proposal.

The STORE statement is changed to:

STORE record-name [SETTING cursor-name [,cursor-name]...]
                  [USING cursor-name [,cursor-name]...]

If the SETTING phrase is used, the specified cursor(s) are set to
the new record. (The explicit specification of set-type cursors
in the USING phrase replaces the implicit use of set-type
currency indicators when SET SELECTION IS CURRENT OF SET.)

Realm and Set-Type Cursors

COBOL is not designed for writing generalized programs such as an
interactive query interpreter. The record selection expression,
for example, does not allow names of objects in a data base to be
specified by a variable. Consistent with this constraint, the
name and selection scope of a cursor is declared in a source
program. The selection scope of a cursor is a particular realm
or set-type. None, one, or more cursors may be declared for each
realm and set-type included in the program's subschema.

A realm cursor identifies a realm and can be set to select any
record in that realm. A set-type cursor identifies a set-type
and can be set to select any record that is a tenant of that
set-type.

If a homogeneous set-type were allowed, we propose that its
cursors be declared as either OWNER or MEMBER to resolve the
ambiguity that arises when the sets of a set-type are not
disjoint. If a record, r, is both owner and member in a
homogeneous set, it is treated as an owner when referenced by an
OWNER cursor and as a member when referenced by a MEMBER cursor.
For example, "NEXT" referencing an OWNER cursor selecting r would
select its first child, while "NEXT" referencing a MEMBER cursor
selecting r would select its next sibling.

Conceptually, there are four types of pointers which a cursor may
contain: a record pointer, a null pointer, a zero pointer, and a
gap pointer.

    A cursor containing a record pointer is selecting a record
    and consequently also identifying a position within its
    selection scope.

    A cursor containing a null pointer is not selecting a record
    and not identifying a position.

    A cursor containing a zero pointer is not selecting a
    record, but, if the selection scope of the cursor is a realm
    or singular set, the cursor is effectively positioned before
    the first and after the last record of its selection scope.

    A cursor containing a gap pointer is not selecting a record, but is effectively positioned before the first record, or after the last record, or between two records within its selection scope.

A positioned cursor can be used for relative selection. For example, if a realm cursor contains a zero pointer, "NEXT" selects the first record of the realm and "PRIOR" selects the last record of the realm.

A cursor cannot be used unless it is in the active state. A cursor is in the active state if any of the records within its selection scope are in a realm that the run unit has placed in ready mode. Upon activation, a cursor contains a zero pointer.

A cursor of a singular set-type always identifies the set. A cursor of a non-singular set-type identifies a set only when it is positioned; that is, when it contains a record pointer or a gap pointer. If a set-type cursor is selecting owner record r, then, as a result of an ERASE of record r, the cursor is assigned a zero pointer and, thus, is no longer positioned.

If a realm cursor is selecting record r, then, as a result of an ERASE of record r, the cursor is assigned a gap pointer. If a cursor of set-type S is selecting member record r, then as a result of an ERASE of record r, or the DISCONNECT of record r from set-type S, the cursor will be assigned a gap pointer. If a set-type cursor is used to identify the object record of a MODIFY statement that causes the record to be repositioned within the set-type, the cursor is assigned a gap pointer and no other cursor is affected. The effect of relative selection with a gap pointer can be described by imagining that the cursor is positioned in the "gap" created by the "removed" record.

A cursor can contain a record pointer only through explicit assignment by a STORE statement or a SET statement. The selected record is known as the current record of that cursor. A cursor can contain a null pointer only as the result of its current record being unlocked by the run unit. Language is required to enable a COBOL program to determine the type of record selected by a cursor, the type of pointer it contains, and whether two cursors contain the same pointer.

Record Locking

To prevent currency confusion, the current record of any cursor must be protected from update by a concurrent run unit. Therefore, a current record must either be part of a locked realm, or the record must have been locked when it was selected by the run unit. Realm locking is specified by the EXCLUSIVE or PROTECTED options of the USAGE-MODE phrase of the READY statement. If a run unit places a realm in ready status and does not specify realm locking, then record locking is in effect for the records of that realm.

When record locking is in effect, a record has three states:
unlocked, locked exclusive, and locked shared. A selection
operation is either an exclusive request or a shared request. If
a record is in the unlocked state, any selection request for that
record will be granted. When a request is granted, the record is
locked accordingly and the run unit is said to "hold the lock".

If a record is in the locked exclusive state, any selection
request from a run unit not holding the lock will be denied. If
a record is in the locked shared state, a shared request from any
run unit will be granted. Thus, any number of concurrent run
units can hold a shared lock for the same record. If a record is
in the locked shared state, an exclusive request will be denied
unless the requesting run unit is the only run unit that holds
the shared lock.

The DBCS may lock records in addition to those explicitly
requested by a run unit and may also defer the execution of
unlocking requests. This implicit locking and deferred unlocking
is implementor-defined and controlled entirely by the DBCS.

To prevent lost updates, a run unit must hold an exclusive lock
for the object record of a MODIFY, ERASE, CONNECT, or DISCONNECT
statement.

To prevent dependency on uncommitted changes, a record that has
been the object of a successful MODIFY, ERASE, CONNECT, or
DISCONNECT statement remains locked exclusive to the run unit
until the transaction terminates. Also, the result of a STORE
statement is that the new record is locked exclusive and remains
locked exclusive to the run unit until the transaction
terminates.

A programming convention that can help to prevent inconsistent
analysis is to lock an owner record before selecting its member
records and not release the owner record lock until such time as
no more member records have to be selected in the set. A safer
strategy is not to release any locks until such time as no more
records have to be selected in the transaction [10]. However,
this strategy is inadequate for some programs and unnecessary for
others. Some programs must use realm locking to prevent
inconsistent analysis; other programs can safely release locks
and then acquire new locks within the same transaction. To
facilitate the latter class of programs, the SET statement not
only locks the record being selected, but can also be used to
unlock a record being unselected.

The full syntax of the SET statement is:

SET cursor-name [,cursor-name]... TO selection-expression

$$[,LOCK [SHARED] [lock-name] [DONTENQ]] \left[, \left\{ \begin{array}{l} RETAIN \\ RELEASE \\ REDUCE \end{array} \right\} HOLD \right]$$

The SET statement has four parts. The first part is one or more cursor names. A cursor named in the first part of a SET statement is called a target cursor.

The second part of a SET statement is the selection expression. The record identified by a selection expression must be within the selection scope of each target cursor and within a realm in ready mode. The result of a selection expression is a pointer or an exception condition. The pointer is assigned to each target cursor. Target cursors are not changed if the result is an exception condition. The selection expression is defined later in this proposal.

The third part of a SET statement is the LOCK phrase. The LOCK phrase applies when record locking is in effect for the record identified by the selection expression.

> If SHARED is specified, the selection operation is a shared request.

> If SHARED is not specified, the type of request is determined as follows:

>> If the realm of the selected record was placed in ready mode by the run unit with a USAGE-MODE of RETRIEVAL, the selection operation is a shared request.

>> If the realm of the selected record was placed in ready mode by the run unit with a USAGE-MODE of UPDATE, the selection operation is an exclusive request.

> If a lock-name is specified, the record is locked under that name. A run unit may hold the locks of many records under the same name. Other records may be locked under a different name. This allows a group of records to be selectively unlocked by the UNLOCK statement.

The DONTENQ option determines what happens when a selection request is denied:

> If DONTENQ is specified, a "request denied" exception condition occurs.

> If DONTENQ is not specified, the run unit is either suspended until the request can be granted or a "transaction backout" exception condition occurs. When

a transaction backout exception condition occurs, the flow of control is similar to privacy lock exception 99000: after execution of the procedure specified in the USE statement, control is transferred to the system for abnormal termination of the run unit.

Syntactically and semantically, the last part of a SET statement is the HOLD phrase. The HOLD phrase applies when record locking is in effect for a record being unselected. Thus, if a target cursor contains a record pointer at the initiation of a successful SET statement, the HOLD phrase applies to the current record of that cursor. However, the HOLD phrase does not change the locked exclusive state of a record that has been changed or stored within the transaction.

If REDUCE is specified, the locked state of the record is changed from locked exclusive to locked shared. If the locked state of the record was locked shared, REDUCE has the same effect as RETAIN.

If RETAIN is specified, or the HOLD phrase is omitted, the locked state of the record is not changed. However, the lock becomes "not releasable", which means that the record can only be unlocked from the run unit by an UNLOCK statement or transaction termination.

If RELEASE is specified, the record is unlocked from the run unit provided the lock is releasable and the record is not selected by another cursor in the run unit.

For example, if a run unit is simply traversing a set with set-type cursor, C, the statement:

SET C TO NEXT, LOCK SHARED, RELEASE HOLD.

will select the next record in the set and unlock the previous record from the run unit. (If no other run unit also held the shared lock, the record will be in the unlocked state.)

The UNLOCK statement has the form:

$$\text{UNLOCK} \left\{ \begin{array}{l} \left. \begin{array}{l} \text{cursor-name} \\ \text{lock-name} \end{array} \right\} \cdots \\ \text{ALL} \end{array} \right\}$$

The identified records are unlocked from the run unit. All cursors in the run unit selecting the unlocked records are assigned a null pointer. A lock name identifies those records whose locks are held by the run unit under that name. ALL identifies all those records whose locks are held by the run unit. However, the UNLOCK statement does not unlock records that have been changed or stored within the transaction. These

records, plus any other records left in a locked state by the run
unit are unlocked by the DBCS at transaction termination.

The Selection Expression

The following proposed selection expression includes more than
the minimum changes necessary to accomodate the cursor concept.
However, the additional changes are entirely syntactic. The
objective is to clarify the language without altering its record
selection capabilities.

The proposal does not include exception conditions. The proposal
does include most of the restrictions specified in the COBOL
Journal of Development. In the appendix we propose that some of
these restrictions be eliminated.

The proposed selection expression has six formats. The set
names, realm names, and record names used in any format must be
defined in the subschema. Any identifiers specified must
reference data items defined in the subschema record description
entry of the specified record-type.

FORMAT 1

cursor-name

>   The result is the content of the cursor.

>   For example, if cursor C1 is selecting record r, then, as a
>   result of:

>   SET C2 TO C1.

>   cursor C2 is also selecting record r.

FORMAT 2

OWNER [WITHIN cursor-name]

>   The result is a pointer to the owner of the set identified
>   by the set-type cursor named in the WITHIN phrase. If the
>   set-type is singular, the result is a zero-pointer. If the
>   WITHIN phrase is omitted, the set is identified by the first
>   target cursor of the SET statement.

>   For example, if C1 is a cursor for set-type S and is
>   selecting record r, then, as a result of:

>   SET C1 TO OWNER.

>   C1 is selecting the owner of r in S. If the owner of r in S
>   is within the selection scope of cursor C2, then, as a
>   result of:

SET C2 TO OWNER WITHIN C1.

C2 is selecting the owner of r in S while C1 is still
selecting r.

Ordinal, Associative, and Relative Selection

Formats 3 and 4 provide ordinal and associative selection,
respectively. Formats 5 and 6 provide relative selection. Each
format requires the specification of a domain of selection; that
is, the records eligible for selection. If a record name is
specified, the domain of selection is records of the specified
type within the specified realm or set. If the record name is
omitted, the domain of selection is all records within the realm
or all member records of the set. The realm or set may be
specified by the WITHIN phrase. If a set name is specified in
the WITHIN phrase, the set is determined by the SET SELECTION
declaration of that set-type. If the WITHIN phrase is omitted,
the realm or set is identified by the first target cursor of the
SET statement.

FORMAT 3

$$\begin{Bmatrix} \text{FIRST} \\ \text{nth} \\ \text{LAST} \end{Bmatrix} [\text{record-name}] \left[\text{WITHIN} \begin{Bmatrix} \text{set-name} \\ \text{cursor-name} \\ \text{realm-name} \end{Bmatrix} \right]$$

The result is a pointer to the first, last, or nth record
within the domain of selection.

"nth" is an integer constant or variable. If nth is zero,
the result of the selection expression is a zero pointer.
If nth is positive, the record selected is the one whose
ordinal position is equal to nth, counting from the first
record in the domain of selection. If nth is negative, the
record selected is the one whose ordinal position is equal
to nth, counting from the last record in the domain of
selection.

FIRST selects the first record in the domain of selection
and is therefore equivalent to a nth of 1. LAST selects the
last record in the domain of selection and is therefore
equivalent to a nth of -1.

For example, if C1 is a cursor for set-type S and is
identifying a set in S, then, as a result of:

SET C1 TO FIRST R1.

C1 is selecting the first R1 record in that set.

FORMAT 4

FIRST   record-name $\left[\text{WITHIN} \left\{ \begin{matrix} \text{set-name} \\ \text{cursor-name} \\ \text{realm-name} \end{matrix} \right\} \right]$

USING identifier[,identifier] ...

The result is a pointer to the first record in the domain of selection that has the specified contents.

If the domain of selection is record-type in realm, the location mode of the record-type must be CALC and the identifier(s) specified must reference the schema-defined CALC key(s) of the record-type. The search arguments are the CALC key values in the record area associated with the specified record-type. The record selected is the first record in the realm with CALC key data items equal to the search arguments.

For example, if C2 is a cursor for realm A, F3 is the CALC key of R1 records, and the value of F3 in the R1 record area is "528671", then, as a result of:

SET C2 TO FIRST R1 USING F3.

C2 is selecting the first R1 record in realm A in which F3 has the value "528671".

If the domain of selection is record-type in set, the record selected is the first record in the set with the specified data item(s) equal to the search argument(s). The data items are specified in the USING phrase and the search arguments are the values of those data items in the record area associated with the specified record-type.

Relative Selection

Formats 5 and 6 require a positioned cursor to identify the starting point for relative selection. This "starting point cursor" may be named in the WITHIN phrase. If the WITHIN phrase is omitted, the starting point cursor is the first target cursor of the SET statement.

To explain formats 5 and 6, we say that the domain of selection has a left part and a right part.

If the starting point cursor is a realm cursor or a cursor of a singular set, the left part and right part are defined as follows:

If the cursor is positioned at a record or between two records, the left part consists of those records in the domain of selection that appear before the position of the

starting point cursor and the right part consists of those
records that appear after the position of the starting point
cursor.

If the cursor contains a zero pointer, the left part and the
right part both consist of all the records in the domain of
selection.

If the cursor is positioned before the first record, the
left part is empty and the right part consists of all the
records in the domain of selection.

If the cursor is positioned after the last record, the right
part is empty and the left part consists of all the records
in the domain of selection.

If the starting point cursor is a cursor of a non-singular
set-type, the left part and right part are defined as follows:

If the cursor is positioned at a member record or between
two member records, the left part consists of those records
in the domain of selection that appear before the position
of the starting point cursor and the right part consists of
those records that appear after the position of the starting
point cursor.

If the cursor is positioned at the owner record, the left
part and the right part both consist of all the records in
the domain of selection.

If the cursor is positioned before the first member record,
the left part is empty and the right part consists of all
the records in the domain of selection.

If the cursor is positioned after the last member record,
the right part is empty and the left part consists of all
the records in the domain of selection.

FORMAT 5

$$\begin{Bmatrix} \text{NEXT} \\ \text{PRIOR} \end{Bmatrix} \text{[record-name]} \text{[WITHIN cursor-name]}$$

If NEXT is specified, the result is a pointer to the first
record in the right part of the domain of selection. If
PRIOR is specified, the result is a pointer to the last
record in the left part of the domain of selection.

For example, if C1 is a cursor for set-type S and is
selecting record r, then, as a result of:

SET C1 TO NEXT R1.

C1 is selecting the first R1 record after r in S.

FORMAT 6

NEXT [record-name] [WITHIN cursor-name]

USING identifier[,identifier]...

The result is a pointer to the first record in the right part of the domain of selection that has the specified contents. (This format provides "relative-associative" selection.)

Although the record-name may be omitted, the domain of selection includes a record-type. The record-type is that of the current record of the starting point cursor. Therefore, if a record name is specified, it must be the same record-type as the current record of the starting point cursor.

If the domain of selection is record-type in realm, the location mode of the record-type must be CALC and the identifier(s) specified must reference the schema-defined CALC key(s) of the record-type. The search arguments are the CALC key values in the current record of the starting point cursor. The record selected is the first record in the right part of the realm with CALC key data items equal to the search arguments.

If the domain of selection is record-type in set, the record selected is the first record in the right part of the set with the specified data item(s) equal to the search argument(s). The data items are specified in the USING phrase and the search arguments are the values of those data items in the current record of the starting point cursor.

For example, if C1 is a cursor for set-type S and is selecting r, a record of type R1 in which F1 has the value 10 and F2 has the value 20, then, as a result of:

SET C1 TO NEXT R1 USING F1,F2.

C1 is selecting the first R1 record after r in S, in which F1 has the value 10 and F2 has the value 20.

CONCLUSION

This paper has explained for need for changes to the COBOL Data Base Facility in regard to currency indicators, concurrency, and the data base key. The most important issue is concurrency and it is clear that monitored mode does not solve the problem of maintaining integrity while allowing the concurrent use of shared data. The COBOL Data Base Facility would be improved if the data

base key were eliminated, monitored mode replaced by record
locking, and currency indicators replaced by cursors.

APPENDIX

Semantically, the proposed selection expression is equivalent to
the record selection expression of the COBOL Data Base Facility
and, therefore, does not provide a generalized selection
capability. Most of the restrictions apply to associative and
relative-associative selection. Curiously, ordinal selection is
unrestricted.

Since the location mode of a record is an attribute appropriate
to an internal schema, the restriction that associative and
relative-associative selection within realm must be by CALC key
is clearly inconsistent with the requirements expressed in the
SPARC DBSG Report. In contrast, selection within set is not
restricted to schema-defined search keys. The USING phrase may
reference any fields in a record. However, the USING phrase is
inherently restrictive because it is a parameter list rather than
a "qualification expression".

The USING phrase qualifies the record to be selected, but the
qualification is limited to an equals condition on one or more
fields. Existing data base management systems, such as IMS/VS,
do not impose this restriction. The inability to express
qualification using any of the relation conditions and logical
operators of COBOL is a step backward for higher level language
and data base management systems.

A qualification expression explicitly specifies operations and
operands. The search arguments are not restricted to data items
in a current record or record area. The conditions are not
limited to EQUALS and AND. An example of a qualification
expression is:

WHERE (F1 IN R1 = F1 IN C1) AND (F2 IN R1 = F2 IN C1)

This expression is equivalent to the USING phrase in the example
of format 6. R1 is the name of a record-type, not a record
area. The search arguments are the values of F1 and F2 in the
current record of C1.

The advantage of a qualification expression is that a difference
in qualification criteria does not force a difference in
programming style. For example, if the above logical condition
were OR, rather than AND, or a relation condition were LESS THAN,
rather than EQUALS, the only difference would be in the
qualification expression. However, with the COBOL Data Base
Facility, the difference is that the search would have to be
programmed because the selection criteria cannot be expressed in
the USING phrase.

As implied by the above example of a qualification expression, the USING phrase can still be useful as a shorthand form of the qualification expression. However, the USING phrase would be improved if the source of the search arguments in format 6 were the same as in format 4.

These comments are an appendix because the subject is beyond the stated scope of the paper. Nevertheless, we propose that the CALC key restriction be eliminated and the USING phrase augmented by a qualification expression. Finally, we note that elimination of the data base key and the CALC key restriction would simplify the SET SELECTION declaration of the schema and propose that the capability of a qualification expression eliminates the need for the SET SELECTION clause of the subschema.

REFERENCES

1. CODASYL Data Base Task Group April 71 Report

2. CODASYL COBOL Journal of Development, Canadian Government Specifications Board, May 1975 Revision

3. Interim Report of the ANSI/X3/SPARC Study Group on Data Base Management Systems, February, 1975

4. CODASYL Data Base Task Group October 69 Report

5. CODASYL Data Description Language Journal of Development, June 1973, NBS Handbook 113, U.S. Department of Commerce

6. "The DDL as an Industry Standard?", by W.J.Waghorn, in Data Base Description, North-Holland American Elsevier, 1975

7. "DMS1100 User Experience", by E.J.Emerson, in Data Base Management Systems, North-Holland American Elsevier, 1974

8. "Data Description for Computer-Aided Design", by Ann Ellis Bandurski and Dr. David K. Jefferson, in ACM SIGMOD International Conference on Management of Data, 1975

9. "An Analysis of the April 1971 Data Base Task Group Report", by Robert W. Engles, in 1971 ACM-SIGFIDET Workshop on Data Description, Access, and Control

10. "Granularity of Locks in a Shared Data Base", by J.N.Gray, R.A.Lorie, and G.R.Putzolu, in Proceedings of the International Conference on Very Large Data Bases, 1975

Modelling in Data Base Management Systems, G.M. Nijssen, (ed.)
North Holland Publishing Company, 1976

Granularity of Locks and Degrees of Consistency
in a Shared Data Base

J.N. Gray, R.A. Lorie, G.R. Putzolu, I.L. Traiger

IBM Research Laboratory
San Jose, California

The problem of choosing the appropriate granularity (size)
of lockable objects is introduced and the tradeoff between
concurrency and overhead is discussed. A locking protocol
which allows simultaneous locking at various granularities
by different transactions is presented. It is based on
the introduction of additional lock modes besides the
conventional share mode and exclusive mode. A proof is
given of the equivalence of this protocol to a
conventional one.

Next the issue of consistency in a shared environment is
analyzed. This discussion is motivated by the realization
that some existing data base systems use automatic lock
protocols which insure protection only from certain types
of inconsistencies (for instance those arising from
transaction backup), thereby automatically providing a
limited degree of consistency. Four degrees of
consistency are introduced. They can be roughly
characterized as follows: degree 0 protects others from
your updates, degree 1 additionally provides protection
from losing updates, degree 2 additionally provides
protection from reading incorrect data items, and degree 3
additionally provides protection from reading incorrect
relationships among data items (i.e. total protection). A
discussion follows on the relationships of the four
degrees to locking protocols, concurrency, overhead,
recovery and transaction structure.

Lastly, these ideas are compared with existing data
management systems.

I. GRANULARITY OF LOCKS:

An important issue which arises in the design of a data base
management system is the choice of lockable units, i.e. the data
aggregates which are atomically locked to insure consistency.
Examples of lockable units are areas, files, individual records,
field values, and intervals of field values.

The choice of lockable units presents a tradeoff between concurrency
and overhead, which is related to the size or granularity of the
units themselves. On the one hand, concurrency is increased if a
fine lockable unit (for example a record or field) is chosen. Such
unit is appropriate for a "simple" transaction which accesses few
records. On the other hand a fine unit of locking would be costly
for a "complex" transaction which accesses a large number of
records. Such a transaction would have to set and reset a large

number of locks, incurring the computational overhead of many
invocations of the lock subsystem, and the storage overhead of
representing many locks. A coarse lockable unit (for example a
file) is probably convenient for a transaction which accesses many
records. However, such a coarse unit discriminates against
transactions which only want to lock one member of the file. From
this discussion it follows that it would be desirable to have
lockable units of different granularities coexisting in the same
system.

This paper presents a lock protocol satisfying these requirements
and discusses the related implementation issues of scheduling,
granting and converting lock requests.

Hierarchical locks:

We will first assume that the set of resources to be locked is
organized in a hierarchy. Note that this hierarchy is used in the
context of a collection of resources and has nothing to do with the
data model used in a data base system. The hierarchy of Figure 1
may be suggestive. We adopt the notation that each level of the
hierarchy is given a node type which is a generic name for all the
node instances of that type. For example, the data base has nodes
of type area as its immediate descendants, each area in turn has
nodes of type file as its immediate descendants and each file has
nodes of type record as its immediate descendants in the hierarchy.
Since it is a hierarchy, each node has a unique parent.

DATA BASE

AREAS

FILES

RECORDS

Figure 1. A sample lock hierarchy.

Each node of the hierarchy can be locked. If one requests exclusive
access (X) to a particular node, then when the request is granted,
the requestor has exclusive access to that node and implicitly to
each of its descendants. If one requests shared access (S) to a
particular node, then when the request is granted, the requestor has
shared access to that node and implicitly to each descendant of that
node. These two access modes lock an entire subtree rooted at the
requested node.

Our goal is to find some technique for implicitly locking an entire
subtree. In order to lock a subtree rooted at node R in share or
exclusive mode it is important to prevent share or exclusive locks
on the ancestors of R which would implicitly lock R and its
descendants. Hence a new access mode, intention mode (I), is
introduced. Intention mode is used to "tag" (lock) all ancestors of
a node to be locked in share or exclusive mode. These tags signal
the fact that locking is being done at a "finer" level and thereby
prevents implicit or explicit exclusive or share locks on the
ancestors.

The protocol to lock a subtree rooted at node R in exclusive or share mode is to first lock all ancestors of R in intention mode and then to lock node R in exclusive or share mode. For example, using Figure 1, to lock a particular file one should obtain intention access to the data base, to the area containing the file and then request exclusive (or share) access to the file itself. This implicitly locks all records of the file in exclusive (or share) mode.

Access modes and compatibility:

We say that two lock requests for the same node by two different transactions are <u>compatible</u> if they can be granted concurrently. The mode of the request determines its compatibility with requests made by other transactions. The three modes X, S and I are incompatible with one another but distinct S requests may be granted together and distinct I requests may be granted together.

The compatibilities among modes derive from their semantics. Share mode allows reading but not modification of the corresponding resource by the requestor and by other transactions. The semantics of exclusive mode is that the grantee may read and modify the resource but no other transaction may read or modify the resource while the exclusive lock is set. The reason for dichotomizing share and exclusive access is that several share requests can be granted concurrently (are compatible) whereas an exclusive request is not compatible with any other request. Intention mode was introduced to be incompatible with share and exclusive mode (to prevent share and exclusive locks). However, intention mode is compatible with itself since two transactions having intention access to a node will explicitly lock descendants of the node in X, S or I mode and thereby will either be compatible with one another or will be scheduled on the basis of their requests at the finer level. For example, two transactions can simultaneously be granted the data base and some area and some file in intention mode. In this case their explicit locks on particular records in the file will resolve any conflicts among them.

The notion of intention mode is refined to <u>intention share mode</u> (IS) and <u>intention exclusive mode</u> (IX) for two reasons: the intention share mode only requests share or intention share locks at the lower nodes of the tree (i.e. never requests an exclusive lock below the intention share node), hence IS is compatible with S mode. Since read only is a common form of access it will be profitable to distinguish this for greater concurrency. Secondly, if a transaction has an intention share lock on a node it can convert this to a share lock at a later time, but one cannot convert an intention exclusive lock to a share lock on a node. Rather to get the combined rights of share mode and intention exclusive mode one must obtain an X or SIX mode lock. (This issue is discussed in the section on rerequests below).

We recognize one further refinement of modes, namely <u>share and intention exclusive mode</u> (SIX). Suppose one transaction wants to read an entire subtree and to update particular nodes of that subtree. Using the modes provided so far it would have the options of: (a) requesting exclusive access to the root of the subtree and doing no further locking or (b) requesting intention exclusive access to the root of the subtree and explicitly locking the lower nodes in intention, share or exclusive mode. Alternative (a) has low concurrency. If only a small fraction of the read nodes are

updated then alternative (b) has high locking overhead. The correct
access mode would be share access to the subtree thereby allowing
the transaction to read all nodes of the subtree without further
locking and intention exclusive access to the subtree thereby
allowing the transaction to set exclusive locks on those nodes in
the subtree which are to be updated and IX or SIX locks on the
intervening nodes.   Since this is such a common case, SIX mode is
introduced for this purpose. It is compatible with IS mode since
other transactions requesting IS mode will explicitly lock lower
nodes in IS or S mode thereby avoiding any updates (IX or X mode)
produced by the SIX mode transaction.   However SIX mode is not
compatible with IX, S, SIX or X mode requests.

Table 1 gives the compatibility of the request modes, where for
completeness we have also introduced the null mode (NL) which
represents the absence of requests of a resource by a transaction.

	NL	IS	IX	S	SIX	X
NL	YES	YES	YES	YES	YES	YES
IS	YES	YES	YES	YES	YES	NO
IX	YES	YES	YES	NO	NO	NO
S	YES	YES	NO	YES	NO	NO
SIX	YES	YES	NO	NO	NO	NO
X	YES	NO	NO	NO	NO	NO

Table 1. Compatibilities among access modes.

To summarize, we recognize six modes of access to a resource:

NL: Gives no access to a node, i.e. represents the absence of a
    request of a resource.

IS: Gives intention share access to the requested node and allows
    the requestor to lock descendant nodes in S or IS mode. (It
    does no implicit locking.)

IX: Gives intention exclusive access to the requested node and
     allows the requestor to explicitly lock descendants in X, S,
     SIX, IX or IS mode. (It does no implicit locking.)

S: Gives share access to the requested node and to all descendants
   of the requested node without setting further locks.   (It
   implicitly sets S locks on all descendants of the requested
   node.)

SIX: Gives share and intention exclusive access to the requested
     node. (In particular it implicitly locks all descendants of the
     node in share mode and allows the requestor to explicitly lock
     descendant nodes in X, SIX or IX mode.)

X: Gives exclusive access to the requested node and to all
    descendants of the requested node without setting further locks.
    (It implicitly sets X locks on all descendants. Locking lower
    nodes in S or IS mode would give no increased access.)

IS mode is the weakest non-null form of access to a resource. It
carries fewer privileges than IX or S modes.   IX mode allows IS, IX,
S, SIX and X mode locks to be set on descendant nodes while S mode
allows read only access to all descendants of the node without
further locking.   SIX mode carries the privileges of S and of IX

mode (hence the name SIX). X mode is the most privileged form of access and allows reading and writing of all descendants of a node without further locking. Hence the modes can be ranked in the partial order (lattice) of privileges shown in Figure 2. Note that it is not a total order since IX and S are incomparable.

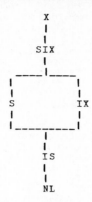

Figure 2. The partial ordering of modes by their privileges.

Rules for requesting nodes:

The implicit locking of nodes will not work if transactions are allowed to leap into the middle of the tree and begin locking nodes at random. The implicit locking implied by the S and X modes depends on all transactions obeying the following protocol:

(a) Before requesting an S or IS lock on a node, all ancestor nodes of the requested node must be held in IX or IS mode by the requestor.

(b) Before requesting an X, SIX or IX lock on a node, all ancestor nodes of the requested node must be held in SIX or IX mode by the requestor.

(c) Locks should be released either at the end of the transaction (in any order) or in leaf to root order. In particular, if locks are not held to end of transaction, one should not hold a lock after releasing its ancestors.

To paraphrase this, locks are requested root to leaf, and released leaf to root. Notice that leaf nodes are never requested in intention mode since they have no descendants.

Several examples:

To lock record R for read:
```
 lock data-base          with mode = IS
 lock area containing R   with mode = IS
 lock file containing R   with mode = IS
 lock record R            with mode = S
```
Don't panic, the transaction probably already has the data base, area and file lock.

To lock record R for write-exclusive access:
```
  lock data-base            with mode = IX
  lock area containing R    with mode = IX
  lock file containing R    with mode = IX
  lock record R             with mode = X
```
Note that if the records of this and the previous example are distinct, each request can be granted simultaneously to different transactions even though both refer to the same file.

To lock a file F for read and write access:
```
  lock data-base            with mode = IX
  lock area containing F    with mode = IX
  lock file F               with mode = X
```
Since this reserves exclusive access to the file, if this request uses the same file as the previous two examples it or the other transactions will have to wait.

To lock a file F for complete scan and occasional update:
```
  lock data-base            with mode = IX
  lock area containing F    with mode = IX
  lock file F               with mode = SIX
```
Thereafter, particular records in F can be locked for update by locking records in X mode. Notice that (unlike the previous example) this transaction is compatible with the first example. This is the reason for introducing SIX mode.

To quiesce the data base:
```
  lock data base with mode = X.
```
Note that this locks everyone else out.

Directed acyclic graphs of locks:

The notions so far introduced can be generalized to work for directed acyclic graphs (DAG) of resources rather than simply hierarchies of resources. A tree is a simple DAG. The key observation is that to implicitly or explicitly lock a node, one should lock all the parents of the node in the DAG and so by induction lock all ancestors of the node. In particular, to lock a subgraph one must implicitly or explicitly lock all ancestors of the subgraph in the appropriate mode (for a tree there is only one parent). To give an example of a non-hierarchical structure, imagine the locks are organized as in Figure 3.

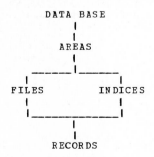

Figure 3. A non-hierarchical lock graph.

We postulate that areas are "physical" notions and that files, indices and records are logical notions. The data base is a collection of areas. Each area is a collection of files and indices. Each file has a corresponding index in the same area. Each record belongs to some file and to its corresponding index. A record is comprised of field values and some field is indexed by the index associated with the file containing the record. The file gives a sequential access path to the records and the index gives an associative access path to the records based on field values. Since individual fields are never locked, they do not appear in the lock graph.

To write a record R in file F with index I:

lock data base	with mode = IX
lock area containing F	with mode = IX
lock file F	with mode = IX
lock index I	with mode = IX
lock record R	with mode = X

Note that <u>all</u> paths to record R are locked. Alternaltively, one could lock F and I in exclusive mode thereby implicitly locking R in exclusive mode.

To give a more complete explanation we observe that a node can be locked <u>explicitly</u> (by requesting it) or <u>implicitly</u> (by appropriate explicit locks on the ancestors of the node) in one of five modes: IS, IX, S, SIX, X. However, the definition of implicit locks and the protocols for setting explicit locks have to be extended for DAG's as follows:

A node is <u>implicitly granted in</u> S mode to a transaction if <u>at least one</u> of its parents is (implicitly or explicitly) granted to the transaction in S, SIX or X mode. By induction that means that at least one of the node's ancestors must be explicitly granted in S, SIX or X mode to the transaction.

A node is <u>implicitly granted in</u> X mode if <u>all</u> of its parents are (implicitly or explicitly) granted to the transaction in X mode. By induction, this is equivalent to the condition that all nodes in some cut set of the collection of all paths leading from the node to the roots of the graph are explicitly granted to the transaction in X mode and all ancestors of nodes in the cut set are explicitly granted in IX or SIX mode.

From Figure 2, a node is implicitly granted in IS mode if it is implicitly granted in S mode, and a node is implicitly granted in IS, IX, S and SIX mode if it is implicitly granted in X mode.

<u>The protocol for explicitly requesting locks on a DAG</u>:

(a) Before requesting an S or IS lock on a node, one should request at least one parent (and by induction a path to a root) in IS (or greater) mode. As a consequence none of the ancestors along this path can be granted to another transaction in a mode incompatible with IS.

(b) Before requesting IX, SIX or X mode access to a node, one should request all parents of the node in IX (or greater) mode. As a consequence all ancestors will be held in IX (or greater mode) and cannot be held by other transactions in a mode incompatible with IX (i.e. S, SIX, X).

(c) Locks should be released either at the end of the transaction
(in any order) or in leaf to root order. In particular, if
locks are not held to the end of transaction, one should not
hold a lower lock after releasing its ancestors.

To give an example using Figure 3, a sequential scan of all records
in file F need not use an index so one can get an implicit share
lock on each record in the file by:

```
lock data base             with mode = IS
lock area containing F     with mode = IS
lock file F                with mode = S
```

This gives implicit S mode access to all records in F. Conversely,
to read a record in a file via the index I for file F, one need not
get an implicit or explicit lock on file F:

```
lock data base             with mode = IS
lock area containing R     with mode = IS
lock index I               with mode = S
```

This again gives implicit S mode access to all records in index I
(in file F). In both these cases, only one path was locked for
reading.

But to insert, delete or update a record R in file F with index I
one must get an implicit or explicit lock on all ancestors of R.

The first example of this section showed how an explicit X lock on a
record is obtained. To get an implicit X lock on all records in a
file one can simply lock the index and file in X mode, or lock the
area in X mode. The latter examples allow bulk load or update of a
file without further locking since all records in the file are
implicitly granted in X mode.

Proof of equivalence of the lock protocol.

We will now prove that the described lock protocol is equivalent to
a conventional one which uses only two modes (S and X), and which
explicitly locks atomic resources (the leaves of a tree or sinks of
a DAG).

Let G = (N,A) be a finite (directed acyclic) graph where N is the
set of nodes and A is the set of arcs. G is assumed to be without
circuits (i.e. there is no non-null path leading from a node n to
itself). A node p is a parent of a node n and n is a child of p if
there is an arc from p to n. A node n is a source (sink) if n has
no parents (no children). Let SI be the set of sinks of G. An
ancestor of node n is any node (including n) in a path from a source
to n. A node-slice of a sink n is a collection of nodes such that
each path from a source to n contains at least one node of the
slice.

We also introduce the set of lock modes M = {NL,IS,IX,S,SIX,X} and
the compatibility matrix C : MxM->{YES,NO} described in Table 1.
Let c : mxm->{YES,NO} be the restriction of C to m = {NL,S,X}.

A lock-graph is a mapping L : N->M such that:
(a) if L(n) ∈ {IS,S} then either n is a source or there exists a
    parent p of n such that L(p) ∈ {IS,IX,S,SIX,X}. By induction
    there exists a path from a source to n such that L takes only
    values in {IS,IX,S,SIX,X} on it. Equivalently L is not equal to
    NL on the path.
(b) if L(n) ∈ {IX,SIX,X} then either n is a root or for all parents
    p1...pk of n we have L(pi) ∈ {IX,SIX,X} (i=1...k). By induction
    L takes only values in {IX,SIX,X} on all the ancestors of n.

The interpretation of a lock-graph is that it gives a map of the
explicit locks held by a particular transaction observing the six
state lock protocol described above. The notion of projection of a
lock-graph is now introduced to model the set of implicit locks on
atomic resources acquired by a transaction.

The projection of a lock-graph L is the mapping l: SI->m constructed
as follows:
(a) l(n)=X if there exists a node-slice {n1...ns} of n such that
    L(ni)=X for each node in the slice.
(b) l(n)=S if (a) is not satisfied and there exists an ancestor a of
    n such that L(a) ∈ {S,SIX,X}.
(c) l(n)=NL if (a) and (b) are not satisfied.

Two lock-graphs L1 and L2 are said to be **compatible** if
C(L1(n),L2(n))=YES for all n ∈ N. Similarly two projections l1 and
l2 are compatible if c(l1(n),l2(n))=YES for all n ∈ SI.

Theorem:

If two lock-graphs L1 and L2 are compatible then their projections
l1 and l2 are compatible. In other words if the explicit locks set
by two transactions do not conflict then also the three-state locks
implicitly acquired do not conflict.

Proof: Assume that l1 and l2 are incompatible. We want to prove
that L1 and L2 are incompatible. By definition of compatibility
there must exist a sink n such that l1(n)=X and l2(n) ∈ {S,X} (or
vice versa). By definition of projection there must exist a
node-slice {n1...ns} of n such that L1(n1)=...=L1(ns)=X. Also there
must exist an ancestor n0 of n such that L2(n0) ∈ {S,SIX,X}. From
the definition of lock-graph there is a path P1 from a source to n0
on which L2 does not take the value NL.

If P1 intersects the node-slice at ni then L1 and L2 are
incompatible since L1(ni)=X which is incompatible with the non-null
value of L2(ni). Hence the theorem is proved.

Alternatively there is a path P2 from n0 to the sink n which
intersects the node-slice at ni. From the definition of lock-graph
L1 takes a value in {IX,SIX,X} on all ancestors of ni. In
particular L1(n0) ∈ {IX,SIX,X}. Since L2(n0) ∈ {S,SIX,X} we have
C(L1(n0),L2(n0))=NO.   Q.E.D.

Dynamic lock graphs:

Thus far we have pretended that the lock graph is static. However,
examination of Figure 3 suggests otherwise. Areas, files and
indices are dynamically created and destroyed, and of course records
are continually inserted, updated, and deleted. (If the data base
is only read, then there is no need for locking at all.)

We introduce the lock protocol for dynamic DAG's by example.
Consider the implementation of <u>index interval locks</u>. Rather than
being forced to lock entire indices or individual records, we would
like to be able to lock all records with a certain contiguous range
of index values; for example, lock all records in the bank account
file with the location field equal to Napa. Therefore, the index is
partitioned into lockable key value intervals. Each indexed record
"belongs" to a particular index interval and all records in a file
with the same field value on an indexed field will belong to the
same key value interval (i.e. all Napa accounts will belong to the
same interval). This new structure is depicted in Figure 4. In [1]
such locks were called predicate locks and and an alternate (more
general but less efficient) implementation was proposed.

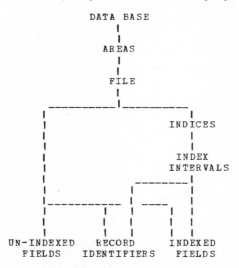

Figure 4. The lock graph with index interval locks.

The only subtle aspect of Figure 4 is the dichotomy between indexed
and un-indexed fields. Since the indexed field value and record
identifier (logical address) appear in the index, one can read the
indexed field directly (i.e. without "touching" the record). Hence
an index interval is a parent of the corresponding field values.
Further, the index "points" via record identifiers to all records
with that value and so is a parent of all such record identifiers.
On the other hand, one can read and update un-indexed fields of the
record without affecting the index and so the file is the only
parent of such fields.

When an indexed field is updated, it and its record identifier move
from one index interval to another. For example, when a Napa
account is moved to the St. Helena branch, the account record and
its location field "leave" the Napa interval of the location index
and "join" the St. Helena index interval. When a new record is
inserted it "joins" the interval containing the new field value and
also it "joins" the file. Deletion removes the record from the
index interval and from the file. index is not a lock ancestor of
such fields.

Since Figure 4 defines a DAG, albeit a dynamic DAG, the protocol of
the previous section can be used to lock the nodes of the DAG.
However, the protocol should be extended as follows to handle
dynamic changes to the lock graph:

(d) Before moving a node in the lock graph, the node must be
     implicitly or explicitly granted in X mode in both its old and
     its new position in the graph. Further, the node must not be
     moved in such a way as to create a cycle in the graph.

Carrying out the example of this section, to move a Napa bank
account to the St. Helena branch:
```
lock data base                     in mode = IX
lock area containing accounts in mode = IX
lock accounts file                 in mode = IX
lock location index                in mode = IX
lock Napa interval                 in mode = IX
lock St. Helena interval           in mode = IX
lock record                        in mode = IX
lock field                         in mode = X.
```
Alternatively, one could get an implicit lock on the field by
requesting explicit X mode locks on the record and index intervals.

Scheduling and granting requests:

Thus far we have described the semantics of the various request
modes and have described the protocol which requestors must follow.
To complete the discussion we discuss how requests are scheduled and
granted.

The set of all requests for a particular resource are kept in a
queue sorted by some fair scheduler. By "fair" we mean that no
particular transaction will be delayed indefinitely. First-in
first-out is the simplest fair scheduler and we adopt such a
scheduler for this discussion modulo deadlock preemption decisions.

The group of mutually compatible requests for a resource appearing
at the head of the queue is called the granted group. All these
requests can be granted concurrently. Assuming that each
transaction has at most one request in the queue then the
compatibility of two requests by different transactions depends only
on the modes of the requests and may be computed using Table 1.
Associated with the granted group is a group mode which is the
supremum mode of the members of the group which is computed using
Figure 2 or Table 3. Table 2 gives a list of the possible types of
requests that can coexist in a group and the corresponding mode of
the group.

Table 2. Possible request groups and their group mode.
Set brackets indicate that several such requests may be present.

MODES OF REQUESTS	MODE OF GROUP
X	X
SIX, {IS}	SIX
S, {S}, {IS}	S
IX, {IX}, {IS}	IX
IS, {IS}	IS

Figure 5 depicts the queue for a particular resource, showing the

requests and their modes. The granted group consists of five
requests and has group mode IX. The next request in the queue is
for S mode which is incompatible with the group mode IX and hence
must wait.

```
**********************************
* GRANTED GROUP: GROUPMODE = IX *
* |IS|--|IX|--|IS|--|IS|--|IS|--*-|S|-|IS|-|X|-|IS|-|IX|
**********************************
```

Figure 5. The queue of requests for a resource.

When a new request for a resource arrives, the scheduler appends it
to the end of the queue. There are two cases to consider: either
someone is already waiting or all outstanding requests for this
resource are granted (i.e. no one is waiting). If no one is waiting
and the new request is compatible with the granted group mode then
the new request can be granted immediately. Otherwise the new
request must wait its turn in the queue and in the case of deadlock
it may preempt some incompatible requests in the queue.
(Alternatively the new request could be canceled. In Figure 5 all
the requests decided to wait.) When a particular request leaves the
granted group the group mode of the group may change. If the mode
of the first waiting request in the queue is compatible with the new
mode of the granted group, then the waiting request is granted. In
Figure 5, if the IX request leaves the group, then the group mode
becomes IS which is compatible with S and so the S may be granted.
The new group mode will be S and since this is compatible with IS
mode the IS request following the S request may also join the
granted group. This produces the situation depicted in Figure 6:

```
*****************************************
* GRANTED GROUP GROUPMODE = S           *
* |IS|--|IS|--|IS|--|IS|--|S|--|IS|--*-|X|-|IS|-|IX|
*****************************************
```

Figure 6. The queue after the IX request is released.

The X request of Figure 6 will not be granted until all the requests
leave the granted group since it is not compatible with any mode.

Conversions:

A transaction might re-request the same resource for several
reasons: Perhaps it has forgotten that it already has access to the
record; after all, if it is setting many locks it may be simpler to
just always request access to the record rather than first asking
itself "have I seen this record before". The lock subsystem has all
the information to answer this question and it seems wasteful to
duplicate. Alternatively, the transaction may know it has access to
the record, but want to increase its access mode (for example from S
to X mode if it is in a read, test, and sometimes update scan of a
file). So the lock subsystem must be prepared for re-requests by a
transaction for a lock. We call such re-requests conversions.

When a request is found to be a conversion, the old (granted) mode
of the requestor to the resource and the newly requested mode are
compared using Table 3 to compute the new mode which is the supremum
of the old and the requested mode (ref. Figure 2).

Table 3. The new mode given the requested and old mode.

	IS	IX	S	SIX	X
IS	IS	IX	S	SIX	X
IX	IX	IX	SIX	SIX	X
S	S	SIX	S	SIX	X
SIX	SIX	SIX	SIX	SIX	X
X	X	X	X	X	X

So for example, if one has IX mode and requests S mode then the new mode is SIX.

If the new mode is equal to the old mode (note it is never less than the old mode) then the request can be granted immediately and the granted mode is unchanged. If the new mode is compatible with the group mode of the <u>other</u> members of the granted group (a requestor is always compatible with himself) then again the request can be granted immediately. The granted mode is the new mode and the group mode is recomputed using Table 2. In all other cases, the requested conversion must wait until the group mode of the other granted requests is compatible with the new mode. Note that this immediate granting of conversions over waiting requests is a minor violation of fair scheduling.

If two conversions are waiting, each of which is incompatible with an already granted request of the other transaction, then a deadlock exists and the already granted access of one must be preempted. Otherwise there is a way of scheduling the waiting conversions: namely, grant a conversion when it is compatible with all other granted modes in the granted group. (Since there is no deadlock cycle this is always possible.)

The following example may help to clarify these points. Suppose the queue for a particular resource is:

```
*******************************
*  GROUPMODE = IS              *
*  |IS|---|IS|---------------------------------
*******************************
```

Figure 7. A simple queue.

Now suppose the first transaction wants to convert to X mode. It must wait for the second (already granted) request to leave the queue. If it decides to wait then the situation becomes:

```
*******************************
*  GROUPMODE = IS              *
*  |IS<-X|---|IS|---------------------------
*******************************
```

Figure 8. A conversion to X mode waits.

No new request may enter the granted group since there is now a conversion request waiting. In general, conversions are scheduled before new requests. If the second transaction now converts to IX, SIX, or S mode it may be granted immediately since this does not conflict with the <u>granted</u> (IS) mode of the first transaction. When the second transaction eventually leaves the queue, the first conversion can be made:

```
******************************
* GROUPMODE = IS             *
*  |IX|-------------------------------------
******************************
```

Figure 9. One transaction leaves and the conversion is granted.

However, if the second transaction tries to convert to exclusive mode one obtains the queue:

```
******************************
*   GROUPMODE = IS           *
*  |IS<-X|---|IS<-X|----------------------
******************************
```

Figure 10. Two conflicting conversions are waiting.

Since X is incompatible with IS (see Table 1), this situation implies that each transaction is waiting for the other to leave the queue (i.e. deadlock) and so one transaction must be preempted. In all other cases (i.e. when no cycle exists) there is a way to schedule the conversions so that no already granted access is violated.

Deadlock and lock thrashing:

Whenever a transaction waits for a request to be granted, it runs the risk of waiting forever in a deadlock cycle. For the purposes of deadlock detection it is important to know who is waiting for whom. The request queues give this information. Consider any waiting request R by transaction T. There are two cases: If R is a conversion, T is WAITING_FOR all transactions granted incompatible requests to the queue. If R is not a conversion, T is WAITING_FOR all transactions ahead of it in the queue granted or waiting for incompatible requests. Given this WAITING_FOR relation computed for all waiting transactions, there is no deadlock if and only if WAITING_FOR is acyclic.

The WAITING_FOR relation may change whenever a request or release occurs and when a conversion is granted. If a transaction may wait for at most one request at a time, then the deadlock state can only change when some process decides to wait. In this special case (synchronous calls to lock system), only waits require recomputation of the WAITING_FOR relation. If deadlock is improbable, deadlock testing can be done periodically rather than on each wait, further reducing computational overhead.

One new request may form many cycles and each such cycle must be broken. When a cycle is detected, to break the cycle some granted or waiting request must be preempted. The lock scheduler should choose a minimal cost set of victims to preempt, so that all cycles are broken, undo all the changes to the data base made by the victims since the preempted resources were granted, and then preempt the resource and signal the victims that they have been backed up.

The issues discussed so far--lock scheduling, detecting and breaking deadlocks--are low level scheduling decisions. They must be connected with a high level transaction scheduler which regulates the load on the system and regulates the entry and progress of transactions to prevent long waits, high probability of waiting (lock thrashing), and deadlock. By analogy, a page management system with only a low level page frame scheduler, which allocates and preempts page frames in a fairly naive way, is likely to produce page thrashing unless it is coupled with a working set scheduler which regulates the number and character of processes competing for page frames.

II. DEGREES OF CONSISTENCY:

We now focus on how locks can be used to construct transactions out of atomic actions. The data base consists of entities which are related in certain ways. These relationships are best thought of as assertions about the data. Examples of such assertions are:
'Names is an index for Telephone_numbers.'
'The value of Count_of_x gives the number of employees in department x.'

The data base is said to be consistent if it satisfies all its assertions [1]. In some cases, the data base must become temporarily inconsistent in order to transform it to a new consistent state. For example, adding a new employee involves several atomic actions and the updating of several fields. The data base may be inconsistent until all these updates have been completed.

To cope with these temporary inconsistencies, sequences of atomic actions are grouped to form transactions. Transactions are the units of consistency. They are larger atomic actions on the data base which transform it from one consistent state to a new consistent state. Transactions preserve consistency. If some action of a transaction fails then the entire transaction is 'undone' thereby returning the data base to a consistent state. Thus transactions are also the units of recovery. Hardware failure, system error, deadlock, protection violations and program error are each a source of such failure.

If transactions are run one at a time then each transaction will see the consistent state left behind by its predecessor. But if several transactions are scheduled concurrently then locking is required to insure that the inputs to each transaction are consistent.

Responsibility for requesting and releasing locks can either be assumed by the user or be delegated to the system. User controlled locking results in potentially fewer locks due to the user's knowledge of the semantics of the data. On the other hand, user controlled locking requires difficult and potentially unreliable application programming. Hence the approach taken by some data base systems is to use automatic lock protocols which insure protection from general types of inconsistency, while still relying on the user to protect himself against other sources of inconsistencies. For example, a system may automatically lock updated records but not records which are read. Such a system prevents lost updates arising from transaction backup. Still, the user should explicitly lock records in a read-update sequence to insure that the read value does not change before the actual update. In other words, a user is guaranteed a limited automatic degree of consistency. This degree of consistency may be system wide or the system may provide options to select it (for instance a lock protocol may be associated with a transaction or with an entity).

We now present several equivalent definitions of four consistency
degrees. The first definition is an operational and intuitive one
useful in describing the system behavior to users. The second
definition is a procedural one in terms of lock protocols, it is
useful in explaining the system implementation. The third
definition is in terms of a trace of the system actions, it is
useful in formally stating and proving properties of the various
consistency degrees.

Informal definition of consistency:

An output (write) of a transaction is committed when the transaction
abdicates the right to 'undo' the write thereby making the new value
available to all other transactions. Outputs are said to be
uncommitted or dirty if they are not yet committed by the writer.
Concurrent execution raises the problem that reading or writing
other transactions' dirty data may yield inconsistent data.

Using this notion of dirty data, the degrees of consistency may be
defined as:

Definition 1:

Degree 3: Transaction T sees degree 3 consistency if:
  (a) T does not overwrite dirty data of other transactions.
  (b) T does not commit any writes until it completes all its writes
      (i.e. until the end of transaction (EOT)).
  (c) T does not read dirty data from other transactions.
  (d) Other transactions do not dirty any data read by T before T
      completes.

Degree 2: Transaction T sees degree 2 consistency if:
  (a) T does not overwrite dirty data of other transactions.
  (b) T does not commit any writes before EOT.
  (c) T does not read dirty data of other transactions.

Degree 1: Transaction T sees degree 1 consistency if:
  (a) T does not overwrite dirty data of other transactions.
  (b) T does not commit any writes before EOT.

Degree 0: Transaction T sees degree 0 consistency if:
  (a) T does not overwrite dirty data of other transactions.

Note that if a transaction sees a high degree of consistency then it
also sees all the lower degrees.

Degree 0 consistent transactions commit writes before the end of
transaction. Hence backing up a degree 0 consistent transaction may
require undoing an update to an entity locked by another
transaction. In this sense, degree 0 transactions are
unrecoverable.

Degree 1 transactions do not committ writes until the end of the
transaction. Hence one may undo (back up) an in-progress degree 1
transaction without setting additional locks. This means that
transaction backup does not erase other transactions' updates. This
is the principal reason one data management system automatically
provides degree 1 consistency to all transactions.

Degree 2 consistency isolates a transaction from the uncommitted data of other transactions. With degree 1 consistency a transaction might read uncommitted values which are subsequently updated or are undone. In degree 2 no dirty data values are read.

Degree 3 consistency isolates the transaction from dirty relationships among values. Reads are repeatable. For example, a degree 2 consistent transaction may read two different (committed) values if it reads the same entity twice. This is because a transaction which updates the entity could begin, update and end in the interval of time between the two reads. More elaborate kinds of anomalies due to concurrency are possible if one updates an entity after reading it or if more than one entity is involved (see example below). Degree 3 consistency completely isolates the transaction from inconsistencies due to concurrency [1].

Each transaction can elect the degree of consistency appropriate to its function. When the third definition is given we will be able to state the consistency and recovery properties of such a system more formally.
Briefly:

If one elects degree i consistency then one sees a degree i consistent state (so long as all other transactions run at least degree 0 consistent)

If all transactions run at least degree 1 consistent, system backup (undoing all in-progress transactions) loses no updates of completed transactions.

If all transactions run at least degree 2 consistent, transaction backup (undoing any in-progress transaction) produces a consistent state.

To give an example which demonstrates the application of these several degrees of consistency, imagine a process control system in which some transaction is dedicated to reading a gauge and periodically writing batches of values into a list. Each gauge reading is an individual entity. For performance reasons, this transaction sees degree 0 consistency, committing all gauge readings as soon as they enter the data base. This transaction is not recoverable (can't be undone). A second transaction is run periodically which reads all the recent gauge readings, computes a mean and variance and writes these computed values as entities in the data base. Since we want these two values to be consistent with one another, they must be committed together (i.e. one cannot commit the first before the second is written). This allows transaction undo in the case that it aborts after writing only one of the two values. Hence this statistical summary transaction should see degree 1. A third transaction which reads the mean and writes it on a display sees degree 2 consistency. It will not read a mean which might be 'undone' by a backup. Another transaction which reads both the mean and the variance must see degree 3 consistency to insure that the mean and variance derive from the same computation (i.e. the same run which wrote the mean also wrote the variance).

Lock protocol definition of consistency:

Whether an instantiation of a transaction sees degree 0, 1, 2 or 3 consistency depends on the actions of other concurrent transactions. Lock protocols are used by a transaction to guarantee itself a certain degree of consistency independent of the behavior of other transactions (so long as all transactions at least observe the degree 0 protocol).

The degrees of consistency can be procedurally defined by the lock
protocols which produce them. A transaction locks its inputs to
guarantee their consistency and locks its outputs to mark them as
dirty (uncommitted).

For this section, locks are dichotomized as _share_ _mode_ _locks_ which
allow multiple readers of the same entity and _exclusive_ _mode_ _locks_
which reserve exclusive access to an entity. (This is the "two
mode" lock protocol. Its generalization to the "six mode" protocol
of the previous section should be obvious.) Locks may also be
characterized by their duration: locks held for the duration of a
single action are called _short_ _duration_ _locks_ while locks held to
the end of the transaction are called _long_ _duration_ _locks_. Short
duration locks are used to mark or test for dirty data for the
duration of an action rather than for the duration of the
transaction.

The lock protocols are:

Definition _2_:

Degree 3: transaction T _observes_ _degree_ _3_ _lock_ _protocol_ if:
  (a) T sets a long exclusive lock on any data it dirties.
  (b) T sets a long share lock on any data it reads.

Degree 2: transaction T _observes_ _degree_ _2_ _lock_ _protocol_ if:
  (a) T sets a long exclusive lock on any data it dirties.
  (b) T sets a (possibly short) share lock on any data it reads.

Degree 1: transaction T _observes_ _degree_ _1_ _lock_ _protocol_ if:
  (a) T sets a long exclusive lock on any data it dirties.

Degree 0: transaction T _observes_ _degree_ _0_ _lock_ _protocol_ if:
  (a) T sets a (possibly short) exclusive lock on any data it
      dirties.

The lock protocol definitions can be stated more tersely with the
introduction of the following notation. A transaction is _well_
formed _with_ _respect_ _to_ _writes_ (_reads_) if it always locks an entity
in exclusive (shared or exclusive) mode before writing (reading)
it. The transaction is _well_ _formed_ if it is well formed with
respect to reads and writes.

A transaction is _two_ _phase_ (_with_ _respect_ _to_ _reads_ _or_ _updates_) if it
does not (share or exclusive) lock an entity after unlocking some
entity. A two phase transaction has a growing phase during which it
acquires locks and a shrinking phase during which it releases
locks.

Definition 2 is too restrictive in the sense that consistency will
not require that a transaction hold all locks to the EOT (i.e. the
EOT is the shrinking phase). Rather, the constraint that the
transaction be two phase is adequate to insure consistency. On the
other hand, once a transaction unlocks an updated entity, it has
committed that entity and so cannot be undone without cascading
backup to any transactions which may have subsequently read the
entity. For that reason, the shrinking phase is usually deferred to
the end of the transaction; thus, the transaction is always
recoverable and all updates are committed together. The lock
protocols can be redefined as:

Definition 2':

Degree 3: T is well formed
        and T is two phase.

Degree 2: T is well formed
        and T is two phase with respect to writes.

Degree 1: T is well formed with respect to writes
        and T is two phase with respect to writes.

Degree 0: T is well formed with respect to writes.

All transactions are required to observe the degree 0 locking
protocol so that they do not update the uncommitted updates of
others. Degrees 1, 2 and 3 provide increasing system-guaranteed
consistency.

Consistency of schedules:

The definition of what it means for a transaction to see a degree of
consistency was given in terms of dirty data. In order to make the
notion of dirty data explicit it is necessary to consider the
execution of a transaction in the context of a set of concurrently
executing transactions. To do this we introduce the notion of a
schedule for a set of transactions. A schedule can be thought of as
a history or audit trail of the actions performed by the set of
transactions. Given a schedule the notion of a particular entity
being dirtied by a particular transaction is made explicit and hence
the notion of seeing a certain degree of consistency is formalized.
These notions may then be used to connect the various definitions of
consistency and show their equivalence.

The system directly supports entities and actions. Actions are
categorized as begin actions, end actions, share lock actions,
exclusive lock actions, unlock actions, read actions, and write
actions. An end action is presumed to unlock any locks held by the
transaction but not explicitly unlocked by the transaction. For the
purposes of the following definitions, share lock actions and their
corresponding unlock actions are additionally considered to be read
actions and exclusive lock actions and their corresponding unlock
actions are additionally considered to be write actions.

A transaction is any sequence of actions beginning with a begin
action and ending with an end action and not containing other begin
or end actions.

Any (sequence preserving) merging of the actions of a set of
transactions into a single sequence is called a schedule for the set
of transactions.

A schedule is a history of the order in which actions were executed
(it does not record actions which were undone due to backup). The
simplest schedules run all actions of one transaction and then all
actions of another transaction,... Such one-transaction-at-a-time
schedules are called serial because they have no concurrency among
transactions. Clearly, a serial schedule has no concurrency induced
inconsistency and no transaction sees dirty data.

Locking constrains the set of allowed schedules. In particular, a
schedule is legal only if it does not schedule a lock action on an

entity for one transaction when that entity is already locked by
some other transaction in a conflicting mode.

An initial state and a schedule completely define the system's
behavior. At each step of the schedule one can deduce which entity
values have been committed and which are dirty: it locking is used,
updated data is dirty until it is unlocked.

Since a schedule makes the definition of dirty data explicit, one
can apply Definition 1 to define consistent schedules:

Definition 3:

A transaction runs at degree 0 (1, 2 or 3) consistency in schedule S
if T sees degree 0 (1, 2 or 3) consistency in S. (Conversely,
transaction T sees degree i consistency if all legal schedules run T
at degree i consistency.)

If all transactions run at degree 0 (1,2 or 3) consistency in
schedule S then S is said to be a degree 0 (1, 2 or 3) consistent
schedule.

Given these definitions one can show:

Assertion 1:

(a) If each transaction observes the degree 0 (1, 2 or 3) lock
    protocol (Definition 2) then any legal schedule is degree 0 (1,
    2 or 3) consistent (Definition 3) (i.e, each transaction sees
    degree 0 (1, 2 or 3) consistency in the sense of Definition
    1).
(b) Unless transaction T observes the degree 1 (2 or 3) lock
    protocol then it is possible to define another transaction T'
    which does observe the degree 1 (2 or 3) lock protocol such
    that T and T' have a legal schedule S but T does not run at
    degree 1 (2 or 3) consistency in S.

In [1] we proved Assertion 1 for degree 3 consistency. That
argument generalizes directly to this result.

Assertion 1 says that if a transaction observes the lock protocol
definition of consistency (Definition 2) then it is assured of the
informal definition of consistency based on committed and dirty data
(Definition 1). Unless a transaction actually sets the locks
prescribed by degree 1 (2 or 3) consistency one can construct
transaction mixes and schedules which will cause the transaction to
run at (see) a lower degree of consistency. However, in particular
cases such transaction mixes may never occur due to the structure or
use of the system. In these cases an apparently low degree of
locking may actually provide degree 3 consistency. For example, a
data base reorganization usually need do no locking since it is run
as an off-line utility which is never run concurrently with other
transactions.

Assertion 2:

If each transaction in a set of transactions at least observes the
degree 0 lock protocol and if transaction T observes the degree 1 (2
or 3) lock protocol then T runs at degree 1 (2 or 3) consistency
(Definitions 1, 3) in any legal schedule for the set of
transactions.

Assertion 2 says that each transaction can choose its degree of
consistency so long as all transactions observe at least degree 0
protocols. Of course the outputs of degree 0, 1 or 2 consistent
transactions may be degree 0, 1 or 2 consistent (i.e. inconsistent)
because they were computed with potentially inconsistent inputs.
One can imagine that each data entity is tagged with the degree of
consistency of its writer: Degree 0 entities are purple, degree 1
entities are red, degree 2 entities are yellow and degree 3 entities
are green. The color of the outputs of a transaction is the minimum
of the transaction's color and the colors of the entities it reads
(because they are potentially inconsistent). Gradually the system
will turn purple or red unless everyone runs with a high degree of
consistency. If the transaction's author knows something about the
systems structure which allows an apparently degree 1 consistent
protocol to produce degree 3 consistent results then this color
coding is pessimistic. But, in general a transaction must beware of
reading entities tagged with degrees lower than the degree of the
transaction.

Dependencies among transactions:

One transaction is said to depend on another if the first takes some
of its inputs from the second. The notion of dependency is defined
differently for each degree of consistency. These dependency
relations are completely defined by a schedule and can be useful in
discussing consistency and recovery.

Each schedule defines three relations: <, << and <<< on the set of
transactions as follows. Suppose that transaction T performs action
a on an entity e at some step in the schedule and that transaction T'
performs action a' on entity e at a later step in the schedule.
Further suppose that T does not equal T'. Then:

```
T <<< T'  if  a is a write action and a' is a write action
       or  a is a write action and a' is a read  action
       or  a is a read  action and a' is a write action

T <<  T'  if  a is a write action and a' is a write action
       or  a is a write action and a' is a read  action

T <   T'  if  a is a write action and a' is a write action
```

So degree 1 does not care about read dependencies at all. Degree 2
cares only about one kind of read dependency. And degree 3 ignores
only read-read dependencies (reads commute). The following table is
a notationally convenient way of seeing these definitions:

$$<<< \; : \; W\text{->}W \; | \; W\text{->}R \; | \; R\text{->}W$$

$$<< \; : \; W\text{->}W \; | \; W\text{->}R$$

$$< \; : \; W\text{->}W$$

meaning that (for example) T <<< T' if T writes (W) something later
read (R) by T' or written (W) by T' or T reads (R) something later
written (W) by T'.

Let <* be the transitive closure of <, then define:
```
  BEFORE1(T) = {T'| T' <* T}
  AFTER1(T)  = {T'| T  <* T'}.
```

The sets BEFORE2, AFTER2, BEFORE3 and AFTER3 are defined analogously from << and <<<.

The obvious interpretation for this is that each BEFORE set is the set of transactions which contribute inputs to T and each AFTER set is the set of transactions which take their inputs from T (where the ordering only considers dependencies induced by the corresponding consistency degree).

If some transaction is both before T and after T in some schedule then no serial schedule could give such results. In this case concurrency has introduced inconsistency. On the other hand, if all relevant transactions are either before or after T (but not both) then T will see a consistent state (of the corresponding degree). If all transactions dichotomize others in this way then the relation <* (<<* or <<<*) will be a partial order and the whole schedule will give degree 1 (2 or 3) consistency. This can be strengthened to:

Assertion 3:

A schedule is degree 1 (2 or 3) consistent if and only if the relation <* (<<* or <<<*) is a partial order.

The <, << and <<< relations are variants of the dependency sets introduced in [1]. In that paper only degree 3 consistency is introduced and Assertion 3 was proved for that case. In particular such a schedule is equivalent to the serial schedule obtained by running the transactions one at a time in <<< order. The proofs of [1] generalize fairly easily to handle assertion 1 in the case of degree 1 or 2 consistency.

Consider the following example:

```
T1 LOCK    A
T1 READ    A
T1 UNLOCK  A
T2 LOCK    A
T2 WRITE   A
T2 LOCK    B
T2 WRITE   B
T2 UNLOCK  A
T2 UNLOCK  B
T1 LOCK    B
T1 WRITE   B
T1 UNLOCK  B
```

In this schedule T2 gives B to T1 and T2 updates A after T1 reads A so T2<T1, T2<<T1, T2<<<T1 and T1<<<T2. The schedule is degree 2 consistent but not degree 3 consistent. It runs T1 at degree 2 consistency and T2 at degree 3 consistency.

It would be nice to define a transaction to see degree 1 (2 or 3) consistency if and only if the BEFORE and AFTER sets are disjoint in some schedule. However, this is not restrictive enough; rather one must require that the before and after sets be disjoint in all schedules in order to state Definition 1 in terms of dependencies. Further, there seems to be no natural way to define the dependencies of degree 0 consistency. Hence the principal application of the dependency definition is as a proof technique and for discussing schedules and recovery issues.

Relationship to transaction backup and system recovery:

A transaction T is said to be <u>recoverable</u> if it can be undone before
'EOT' without undoing other transactions' updates. A transaction T
is said to be <u>repeatable</u> if it will reproduce the original output if
rerun following recovery, assuming that no locks were released in
the backup process. Recoverability requires system wide degree 1
consistency, repeatability requires that all other transactions be
at least degree 1 and that the repeatable transaction be degree 3.

The <u>normal</u> (i.e. trouble free) operation of a data base system can
be described in terms of an initial consistent state S0 and a
schedule of transactions mapping the data base into a final
consistent state S3 (see Figure 11). S1 is a checkpoint state,
since transactions are in progress, S1 may be inconsistent. A
<u>system crash</u> leaves the data base in state S2. Since transactions
T3 and T5 were in progress at the time of crash, S2 is potentially
inconsistent. <u>System recovery</u> amounts to bringing the data base in
a new consistent state in one of the following ways:

(a) Starting from state S2, <u>undo</u> all actions of transactions
    in-progress at the time of the crash.

(b) Starting from state S1 first undo all actions of transactions in
    progress at the time of the crash (i.e. actions of T3 and T4
    before S1) and then <u>redo</u> all actions of transactions which
    completed before the crash (i.e. actions of T2 and T3 after
    S1).

(c) starting at S0 redo all transactions which completed before the
    crash.

Observe that (a) and (c) are degenerate cases of (b).

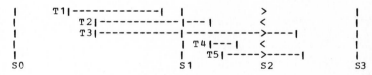

```
|     T1|-------------|  |              >            |
|       T2|------------ |--- |          <            |
|        T3|------------|------------>----|           |
|                       |  T4|--- |    <              |
|                       |   T5|----->-----|           |
S0                      S1          S2              S3
```

Figure 11. System states, S0 is initial state, S1 is checkpoint
state, S2 is a crash and S3 is the state that results in the absence
of a crash.

Unless all transactions run at least degree 1 consistency, system
recovery may lose updates. If for example, T3 writes a record, r,
and then T4 further updates r then undoing T3 will cause the update
of T4 to r to be lost. This situation can only arise if some
transaction does not hold its write locks to EOT.

(a) If all the transactions run in at least degree 1 consistency
    then system recovery loses no updates of complete
    transactions. However there may be no schedule which would
    give the same result because transactions may have <u>read</u> outputs
    of undone transactions.

(b) If all the transactions run in at least degree 2 then the
     recovered state is consistent and derives from the schedule
     obtatined from the original system schedule by deleting
     incomplete transactions. Note that degree 2 prevents read
     dependencies on transactions which might be undone by system
     recovery. of all the completed transactions results in a
     meaningful schedule.

(c) If a transaction is degree 3 consistent then it is
     reproducible.

Transaction crash gives rise to transaction backup which has
properties analogous to system recovery.

Cost of degrees of consistency:

The only advantage of lower degrees of consistency is performance.
If less is locked then less computation and storage is consumed.
Further if less is locked, concurrency is increased since fewer
conflicts appear. (Note that the granularity lock scheme of the
first section was motivated by minimizing the number of explicit
locks set.)

We will make some very crude estimates of the storage and
computation resources consumed by the locking protocols as a
function of the consistency degree. For the remainder of this
section assume that all transactions are identical. Also assume
that they do R reads and W writes (and hence set approximately R
share mode locks and W exclusive mode locks). Further we assume
that all the transactions run at the same consistency degree.

Each outstanding lock request consumes a queue element. The maximum
per-transaction space for these queue elements as a function of
consistency degrees is:

Table 4. Consistency degrees vs storage consumption.

CONSISTENCY DEGREE	STORAGE (in queue elements)
0	1
1	W
2	W+1
3	W+R

Observe that degrees 1 and 2 consume roughly the same amount of
storage but that degree 3 consumes substantially more storage. This
observation is aggravated by the fact that reads are typically ten
times more common than writes.

The estimation of computation (CPU) overhead is much more subtle.
We make only a crude estimate here. First one may consider the
overhead in requesting and releasing locks. This is shown in Table
5 as a function of consistency degrees.

TABLE 5. Computational overhead vs degrees of consistency.

```
 ---------------------------------------------------------
|                     |                                   |
| CONSISTENCY DEGREE  | CPU (in calls to lock sys)        |
|---------------------|-----------------------------------|
|                     |                                   |
|         0           |               W                   |
|         1           |               W                   |
|         2           |              W+R                  |
|         3           |              W+R                  |
|                     |                                   |
 ---------------------------------------------------------
```

Table 5 indicates that the computational overhead of degrees 2 and 3 are comparable and are greater than the overhead of degrees 0 or 1. These pairs of degrees set the same locks, they just hold them for different durations.

Table 5 ignores the observation that some lock requests are trivially satisfied (the request is granted immediately) while others require a task switch and hence are quite expensive. The probability that a read lock will have to wait is proportional to the number of conflicting locks (write) currently granted. The probability that a write lock will have to wait is proportional to the number of conflicting (read or write) locks that are currently granted. Table 4 gives a guess of the maximum number of locks of each type held by each transaction. If there are 2*N+1 transactions one can multiply the entries of Table 4 by N to get an average number of locks held by all others. If a wait lock request is C+1 times as expensive as an immediately granted request and if P is the probability that two different requests are for the same resource then the relative computational costs are roughly computed:

degree 0 overhead: W   cost of setting locks
                      P*C*N*W   cost of waits

degree 1 overhead: W   cost of writes
                      P*C*N*W*W   cost of waits

degree 2 overhead: W+R   cost of setting locks
                      P*C*N*W*(W+1)   cost of write waits
                      P*C*N*R*W   cost of read waits

degree 3 overhead: W+R   cost of setting locks
                      P*C*N*W*(W+R)   cost of waiting for writes
                      P*C*N*R*W   cost of waiting for reads

TABLE 6. Computational overhead vs degrees of consistency.

```
 ---------------------------------------------------------
|                     |                                   |
| CONSISTENCY DEGREE  | CPU (in calls to lock sys)        |
|---------------------|-----------------------------------|
|                     |                                   |
|         0           |       W+P*C*N*W*(1)               |
|         1           |       W+P*C*N*W*(W)               |
|         2           |     W+R+P*C*N*W*(W+R+1)           |
|         3           |     W+R+P*C*N*W*(W+2*R)           |
|                     |                                   |
 ---------------------------------------------------------
```

To consider a specific example, a simple banking transaction does five reads (R=5) and six (W=6) writes. A transaction accesses a random account and there are millions of accounts so the probability of collision, P, is roughly .000001.   Suppose there are one hundred transactions per second.   A lock takes one hundred instructions and a wait   requires five   thousand instructions;   hence, C=50.   So the term P*C*N*W evaluates   to 0.015.   This implies that Table 5 gave a good estimate of the CPU overhead because the last term in Table 6 is miniscule compared to the term W+R.   Of course this analysis is very sensitive to P   and one must   design the data base so   that P takes on a very small value.

The striking thing about these estimates is that degree 2 and degree 3 seem to have similar computational   overhead which   seems to be substantially   larger   than the   overhead of   degree 0   or 1 consistency. We suspect that this conclusion would   survive a more careful study of the problem.

ISSUE	DEGREE 0	DEGREE 1	DEGREE 2	DEGREE 3
COMMITTED DATA	WRITES ARE COMMITTED IMMEDIATELY	WRITES ARE COMMITTED AT EOT	SAME AS 1	SAME AS 1
DIRTY DATA	YOU DON'T UPDATE DIRTY DATA	0 AND NO ONE ELSE UPDATES YOUR DIRTY DATA	0,1 AND YOU DON'T READ DIRTY DATA	0,1,2 AND NO ONE ELSE DIRTIES DATA YOU READ
LOCK PROTOCOL	SET SHORT EXCL. LOCKS ON ANY DATA YOU WRITE	SET LONG EXCL. LOCKS ON ANY DATA YOU WRITE	1 AND SET SHORT SHARE LOCKS ON ANY DATA YOU READ	1 AND SET LONG SHARE LOCKS ON ANY DATA YOU READ
TRANSACTION STRUCTURE	WELL FORMED WRT WRITES	(WELL FORMED AND 2 PHASE) WRT WRITES	WELL FORMED (AND 2 PHASE WRT WRITES)	WELL FORMED AND TWO PHASE
CONCURRENCY	GREATEST: ONLY WAIT FOR SHORT WRITE LOCKS	GREAT: ONLY WAIT FOR WRITE LOCKS	MEDIUM: ALSO WAIT FOR READ LOCKS	LOWEST: ANY DATA TOUCHED IS LOCKED TO EOT
OVERHEAD	LEAST: ONLY SET SHORT WRITE LOCKS	SMALL: ONLY SET WRITE LOCKS	MEDIUM: SET BOTH KINDS OF LOCKS BUT NEED NOT STORE SHORT LOCKS	HIGHEST: SET AND STORE BOTH KINDS OF LOCKS
TRANSACT-ION BACKUP	CAN NOT UNDO WITHOUT CASCADING TO OTHERS	UN-DO ALL INCOMPLETE TRANSACTIONS IN ANY ORDER	UN-DO ANY INCOMPLETE TRANSACTIONS IN ANY ORDER	SAME AS 2
PROTECTION PROVIDED	LETS OTHERS RUN HIGHER CONSISTENCY	0 AND CAN'T LOSE WRITES	0,1 AND CAN'T READ BAD DATA ITEMS	0,1,2 AND CAN'T READ BAD DATA RELATIONSHIPS
SYSTEM RECOVERY TECHNIQUE	APPLY LOG IN ORDER OF ARRIVAL	APPLY LOG IN < ORDER	SAME AS 1: BUT RESULT IS SAME AS SOME SCHEDULE	2 AND SCHEDULE IS SERIAL
DEPENDENCIES	NONE	W->W	W->W W->R	W->W W->R R->W
ORDERING	NONE	< IS AN ORDERING OF THE TRANS-ACTIONS	<< IS AN ORDERING OF THE TRANS-ACTIONS	<<< IS AN ORDERING OF THE TRANS-ACTIONS

Table 7. Summary of consistency degrees.

III. LOCK GRANULARITY AND DEGREES OF CONSISTENCY IN EXISTING SYSTEMS:

IMS/VS with the program isolation feature [2] has a two level lock hierarchy: segment types (sets of records), and segment instances (records) within a segment type. Segment types may be locked in EXCLUSIVE (E) mode (which corresponds to our exclusive (X) mode) or in EXPRESS READ (R), RETRIEVE (G), or UPDATE (U) (each of which correspond to our notion of intention (I) mode) [2, pages 3.18-3.27]. Segment instances can be locked in share or exclusive mode. Segment type locks are requested at transaction initiation, usually in intention mode. Segment instance locks are dynamically set as the transaction proceeds. In addition IMS/VS has user controlled share locks on segment instances (the *Q option) which allow other read requests but not other *Q or exclusive requests. IMS/VS has no notion of S or SIX locks on segment types (which would allow a scan of all members of a segment type concurrent with other readers but without the overhead of locking each segment instance). Since IMS/VS does not support S mode on segment types one need not distinguish the two intention modes IS and IX (see the section introducing IS and IX modes). In general, IMS/VS has a notion of intention mode and does implicit locking but does not recognize all the modes described here. It uses a static two level lock tree.

IMS/VS with the program isolation feature basically provides degree 2 consistency. However degree 1 consistency can be obtained on a segment type basis in a PCB (view) by specifying the EXPRESS READ option for that segment. Similarly degree 3 consistency can be obtained by specifying the EXCLUSIVE or UPDATE options. IMS/VS also has the user controlled share locks discussed above which a program can request on selected segment instances to obtain additional consistency over the degree 1 or 2 consistency provided by the system.

IMS/VS without the program isolation feature (and also the previous version of IMS namely IMS/2) doesn't have a lock hierarchy since locking is done only on a segment type basis. It provides degree 1 consistency with degree 3 consistency obtainable for a segment type in a view by specifying the EXCLUSIVE option. User controlled locking is also provided on a limited basis via the HOLD option.

DMS 1100 has a two level lock hierarchy [4]: areas and pages within areas. Areas may be locked in one of seven modes when they are OPENed: EXCLUSIVE RETRIEVAL (which corresponds to our notion of exclusive mode), PROTECTED UPDATE (which corresponds to our notion of share and intention exclusive mode), PROTECTED RETRIEVAL (which we call share mode), UPDATE (which corresponds to our intention exclusive mode), and RETRIEVAL (which is our intention share mode). Given this transliteration, the compatibility matrix displayed in Table 1 is identical to the compatibility matrix of DMS 1100 [3, page 3.59]. However, DMS 1100 sets only exclusive-locks on pages within areas (short term share locks are invisibly set during internal pointer following). Further, even if a transaction locks an area in exclusive mode, DMS 1100 continues to set exclusive locks (and internal share locks) on the pages in the area, despite the fact that an exclusive lock on an area precludes reads or updates of the area by other transactions. Similar observations apply to the DMS 1100 implementation of S and SIX modes. In general, DMS 1100 recognizes all the modes described here and uses intention modes to detect conflicts but does not utilize implicit locking. It uses a static two level lock tree.

DMS 1100 provides level 2 consistency by setting exclusive locks on the modified pages and and a temporary lock on the page corresponding to the page which is "current of run unit". The temporary lock is released when the "current of run unit" is moved. In addition a run-unit can obtain additional locks via an explicit KEEP command.

The ideas presented were developed in the process of designing and implementing an experimental data base system at the IBM San Jose Research Laboratory. (We wish to emphasize that this system is a vehicle for research in data base architecture, and does not indicate plans for future IBM products.) A subsystem which provides the modes of locks herein described, plus the necessary logic to schedule requests and conversions, and to detect and resolve deadlocks has been implemented as one component of the data manager. The lock subsystem is in turn used by the data manager to automatically lock the nodes of its lock graph (see Figure 12). Users can be unaware of these lock protocols beyond the verbs "begin transaction" and "end transaction".

The data base is broken into several storage areas. Each area contains a set of relations (files), their indices, and their tuples(records) along with a catalog of the area. Each tuple has a unique tuple identifier (data base key) which can be used to quickly (directly) address the tuple. Each tuple identifier maps to a set of field values. All tuples are stored together in an area-wide heap to allow physical clustering of tuples from different relations. The unused slots in this heap are represented by an area-wide pool of free tuple identifiers (i.e. identifiers not allocated to any relation). Each tuple "belongs" to a unique relation, and all tuples in a relation have the same number and type of fields. One may construct an index on any subset of the fields of a relation. Tuple identifiers give fast direct access to tuples, while indices give fast associative access to field values and to their corresponding tuples. Each key value in an index is made a lockable object in order to solve the problem of "phantoms" [1] without locking the entire index. We do not explicitly lock individual fields or whole indices so those nodes appear in Figure 12 only for pedagogical reasons. Figure 12 gives only the "logical" lock graph; there is also a graph for physical page locks and for other low level resources.

As can be seen, Figure 12 is not a tree. Heavy use is made of the techniques mentioned in the section on locking DAG's. For example, one can read via tuple identifier without setting any index locks but to lock a field for update its tuple identifier and the old and new index key values covering the updated field must be locked in X mode. Further, the tree is not static, since data base keys are dynamically allocated to relations; field values dynamically enter, move around in, and leave index value intervals when records are inserted, updated and deleted; relations and indices are dynamically created and destroyed within areas; and areas are dynamically allocated. The implementation of such operations observes the lock protocol presented in the section on dynamic graphs: when a node changes parents, all old and new parents must be held (explicitly or implicitly) in intention exclusive mode and the node to be moved must be held in exclusive mode.

The described system supports concurrently consistency degrees 1,2 and 3 which can be specified on a transaction basis. In addition share locks on individual tuples can be acquired by the user.

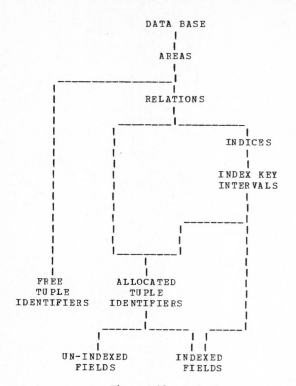

Figure 12. A lock graph.

ACKNOWLEDGMENT

We gratefully acknowledge many helpful discussions with Phil Macri,
Jim Mehl and Brad Wade on how locking works in existing systems and
how these results might be better presented.   We are especially
indebted to Paul McJones in this regard.

REFERENCES

[1]   K.P. Eswaran, J.N. Gray, R.A. Lorie, I.L. Traiger, On the
       Notions of Consistency and Predicate Locks, Technical Report
       RJ.1487, IBM Research Laboratory, San Jose, Ca., Nov. 1974. (to
       appear CACM).

[2]   Information Management System Virtual Storage (IMS/VS). System
       Application Design Guide, Form No. SH20-9025-2, IBM Corp.,
       1975.

[3]   UNIVAC 1100 Series Data Management System (DMS 1100). ANSI
       COBOL Field Data Manipulation Language. Order No. UP7908-2,
       Sperry Rand Corp., May 1973.

Modelling in Data Base Management Systems, G.M. Nijssen, (ed)
North Holland Publishing Company, 1976

INTEGRITY OF DATA BASES :
A GENERAL LOCKOUT ALGORITHM
WITH DEADLOCK AVOIDANCE

G. GARDARIN and S. SPACCAPIETRA
Institut de Programmation
Université Paris VI, Paris, France

Abstract : Allowing simultaneous access to a data base by many
different users implies that protections have to be used to
assure data integrity.

We first propose elements for a theory on data base concurrency,
in which lockout rules are defined on "objects" of any level and
the concept of "operation" is used as a generalization of the
type-of-access notion. Permitted operations on any object and
compatibilities between these operations are defined by the administrator in the schema rules. Once this has been done, a very
simple algorithm avoids simultaneous execution of non compatible
operations.

Secondly, the deadlock problem is discussed. We present a detection algorithm, which uses a graph representing the waitings between users and looks for the existence of a circuit in it.

Finally, using the external schema to anticipate possible operations on objects and A.N.HABERMANN's method to construct a deadlock avoidance algorithm starting from a detection algorithm,
we propose a general method avoiding simultaneous execution of
non compatible operations on an object and avoiding deadlock
situations to become effective.

1. INTRODUCTION

Allowing simultaneous access to a data base by many different users implies that
protections have to be used to assure data integrity.

Usually, a lockout mechanism resolves the concurrency problem : a lock is associated with a given data set (an area in CODASYL [2], a data item in ANSI/SPARC [1])
and a number of operations on that set are identified (exclusive, protected and
unprotected access for retrieval or update in CODASYL, update or non update access in ANSI/SPARC).
In each case, the problem is viewed at in a particular way and a particular solution is proposed.

A general method dealing with access conflicts must provide the possibility of
associating a lock with any data set (data base, data set, area, record, data
item, ...) according to user's needs and to conceptual sharing possibilities.

Furthermore, possible operations on these data sets and compatibilities of these
operations should not be arbitrarily limited by the system designers : they should
be defined by the administrators while defining the schemas.
Of course, the internal structure of the data base as well as the implementations
options of the data base system limit the possibilities of sharing data : the
mapping between conceptual schema and internal schema has to be concerned with
these limitations.

Section 2 develops these ideas which, in our opinion, are a sound basis for a
theory of concurrency (i.e. simultaneous sharing of data).

Section 3 proposes a tool for the administrators to declare possible operations
and compatibilities of simultaneous execution of these operations on each data set.
A very simple algorithm is then described, avoiding simultaneous execution of non
compatible operations.

Section 4 deals with the deadlock problem. In fact, as the possibilities of sharing data increase, this problem becomes very important.
An algorithm for deadlock detection, in a concurrency context, is presented.
Using this algorithm and predicting the possible operations, by means of the external schema, a method is proposed to avoid deadlock situations to become effective.

Combining the different proposed algorithms results in a general method to solve
the concurrency problem.

2. ELEMENTS FOR A THEORY OF CONCURRENCY

It is evident that it is not possible to allow any kind of usage to run concurrently on a data base.

If no user modifies the data base, concurrent access is allowed. Contrarily, if
one or more users may modify the data base, then "transitory" states may appear in
which parts of the data base are not consistent.
In this case, a restriction of the concurrent activities of the different users is
needed to inhibit concurrent access to those parts of the data base.

Let us examine two different methods proposed by working groups on data bases to
solve this first aspect of the concurrency problem (the second one - deadlock -
is discussed later).

CODASYL proposes a solution in which the problem is dealed with at the area level and the difference in usage is made between exclusive, protected and unprotected access for retrieval or update.

ANSI/SPARC is not very precise on this subject ; it seems to propose a distinction between update and non update access, at a data item level.

These approaches are very particular and, in our opinon, insatisfactory.

For example, suppose the data base contains records describing motor-cars, these records being grouped into areas by departement (or state) of registration (one area for each departement).
On the other hand, the data-set of motor-cars which colour is orange has been defined ; the owner record of this data-set contains the number of orange motor-cars.

Consider now the two following operations :
  - adding a new motor-car ;
  - editing the number of orange motor-cars together with the list of theirs index numbers.

Simultaneous execution of these two operations can lead to obtain a listing where the number of motor-cars is said to be n and only $n-1$ index numbers are listed below. Therefore, these two operations can be defined as not compatible (in fact, it depends on the precision wanted in the result).
To correctly solve this example, CODASYL urges to lock every area containing an orange motor-car : such a constraint is much too strong.

Following ANSI/SPARC, we have to lock every record, comprising the owner record, successively : if done at the item level this can be very awkward and leads to non trivial deadlock problems (which could be managed using the solution we propose in Section 4).

Finally, both solutions are insatisfactory, due to the fact that they are technical solution, implemented at the internal level regardless of the user's needs of sharing.

A general method must provide the administrators with a tool to specify the concurrency aspects in theirs own terms, at their own level (external, conceptual, internal), using the following steps :

1.- define the objects that have to be shared,
2.- define the operations that can be made on these objects,
3.- define the compatibilities, i.e. the possibilities of simultaneous execution of these operations.

This seems to be the method used by persons collaborating to perform some common general task.

Defining the concurrency specifications appears to be a problem with two degrees of freedom :

  - choice of objects,
  - choice of operations on these objects.

Further, the problem is different according to the level in which it is considered:

  - at the external level, each user has his own particular view of objects and operations he wants to do on them ;
  - at the conceptual level, concurrency specifications should consist in a realistic appropriate integration of user's needs with regard to the interest of the enterprise ;
  - at the internal level, sharing constraints result of concurrency specifications defined at the conceptual level and limitations dues to storage technologies

in use. Concurrency specifications have to respect these constraints.

Finally, the concurrency problem can be represented by a threedimensional diagram, as seen in figure 1, where one axis represents the levels in which the problem has to be considered (each level implies a different context), the two other axes representing the two degrees of freedom in specifying the problem (objects, operations).

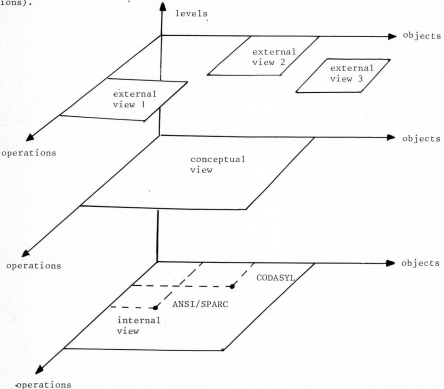

Figure 1 : concurrency as a two-dimensional problem which can be considered at three different levels

Actual systems, as well as the proposals or requirements from working groups, arbitrarily choose a point in the two-dimensional space of the internal level.

As we find it unsatisfactory, in the following Sections we propose a method and some algorithms which, if supported by the data base system, allow each administrator to choose his point at his level.

However, methods and algorithms can only be applied to "independent" objects. There are two kinds of dependency :
- structural dependency, between overlapping objects,
- semantic dependency, between objects bound by some integrity constraint.

In such a context, to operate on an object it is necessary to lock every dependent object. There is a need for general locking protocols dealing with dependent objects. J.N. GRAY u.a. [5] propose a protocol to lock structural dependent objects in a hierarchical or directed acyclic graph context. In a forthcoming paper we will propose a general method handling both kinds of dependency.

3. THE LOCKOUT METHOD

In the present and following sections, we deal with the concurrency problem on objects, regardless of their scope and of the level in which they are considered.

It is clear that it exists a correspondence between objects in the different levels and that mappings exist to realize this correspondence.

The method and algorithms we develop can be implemented at the different levels. Limitation of concurrent access must be effective at the internal level ; moreover, we recommand to perform it at the conceptual level too.

At the internal level it is assumed that constraints on objects result from both conceptual and technological constraints and that user's intents are recognized using the appropriate external schemas.

The following notations are used hereinafter :

- $\subset$ logical inclusion,
- $\neg$ logical negation,
- $\wedge$ logical intersection,
- $\vee$ logical union,
- $\star$ boolean matrix multiplication
  (defined by : element (i,j) of the product matrix is the union of the intersections of elements having the same rank in the ith line of the left matrix and in the jth colum of the right matrix),
- ϵ is member of,
- $\notin$ is not member of,
- $\vee$ for any,
- $\exists$ there exists.

3.1. Définition of the operations

Be F_i an object (field, group, record, record-set, data base, ...). The operations defined on this object are said to be the possible operations on F_i. They are identified by a name, here noted

$$O_1^i \ , \ O_2^i \ , \ \ldots, \ O_j^i \ , \ \ldots, \ O_l^i \ .$$

Of course, the administrator does not need to define the possible operations for every object ; this is only needed for sharable objects, according to the degree of sharing which is of interest to him. In certain cases, a sufficient degree of sharing will be obtained by just defining operations on the data base.

The compatibilities of the possible operations on object F_i are drawn in a boolean matrix C^i , called the matrix of compatibilities of operations.
This matrix is defined assuming $C^i = (c_{mn}^i)$, where $c_{mn}^i = 1$ if operations O_m^i and O_n^i are simultaneously executable on object F_i, $c_{mn}^i = 0$ otherwise.

Of course, the matrices C^i are symmetric.
If no sumultaneous sharing is allowed then all elements c_{mn}^i are equal to 0. The existence of one $c_{mn}^i = 1$ shows that operation O_m^i is no more exclusive with all other ones ; thus, a possibility of simultaneous access exists on object F_i.

3.2. Current sections of operations on an object

Data sharing is not handled on a single operation bases. Inded, users are interested in being able to perform a sequence of the requested operations during a given section of his program. Therefore, objects are locked for a "section of operation(s)", starting with a user's "request for section of operations" up to the "end of section of operations" request.

Sections of operations that users are executing on objects in the data base are registered by means of boolean vectors

$$
A_j^i(t) = \begin{bmatrix} a_1^i \\ \vdots \\ a_m^i \\ \vdots \\ a_l^i \end{bmatrix}
$$

these vectors are defined by setting $a^i = 1$ if operation O_m^i is being executed (on object F_i) by user P_j at the time t ; $a_m^i = 0$ if not.

As in ANSI/SPARC, at the time the users request an object, the system must be capable of recognizing which operation(s) the user intents to execute on this object.
Before allowing the user to proceed, the system has to check that no section of operation non compatible with the requested one(s) is being executed on this object by any other user.

3.3. Definition of requests

A request, by user P_j, at the time t, to execute a section of one or more operations on an object F_i is described by means of a boolean vector

$$
Q_j^i(t) = \begin{bmatrix} q_1^i \\ \vdots \\ q_k^i \\ \vdots \\ q_l^i \end{bmatrix}
$$

defined by setting $q_k^i = 1$ if and only if user P_j request to execute operations O_k^i.

3.4. The basic theorem

The following theorem is a premise for the construction of general algorithms to be run at the begining and at the end of a section of operations on an object, to determine whether or not the requested section can be allowed, regarding to the defined compatibilities.

Theorem 1 : A necessary condition to accept a request for a section of operations $Q_p^i(t)$ by user P_p on an object F_i is

$$
Q_p^i(t) \subset \neg(\neg C^i \star \underset{j \neq p}{\vee} A_j^i(t))
$$

Proof : be

$$c^i = \begin{bmatrix} c^i_{11} & \cdots & c^i_{1m} & \cdots & c^i_{1l} \\ \vdots & & \vdots & & \vdots \\ c^i_{k1} & & c^i_{km} & & c^i_{kl} \\ \vdots & & \vdots & & \vdots \\ c^i_{l1} & & c^i_{lm} & & c^i_{ll} \end{bmatrix} \qquad \text{the compatibilities,}$$

$$\underset{j \neq p}{\vee} A^i_j (t) = \begin{bmatrix} a^i_1 \\ \vdots \\ a^i_m \\ \vdots \\ a^i_l \end{bmatrix} \qquad \text{the current operations,}$$

$$Q^i_p (t) = \begin{bmatrix} q^i_1 \\ \vdots \\ q^i_k \\ \vdots \\ q^i_l \end{bmatrix} \qquad \text{the request.}$$

Then, the boolean product in the condition above is :

$$\neg c^i \star \underset{j \neq p}{\vee} A^i_j (t) = \begin{bmatrix} \underset{m=1,l}{\vee} (\neg c^i_{1m} \wedge a^i_m) \\ \vdots \\ \underset{m=1,l}{\vee} (\neg c^i_{km} \wedge a^i_m) \\ \vdots \\ \underset{m=1,l}{\vee} (\neg c^i_{lm} \wedge a^i_m) \end{bmatrix}$$

and we can see that

$$Q^i_p (t) \subset \neg(\neg c^i \star \underset{j \neq p}{\vee} A^i_j (t))$$

$$\Longleftrightarrow \quad \forall k, \ q^i_k \subset \neg(\underset{m=1,l}{\vee} (\neg c^i_{km} \wedge a^i_m))$$

$$\Longleftrightarrow \quad \forall k \ \text{such as} \ q^i_k = 1 : \ \underset{m=1,l}{\vee} (\neg c^i_{km} \wedge a^i_m) = 0$$

$\Longleftrightarrow \quad$ for each operation O^i_k requested by the user P_p there does not exist m sot that $\neg c^i_{km}=1$ and $a^i_m=1$.

Now, according to the given definitions we have :
- $\neg c^i_{km} = 1$ if and only if operations O^i_k and O^i_m are not compatible,
- $a^i_m = 1$ if and only if a section of operations O^i_m is actually being executed on object F_i by any other user.

Finally, the suggested condition is equivalent to the fact that there are no cur-

rent sections of operations being executed by any other user which are non compatible with the requested ones.
Therefore, the request can be accepted : the theorem is demonstrated.

3.5. Algorithms handling requests and ends of sections of operations

The system must be capable to maintain a queue associated with each shared object, in which it accumulates the requests which are not compatible with the current state, until execution of all non comaptibles sections of operations is completed [2].

We present here two algorithms dealing with (1) the requests for sections of operations, occasionally inserting the request in the associated queue, and (2) the ends of sections of operations, occasionally deleting now acceptable request from the associated queue.

3.5.1. Request for sections of operations

User P_p's request on object F_i is described by the boolean vector Q.

<u>Procedure</u> ROP (i,Q,p) ;

<u>begin</u> <u>if</u> $Q \subset \neg(\neg C^i \star \bigvee_{j \neq p} A_j^i)$ <u>then</u> <u>begin</u>

$$A_p^i = A_p^i \vee Q ;$$

<u>end</u>

<u>else</u> <u>begin</u>
"insert the request Q, together with the user number p, in the queue associated to object F_i." ; "desactivate user P_p " ;
<u>end</u>

<u>end</u>

3.5.2. End of sections of operations

User P_p has completed the section of operations on object F_i described by the boolean vector Q.

<u>Procedure</u> EOP (i,Q,p) ;

<u>begin</u> $A_p^i = A_p^i \wedge \neg Q$;

<u>for</u> "each request R, issued from a user P_q, in the queue associated to object F_i."

<u>do begin</u>
<u>if</u> $R \subset \neg(\neg C^i \star \bigvee_{j \neq q} A_j^i)$ <u>then</u> <u>begin</u>
$A_q^i = A_q^i \vee R$;
"activate user P_q " ;
<u>end</u>

<u>end</u>

<u>end</u>

3.6. Example

Be F_1 an object shared by users P_1, P_2.
The possible operations on object F_1 are :

O_1^1 : reading some elements in F_1

O_2^1 : modifying some elements in F_1,

O_3^1 : adding some elements into F_1'.

We have $C^1 = \begin{bmatrix} 1 & 0 & 1 \\ 0 & 0 & 0 \\ 1 & 0 & 0 \end{bmatrix}$; the initial state is $A_1^1 = A_2^1 = \begin{bmatrix} 0 \\ 0 \\ 0 \end{bmatrix}$.

A possible evolution is :

1) user P_1 wants to read F_1 ; he executes :

ROP $(1, \begin{bmatrix} 1 \\ 0 \\ 0 \end{bmatrix}, 1)$

$\begin{bmatrix} 1 \\ 0 \\ 0 \end{bmatrix} \subset \neg (\neg C^1 * A_2^1)$ is true ; therefore this request is accepted and A_1^1 is set to $\begin{bmatrix} 1 \\ 0 \\ 0 \end{bmatrix}$.

2) user P_2 wants to modify F_1 ; he executes :

ROP $(1, \begin{bmatrix} 0 \\ 1 \\ 0 \end{bmatrix}, 2)$;

$(\neg C^1 * A_1^1) = \begin{bmatrix} 0 & 1 & 0 \\ 1 & 1 & 1 \\ 0 & 1 & 1 \end{bmatrix} * \begin{bmatrix} 1 \\ 0 \\ 0 \end{bmatrix} = \begin{bmatrix} 0 \\ 1 \\ 0 \end{bmatrix}$ and $\begin{bmatrix} 0 \\ 1 \\ 0 \end{bmatrix} \subset \neg (\neg C^1 * A_1^1)$ is false ;

therefore this request is rejected and $\left(\begin{bmatrix} 0 \\ 1 \\ 0 \end{bmatrix}, 2 \right)$ is inserted in the queue associated with F_1 ; user P_2 is desactivated.

3) user P_1 wants to add some elements into F_1 ; he executes:

ROP $(1, \begin{bmatrix} 0 \\ 0 \\ 1 \end{bmatrix}, 1)$;

$\begin{bmatrix} 0 \\ 0 \\ 1 \end{bmatrix} \subset \neg (\neg C^1 * A_2^1)$ is true ; therefore this request is accepted and A_1^1 is set to : $\begin{bmatrix} 1 \\ 0 \\ 0 \end{bmatrix} \vee \begin{bmatrix} 0 \\ 0 \\ 1 \end{bmatrix} = \begin{bmatrix} 1 \\ 0 \\ 1 \end{bmatrix}$

4) user P_1 releases all operations he is actually performing on object F_1 ; an EOP $(1, \begin{bmatrix} 1 \\ 0 \\ 1 \end{bmatrix}, 1)$ is executed.

First, A_1^1 is set to $\begin{bmatrix} 1 \\ 0 \\ 1 \end{bmatrix} \wedge \neg \begin{bmatrix} 1 \\ 0 \\ 1 \end{bmatrix} = \begin{bmatrix} 0 \\ 0 \\ 0 \end{bmatrix}$

Next, the queue associated to F_1 is searched ; one request $\left(\begin{bmatrix} 0 \\ 1 \\ 0 \end{bmatrix} , 2\right)$ exists, for which :

$$R \subset \urcorner (\urcorner C^1 * A_1^1) \quad \text{is true.}$$

Therefore A_2^1 is set to $\begin{bmatrix} 0 \\ 1 \\ 0 \end{bmatrix}$; user P_2 is activated having his request now accepted.

4. DEADLOCK DETECTION

So far we discussed a general method to manage access conflicts which, in our opinion, could suppress the disadvantages due to the choice of a given particular solution in CODASYL and ANSI/SPARC.

We consider now the deadlock (or deadly embrace) problem.

First, we propose a deadlock detection algorithm. This one, as well as the following avoidance algorithm, is presented in a data base context as a part of a general theory on concurrency.

These, and more, detection and avoidance algorithms were developed by G. GARDARIN in a context of simultaneous sharing of files. Further information on the basis of these algorithms can be found in [4].

It is also of interest to refer to A.N. HABERMANN [6] and R.C. HOLT [7] : both have proposed detection/avoidance algorithms in a context of exclusive sharing of resources. Unfortunately, these algorithms can not be used in simultaneous sharing.

4.1. The graph of waitings between users

Waitings between users can be represented by a directed graph, in which the nodes stand for the users [8].
An arc goes from node P_i to node P_j if and only if user P_i is waiting on user P_j's completion of at least one section of operation on an object.

This means that user P_i has been desactivated due to a request from him on an object which was currently used, in a non compatible way, by user P_j.

Formally : $\exists$ arc $P_i \to P_j \Leftrightarrow \exists F^k, O_m^k, O_n^k / a_{jm}^k \wedge q_{jn}^k \wedge \urcorner c_{mn}^k = 1$.

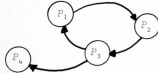

P_1 waits for P_2

P_2 waits for P_3

P_3 waits for P_1 and P_4

P_4 does not wait

figure 2 : example of
the waiting's graph

A deadlock situation is equivalent to the existence of a circuit in such a graph [8].
In the above example, P_1, P_2 and P_3 are in a deadlock situation ; contrarily, P_4 can proceed his execution.

4.2. The principle of a detection algorithm

Detection of deadlock situations can be achieved by detecting the existence of circuits in the graph representing the waitings between users. To this purpose, ROY's algorithm [9] is used.

An implementation of this algorithm consists in first associating to each node the number of arcs whose origin is that node ; secondly, the nodes whose associated number is 0 are canceled, which implies to decrement, by 1, the numbers associated to the nodes from which an arc existed to the deleted node. This implementation is shown in figure 3.

Figure 3 : example of ROY's algorithm.

The graph has a circuit, which has been isolated by the algorithm.

4.3. The proposed detection algorithm

In practice, it is difficult to maintain the number of arcs leaving from a node. On the contrary, it is simple to know the number of objects each user is waiting for. Let us note N(p) the number of objects that user P_p is waiting for.

Theorem 1, from section 3.3, and the implementation of ROY's algorithm result in the following detection algorithm, whose value is TRUE if a deadlock situation exists FALSE if not.
It is assumed that $\underset{j \in P}{\vee} A_j^i = (0)$ if P is empty.

Boolean **procedure** DETECT ;

begin

$P = \{$list of users P_j where $N(j) = 0\}$;

$F = \{$list of objects actually used by users in $P\}$;

for "each entry F_i in F"

  do begin

    for "each $P_k \notin P$ waiting for object F_i such as

$$Q_k^i \subset \neg (\neg C^i \star \underset{\substack{P_j \notin P \\ j \neq k}}{\vee} A_j^i)"$$

      do begin

        "P_k is no more waiting for object F_i"

        $N(k) = N(k) - 1$;

        if $N(k) = 0$ **then** **begin**

            "add P_k to list P" ;

            "add objects used by P_k to list F" ;

            end

      end

  end

<u>if</u> "all actual users are in P" <u>then</u> DETECT = FALSE ;

<u>else</u> DETECT = TRUE ;

<u>end</u> ;

The result of this algorithm does not depend on the order in which objects F_i are added to list F. The proof of this is given in appendix A.

4.4. Example

Be F_1 , F_2, F_3 three objects.
The possible operations on object F_1 are :
- reading,
- modifying some elements.
The matrix of compatibilities of these operations is $\begin{bmatrix} 1 & 0 \\ 0 & 0 \end{bmatrix}$.

On object F_2 , the possible operations are :

- reading,
- adding some elements.
The matrix of compatibilities of these operations is $\begin{bmatrix} 1 & 1 \\ 1 & 0 \end{bmatrix}$.

On object F_3 , the only possible operation is suppressing some elements. The matrix of compatibility of this operation is (0).

Consider now the following current state with four users sharing the three objects :
- P_1 is reading F_2 and modifying F_1 ,
- P_2 is reading F_2 and waits to modify F_1 ,
- P_3 is adding elements in F_2, suppressing elements from F_3 and waits to read F_1 ,
- P_4 waits to add elements in F_2 ,

Using the notations we introduced, this current state is described by :

- user P_1 : $N(1) = 0$, $Q_1^1 = \begin{bmatrix} 0 \\ 0 \end{bmatrix}$, $Q_1^2 = \begin{bmatrix} 0 \\ 0 \end{bmatrix}$, $Q_1^3 = (0)$,

  $A_1^1 = \begin{bmatrix} 0 \\ 1 \end{bmatrix}$, $A_1^2 = \begin{bmatrix} 1 \\ 0 \end{bmatrix}$, $A_1^3 = (0)$;

- user P_2 : $N(2) = 1$, $Q_2^1 = \begin{bmatrix} 0 \\ 1 \end{bmatrix}$, $Q_2^2 = \begin{bmatrix} 0 \\ 0 \end{bmatrix}$, $Q_2^3 = (0)$,

  $A_2^1 = \begin{bmatrix} 0 \\ 0 \end{bmatrix}$, $A_2^2 = \begin{bmatrix} 1 \\ 0 \end{bmatrix}$, $A_2^3 = (0)$;

- user P_3 : $N(3) = 1$, $Q_3^1 = \begin{bmatrix} 1 \\ 0 \end{bmatrix}$, $Q_3^2 = \begin{bmatrix} 0 \\ 0 \end{bmatrix}$, $Q_3^3 = (0)$,

  $A_3^1 = \begin{bmatrix} 0 \\ 0 \end{bmatrix}$, $A_3^2 = \begin{bmatrix} 0 \\ 1 \end{bmatrix}$, $A_3^3 = (1)$;

- user P_4 : $N(4) = 1$, $Q_4^1 = \begin{bmatrix} 0 \\ 0 \end{bmatrix}$, $Q_4^2 = \begin{bmatrix} 0 \\ 1 \end{bmatrix}$, $Q_4^3 = (0)$,

  $A_4^1 = \begin{bmatrix} 0 \\ 0 \end{bmatrix}$, $A_4^2 = \begin{bmatrix} 0 \\ 0 \end{bmatrix}$, $A_4^3 = (0)$.

Excution on the detection algorithm results in the following steps :

$P = \{P_1\}$; $F = \{F_1, F_2\}$;

<u>for</u> F_1 :

- P_2 waits for F_1 and we have $Q_2^1 = \begin{bmatrix} 0 \\ 1 \end{bmatrix}$

  and $\neg\,(\neg\,C^1 \star \underset{\substack{P_j \notin P \\ j \neq 2}}{\vee} A_j^1) = \begin{bmatrix} 1 \\ 1 \end{bmatrix}$

  so $Q_2^1 \subset \neg(\neg\,C^1 \star \underset{\substack{P_j \notin P \\ j \neq 2}}{\vee} A_j^1)$ is true <u>then</u> <u>begin</u>

  $\qquad N(2) = N(2) - 1 = 0$;

  $\qquad P = \{P_1, P_2\}$;

  $\qquad F = \{F_1, F_2\}$;

  $\qquad$ <u>end</u>

- P_3 waits for F_1 and we have $Q_3^1 = \begin{bmatrix} 1 \\ 0 \end{bmatrix}$

  and $\neg(\neg\,C^1 \star \underset{\substack{P_j \notin P \\ j \neq 3}}{\vee} A_j^1) = \begin{bmatrix} 1 \\ 1 \end{bmatrix}$

  so $Q_3^1 \subset \neg(\neg\,C^1 \star \underset{\substack{P_j \notin P \\ j \neq 3}}{\vee} A_j^1)$ is true <u>then</u> <u>begin</u>

  $\qquad N(3) = N(3) - 1 = 0$;

  $\qquad P = \{P_1, P_2, P_3\};$

  $\qquad F = \{F_1, F_2, F_3\};$

  $\qquad$ <u>end</u>

<u>for</u> F_2 :

- P_4 waits for F_2 and we have $Q_4^2 = \begin{bmatrix} 0 \\ 1 \end{bmatrix}$

  and $\neg(\neg\,C^2 \star \underset{\substack{P_j \notin P \\ j \neq 4}}{\vee} A_j^2) = \begin{bmatrix} 1 \\ 1 \end{bmatrix}$

  so $Q_4^2 \subset \neg(\neg\,C^2 \star \underset{\substack{P_j \notin P \\ j \neq 4}}{\vee} A_j^2)$ is true then <u>begin</u>

  $\qquad N(4) = N(4) - 1 = 0$;

  $\qquad P = \{P_1, P_2, P_3, P_4\};$

  $\qquad F = \{F_1, F_2, F_3\};$

  $\qquad$ <u>end</u>

as P contains all actual users <u>then</u> there is no deadlock situation.

5. DEADLOCK AVOIDANCE

5.1. The method

To avoid deadlock situations, we have to know in advance the requests on objects
that users are able to do. This is achieved by examining the external schemas
corresponding to the current users. Using the external schema of user P_j , it is
possible to define, associated to each sharable object F_i , a boolean vector D_j^i
in which are recorded the sections of operations that user P_j is able to do.

Then, considering all these sections of operations on objects as waiting requests,
the following rule allows to decide if a request can be accepted without any
danger of deadlock :

- when the users request for a section of operations on an object, the system
  will accept it if the new current state, after the request has been accepted,

is without any danger of deadlock (assuming all requests as potentially
waiting, the new state is not a deadlock situation) ; otherwise, the system
will memorize the request as an effectively waiting one.

Finally, deadlock avoidance is achieved by running the above detection algorithm
before the request is accepted ; input to the algorithm are the D_j^i (instead of
Q_j^i) vectors and the A_j^i vectors which would be created if the request was
accepted.
Moreover, this is an usual way to obtain an avoidance method from a detection
algorithm [8].

However, we have trouble in applying the detection algorithm : indeed, the number
of objects each user is potentially waiting for must be calculated for each request. To prevent this, we modify the definition of initialisations ($N(p)$, lists
P and F) in the algorithm : the number $N(j)$ of objects user P_j is potentially
waiting for is defined as the number of matrices D_j^i in which at least one
element has value 1 ; list P is empty , list F contains all shared objects.

5.2. Example

Be F_1, F_2 two objects shared by users P_1, P_2.
On object F_1, read -0_1^1- and modify -0_2^1- operations are defined, with
$C^1 = \begin{bmatrix} 1 & 0 \\ 0 & 0 \end{bmatrix}$. On object F_2 only one exclusive operation "use" is considered :
$C^2 = (0)$.

Assume that user P_1 is allowed to read F_1 and use F_2 , and that user P_2 is
allowed to use F_2 and modify F_1 .
We have : $D_1^1 = \begin{pmatrix} 1 \\ 0 \end{pmatrix}$, $D_2^1 = \begin{pmatrix} 0 \\ 1 \end{pmatrix}$, $D_1^2 = (1)$, $D_2^2 = (1)$.

1) User P_1 requests to read F_1 : ROP $(1, \begin{bmatrix} 1 \\ 0 \end{bmatrix}, 1)$.
First we apply the ROP algorithm : this request is accepted and A_1^1 is set to
$\begin{bmatrix} 1 \\ 0 \end{bmatrix}$.
Secondly we apply the deadlock detection algorithm, using as requests the matri-
ces D_k^i instead of Q_k^i ; the initial state is :

$\qquad N(1) = 2, \; N(2) = 2, \; P = \emptyset, \; F = \{F_1, F_2\};$

For F_1 :

$\qquad \exists P_1 / \; D_1^1 \subset \neg(\neg C^1 \star A_2^1)$ is true, then $N(1) = 1$;

For F_2 :

$\qquad \exists P_1 / \; D_1^2 \subset \neg(\neg C^2 \star A_2^2)$ is true, then : $N(1) = 0$; $P = \{P_1\}$
$\qquad\qquad\qquad\qquad\qquad\qquad\qquad\qquad\qquad\qquad\qquad F = \{F_1, F_2, F_1\}$

$\qquad \exists P_2 / \; D_2^2 \subset \neg(\neg C^2 \star A_1^2)$ is true, then $N(2) = 1$;

For F_1

$\qquad \exists P_2 / \; D_2^1 \subset \neg(\neg C^1 \star \begin{bmatrix} 0 \\ 0 \end{bmatrix})$ is true, then $N(2) = 0$; $P = \{P_1, P_2\}$

There is no potential deadlock situation. The request is definitively accepted.

2) User P_2 request to use F_2 : ROP (2,(1),2)

First we apply the ROP algorithm : this request is accepted and A_2^2 is set to (1). Secondly, we apply the deadlock detection algorithm, as above. Initial state is :

$N(1) = 2$, $N(2) = 2$, $P = \emptyset$, $F = \{F_1, F_2\}$

For F_1 :
$$\exists\, P_1 / D_1^1 \subset \neg(\neg\, C^1 \ast A_2^1) \text{ is true, then } N(1) = 1 ;$$

For F_2 :
$$\exists\, P_2 / D_2^2 \subset \neg(\neg\, C^2 \ast A_1^2) \text{ is true, then } N(2) = 1 ;$$

There is no more object in F and P does not contain all users : the new state occasion a danger of deadlock. Therefore the request is rejected and inserted in the queue associated with F_2 . A_2^2 is reset to (0).

3) If we go on with the example, user P_1 requests to use F_2 and his request is accepted. So execution of P_1 is possible. Once P_1 has released F_1 and F_2 , execution of P_2 is possible.

6. CONCLUSION

This paper focuses on three original results :

- some elements for a theory on data base concurrency ;
- a lockout approach, allowing a high level of sharing in data bases ;
- a detection and avoidance algorithm for the deadlock problem in the context of concurrency.

These results are rather independent : it is not necessary to use the lockout approach to implement the deadlock algorithms. Deadlock algorithms can be directly implemented on CODASYL or ANSI/SPARC reports.

Finally, we consider that the definition of a conceptual model, which is the essential aspect of ANSI/SPARC report, is a tool to considerably improve solutions to the sharing problem : possibilities of simultaneous sharing have to be defined at the conceptual level, regardless of the storage constrains.

Storage constraints have to be considered only when dealing with the mapping of the conceptual schema to the internal schema. Methods and algorithms for this purpose have still to be developed.

APPENDIX A

Assertion : the result of the detection algorithm (section 4.3.) does not depend on the order in which objects F_i are added to list F.

Proof : Be P_k an user utilizing objects $F_1, F_2, \ldots, F_m$. We shall demonstrate that, while adding these objects to list F, permutation of two adjacent objects F_i and F_{i+1} does not change the result of the algorithm.

If not, this means that a user $P_a \in P$ becomes a pending user $(P_j$ is said to be a pending user $\Leftrightarrow N(j) = 0)$ if we examine list F in the order F_i F_{i+1} and that this user P_a does not become a pending user if we examine list F using order F_{i+1} F_i .

To obtain this, P_α must be :

1) Waiting for F_{i+1} : otherwise he would become a pending user in second case too (order F_{i+1} F_i.) while considering F_i,

2) Waiting for another user P_β, $P_\beta \notin P$ before consideration of F_i and $P_\beta \in P$ after : otherwise he would become a pending user during examination of F_i using order F_i F_{i+1}.

This situation is shown in the following figure :

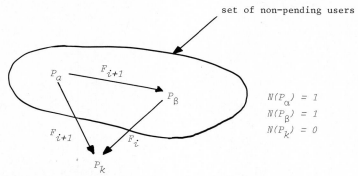

set of non-pending users

$N(P_\alpha) = 1$
$N(P_\beta) = 1$
$N(P_k) = 0$

P_α waits for release of F_{i+1} by P_β and P_k
P_β waits for release of F_i by P_k

Such a situation implies that P_β is using F_{i+1}.

Therefore, using order F_{i+1} F_i , while adding P_β to P object F_{i+1} is added to F. Finally, while examining F_{i+1} again, P_α is added to P.

Thus the hypothesis that P_α be never added to P is false ; therefore two adjacent objects may be permuted while adding them to F. Using successive permutations, we ascertain that any order can be used in adding objects to F.

The stated assertion is demonstrated.

APPENDIX B   (Cross reference)

For some of the concepts we discussed in this paper a reference can be made to a corresponding concept in the paper by GRAY u.a. [9].

Sometimes it is only a matter of terminology. Thus, the reader may use the following table for correspondences :

GRAY u.a (Section I)	this paper
transaction	user
lock mode access mode } mode	Section of operation
lock request	request for section of operations

In other cases, concepts are similar but somewhat different. Thus for :

GRAY u.a. (Section II)   this paper

action	operation
transaction	section of operations
begin action	request for section of operations
end action	end of section of operations

REFERENCES

[1] ANSI/SPARC March 1975 Interim Report

[2] CODASYL DBTG Report
     April 1971

[3] E.G. COFFMANN, M.J. E.LPHICK, A. SHOSHANI
     "System deadlocks"
     Computing Surveys, vol.3, number 2, june 1971, pages 67-68

[4] G. GARDARIN
     "Une solution au problème du verrou mortel en partage simultané de fichiers"
     Thèse de 3ème cycle, Université Paris VI, Paris, Avril 1974

[5] J.N. GRAY, R.A. LORIE, G.R. PUTZOLU, I.L. TRAIGER
     "Granularity of locks and degrees of consistency in a shared data base"
     IFIP TC-2 Working Conference on Modelling in Data Base
     Management Systems, january 1976, Freudenstadt, Germany

[6] A.N. HABERMANN
     "Prevention of systems deadlocks"
     CACM, vol. 12, number 7, july 1969, pages 373-377

[7] R.C. HOLT
     "Some deadlocks properties of computer systems"
     Computing Surveys, vol.4, number 3, september 1972, pages 179-196

[8] J.E. MURPHY
     "Resource allocation with interlock detection in a multi-task system"
     AFIPS FJCC, vol.33, part 2, 1968, pages 1169-1176

[9] B. ROY
     "Cheminement et connexité dans les graphes ; application aux problèmes
     d'ordonnancement"
     Revue METRA, série spéciale, n°1, 1962

AUTHOR INDEX

M. ADIBA
Université Scientifique et Médicale
de Grenoble
Math. Appliquées - Information
Boite Postale 53
GRENOBLE CEDEX, FRANCE

Prof. Dr. K. BAUKNECHT
Institut für Informatik der
Universität Zürich
Kurvenstrasse 17
CH - 8006 ZURICH, SWITZERLAND

G. BENCI
IRIA
Domaine de Voluceau
Rocquencourt
LE CHESNAY, FRANCE

H. BILLER
Institut für Informatik
Universität Stuttgart
Herdweg 51
STUTTGART 1, GERMANY

F. BODART
Institut d'Informatique
Facultes Universitaires
Rue Grandgagnage 21
NAMUR, BELGIUM

HENRI BOGAERT
Institut d'Informatique
Rue Grandgagnage 21
NAMUR, BELGIUM

Prof. BROCKHAUS
Techn.·Universität Wien
KARLSPLATZ 13, WIEN, AUSTRIA

A. CABANES
Institut d'Informatique d'Entreprise
C.N.A.M.
292 Rue St. Martin
75141 PARIS CEDEX 3, FRANCE

LARRY COHN
IBM Corporation
1501 California Avenue
PALO ALTO, CA 94304, U.S.A.

M. CREHANGE
Uer de Mathematiques
Université de Nancy 1
Boulevard des Aiguillettes
VANDOEUVRE, FRANCE

C. DELOBEL
Directeur de la MIAG
Université Scientifique et Médicale
de Grenoble
Boite Postale 53
GRENOBLE CEDEX, FRANCE

B. DOUQUE
Philips-Electrologica B.V.
Data Systems
Postbus 245
NL. APELDOORN, THE NETHERLANDS

R. DURCHHOLZ
Gesell. für Mathematik und
Daterverarbeitung MBH
Schloss Birlinghoven
Postfach 1240
ST. AUGUSTIN 1, GERMANY

R.W. ENGLES
IBM Corporation
1501 California Avenue
PALO ALTO, CA 94304, U.S.A.

C. ESCULIER
STERIA
F-78140 VELIZY-VILLACOUBLAY, FRANCE

E. FALKENBERG
Universität Stuttgart
Institut für Informatik
Herdweg 51
STUTTGART 1, GERMANY

J. GALLITAND
Box 608
Hunter College
695 Park Avenue
NEW YORK, NY 10021, U.S.A.

G. GARDARIN
Institut de Programmation
Université de Paris VI
Place Jussieu, 4
PARIS CEDEX 05, FRANCE

W. GLATTHAAR
Institut für Informatik
Universität Stuttgart
Herdweg 51
STUTTGART 1, GERMANY

F. GROTENHUIS
N.V. Philips
ISA-AS VN 321
EINDHOVEN, THE NETHERLANDS

P. HALL
British Ship Research Ass.
WALLSEND, TYNE-WEAR, NE28 6UY, U.K.

W.H. HENGST
N.D.U. - B.V.
Dept. of ADM.-Autom. Data Processing
West-Blaak 1 PO
ROTTERDAM, THE NETHERLANDS

P. HEYDERHOFF
Gesell. für Mathematik und
Datenverarbeitung MBH
Schloss Birlinghoven
Postfach 1240
ST. AUGUSTIN, GERMANY

Dr. HAROLD HOEHNE
Computer Gesell. Konstanz
Max-Stromeyerstr. 116
KONSTANZ, GERMANY

M.H.H. HUITS
N.V. Philips
Dept. ISA Research
VN 624
EINDHOVEN, THE NETHERLANDS

A.T.F. HUTT
Southampton University
Dept. of Mathematics
The University
Highfield
SOUTHAMPTON, U.K.

F. KIRSHENBAUM
Equitable Life Assurance Society
1285 Avenue of the Americas (7-F)
NEW YORK, NY 10019, U.S.A.

H.S.M. KRUYER
Koninklyke Shell Lab. Amsterdam
Badhuisweg 3
AMSTERDAM NOORD, THE NETHERLANDS

P. LOCKEMANN
Universität Karlsruhe
Fakultät für Informatik
Karlsruhe
Postfach 6380
ZIRKEL NR. 2, GERMANY

C. MACHGEELS
Université Libre de Bruxelles
50 Avenue F.D. Roosevelt
BRUSSELS, BELGIUM

L.I. MERCZ
Control Data Corporation
B.P. 47
FERNEY-VOLTAIRE, FRANCE

BERNARD MEYER
TU Berlin
FB Kybernetik (20)
Institut für Softwaretechnik
U. Theor. Informatik
Otto-Suhr-Allee 18-20
BERLIN 10, GERMANY

I. MIJARES
Computer Communications Network Group
Dept. of Computer Science
University of Waterloo
WATERLOO, ONTARIO N2L 3G1, CANADA

W.G. MOORHEAD
CERN
CH-1211 GENEVE, 23, SWITZERLAND

P. MOULIN
E.D.F./G.D.F.
S.T.I.
Rue J. Bara, 21
ISSY-LES-MOULINEAUX, FRANCE

H. MUNZENBERGER
GMD Bonn
Schloss Birlinghoven
Postfach 1240
ST. AUGUSTIN 1, GERMANY

R. MUNZ
TU Berlin
FB Kybernetik (20)
Inst. für Softwaretechnik
U. Theor. Informatik
Otto-Suhr-Allee 18-20
BERLIN 10, GERMANY

M. NANCI
Institut d'Administration des
Entreprises
29 Avenue Robert Schuman
AIX EN PROVENCE, FRANCE

E. NEUHOLD
Universität Stuttgart
Institut für Informatik
Herdweg 51
STUTTGART, GERMANY

G.M. NIJSSEN
Control Data Corporation
46 Avenue des Arts
BRUSSELS, BELGIUM

M. NOKSO-KOIVISTO
University of Tampere
Project Tiski
PL 607
TAMPERE 10, FINLAND

LINDA PAGLI
Ist. Scienze dell'Informazione
Corso Itailia 40
I-5600 PISA, ITALY

G. PELAGATTI
Politechnico di Milano
Instituto di Elettronica
Piazza L. Da Vinci 32
MILANO, ITALY

A. PIROTTE
MBLE Research Laboratory
2 Avenue van Becelaere
BRUSSELS, BELGIUM

G.R. PUTZ LU
IBM Research Laboratory
Monterey & Cottle Roads
SAN JOSE, CA 95114, U.S.A.

J. RANDON
E.D.F./G.D.F. (S.T.I.)
Rue J. Bara 21
ISSY-LES-MOULINEUX, FRANCE

F. REMMEN
University of Technology
Mathematics Dept.
P.O. Box 513
EINDHOVEN, THE NETHERLANDS

U. RETHFELD
Siemens AG
Leopoldstrasse 208
MUNCHEN 40, GERMANY

G. RICHTER
Gesell. für Mathematik und
Datenverarbeitung MBH
Schloss Birlinghoven
Postfach 1240
ST. AUGUSTIN 1, GERMANY

M. ROLLAND
UER Mathématiques et Informatique
42 Avenue de la Libération
F-5400 NANCY, FRANCE

J. RUCHTI
EAWAG an der ETH
Uberlandstrasse 133
DUBENDORF, SWITZERLAND

G. SCHLAGETER
Universität Karlsruhe
Inst. für Angew. Informatik
Kollegium am Schloss
Postfach 6380
KARLSRUHE, GERMANY

H.A. SCHMID
Universität Stuttgart
Institut für Informatik
Pfaffenwaldring 64
STUTTGART 80, GERMANY

Dr. H. SCHMUTZ
IBM Heidelberg
Scientific Center
Tiergartenstr. 15
D-6900 HEIDELBERG, GERMANY

H.J. SCHNEIDER
TU Berlin
FB Kybernetik (20)
Inst. für Softwaretechnik
U. Theor. Informatik
Otto-Suhr-Allee 18-20
BERLIN 10, GERMANY

M.E. SENKO
IBM
T.J. Watson Research Center
P.O. Box 216
Yorktown Heights
NEW YORK, NY 10598, U.S.A.

F. SIMON
SOBEMAP
Place du Champ de Mars 5
A.G. Building
BRUSSELS, BELGUIM

S. SPACCAPIETRA
Institut de Programmation
Université Paris VI ·
4 Place Jussieu
75230 PARIS CEDEX 05, FRANCE

T.B. STEEL JB.
Equitable Life Assurance Society
1285 Avenue of the Americas
NEW YORK, NY 10019, U.S.A.

P. STOCKER
University of East Anglia
School of Computing Studies
NORWICH, U.K.

H. TARDIEU
CETE - Div. Informatique
Service Etudes
Zone Industrielle
LES MILLES, FRANCE

M. TEBOUL
Personnel
E.D.F./G.D.F.
S.T.I.
Rue J. Bara 21
ISSY-LES-MOULINEAUX, FRANCE

S. TODD
IBM United Kingdom Ltd.
UK Scientific Centre
Neville Road
Peterlee
COUNTY DURHAM SR8 1BY, U.K.

Dr. F.W. TOMPA
Dept. of Computer Science
University of Waterloo
WATERLOO, ONTARIO N2L 3GI, CANADA

H. WEBER
Technische Universität Berlin
Otto-Suhr-Allee 18-20
BERLIN 10, GERMANY

E. WILDGRUBE
Siemens AG
Leopoldstr. 208
MÜNCHEN 40, GERMANY

Dr. K. ZIMMERMANN
IBM Austria
IBM Laboratorium
A-1010 WIEN, AUSTRIA